AIREDALE & WHARFEDALE COLLEGE

Calverley Lane, Horsforth, LEEDS LS18 4RQ.

AUTHOR	TRAINING TECHNOLOGY PROGRAMME
TITLE	Volume 6
CLASSNo. 374	Copy No.
DEPARTMENT	LIBRARY

This book must be returned by the latest date shown. Please bring the book with you if you wish to extend the period of loan.

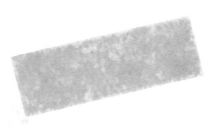

THE TRAINING TECHNOLOGY PROGRAMME

Volume 6

ASSESSMENT AND EVALUATION IN TRAINING

TRAINING TECHNOLOGY PROGRAMME
Produced by the North West Consortium

Volume 6

ASSESSMENT AND EVALUATION IN TRAINING

John Stock, John Macleod, John Holland, Andy Davies, Peter Jennings, Mike Cross, Joe Richards and Jim Garbett.

Supported by OPEN TECH

Parthenon Publishing
THE PARTHENON PUBLISHING GROUP LIMITED

The Training Technology Programme is published on behalf of the North West Consortium by:

In the U.K. and Europe

    The Parthenon Publishing Group Ltd
    Casterton Hall
    Carnforth
    Lancashire LA6 2LA
    England

ISBN 1-85070-163-6

In the U.S.A.

    The Parthenon Publishing Group Inc
    120 Mill Road
    Park Ridge
    NJ 07656
    U.S.A.

ISBN 0-940813-35-1

Editorial Note
The male pronoun has been used throughout the Training Technology Programme for stylistic reasons only. It covers both masculine and feminine genders.

THE TRAINING TECHNOLOGY PROGRAMME

The Training Technology Programme (TTP) aims to provide materials which will help improve training and learning.

The Programme is presented by the North West Consortium, consisting of Lancashire Polytechnic, S. Martin's College and Lancashire College.

TTP is a set of distance learning materials in two versions. There is a choice between a hard-back Volume edition and a soft-back Package edition.

PROGRAMME PRODUCTION

Project Manager .... *Bob Wilson*
Co-ordinator .... *John Stock*
Programme Co-ordinator .... *Kath Litherland*
Video Advisor .... *Fred Fawbert*
Audio Advisor .... *Peter Darnton*
Main Illustrators .... *Angela Pour-Rahnema*
David Hill & Lesley Sumner
Editors .... *Andy Davies & Derek Oliver*
Production Team Members .... *Lynne Hamer, Judith Hindle*
Caroline Nesfield (Programme Secretary)
Susan Western, Bobby Whittaker

ACKNOWLEDGEMENTS

With gratitude and appreciation to the many who have supported the Programme including the Directorate, Principals and mangement of Lancashire Polytechnic, S. Martin's College and Lancashire College; David Bloomer, Norma Brennan, Cyril Cavies, Ryland Clendon, Noel Goulsbra, Stanley Henig, Tony James, Peter Knight, Joe Lee, Ken Phillips, Alan Sharples, Ross Simpson; The Director and members of MSC Open Tech, especially Steve Emms, Les Goodman, Fiona Jordan; last, but certainly not least, The Authors' Families.

FOR FURTHER INFORMATION

Write to Bob Wilson, Programme Director,
Training Technology Programme, Lancashire Polytechnic,
PRESTON, PR1 2TQ.   Tel. (0772) 22141

Foreword
to the Training Technology Programme

Today we see technology being applied to every department of civilised living. It comes in many forms and its applications are virtually limitless. What we see today, although it is transforming society, is but the beginning, and the extent and pace of change is likely to increase many times.

It is most fitting and timely therefore that a systematic effort is being made to apply technology to training. The techniques available are very varied ranging from computers to audio visual equipment. It will enable training to be undertaken privately at home or at the work place in a group, in the remote croft or in the city.

Technology is revolutionising training; I welcome therefore this Training Technology Programme developed by the North West Consortium and Parthenon Publishing, supported by the Manpower Services Commission. It brings training in technology, through the medium of technology, to more people than ever before.

I commend it and I am delighted to have been invited to contribute this foreword.

John Banham
Director General CBI

Contents

Study Unit 1

Introduction to Assessment and Evaluation

Component 1:

Assessment — What is it? Why bother?

Key Words

 Assessment; assessment/testing of; prior knowledge; ability; aptitude; learning progress; achievement; performance; skills; knowledge; interest; attitudes.

Introduction

We are all busy assessing (and evaluating) most of the time:

'That's a nice coat you're wearing.'

'John didn't look well tonight.'

'What terrible weather.'

'I'm not going to have the car serviced there again.'

'Gosh, that meat was tough.'

'The coach is cheaper.'

'At least the beer's good.'

No doubt you can think of many other similar examples.

All these comments are based on some sort of assessment of a situation, often relative to an implied standard of reference or normal condition. What we are doing is observing something — and then comparing our observation with an established standard.

Most of our day-to-day assessing is at this informal and often subjective level, but we do come across attempts at being more systematic, e.g. judges marking an ice skating competition; comparing sunshine, rainfall and temperature figures for holiday resorts; and possibly even beauty contests!

Thus we see that the term assessment is used in a number of different ways, and often very casually and in everyday speech. An appropriate dictionary definition is 'to estimate the magnitude, quality or value of something', hence the word 'assessor' to describe someone who is engaged in assessing.

In the areas of more direct interest to us, exactly the same principle applies, but obviously the range/scope covered by the word 'something' is narrowed down to include only those features which we regard as appropriate. For example:

In the training context, assessment is generally used to refer to the process of obtaining information about trainees' learning, progress and achievement, that is, **what** and **how well** your trainees have learned.

In psychology, it is often used to refer to the process of applying tests to measure people's skills, aptitudes, abilities, personalities etc.

In management education the special concern is with selection and appraisal.

For the time being we will use a general definition of assessment to include aspects of all three of the above.

In all of these, what we are aiming to do is to identify **what** information we need to obtain, set up procedures to **collect** the information and then examine and interpret it.

What to Assess

As an initial step, let's consider an example where assessment might be required at a number of times or stages in a trainee's progress.

Imagine you have been given the job of training someone as a check-out operator, in a supermarket. What, if anything, might you want to assess? (Note: Consider each of the following items, and mentally tick or cross out each one before proceeding.)

I might want to assess the trainee's:

a. existing knowledge (how much he already knows)
b. aptitude for this type of job
c. general ability
d. ability to learn new skills and knowledge
e. overall levels of interest and motivation
f. learning and performance during training
g. standard of performance after a period of actually doing the job.

Let us consider each of the above items in turn.

a. Assessing how much the trainee already knows.
Seems a good idea, but is it practicable? In the case of the trainee check-out operator, what might we want to find out about?
Whether he has

* handled cash, and given change
* operated a till
* ever operated a check-out position
* been a customer in the particular store or chain of stores for which training will be given?

Write down any other items you can think of (for your own reference).

Now, how would **you** go about assessing the above? (Again, make a mental note against each item.)
Would you assess them

* formally/informally?
* using oral questions/written questionnaire?
* using practical test/simulation?

Do you think it will be sufficient to ask the trainee (by using informal oral questions)?

Probably 'Yes', provided the trainee understands the questions and answers truthfully!

In any case, if in any doubt you could ask additional questions or devise simple practical tests.

4

▨▨▨ Checkpoint

But why is this assessment necessary?
(Try to answer this in your own words before proceeding.)

Well, it should allow training to start at an appropriate point/level and avoid wasting both your time and the trainee's.

▨▨▨

Can you think of anything that the above answer assumes?

It seems to assume that training is going to be on a one-to-one basis — where the trainer can tailor the instruction to the particular needs of an individual trainee.

In some cases, more formal and systematic assessment or pre-testing may be necessary, e.g. in order to find out if a trainee has certain pre-requisite skills or knowledge on which training depends (not everyone has the aptitude to become a helicopter pilot, for example!).

Of course, many organisations build such assessment into their selection procedures, sometimes using pencil-and-paper tests of particular abilities (e.g. clerical, spatial, numerical) which can be administered to groups of applicants.

In our case, if the trainee is assumed to have knowledge of decimals and fractions, it may be as well to check it out first.

To sum up, 'finding out how much the trainee already knows' is a good guiding principle, but in practice each case should be considered and dealt with separately.

b. Assessing the trainee's aptitude for this type of job.

Aptitude is another everyday word which in our case refers to a pre-disposition or inherent ability to act or behave in a particular way. For example, Zola Budd would appear to have an aptitude for running and Laurence Olivier for acting.

Here it is very easy to 'run wild'!

▨▨▨

If, from a group of applicants, you were selecting someone for training to become a fork-lift truck driver, it is probably easy to list some of the aptitudes you consider important. Try to write out a few now on a separate sheet before looking ahead.

I don't know what you have written, of course, but here are some which come to mind:
* *Co-ordination; hand-eye, hand-foot.*
* *Spatial ability and judgement of distance.*
* *Eyesight and hearing.*
* *'Feeling' for machinery.*

The trouble is, when you have listed these aptitudes, what is their relative importance and, more critically, how can they be measured?

To digress for a moment:

Reliability and Validity

Although reliability and validity will be dealt with more fully later on, these two important and related concepts merit a brief introduction here.

A test is reliable if it gives consistent and repeatable results. A clock is not reliable if it gains one day and loses the next, and a tape measure is not reliable if it stretches in use by variable amounts. Thus a test would not be reliable if the same person obtained different scores on different occasions (after allowing for any greater familiarity with the test on the later occasions).

A test is valid if it measures exactly what it is designed to measure (and hopefully nothing else). Thus an eyesight test should be valid, provided it is given under controlled and standardised conditions.

You might like to consider whether the driving test is both reliable and valid!

To return. Home-made tests of, say, co-ordination are likely to be difficult to construct and **unreliable** — and you may end up measuring something different from the original intention, i.e. they may be **invalid** and not measure the desired aptitude.

Published aptitude tests may seem to fit the bill, but unfortunately experience indicates that people often use such tests because they are there — rather than because they measure precisely the desired aptitude.

So, apart from assessing physical requirements (e.g. eyesight, hearing) you are advised to go easy on this one, unless you have well-tried and suitable aptitude tests available.

c. Assessing the trainee's general ability.

There are numerous general ability tests published and available, but again you must have a very clear reason for wanting to use them. If someone is going to spend most of the time doing a straightforward routine job, measuring his level of **general** ability is likely to be a waste of time. Measuring specific abilities (e.g. clerical ability, spatial ability, manual dexterity) might be desirable in some cases.

d. Assessing the trainee's ability to learn new skills and knowledge.

Wouldn't it be nice! Unfortunately, this is almost impossible to measure precisely. The best bet here is to talk to the trainee and look for evidence in his previous experience which suggests the existence of such abilities.

e. Assessing overall levels of interest and motivation.

▨▨▨

If you felt this was an important item, how would you try to measure it? Write down one or two ideas on a separate sheet.

As in (d.) above, talking to the trainee and asking relevant questions is one way. Another would be to use a questionnaire. The difficulty here is in trying to decide how truthful the answers are likely to be, as the trainee may be trying to make a good impression!

'We have ways of making you talk'

f. Assessing the trainee's learning and performance during training.

I hope you agree that this is absolutely vital — an essential requirement. Unfortunately, it is often overlooked, or dealt with in a very haphazard way, because it requires a disciplined and systematic approach to specifying the desirable outcomes of training, step-by-step and stage-by-stage.

The trainee needs to feel that he is making progress — and assessing learning/performance from time to time during training is a good way of providing this feedback. This is particularly important in the case of skills (e.g. keyboard, hand/eye co-ordination) where the same basic skill is being developed progressively, and highlighting achievement is a strong motivator.

g. Assessing performance at the end of training.

Obviously, another **must**. In fact, when 'assessment' is mentioned, most people think immediately of this 'end of course' examination or test. Several of the standard text books on assessment make the assumption that this is the only form of assessment to be covered! It **is** important, but in many training situations the previous category, assessing during training, is at least as vital.

It should be recognised that this 'end of training' assessment needs to be based on measuring performance in situations as close as possible to the real thing, e.g. written tests are likely to be quite inappropriate if the training is geared to doing a practical job. Imagine if the official driving test were to consist solely of a written examination!

h. Assessing standard of performance after a period of actually doing the job.

No doubt this is done informally in most cases, but you would have to decide whether it should be done more systematically. One reason for doing this would be to 'refresh' correct methods of doing things, and to reduce the possibility of bad habits developing. In the case of the check-out operator, a good liaison between trainers and supervisors (who should be monitoring standards of performance 'on the job'), is essential.

Summary

We have now looked at each of the items a. to h. in turn. These cover the main areas where assessment might be used before, during and after training.

Before Training covers assessment of:

* existing knowledge (sometimes called entry behaviour or pre-requisite knowledge).

* any special aptitudes required, and which may need to be measured.

* overall (general) ability.

* ability to learn new skills and knowledge — difficult to measure, but the rate of progress during training will depend on this.

* overall levels of interest and motivation — which are likely to change during and after training, and which may need to be monitored later on as well.

During Training covers any assessment of learning, performance, progress, attitudes etc. made while training is still going on, and is linked to the third category.

After Training which covers assessments made immediately training has been completed (the most usual form of assessment), plus any assessment made at a later stage after some experience of doing the job has been obtained.

■///

I would suggest that you now try to apply the items to a training situation with which you are familiar, placing them in order of priority (1 to 8) from most important to least important.

If you find this difficult, you could choose one of the following examples to consider:

a. Machinist in a clothing factory.
b. Telephone switchboard operator/receptionist.
c. Gardener.
d. Hairdresser (ladies, gents or unisex!).
e. Occupational therapy helper.
f. Removal man.
g. Computer programmer.

Then see how closely your original 'ticks and crosses' compare with these rankings and your ideas now, after having worked through this introductory Component on assessment.

Finally, remember that we have been using the term assessment in a fairly broad sense, but essentially it covers the procedures for deciding what information we need to obtain about abilities, learning and performance, then actually obtaining the information, and finally analysing the results.

In the next two Components we shall be considering what exactly can be assessed and how to go about it.

Tutor Contact

Please contact your tutor if you wish to clarify any of the points in this Component or discuss your answers to any of the questions or exercises.

Component 2:

What Can We Assess?

Introduction

Component One has already raised the question **'what might you want to assess?'** — relating it to a particular example, the check-out operator.

In Component Two we'll look at a slightly different question **'what can we assess?'**

Inevitably, this second question is linked to other key questions raised elsewhere in this introductory Study Unit and then treated more fully in later Study Units of Package Four, for example:

why are we assessing at all?

and

how are we going to assess?

One way of starting to think about **what we can assess** is to ask ourselves questions about what we **do** assess, before we judge or evaluate something or somebody. After all, we do actually **assess** quite a lot, at home, in leisure and at work. Every day we look at somebody or something in a particular way and, according to our interest, we assess a number of aspects of presentation or performance.

Look at the house in Figure One.

Figure 1

After a quick look, Jim assessed it as isolated, out of date, poky, a liability, whereas Joe sees it as idyllic, quaint, a cottage with potential.

▨▨▨ Checkpoint

No doubt you will quickly work out your own assessment of the subject of the picture overleaf. Choose a few words which indicate your assessment of the car in the picture.

9

To you, the car may be 'out of date', slow (therefore bad), expensive to buy and maintain. But it might equally be 'vintage', slow (therefore good), occasional use only, so cheap to run — an investment.
It all depends on your point of view.

One of the difficulties of this kind of everyday assessment is that it **is** so random and it may rely on very scanty information and subjective observation.

Because it tends to be subjective and unfocussed, any information of this sort we may pass on to somebody else may be worthless, misleading or even harmful. We all use the information we collect, the assessments we or others make, in order to make judgements or reach decisions. In effect, to **evaluate**. This is why it is so important to be clear about what we **can** assess.

Assessing People and Things — the realities and problems

a. Everyday Life

If people do tend to assess in a random and unstructured way in everyday life, and if we are aware of this, we will probably want to ask **'what has been assessed?'** when we consider any statement they make. That is to say, we can assume that the person giving the assessment has some criterion in mind, some **measure, standard** or **principle** by which he is operating.

The point of view, possibly quite subjective or even self-interested, of the person making the judgement, is very important. It will affect both the judgement itself and the way that other people view it. Of course, we may not always be sure of the stand-point of the person concerned but, often, with everyday judgements, it may be only too obvious that the 'evaluator' has a particular **criterion** in mind, his own way of measuring the worth of the person or thing he is considering.

But it's also true that **any** attempt at **serious assessment**, or judgement or evaluation arising from that assessment, will be based on particular **criteria**, that is to say **principles** or **standards** which have probably been formally proposed, in advance, by the evaluator or evaluators.

b. The Training Context

Let's transfer this pattern of assessing to the training context, first, your own situation and then an example from elsewhere.

Your own situation

If you are about to be involved in training somebody in some aspect of your work, or if you are doing this already, try listing some methods of assessing how well a trainee has done. If you are not training somebody at the moment, one way of looking at the problem might be to think of the job **you** do and to work out ways you think someone might assess **you** in order to have a clear, comprehensive and fair picture of what you do and how well you do it. Thinking about yourself does help to concentrate the mind. Would you be happy if you were assessed on just one aspect of your work, perhaps chosen at random by someone else and magnified out of all proportion? Obviously not. We would all prefer a balanced view which considers the range of work that we do and the abilities we need in order to be able to do the job.

'Some aspect of your work . . . magnified out of all proportion'

I suggest you divide a sheet of paper into two halves. On one side, list what the job involves and on the other how you would suggest assessing a particular ability. It may be helpful to have three groups. (Prepare your sheet of paper now.)

A. Knowledge
What does someone need to **know** in order to do this job (the theory, if you like)?

B. Skills
What does the person need to be able **to do**?

C. Attitudes
What sort of **approach** to his work does a person doing this job need to have?

Now list some suggestions of how to assess performance in your chosen area, under each heading.

---

*Well, of course I don't know which job you have chosen or the knowledge, skills and attitudes you feel are required. But I would guess that when it came to the suggestions for assessment you found it quite difficult to formulate 'tests' which **clearly** did the job you wanted them to do. Probably you found any **attitudes** you listed especially difficult to assess. Don't worry — an introduction to the 'how' of assessment comes in the next Component and there is heavy emphasis on it in later Study Units in this Package. (The idea of Self Assessment is taken up thoroughly in Study Unit Five.)*

Another example
As another example, let's consider the trainee laboratory technician in some area of work involving food preparation or food hygiene. We start to list abilities in the groups suggested, possibly as shown below.

As we start to think of appropriate ways of assessing, it becomes obvious that assessment must be very closely linked to a very clear understanding of what a person working in a particular job needs to be able to do. Any statement about this must be equally clear. Let's look at just one of our examples in the table below and see how well they stand up.

In A.1 **two** abilities seem to be listed. At first sight, one appears to be easy to test, possibly through observation. Does the trainee **apply** rules of personal hygiene in food areas? A yes/no answer would seem to suffice, but if you had to devise tests to assess this ability, would you be satisfied with this?

Write down any doubts you might have about the yes/no solution suggested.

The thoughts which crossed my mind included:
* *would he have to do this **all** of the time?*
* *how could we check? (impossible?)*
* *should we insert the word 'consistently' in the description of the ability? This would mean he would have to be doing so whenever we did check. Is this adequate?*

Abilities	Suggested Assessment
A. Knowledge 1. Ability to understand and apply rules of personal hygiene in food areas. 2. etc. 3. etc. **B. Skills** 1. Ability to observe accurately. 2. Ability to record results clearly. 3. Ability to prepare microscopic slides. 4. etc. **C. Attitudes** 1. Ability to work responsibly even when unsupervised. 2. etc.	

Figure 2

The second ability in A.1, 'Ability to **understand** rules . . .', raises other questions for me.

▰▰▰

Write down any questions which arise in your mind.

I ask myself:
*What does **understand** mean? It doesn't help us to know what he should actually **do**. If he applies the rules, does it show that he understands them? Should we use another word instead of 'understand' or 'know', some kind of 'action word', which will enable us to test more easily whether he has the ability or not?*

c. Objectives and Assessment
I seem to have got myself into a terrible tangle with just the first item on my list in the table.

What lessons can be learned here?

It seems clear that stating how to assess something is very difficult indeed unless you have also stated clearly and simply the 'outcome' or behaviour you are expecting to see arising from the training.

It follows that abilities may best be stated in the form of **objectives**. If those objectives contain 'action' verbs (like 'list', 'assemble correctly') it will be easier to see exactly what the trainee has to be able to do and later, when we assess, whether he can do it.

It is easier to decide on how to assess whether an objective has been achieved if statements are kept clear and simple, so it's better not to muddle your objectives by listing more than one ability at a time.

So far so good . . .

BUT, can you spot any flaws in the approach — listing 'abilities' or 'outcomes' of the training, through objectives?

▰▰▰

Try to suggest three or four.

Possibly you thought of one or two of the following:
* *Wouldn't it be rather easy to miss some important aspect of the job by doing it this way?*
* *What happens if there are important unintended outcomes which appear, but you haven't thought of them, so you don't assess?*
* *What allowance does such a system make for the* **conditions** *in which a person works? These could be very different, from trainee to trainee.*
* *Even if we do succeed in listing objectives clearly and concisely, how easy is it to devise tests which really measure the achievement of the objectives? Testing knowledge and skills is one thing. What about attitudes? Will there be a tendency for us to leave out attitudinal objectives because they are difficult to assess? Maybe we'll even argue that they don't really matter.*
All of these are important reservations and you have probably listed others. It may depend on your own work situations.

▰▰▰

Even if you haven't listed one or two of my points, try to apply them all to your own place of work and see whether you have missed something. Consider the question of attitudinal objectives even if, or perhaps especially if, your kind of work doesn't seem to demand them. **Look again at the Checkpoint on your own situation.**

d. Attitudinal Objectives and Assessing Attitude — difficult but important
Some jobs, for example assembling a bicycle, may not seem to demand more than certain knowledge and particular skills, but one well known British manufacturer of bicycles advertises one of the top three models in the range as follows:

The light-weight frames are individually built and brazed by craftsmen, then hand finished and hand sprayed. This frame is carefully assembled by one person into a finished bicycle. Each assembler attaches his own personal card with photograph to the finished bicycle. It is your guarantee of quality, individuality and satisfaction.

It's clear that this manufacturer would be likely to value very highly the trainee who demonstrates enthusiasm and commitment and other **attitudes** not easily measured and not necessarily associated immediately with the knowledge and skills which must be involved in the assembling of bicycles.

Driving a motor vehicle may at first sight seem to demand largely physical behaviour and to be principally a **skill**, but clearly there are other elements.

List for yourself one item in the knowledge area and another in the attitudes area.

*I expect you listed something from the Highway Code under knowledge, the table of Shortest Stopping Distances or a rule such as 'You **must** wear an approved type of seat belt'. Under attitudes, perhaps consideration towards other road users — or, maybe, satisfaction in being a good driver, or something like that.*

e. Towards a Balanced Programme

I hope you may agree that a balanced assessment programme needs to consider all three areas, if it is to be appropriate. And if it is to be valid, we have to devise methods of assessment which really do measure the achievement of those objectives which they are designed to measure. Study Units Two, Three and Four of this Package will focus on just these problems.

Conclusion

Many of the issues raised in this Component may make you feel that you really do **need** to work through a lot more of this Package on **'Assessment and Evaluation'**. You may even feel that you **want** to do so, in which case one of **our** attitudinal objectives will have been achieved!

For the trainer, the key issue is whether the information he collects is **useful**. Is it sensitive in highlighting the problems of a particular trainee — or indeed all trainees? How well does it help the trainer to judge the effectiveness of the training he offers in relation to the objectives he has stated? (Component Six of the present Study Unit takes up this point in more detail.)

But this is a long way from our first 'instant judgement' approach and it is very important, because it concerns our trainees' and our own performance!

A final concern in this brief introduction to the 'what' of assessment must be whether the procedures we select are **reliable**. Is what we end up with any better than the off-the-cuff method, just because it is more complicated? At least part of the answer to this question depends on the questions 'when and how do we assess?' which are raised in the next Component.

Component 3:

Further Assessment Questions

Key Words

 Formal; informal; summative; formative; subjective; objective; continuous assessment; periodic assessment; coursework.

We have already looked at questions of 'what' to assess. Now we shall consider 'how', 'when', 'by whom' and 'of whom'.

First of all, I would like to suggest that you might think of two different approaches to the question of assessment overall, both of which are important to most trainers.

The pragmatic approach, that is, where you look at what is 'going on' in your training programme and, without taking into account what you or others think 'should' be happening, you are able to consider results or reactions which you did not expect from that programme, as well as the more predictable ones.

This is not likely to be written into the official handbook on how to assess your course, but it is an important ingredient in 'informal' (see page 15) and 'formative' or 'on-going' assessment (see page 17).

The predetermined approach, where the results you want to see are specified beforehand, as are the criteria by which you will judge success (or failure).

This is much more likely to be the approach taken by an official handbook and will certainly be the approach which is used before the award of a certificate of competence, a 'pass' on a course, or a promotion is granted.

However, there are also other questions arising from the detailed practice of assessment within the two main approaches I have just suggested. Some of these are often seen as contrasting techniques of assessment, and the more commonly suggested are listed here:

Formal v. Informal

Formative v. Summative
Coursework v. Examination
Internal v. External
all will be looked at in more detail in the following pages. Clearly some of them are to do with timing (the 'when' questions) and we will deal with these a little later (page 17) and the last pair with 'who' questions (pages 18 and 19).

How?

Firstly let's look at the **formal/informal** question.

Informal assessment goes on all the time (or at least it should do if you are awake as a trainer). You are constantly checking the simple observation whether or not the trainees appear to be taking any notice of the programme (or of you!), whether or not they are improving, making progress or learning and what the general 'feeling' of the training programme is.

The formal/informal contrast is often linked with the subjective/objective distinction. Informal assessment is often subjective i.e. it is something you 'feel' rather than can prove with facts and figures. Do not ignore it because of this. It can be very valuable in terms of your relationships with the trainees and has a great deal to do with your sensitivity as a trainer. It is very difficult and far too time-consuming to reduce the day-to-day interaction between you and your trainees to numerical data, such as marks given to each task or response, which are then subjected to objective analysis. Because this approach is often not worth it, we rely heavily and properly on the 'feelings' we get of the training atmosphere.

'My informal assessment is that this is not working'

Our informal observations may never be recorded anywhere, though you may wish to jot down certain points you notice about a trainee's progress, attitudes, or particular difficulties or successes.

One great advantage of informal assessment is that it can be unobtrusive. This reduces the strain on the trainee which assessment often brings and allows you to see him in a more natural light, not straining to perform as in the test situation.

Even so, however much you use informal assessment and subjective judgements you will probably be called upon to undertake some formal assessment with an element of objectivity i.e. carefully worked out, marked and properly recorded assessments, with answers or skills demonstrated which are either right or wrong with no room for argument.

Formal methods include:

* Tests of competence in carrying out tasks.
* Written papers to check on knowledge either of facts or arguments.
* Checklists for a series of skills or for assessing materials for use in a training programme.
* Using commercially produced aptitude or other tests.

(These formal methods will all be dealt with in more detail in later Study Units in this Package.)

Even in these formal strategies you may find some elements of subjectivity coming in, e.g. you may have to decide on the level of pleasantness being shown by a trainee to a member of the public. We can be clear and objective about facts, e.g. can the trainee give the colour coding of the wiring of a standard 13 amp plug, and this leaves no room for dispute or for the trainee's

feeling 'hard done by' when you have decided whether he is right or wrong, but it is more difficult with the subjective bits.

You should try to clarify in your own mind what parts of your assessment of trainees are informal/ formal, subjective/objective.

Try it as an exercise now. You may find it helpful to put the headings 'formal' and 'informal' at the top of a page and list the parts of your assessment procedures under these with 's' or 'o' next to them for subjective or objective. By the way, are all your informal assessments subjective? They need not be.

▰▰▰ Checkpoint
Write down the different strengths of informal and formal assessments and compare yours with my list. You may well come up with more strengths than I have listed!

FORMAL
More likely to be objective.
Gives data on which to make judgements.
Is easier to put in a written form, i.e. a report or record.
Allows you to check on the success in achieving the outcomes you planned.

INFORMAL
Does not put so much strain on the trainee.
May reflect certain attitudes of the trainees more accurately, because they are more prepared to be open in an informal situation.
Allows you to spot the unexpected outcomes.

When

We may want to make assessments before, during and/or after the actual training programme.

Before

During

After

We shall be considering:
Formative v. Summative
Coursework v. Examination
(From my earlier list).

Formative assessment is that which you make as the training programme is going on and therefore, it may enable you to make adjustments to the programme if it seems not to be working as well as you would like i.e. to change the form of the training. It may often be informal and subjective.

Summative assessment, on the other hand, comes at the end of the programme and allows you to sum up both the trainee's progress and the effectiveness of the programme itself. This assessment is usually formal and often strictly objective.

Summative assessment is sometimes called terminal assessment. It should really concern itself with all that the trainee has learned during the programme and this raises a major problem with it: can you include everything you wanted the trainee to pick up? With a short programme the answer might be yes, but with longer ones you will almost certainly have to make a selection of what is to be tested if the test is not to be too long. Can you do this? Are the skills and attitudes best assessed in one test at the end?

You may want to consider some form of formative assessment which is not informal. Sometimes you will hear the term **'continuous assessment'**, but usually it is incorrectly used. It is strictly a continuous review of the information you are picking up from the trainee, together with the consequent adjustments you make to your programme. Rather like an aeroplane on an instrument approach to a runway, where the aircraft computer receives and analyses data from the ground continuously and makes the necessary adjustments to the flight path all the time.

If we did implement such a programme of continuous assessment it would run away with our time, lead us into committing the mistake of 'if it moves assess it' and put undue pressure on the trainee.

What is often called 'continuous assessment' is, in fact, **periodic assessment**, where we have a series of intermittent probes taken of trainee attainment over a period of time. These might take the form of short coursework items. Although these might be 'mini examinations', coursework is usually taken to mean the production of a piece of work, written or practical, where the trainee has had as much time as he wanted and access to any reference material he required, or is working in something like the real job situation. This is in contrast to most examinations where this is not usually the case.

It may also be the checking of certain sub-skills which are necessary before the trainee can tackle the major skill or set of skills at the end of the course. The advantage of doing it this way is that it allows you to give feedback (more on this in Component Four) to the trainee and also to adjust your programme to suit his needs or capabilities.

Summing up then:
End of course tests or examinations usually carry more

prestige and are often demanded before awards, promotions or certificates are given. However, the assessment from an examination at the end of a course (summative assessment), whilst it can provide the trainer with information with which to grade the trainee, or to say whether he is satisfactory or not, does little to help trainees with their learning, nor is it particularly helpful to the trainer who wishes to take action on the information received to diagnose problems and to improve training and/or learning.

Assessment during the training programme (formative assessment) is used to make adjustments, check on trainee progress at regular intervals before a problem becomes a disaster, and to motivate the trainee (see Component Four). A series of formative assessments may be used instead of one terminal examination, giving you a greater breadth and coverage of items you can assess.

Further points on timing
a. If you plump for **summative assessment** it becomes more than ever necessary to make sure that your objectives or desirable outcomes are clear from the start, not only to yourself, but also to your trainees. Preferably, the trainees should have them in writing and should be able to discuss them with you.

b. If you decide on **formative assessment**, then make sure that your periodic assessments are not too frequent or the trainees will feel that they are on some sort of treadmill. If that is the case then the good by-products of periodic formative assessment, in terms of trainee motivation, will disappear.

Make sure that you can tell the difference between:
* **Formative/summative assessment**
* **Coursework/examination**
* **Continuous/periodic assessment**
The answers are all in the preceding paragraphs on 'When?'

By Whom?
Here you should consider who will do the assessing. Should it be internal or external, i.e. will it be done by yourself or those who did the training or by someone from outside? From outside could mean from an independent body or it could mean someone inside your own organisation who had nothing to do with the training.

There are clear advantages and disadvantages for both internal and external assessment. Try thinking of some. Write them down and then compare them with my suggestions.

a. *The more objective you want to be the more you need to have somebody removed from the training.*
b. *The more frequent the assessment the more convenient to have it done by trainers on the spot.*
c. *The more you want to take account of the individuality of the trainees, the better it is to have someone who knows them doing the assessment.*
d. *The more you want to adjust the training programme as a result of assessment, the better to have someone who knows the programme.*
e. *The more prestige you want the programme to have, the more you need outside (external) rather than internal assessment.*
f. *If the assessment is external, it can be more easily standardised across many organisations or branches. The driving test is a clear example of this.*
g. *External standardisation could make the results transferable to another organisation or to another branch or division in your own organisation. (Is this good or bad, and for whom?)*

How far should the trainees assess themselves? Are you going to have self-assessment in your programme?

Self-assessment is not generally used for gaining formal qualifications but we all do it all of the time. You are doing it on this course and your trainees will be thinking about and assessing how well they are doing throughout your training programme. If this is the case, then why not make use of it by asking the trainees to take part in the assessment process? As an example they could do some of their own formative evaluation and let you know how well they see themselves as doing.

Of Whom?

Are you assessing yourself as a trainer or your trainees' progress?

(Notice that the first cartoon in this Component is not about an assessment of the trainees. It is either an assessment of the course, or more probably, of the trainer).

In fact we usually assess both ourselves and the trainees. We will make the informal/formative assessments of our own performance as trainers whether we are obliged to or not. But we may be given, or make for ourselves, a checklist for more formal/summative assessment of how we have done. However, we will probably see our main assessment task as being the assessment of trainee performance which will be taken much further later in this Package.

Thinking of the first three Components which you have now worked through and perhaps using the formal/informal list you previously compiled, consider your training programme, or one with which you are familiar, and see if you can analyse it in terms of what is being assessed, how, when, and by whom.

Why do you think it was decided to do the assessment in this way?

Component 4:

The Purpose of Assessment

Key Words

 Feedback; minimum competency; potential; motivation; standards; norm referenced criterion referenced; skill-mastery testing.

The question — why assess? — must be linked to the question — why train?

Only by making an assessment can we tell if our training is being effective and presumably we want it to be effective or we would not have a training programme.

Why do we have training programmes?

 Checkpoint

Try to list three or four reasons and then see if they are similar to mine.

There may be particular reasons in your situation but your list might well include:
a. Introducing and orienting new personnel.
b. Improving the performance of present employees.
c. Enabling present employees to gain new knowledge or skills required by changes in operation.

If the reasons you had given are good reasons for training, then surely it is important that you know whether or not the training programme is having the desired effect.

In other words, the major reason for assessment is to provide **feedback**, that is, provide information on the trainee's progress in our training programme, both to ourselves as trainers and to the trainee.

We can ask different kinds of questions to provide different kinds of feedback. These might be asked at different stages of the training programme.

Some of them are given here:
a. What progress did the trainees feel they were making?
b. How well did the trainees like the programme?
c. What principles, skills, facts or techniques were learned?
d. What changes does the programme need, to make it more efficient for teaching?
e. What changes in job behaviour resulted from the programme?
f. What were the tangible results of the programme in terms of reduced cost, improved quality, better job performance etc.?
g. Was likely potential for further advancement or promotion of the trainee revealed?

As you see, assessment can give you information about different things in your training programme. Here are some differing approaches.

You may want to find what **attitudes** the trainees have towards the training by letting them fill in reaction sheets, that is, where you ask them, in writing, specific questions about different parts of the programme but also having some less specific questions, allowing them to give you their overall reaction to the training. (You may need to make these anonymous!)

You may want to measure the **learning** achieved by the trainees, either by a written test or by giving a set practical task to do. You may be satisfied here by a test of **minimum competency**, that is, has the trainee reached what can be judged a satisfactory level of performance?

More complicated is to try to **assess the change** in

21

job performance as a result of the training programme. This is often time consuming and, since few tests are available 'off-the-shelf' for this, it is highly likely you will have to devise your own or have ones specifically produced for you, if you wish to assess this area effectively.

Another approach still, would be try to assess the trainee's **potential** for taking on further training and/or promotion.

Having concentrated on what assessment can give us as trainers, we ought now to spend a little time on the question of what it can give to the **trainee.** That is, using assessment **to help learning.**

There are many ways in which assessment can help the trainee. Here I suggest three:

a. Small pieces of assessment during the programme can provide visible, short-term goals or targets for the trainee, and these have been shown to provide great stimulus and to influence the effort the trainee will put into the programme.

b. Trainees can be provided with information from these assessments on their strengths and weaknesses and they can then take action to improve their performance before the final assessment.

c. The feeling of achievement experienced in mastering the skills and/or knowledge necessary to perform satisfactorily on an intermediate test, can be a powerful stimulus for further effort.

Note these are all to do with **formative assessment** (remember Component three), but the final assessment too, can act as an important target.

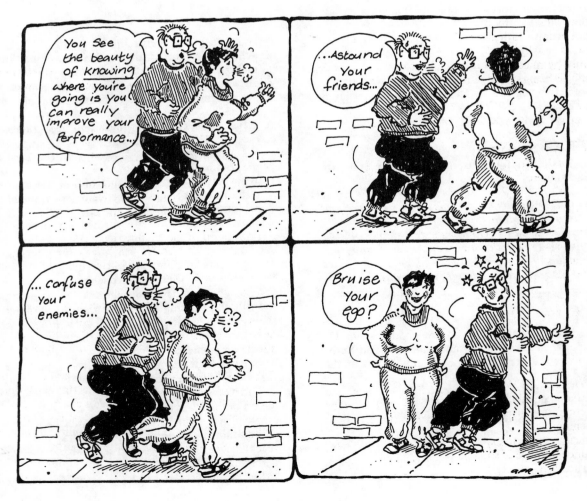

We are now clearly into the area of the **motivation** of the trainee.

Whether the assessment we make as we go along is formal or informal we should make sure that we:

* Give the trainees feedback. (It does no good if they do not know what we think or what the results are.)
* Give that feedback promptly.
* Give them some descriptive appraisal as well as/instead of just a mark or a grade, that is, talk to the trainees about their performance.
* Give them supportive comments, that is, try to find something worthy of praise.
* Are positive rather than negative.

HOWEVER, BEWARE THE DANGER!

If you have too much assessment or allow it to override your common sense, you may find certain side-effects happening:

a. You may come to expect too much, or too little, of a trainee because of some particularly good, or some particularly bad, test result.

b. Because a trainee is good in one area you may expect him (without proof) to be good in others.

c. Trainees will tend to live up (or down) to your expectations.

d. All measuring instruments (tests) are fallible and you may make the wrong judgement based on them.

e. Beware the 'treadmill' effect (see Component Three).

▰▰▰

Make a list of the ways in which an assessment programme might encourage (motivate) your trainees in following the training programme. (The answers are in the paragraphs above this Checkpoint).

We have now raised the question of what **standards** to expect of our trainees and this is an important consideration to be kept in mind when we think of why we are assessing.

We need to return to the question of what are we training for? Answer — we want the trainees to achieve certain standards of knowledge, skills and/or attitudes.

Criterion and Norm Referencing

Now there are two broad categories into which we can put the standards we set:

a. They can be **Norm** referenced
b. They can be **Criterion** referenced

With **norm referencing** we are comparing one trainee's performance with that of another. At its simplest we are saying that one trainee is **better or worse** than another one.

With **criterion referencing** we are judging the trainee's performance against some **standard** which we have prescribed beforehand. For example, can the trainee in say the D.H.S.S. list the leaflets which are available to help the public claim disability allowance?

Perhaps you can now see why purpose is very important in looking at why you should assess and in what way.

If your training programme is meant to find those trainees most suitable to take on particular tasks or to be promoted, then norm referenced testing will be important. If, on the other hand, you want to make sure that all the trainees reach a particular standard of work or competence, then you will go for criterion referenced tests.

The outcomes or the results you get from the different types of test can look very different. (Study Units Three and Four in this Package will give more practical advice on the different kinds of test.)

Study the graphs which follow. They represent the results of different approaches to assessment. In each case the trainees have a mark out of 100, shown on the horizontal axis, and the percentage of trainees gaining each range of scores, e.g. 30-40, is taken from the vertical axis. Try to write down what the two different tests could have been used for, before going on to the rest of this section.

In the first diagram the test has been set so that even the best trainee will not achieve 100% and the bulk of the trainees will achieve around 50%. This kind of testing, often in the form of long written answers to questions asking, say, for a discussion of a topic such as 'What are the best ways of dealing with questions from the public?', is typical of public examinations at school level. However, it may be of limited use in checking skill acquisition by all trainees and in checking on the quality of the training programme.

The second diagram shows the kind of results which may be obtained out of criterion referenced tests. Here the objective is not to stretch the best trainee to the extent of his knowledge or skill but to see whether or not a batch of trainees can meet certain requirements or criteria. You might want to set that level of competence at an 'absolute' standard, for example, that a trainee should be able to list all fourteen of the firm's product lines. On the other hand, you might well

NORM REFERENCED

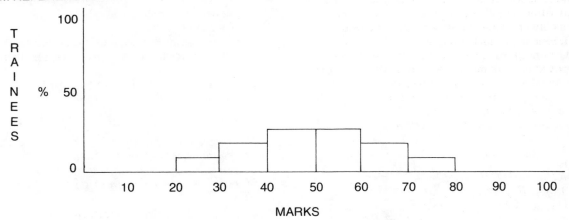

CRITERION REFERENCED

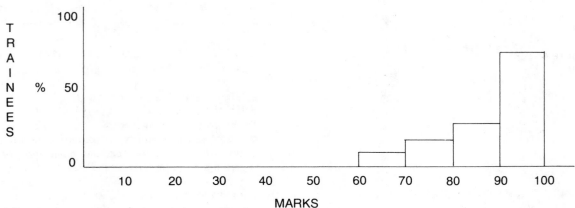

Figure 3

24

decide to have a criterion set below perfection, for example, that the trainee can name twelve out of the fourteen product lines or can work within certain defined tolerances in producing finished goods.

Whilst the distinction between the two kinds of test may look clear in theory, in practice there is some blurring of the edges.

In what is ostensibly a criterion referenced test, it is usually not acceptable to the trainer nor to his superiors to have a nil success rate. If that were to happen then the level of acceptable performance might well be adjusted to suit the trainees more closely. In other words, an element of norm referencing has crept in.

At the other end of the scale you might decide that it is not good for motivation or morale for there always to be a 100% pass rate and as the trainees get better (or you get better at training) you might decide to raise the qualifying standard — just as they do in the Olympic Games — and you have introduced again an element of norm referencing.

A norm referenced test, on the other hand, might be pushed one way or the other by the tester's ideas about standards in his field of expertise. He may decide that no-one's work comes near his idea of the good answer or finished product and his results might look something like Figure 4, even though he was only supposed to be comparing one trainee with another.

He has used outside criteria in his supposedly norm referenced test.

For **skill mastery testing** and perhaps for formative as opposed to summative assessment, criterion referenced testing would appear to be the answer to your prayer, but remember two things:

a. It only shows you what trainees can do, not what they will necessarily do in practice on the job. You may need to follow up criterion referenced tests with longer-term follow-up on the job. Probably the best remembered example of this particular weakness is the handwriting test in school. We all know that in the test situation we could produce at least acceptable writing only to come out with illegible scrawl in our next piece of written work where handwriting was not marked. What is the level of your trainees' performance outside test conditions?

b. It usually does not allow the trainee with exceptional flair or talent to shine nor show that he has gained things from the training which you did not expect (and which might be good).

Make a list of the uses of norm referenced and criterion referenced tests and compare them with mine.

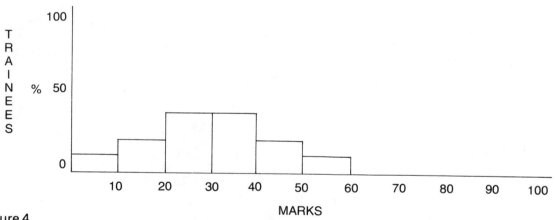

Figure 4

NORM
* *For classifying trainees.*
* *For selecting trainees for fixed quota requirements.*
* *For making decisions on how much (more or less) a trainee has learnt in comparison with others.*

CRITERION
* *For diagnosing trainee difficulties.*
* *For showing trainee ability in a particular area.*
* *For measuring what the trainee has learned.*
* *For certification of competency.*
* *For controlling entry to successive units of instruction.*

* *Whenever mastery of a subject or skill is of prime concern.*
* *Wherever quota-free selection is being used.*

Two Further Points

We assess in order to increase accountability for what the trainees are doing.

Are they learning?

How effective is the training programme?

How good are you as a trainer?

Some assessment questions make the trainees accountable to you whilst others make you accountable to those up the line.

Assessment is really a collection of information. All of which is necessary in order to make judgements — evaluations of the situation (see Component Six).

Think of a training programme with which you are familiar. What is the purpose of the assessment in it and, having categorised the parts of that assessment as either norm or criterion referenced, does the assessment seem appropriate?

Component 5:

The Effects of Assessment

 Key Words

Assessment; choices; formal assessment; certification; trainee; trainer; training programme; organisation; continuous/terminal assessment; administration; costs.

Introduction

In the first four Components of this Study Unit, we have considered a number of fundamental questions about assessment:

Why bother to assess?

When might assessment be desirable?

What to assess?

What can we assess?

How and when to assess?

Who does it?

What is the purpose of assessment?

What standards should we set or expect?

Having attempted to answer these questions, we are now going to stand back a little way and look at the direct effects of any decision to introduce some form of assessment. In order to focus on this central issue, we will consider fairly straightforward examples — the more detailed decisions about methods, techniques, marking systems etc. will be covered later on in the Package.

Assessment Choice

▰▰▰ Checkpoint

A large retailing company runs regular 'in-house' training courses on 'Effective Supervision'. Which of the following do you think would be affected by a decision to issue Company Certificates to trainees completing the course 'successfully'? (It is anticipated

that about 80% of participants will receive Certificates.)

The trainees (participants)

The trainers

The training programme itself

The company?

I hope you agree that all the above will be affected to a greater or lesser extent.

Let us see why, taking each item in turn.

The Trainees

Before we can consider the impact on the trainees themselves, we will need more information about the type of assessment involved. Let us assume that the trainees are to be formally assessed at the end of a training course, by means of a test which will be marked out of 100. Results will be ranked (first, second etc.) and made known. Certificates will be issued to those obtaining above a certain agreed percentage.

Take a piece of paper and divide it into two columns, headed advantages and disadvantages. Write down as many advantages and disadvantages **to the individual trainee** resulting from the above decision as you can think of (without spending more than, say ten minutes on this task).

Now compare your list with mine:

Advantages
* *Provides motivation*
* *Provides a goal*
* *Provides a challenge*
* *Provides competition*
* *Provides feedback (knowledge of results)*

Disadvantages
* *Fear of failure*
* *May 'turn off' the less able*
* *High standard expected?*
* *Actual failure (for some)*
* *'Lost face' if poor results made public*

If successful,
* *Satisfaction and*
* *Increased self confidence*
* *Certification*
* *Qualification*
* *Pay/Promotion*

I hope you got some additional ones, while agreeing with most of the above.

As trainers, if we had to apply the above pattern of assessment, it would be our job to try to capitalise on the advantages and remove or reduce the disadvantages. We might want:
* To play down the fear of failure in some way.
* To restrict the way(s) in which the results are made known.
* To allow 'second chances' at assessment. After all, most people are not too dismayed if they fail the driving test at the first attempt (apart from the cost, time and trouble involved in re-taking it).
* To give each individual trainee a detailed report of strengths and weaknesses — stressing the former rather than the latter, i.e. 'sugaring the pill'.

* To introduce informal mini-tests during the course in order to provide practice and feedback on progress.
* To encourage self-assessment as a way of building up confidence.

The Trainer

Let us now focus on the trainer. This time we will take the above pattern of assessment, but we will also assume that the trainer will be responsible for producing and marking the test(s).

Repeat the exercise of writing down as many advantages and disadvantages as you can think of, but this time **to the trainer**.

Again, compare your list with the following:

Advantages
* *Feedback*
* *Motivation*
* *Goal*
* *Measurement of learning*
* *Information about trainees' performance*
* *Records*
* *Monitoring effectiveness of teaching*

Disadvantages
* *Providing/making up tests*
* *Marking/reporting*
* *Time (testing, not teaching)*
* *Halo effect (allowing test results to colour other assessments)*
* *Effect on trainer/trainee relationship*
* *'Tail wagging the dog'*

If we now compare the **four** sets of advantages and disadvantages (yours and mine!), what do we find? Is there a greater similarity between the two sets of advantages than between the disadvantages to the trainee and the trainer?

If your lists are anything like mine, it would seem that the disadvantages **to the trainee** are more to do with fear of failure, whereas the disadvantages **to the trainer** are more to do with constraints and increased administration.

The Training Programme

Looking at the training programme itself; we already have some clues from the disadvantages to the trainer. Effects on the programme will include:

* Reducing available teaching time, (by time taken for assessment, revision etc.)
* Focussing attention on assessment, rather than on the course content itself.
* Narrowing the content of the teaching programme towards those items likely to be assessed.
* Highlighting the behaviour and performance of the trainees which will help them in the test (rather than more general development).

On the whole, do these items seem to be advantages or disadvantages? To me, they seem to be more disadvantages.

The Company

Moving on to the effects on the organisation/ company, again see if you can generate a number of possible advantages and disadvantages. You will have to widen the scope of your thinking to tackle this one successfully, and you may find it necessary to spell-out your ideas in more detail.

Here is my list:

Advantages
* *Certification of successful trainees may be useful*
  a. as recognition and
  b. as a way of providing indicators for advancement.
* *Records of standards of performance and attainment.*
* *Indicates efficiency of training programme.*
* *Justification to management of cost-effectiveness of training.*

Disadvantages
* *Takes time.*
* *Costs money.*
* *Extra administration.*
* *Problems of trainees who 'fail'.*

I don't expect your list will look quite the same as mine, as the issues here are not perhaps as clear-cut or obvious.

Conclusion

From what we have looked at so far in this Component, I hope you will see that the choice of any form of assessment has far-reaching consequences throughout an organisation, and not just in the 'front-line'.

Because it requires systematic observation and/or measurement, assessment produces information in various forms. This information is often open to 'public' scrutiny, which throws a spotlight on the whole training activity. Assessment is bound to affect to some extent all those involved in training, and it creates an effect which is sometimes out of all proportion to the original intention.

To take a further instance, if we decided to replace the end-of-course test with a more relaxed programme of continuous assessment (but still leading to certification), this would be likely to affect particularly the trainers and trainees. Trainees may feel under more/less pressure depending on their temperaments and personalities, and it would certainly affect the interpersonal relationships between trainer and trainees. The big advantages would be that trainees would get earlier and more frequent feedback on progress and attainment, and remedial action could be taken by the trainer if difficulties arose.

Further Example

Here is another example for you to consider.

A group of trainee computer programmers/systems analysts is being given a number of projects to tackle, after completion of a general introductory course of training. Trainees will be split into groups of three or four to work on a syndicate basis. They will be expected to pool their varying specialist background knowledge (e.g. in science, engineering, mathematics) in contributing to their syndicate's performance.

The projects are fairly open-ended, and designed to encourage initiative and novel approaches and solutions. Tutorial advice will be available, but syndicates will be encouraged to 'press-on' on their own as much as possible. Assessment of results will be made jointly by trainers and other 'in-house' experts, and marks awarded for each project under a number of headings.

Consider the effects of choosing each of the following alternative courses of action, and write down your ideas in note form.

1. Each syndicate is allowed to decide how to proportion out the marks awarded to it for each project, to its individual members.
2. Marks awarded will be considered to be divided equally between the members of each syndicate.
3. A wallchart, mounted in a prominent position and regularly up-dated, will compare the progress of the different syndicates (projects started and completed, marks awarded).
4. Marks awarded for each project will be made known privately to each syndicate, and no official attempt made to compare the relative performance of syndicates, or individual members thereof.
5. Completed projects will be carefully considered by the experts and detailed comments made, but not marked or graded in any way.
6. A fixed time will be allowed for the completion of each project, which will then be marked and results discussed by the whole group. 'Fresh' syndicates will then be formed for the next project.

There are obviously no right or wrong answers to these choices, but here are one or two points to compare with your answers.

1. *The effects of this will depend very largely on how the individuals value the marks they receive. If the course is highly competitive and promotion prospects are at stake, it will be a good test of the extent to which each syndicate has developed as a team, and is aware of the different contribution of each member.*
2. *In a cohesive group this may be readily accepted and cause no problems. In other cases it may be somewhat de-motivating for individual syndicate members — they may not try as hard as they might.*
3. *The effects of this will depend on the 'culture' of the organisation — whether it encourages this type of open competition or not.*
4. *Again this will depend on how important the marks are seen to be, and whether they are recorded for future reference.*
5. *Nice and relaxed — if the organisation is willing to accept this approach. Motivation will depend more on the perceived value of the projects to the individuals themselves.*
6. *'Working against the clock' is often used as a technique to encourage activity. In open-ended and creative work situations it can be counter-productive.*

 Tutor Seen Work

In what ways do training sessions and courses run in your organisation try to respond to the learning needs of adults?

On the basis of what you have learnt so far in this Study Unit, try out the following exercise, referring back to the Unit and your own notes as much as possible. (You may, if you wish, decide to leave this exercise until later on in the Package).

Case Study — Maltons

Maltons is a large supermarket chain, with stores in the Midlands within a radius of fifty miles of the city of Potcham. There is a modern training centre in the town of East Benster about 20 miles North-East of Potcham. The Training Manager, Alan Brindle, is supported by two full-time training officers/instructors. Alan also employs external staff on a part-time basis to run courses as required. Maltons has several thousand full-time and part-time employees. Three new stores are due to open in the next nine months.

It has been agreed that the training manager can introduce a limited number of new courses of one to three weeks' duration for full-time employees. These courses will be held at the training centre and participants will be expected to stay at a local hotel adjacent to the centre during the week (Monday to Thursday nights). The 'star' course will be a three week one for employees in supervisory categories who have been identified as being suitable for possible promotion, i.e. to departmental heads.

Five of the topics to be covered in the course are:

* Company Policy and Administration
* Health and Safety at Work
* Effective Supervision
* Interpersonal Skills
* Self-development

Task

Acting as one of the full-time training officers, prepare a short report to the training manager recommending particular strategies for assessing trainees' achievement in the above topics, including reasons for your choices. It has already been decided that assessment on this course will be accumulated to form a total assessment 'profile' for each individual.

Component 6:

What's It All About? — Assessment for Evaluation (A Summary)

Key Words

 Assessment; evaluation; feedback; improvement; decision making.

What's it all about?

Most of this introductory unit has focussed on assessment but the Unit title promises an introduction to assessment and evaluation. This final Component will therefore look particularly at evaluation and how it relates to assessment and it will raise a number of issues which will be treated in detail in later Study Units.

Assessment for Evaluation

 Checkpoint

In earlier Components we have already thought quite extensively about assessment. Try to list about six key points which seem to you to best show what assessment is about.

* *Assessment means finding out about a trainee's abilities and attitudes and how these have changed as a result of the training.*
* *Assessment should be as accurate, objective and wide-ranging as possible.*
* *Assessment is concerned with having information which can be used as feedback, telling a trainee about his strengths and weaknesses.*
* *Assessment is to help the trainee by telling him how well he has done . . . and to help the trainer to see how well he has done.*

* *Assessment helps a trainee to see where he is now and what he should do or aim for next.*
* *Assessment can help motivation by giving trainees short-term, quickly achievable goals.*

This is my list, mostly derived from the first five Components. I expect you have included at least some of these, perhaps worded somewhat differently — and also some which I have left out. **The main thing is to be clear in your own mind about why assessment is important to you and how it can help you in your training programme.**

More details of the actual tools of assessment will be offered in later Study Units of this Package, but I'm sure it's clear from what we have seen in this first Study Unit that trainers who want to assess meaningfully need to **plan** a scheme to make sure that nothing is missed. Random methods are seldom likely to give a full picture of the knowledge, skills and attitudes which the training is designed to foster.

Evaluation

I have suggested that the emphasis in Components One to Five has been on assessment. But there have been a number of references to evaluation and how it differs from assessment. Write down three or four key points which you think show what evaluation is about. (If you get stuck on this one, skim earlier Components, particularly Two and Four for some clues.)

*Evaluation is about **using the information** of assessment to make **judgements.***

*Evaluation is concerned with **improving performance** — our own performance and the effectiveness of the training we give — and our trainees' performance.*

*Evaluation tries to **demonstrate the effects** of training — to show what has actually happened.*

*Evaluation is concerned with **the real situation** and the **decisions** which have to be taken in relation to it.*

*Evaluation is not just for 'experts' — it is about **practical problems** in our training programmes which assessment constantly throws up.*

Once again, your list will contain at least one or two of these, I expect — probably worded a little differently. I have emphasised a number of key words or phrases in my answers. Check off any of these in yours.

Now, against my list, number the points in order of importance, as you see them. Add and number any important point you think I've missed.

*There can't really be a 'right answer' to this task. It may well depend on your situation and experience. But I expect you will have rated highly, **improving performance** — both your own as a trainer and that of your trainees. Certainly most good teachers and trainers tend to want to look very carefully at their own performance as they are aware just how much the performance of their trainees actually depends on this. (Study Unit Five will concentrate on ways of looking at one's own performance).*

The Importance of Evaluation for the Trainer

Improvement of Training

In the 'literature' there are many examples of the way in which evaluation can affect training and lead to improvement. A dramatic illustration is given in a book by Rowntree (*Educational Technology and Curriculum Development*; Harper and Row). He himself draws this material from Warr, Bird and Rackham — *Evaluation of Management Training* (Gower Press; 1970).

In the training of airline managers, two series of courses are evaluated. In each series (A and B) the course was given five times and, on each occasion, the attitudes and knowledge of each group were measured. For Series B the trainers were informed of the test results; for Series A they were not. The Series B Trainers were thus able to use the data to improve

their course. The graph below shows that the gain in knowledge by successive groups increased through Series B — up to 70% above what it had been the first time through. In Series A, with no feedback from evaluation, average gain in knowledge in the final course was only about 10% above the first run.

From Rowntree, D., *Educational Technology in Curriculum Development*, Harper and Row

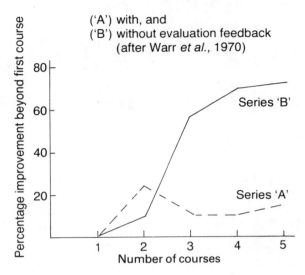

Improvement in Course-Effectiveness

Figure 5

On a day-to-day basis, the trainer's decisions and what he does are also informed by feedback and the training is modified and improved as he gradually finds out about how problems appear from the individual trainee's point of view. Feedback which the trainer obtains from gathering information **as the training proceeds** may well be crucial to the success of a course and help trainees through frustration, boredom or worry. This point has already been well made in Component Four and will be returned to in later Study Units, but it is worth reminding ourselves constantly that **formative** evaluation, as this day-to-day process is called, is vitally important. It is wrong just to consider the more obvious **summative** evaluation when, at the end of the course, we look back at everything that has happened or perhaps, all too often, only at the figures showing the results. This point was made in Component Three.

Improvement of Materials

Any trainer will want to know how well he is doing. One of the difficulties of distance learning, our present medium, is that you can't see me and I can't see you; perhaps you are switching off as you get bored.

'Personality to help the materials along . . .'

I can't modify my approach as we proceed; I've got to rely on the materials rather than my personality to keep you working. Yet many good trainers and teachers in face-to-face learning do rely heavily on personality to help the materials along.

Keeping a student on track is one of the reasons why those who design distance learning materials tend to try to state objectives clearly. The aim is also to give the student frequent opportunities to self-assess, through checkpoints, to test where he is against where the materials have told him he should be. A famous American expert, Robert Mager, makes the point that if the student doesn't know where he is going, how will he know whether he has arrived 'some place else?'

Obviously, face-to-face trainers also want to know something about the effectiveness of their materials. Is this particular topic or that specific section **valuable**? Are these new materials better than those I used before? A detailed consideration of how best to look at training materials occurs in Package Seven, but these general principles of assessment and evaluation which are outlined in the present Study Unit are the key to the evaluation of materials.

Improvement in Communicating the Results of the Training
(Evaluation as proof of a job well done)
Training costs money and it is important to be able to show that the results justify the expenditure. A training programme without open and proper evaluation invites others, perhaps not directly concerned with the training itself, to use their evaluative procedures, which may be neither systematic nor appropriate. So it's in our interest as trainers to build in measures which will **demonstrate** the value of the programme.

It's important that those who are responsible for making decisions, from the individual trainer to those with a wider responsibility, have access to a **range** of assessment information of the type that this Study

Unit has briefly introduced and which will be pursued in much greater detail in later Study Units of this Package. Of course, what actually **happens** as a result of evaluation will depend very much on who is making the decisions and on what kind of decision has to be made, from whether the programme is to continue or cease, to how a particular detail of the programme might be changed.

Improving the decision-making process
It would be nice to think that decisions are easy to make when all the information one might need is available. But, even in the unlikely event of the decision maker having a comprehensive range of information from which to work, there will always be a number of possible reasons why the process of evaluating may not be easy.

List two or three reasons why, even with lots of information from assessment etc., the process of evaluation may prove to be difficult.

Again, our reasons may differ in some detail, but I suspect that you may agree in some of the areas I have listed on the next page.

1. Sometimes, when we collect information, we do not really know what is likely to be relevant. We may collect more than we need and perhaps not in quite the right form, so we may suffer from a sort of **information over-load** *which clouds our vision.*

'Information overload . . . clouds our vision'

2. **We may lack the information we really need.** *Sometimes we may find that we have failed to plan to collect the very information which is really crucial to our evaluation (for example, possibly a questionnaire to those people directly responsible for individual trainees in their day-to-day jobs immediately after training).*
3. *The point of view of the person making the decisions often intrudes.* **Value questions** *about this or that aspect of training may be a very powerful factor in decision-making (for example, whether to adopt new media).*
   The very **selection** *of assessment data for evaluation may well reflect values.*
4. *The* **context** *of the training may be crucial. Decisions are not made in a vacuum. Your particular situation may involve you in facing any number of* **constraints.**

List, off the cuff, three or four obvious constraints which are likely to affect the training context.

Possible answers will include: time; material resources/ money; space; facilities; quality of the trainee; priorities in the training programme.

I expect that, as usual, we may differ slightly but I would guess that time, money and possibly space figured in your list.

Any or all of these may mean that **you can't make the ideal decision**, whatever the evidence you have collected seems to suggest. Your own context is clearly crucial to the way you will evaluate your training programme and this theme will recur in Study Unit Two.

As we have noted, it may be that the evidence you collect is to inform the decision-making of others, that it is out of your hands. If this is the case, the points raised above may be even more important, but the question remains complex. Whose ideas about what information in which context are relevant to a decision to be taken?

Conclusion

This brief introduction to evaluation has raised a number of issues which will be pursued in detail in this Package. It is clear that evaluation is not the same thing as assessment, but an extension of it. One of the purposes of this introductory unit has been to draw this distinction.

Although the input/output model is a part of this process, looking at what goes into the training 'machine' and observing what comes out and noting the change, this is only a part of the evaluation process.

'Looking at what goes into the training machine
and what comes out'

Evaluation may properly involve a far greater range of activities than just the consideration of the change in the trainee. Clearly we can and must think about evaluation in relation to the end product and what trainees in general should be able to do as a result of the training. But the good chalk-face trainer will also be thinking about evaluation in relation to the individual trainee (what about the trainee who is already tall and thin before he enters the machine?) and this means that he will be thinking about evaluating his own performance and the materials he uses (do they account for individual differences?). Evaluation **may** be large-scale, something carried out by others, but in day-to-day training, it's likely to be a tool of the trade, involving a range of simple, common-sense techniques — opinions, impressions, judgements, as well as more objective methods. The face-to-face trainer will probably be only too well aware of many of the questions he wants to answer about the training he is offering, so the methods he will prefer will tend to be those he thinks focus best on aspects which he hopes will increase his own understanding of the problem.

Far from something done by 'experts', often outsiders, do-it-yourself evaluation enables ordinary trainers to look realistically and systematically at their own situation and to see more clearly than they might have done through a random glance, just what needs to be done to improve performance.

Tutor Contact

This first Study Unit in the seven Study Unit Package on Assessment and Evaluation has been an Introduction. For you it may have been very much a brief run through what you know already, or it may indeed have introduced you to some new ideas about the work you do as a trainer or are about to do. We hope that, in either case, it has encouraged you to proceed to the Study Units which follow and which deal in much more depth with issues which have been raised here.

If you have any queries or if you wish to clarify any points in this Study Unit, don't hesitate to contact us.

Objectives

On completion of the Study Unit the student will:
* Be able to define assessment and to list six common characteristics of assessment;
* Be able to define evaluation and to list four common characteristics of it;
* Be able to identify several common uses of assessment;
* Be able to identify the different strengths of formal and informal assessment;
* Be able to identify ways in which every-day assessments are made;
* Accept that structured methods of assessment should be considered by trainers;
* Be willing to look at his own situation as a starting point in thinking about assessment;
* Be able to list at least three main areas of performance which may appropriately be assessed;
* Demonstrate an awareness of some of the strengths and pitfalls of assessment linked to objectives;
* Accept that, to be useful, assessment must be balanced and valid;
* Be able to differentiate between:
  formative and summative assessment
  coursework and examination
  continuous and periodic assessment;
* Be able to state the advantages/disadvantages of internal and external assessment;
* Be able to list ways in which an assessment programme might motivate trainees;

* Be able to differentiate between and identify uses of:
  norm referenced tests
  criterion referenced tests;
* Be able to evaluate examples of assessment
  from the point of view of the trainee
  from the point of view of the trainer;
* Accept that the choice of any form of assessment will have far reaching effects within an organisation;
* In a given situation, be able to recommend particular strategies for assessing the achievement of trainees;
* Be aware of the contribution of evaluation to the improvement of performance;
* Be aware of some of the difficulties of using the results of assessment for evaluation;
* Be aware of some of the constraints which operate in various training contexts.

Acknowledgement: Permission to use material from Rowntree, D. *Educational Technology in Curiculum Development* Harper & Row, is gratefully acknowledged.

Study Unit 2

The Process of Assessment and Evaluation

Component 1:

Making Decisions About Assessment

Key Words

 Congruence; validity; graded stages; process.

The Study Unit

In this Study Unit we will be looking at the implementation of an assessment scheme within a training programme.

Having reviewed general considerations in Study Unit One, we start this unit by considering the taking of decisions about assessment.

Before any decisions about assessment are taken by you, you will need to look at your own position. At what point do you influence Company decisions on assessment?

Are you:

(a) in control of the training course to the extent that you set objectives, devise a training programme and decide on the assessment for that programme?

(b) in control of the training course but have to meet objectives set by others in a training and assessment programme which you devise?

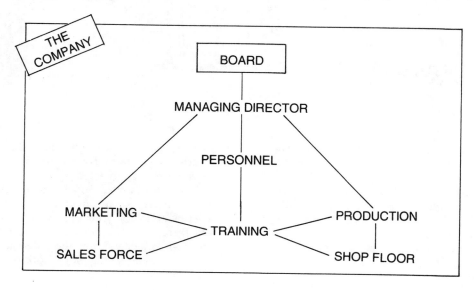

Figure 6

(c) in control of a training programme which meets objectives set by others and is assessed by others?

or

(d) instructing on a training and assessment programme which is given to you to implement by others?

Position (a) is probably rare since a decision to set up a training programme in an organisation seems to imply that those who take the decision to set it up have some objectives in mind for that programme. In positions (b), (c) and (d), however, you need to consider whether you can, or want to, influence the decisions taken by others.

Remember your assessment and evaluation of the training programme might be very useful in enabling you to produce the evidence for all the changes you might wish to suggest.

Where you do not find yourself in position (a) you need to consider what lay behind the decisions that those in authority took. As far as assessment is concerned this is most important in (b) and (c), but even if you are in position (d) you must consider in your implementation of the training course what was in the mind of the authors of it.

If you know the reasons for the setting of certain objectives or for the form which assessment takes then you are in a position to develop an instructional programme which is congruent throughout. That is, it has objectives, a training method and assessment programme which all support each other and which aim for, lead to and test the same things.

What did the Board have in mind?

What the planners wanted clearly makes a difference. For example, is your training course on the shop-floor intended

(a) as an introduction to that section of the work-place for would-be executives?

(b) as part of a long course for the production of highly skilled personnel?

(c) as a complete short course for personnel who are to be given limited skills?

or (d) for some other purpose?

Whatever it is it might carry the same general description or title as a course but the way it is run and assessed must be dictated by what it is all for.

(The rest of this component makes the assumption that you have some say in what goes on, but even where you do not, you need to consider the decisions which are brought up in the rest of this component in order to understand how these decisions might have been arrived at, so that your work can be congruent with them.)

What form of assessment for congruence?

For the assessment itself a key decision is "What form is the assessment to take?" An issue that was raised in Unit One, Component Three.

If you are to achieve congruence between the way you instruct and your assessment programme then a key idea is that of the validity of the instrument, an idea which is expanded in Units Three and Four. In simple terms your assessment programme must test what it claims to be testing. We all know that we are capable of saying one thing and doing another or vice versa. It is little use therefore, to ask trainees in a written test what their attitude to customers ought to be because we will get their parroted answers which may be of no use whatsoever in demonstrating how they really behave towards the general public.

The only way to be sure that skills and attitudes have been grasped is to see them demonstrated not written or talked about.

Written examinations can test recall of information very well. They can also test the ability to organise that information in a worthwhile form and to make deductions from it. You have to consider whether or not that is what you are training for.

It is often said of the kind of examinations most of your trainees will have done in school, that they merely demonstrate the ability (or otherwise) to pass examinations. This is somewhat unfair since success in them also shows the ability to apply oneself to a task over a period and some skill in handling knowledge. Your firm may use the results in its recruitment policy

because of this. However, these examinations are not job specific. Even the practical ones do not have a particular post in mind. That is not their purpose. Your requirements may need you to avoid giving the trainees some sort of "poor-man's" C.S.E., G.C.S.E. or G.C.E. because it would not be congruent with your objectives nor a valid test of your training. Instead you will need to see your trainees demonstrating the qualities you are looking for in a realistic situation.

Time and Timing

If you develop the idea of congruence or appropriateness of the assessment to your training programme, decisions are needed on the time and timing of the assessment. Questions of formative and summative assessment and formal and informal assessment were raised in Unit One Component Three. Now we need to consider them again as they are important in making decisions about our assessment programme.

You may decide that in order to improve your training and give better feedback there will be some formative assessment (i.e. taking place during the training programme) whether this is formal or informal. Even so, virtually every programme will need a form of summative assessment at the end.

Everyone concerned with the training process, the company, you, as trainer, and the trainees themselves need to know that the process of training has gone satisfactorily, hence the importance of the final assessment.

The word 'passed' was avoided in the preceding paragraphs because it may imply an attitude to training which you do not wish to foster. The trainee may see a final assessment as a hurdle to be jumped which, once successfully negotiated, he can forget.

We have probably all met this attitude. At its most extreme it might be the teenager who has just passed his motor-cycle driving test and believes that he no longer has to obey the rules of the road or any of the safety and defensive riding techniques he has been taught. In the workplace it may be the trainee who believes that you only avoid the 'short-cuts' until after passing the 'test' or final assessment.

If this situation is happening, or looks likely to happen, we need to ask certain questions;

(a) Is the assessment, particularly the final one, claiming undue importance in everybody's eyes in the training programme? (This question will be dealt with below.)

(b) Is the assessment out of touch with the real demands of the job?

(c) Can the assessment be broken down into a series of graded stages?

(d) Is it necessary to change attitudes so that training is not seen as something which is never fully completed?

If (b) is true and the assessment is out of touch with the job as it is actually done is this because:

(i) The assessment is not valid i.e. in line with the training?

(ii) The training is not congruent with the job as done?

(iii) The job as done is not the way the company would want the job done?

Clearly those in charge of training, including yourself, can take decisions which will put (i) and (ii) to rights, but dealing with (iii) is a problem requiring tact, a company-wide policy and a commitment to re-training as opposed to initial training. A decision over which you as a trainer may have little control.

It is obvious that there is little point in training people to do a job in a way which, in practice, is found not to be the best way. There will be many instances, however, where the trainee has to go more slowly or painstakingly or with greater conscious attention to rules in order to develop the good habits that are second nature to the trained worker. This is not the same as the situation where the trained worker can say to the newly-fledged trainee "Now you can forget all that rubbish on the training course."

Any 'final' assessment therefore should represent the job as actually performed by the skilled practitioner.

If you could answer "Yes" to questions (c) and (d) then the answer to one may help the other, because breaking the assessment down into a series of graded stages may be a way of developing an attitude which says that we never stop learning about a job and we can go on getting better at it.

Taking this line may seem to be more appropriate to the more highly skilled positions, but at almost every level a division can be made of different knowledge, skills and attitudes required and some breakdown made to produce a series of tests creating a climate where the trainee feels he is adding additional skills etc. at frequent intervals to those already acquired, and has less a sense of being untrained one minute and

fully-trained the next because a single hurdle has been jumped.

How important is your assessment?

This brings us on to questions of how important the assessment is seen to be within the training programme as a whole. This is tied in with the decision considered in the next section on the end result for the trainee. However, you need to consider whether you should emphasize the process which the trainee is going through or the final outcome as revealed in an assessment test. The distinction may seem somewhat artificial in many cases since, in virtually all programmes of training, both the process the trainee goes through and the final outcome will be important. However, the emphasis which you give to either one and which you communicate to the trainees can make a significant difference.

If we use this course as an example, process is all important. You are working through the course and learning by doing this. The outcome, if we have got it right, ought to be a better trainer. By giving instruction and making you think through your own training scheme in the way we suggest, we have committed ourselves to a 'process' approach. There is no terminal assessment of your performance. Nevertheless this is a useful training course if it meets your needs.

That said, we do not have the motivating power of a final assessment and qualification to egg you along.

Final assessment might be taking up too high a proportion of the training time and if you bear in mind what we have said above then you might decide to monitor your trainees' progress throughout their training programme and build up a profile of their performance as you observe them in training and performing the work tasks. This method might meet all the criteria for congruence, validity and avoiding the 'jumping the hurdle' syndrome, but it is time-consuming; you need skills in developing a profile (which is dealt with elsewhere) and the trainees may feel that it lacks objectivity (see Unit One Component Three). You have also got to recognise that your very presence may alter the situation considerably.

▨ Checkpoint

(1) make a list for yourself of the advantages and disadvantages of:

    (a) a single terminal assessment

    (b) a series of assessments (does it matter whether or not these are of graded difficulty?)

    (c) continuous monitoring to produce a profile.

(2) What is the pattern of the timing of assessment on your training course?

Why is it organised in this way?

Are there any changes you would now like to make to the timing?

The end result

Somebody has to decide what the end result of the assessment is going to be and this influences decisions about how it is conducted. Unless you take the extreme view of profiling, that is, that all it does is describe a person's performance without judging it and that therefore no one can be said to have 'failed', then a decision has to be taken about the pass level.

Is this going to be based on norm or criterion referencing (see Unit One, Component Four)?

Is the hurdle, or series of hurdles, intended only to catch the downright incompetent or is it more like the Olympic high-jump, intended to weed out all but those with a very special talent?

If job security, promotion or enhanced payments are attached to performance in assessment, then the trainees are likely to want what they would consider as objective an assessment scheme as possible.

This is where trainees in a written test may feel safest with single word answers that are either right or wrong or practical tests where performance is judged on very strict criteria.

Such a view tends to discourage initiative and whilst it is a suitable approach for the most simple and mechanical of jobs, it does not reflect the complexity of most jobs whether it be in the motor-repair workshop, the office or those jobs most directly involving contact with the public.

What for?

The final decision we have to consider, which might well really be regarded as the first, harks back to the whole of the previous unit. What is it all for?

What purpose does the assessment programme serve for the trainee and for you?

The trainee needs to feel that some targets have been reached and that this has been recognised. He needs feedback in order that his performance can improve.

You need to be able to show that something worthwhile has happened. This may have involved you in pre-testing the trainees and then testing them again to show the change that has taken place over a period of time or in demonstrating that your trainees' performance now meets some strict criteria for success.

It doesn't need to be this elaborate but the trainee does need some recognition of success.

You need feedback on:

    (a) the trainee's performance

    (b) the programme

    (c) the training materials

    (d) your own performance as a trainer.

The trainee and yourself have probably got a very different view of the process.

There is little point in your taking one or other of two extreme views of what assessment reveals. The first would be that if a trainee does badly it is all the fault of the trainee and no questions need to be asked about the training. (Funnily enough when the trainee does well we are much more likely to think that the training has something to do with it.) Equally it is wrong to take a self-condemnatory attitude as a trainer and feel that it must be our fault if the trainees do not do well. Clearly there is a middle path. Trainees do fail through their own fault or lack of ability, and some training is very poor. We need to use assessment to come to a reasoned judgement on all the areas mentioned in (a) to (d) above to improve the course.

The truth is that the trainee has to do the learning. You cannot do it for him. You can only help by running a good programme, which the trainee sees as good and useful. (Hence the suggestion of reaction sheets in Study Unit One Component Four.) Having such a good programme involves having the right materials and helping the trainee to learn through your explanations and your motivation of the trainees.

You ought to judge the decisions that are taken about the assessment of the training programme in the light of what we have just said above.

▰▰▰

In your own training programme does the assessment help you to bring the trainees to the final objectives set by the programme, or do you see it as a 'necessary evil' rather than a positive contribution to the training?

Write down how your assessment programme helps the trainee. If you take the 'necessary evil' line, try to write down a different scheme which would help the trainees to the objectives.

Which parts of your assessment programme help you to judge the materials you use and your own performance? If you think none do, then try to devise some.

Component 2:

Planning an Assessment Programme

Key Words

 Briefing; 'mock' tests; external examiner; sub-skills.

Now that you have thought about the strategy of the whole decision-making process in the assessment of the training programme, we need to turn to the actual tactics of devising a programme and running it.

Pretesting

In order to train your people effectively you must know at what level you are starting. If you make assumptions about knowledge, skills or attitudes which are not there, then your training can only be confusing or ineffective. If, on the other hand, you fail to make use of what the trainee already possesses then he is likely to become bored and to feel that the training programme is not worthwhile.

In order to avoid this you must make some assessments before the training begins, as was suggested in previous discussions on timing. What does this mean in practice?

(a) Do you have information on the trainees from their files? Can you, for example, assume certain mathematical processes are understood because you know they all have at least Grade 2 in C.S.E. mathematics?

If such information is not available or the trainees were not selected on the basis of such formal qualifications, you may still need to know about specific skills in such things as computation in mathematics. If you do, then you need to give some kind of test on these specific skills: addition, use of decimals, whatever. Such a test should be concerned only with what you need the trainees to know for your training programme.

The results of such a test may well, of course, throw up a further problem, viz. that not all your trainees will be at the same level and you may well have to adapt your training programme to cater for this, but this would be a small price to pay to make sure all your trainees were comfortable with the programme.

Even if you do have information on formal educational qualifications, these may well not be tailored to your requirements and trainees who have followed different courses for different examination boards can have very different areas which they have covered/not covered in their courses and you may still need to run specific tests.

(b) Are you part of the selection panel for trainees before they enter the training programme? If you are then you can regard this as part of pretesting or preassessment. If not, then a written report on the selection could be very useful to you. In any case an interview with you before embarking on the training programme could be a very useful way for you to judge attitudes (though you might also want to use a formal written attitude test) and to give you some idea of where you need to start in the training for particular trainees.

Hopefully the cases will not be as extreme as the one illustrated.

Nor need your meeting with them be all a one-to-one situation. You can gain a great deal of information by assessing the trainee's present stage of development through organising a group discussion. You can also use this to allow those who know something to bring those who don't on to a common starting point for the training.

(c) Have the trainees already had some experience within the area? This will make a considerable difference to the assessment programme at this pretesting stage.

Trainees who have had some experience could be seen as falling into two categories.

(i) a 'mixed-bag' who have volunteered for training or have come on training because that is company policy. Here your pretesting could take the form of actually performing the work task and assessing how well, or badly, it is done. This again gives you the starting point or points for your training and also gives you and the trainees a benchmark against which progress following training can be judged.

(It is not usually a good idea to put those without experience into a situation where you are testing their ability in the work task. It might actually be dangerous if machinery is involved and it may well discourage the trainee, particularly if you find they know nothing about the job, which is something you could have found out by asking anyway.)

(ii) a carefully selected group who having shown a certain level of proficiency already are considered by the company as ready to proceed to training or further training. Clearly such a group is easier for you to deal with since you can feel that they are already pretested and that you can safely make specific assumptions about the stage they have already reached.

Checkpoint
Can you now decide for your own training programme what level of pretesting you can have or would like to see?

Write down what it is you are trying to find out and what the consequences of such knowledge might be for your programme.

Frequency

We have already said in Component One of this Unit that most programmes will have some final assessment as the ultimate goal. You now have to decide on the pattern of frequency for your programme.

It has been suggested that you might like to break the large assessment down into its component skills etc. and test them separately, but when devising a programme you need to balance the pros and cons. The one final assessment often fails to motivate the trainee in the middle of the training programme. This can lead to rushed preparation at the end and a course dominated in the trainee's mind by this one tremendous task at the end. In all but the shortest training programmes it is difficult to devise an assessment of reasonable length which effectively tests all that has been covered in the programme. This may or may not be important to you but you need to think about it.

On the other hand, frequent assessment has its drawbacks as well. It may simply become too time-consuming, taking up the training time in constant assessment. Whereas the one final assessment may mean that familiarity breeds contempt and it is not taken seriously enough. Conversely too frequent bouts of assessment may mean that the trainee never feels that he can relax. (See Component Three of Study Unit One.)

Assessment which follows too closely on the training may only be testing short-term retention of knowledge or skills. Frequent small assessments may not be the best means of testing whether a series of complex, interrelated skills can be used in an interrelated way by the trainee, though you might use the small tests as part of the training programme leading to the big final and interrelated assessment.

It is possible to build in assessments which are a series of carefully graded projects to be undertaken by the trainee such as those set for trainee computer programmers. Here the assessment is integral to the training because satisfactory completion of each project provides the assessment as well as the training. This is a form of continuous assessment, which, as we have seen in Component Three of Study Unit One, can take assessment pressure off the trainees or, conversely it can make them feel that it is ever-present, oppressive and intolerable.

If you have more than one element of assessment you will not only have to decide which will be formally and which informally assessed but also the relative weighting of the different parts of the formal assessment. Is an assessment in week one to carry the same weighting as an assessment later in the training programme? This is a question that will be explored in the next component.

Kind of assessment

The technicalities and appropriateness of different kinds of assessment tests for differing situations will be dealt with in detail in Units Three and Four, but even at this stage of overall planning you must bear in mind questions of the objectives you wish to achieve and therefore what kind of test is going to give valid results and also how important the actual assessment of trainees is in your training programme. Are you testing mainly for knowledge, skills or attitudes or some combination of the three, and what kind of tests would be congruent with your original objectives?

Trainee involvement

A structured assessment programme can only work if it is planned as part of the training programme itself and can therefore be congruent with it. With this in mind it is important that the trainees have a briefing and a chance to discuss with you at the beginning of the programme the relationship between the training and the assessment of it.

They need to know (and to have in writing):
(a) exactly how important the assessment is.
(b) what the criteria are that you will be using to judge their performance.
(c) what kind of tests they will be facing. This may well mean building into the training programme 'mock' tests to familiarise trainees with the kind of test that will be coming up. This will help to make your results more valid i.e. reflect what the trainees can really do rather than what they did when confused by the unfamiliar and unexpected.
(d) which parts of the assessment are formal and which informal.
(e) how you will give feedback on the performance of the trainees.

You must try to avoid the 'it's not fair' syndrome amongst your trainees.

After the practical test

In written test

After results

Think of drawing up an assessment timetable for your training programme.

What factors are you going to have to consider?

Write these down and then compare them with my list. You may well come up with different factors for your particular programme and they will certainly be in a different order!

Possible list of factors

(i) The need to provide sufficient time for the trainees to make use of feedback before further assessment.

(ii) The need to build into your personal workload time for giving feedback to the trainees. (Can you give yourself time to make sure they get the feedback quickly?)

(iii) The need to provide practice in the kinds of assessment used.

(iv) The need to provide adequate time for the trainees to prepare for the assessment tasks.

(v) The overall length of the course.

(vi) The importance attached to the assessment results.

Detailed consideration of an example of training and assessment

The time has now come to put the work of the first unit in this package and the work so far in this unit together. Let's have a close look at a training programme and assessment situation with which most of us are very familiar. At the same time we will try to analyse it using the questioning techniques introduced so far.

For this we have chosen training for and the taking of the Driving Test. Please note that this section is not based on official information but is the thinking outsider's analysis.

The first point worth noticing is that we all regard it as the 'driving test' rather than the 'driving course' which tells us a great deal about the importance of assessment in this exercise. It is the be-all-and-end-all of the entire sequence of events. The process i.e. what the learner-driver experiences on the training course is of little consequence provided that it leads to a 'pass' in the test at the end.

The trainer, i.e. the driving instructor, does not control the content of the training programme to any major degree because he knows what the criteria are for 'passing' the assessment and it would not pay him to deviate from the content implied by those criteria since his trainees would fail. He can, however, control the way in which he trains the learner drivers. He may, for example, include several exact replicas of the final test in his training programme in order to familiarise the learner with what is to be expected in the test.

The final assessment is not conducted by the trainer but by an external agency, the examiner.

It is a 'pass/fail' situation. There is no degree of passing or failing, no moving on to a conditional licence to drive on a second level pass. Because of this and its importance to most people the assessment may be retaken until a pass is finally obtained, and thus the instructor has two kinds of people to train:

(a) those who have never taken the test,

and (b) those who have and have failed.

This will call for different training and assessment techniques.

The test itself provides little feedback for the learner. If you fail you will be told the areas of weakness, and if you pass you may be given some idea of what you still need to improve on, but there is no

discussion. A failed trainee must go back to his trainer with his failure slip and they have to reconstruct why the learner failed. A successful trainee is not followed up by anyone to see if the training is being improved upon.

Many people do regard passing the assessment as a licence to forget their training. Is this because the training programme is bad or because the assessment test is out of line with common practice? As an example we could take the manoeuvre when cars travelling in opposite directions pass each other when both are wishing to turn right at traffic lights.

Is it this?

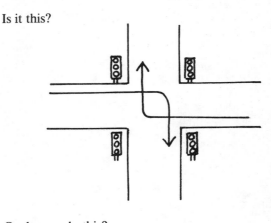

Or do you do this?

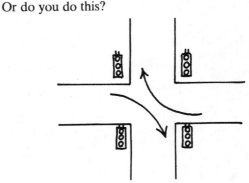

Though you must remember that good training will have made such things as the 'mirror, signal, gear, manoeuvre' sequence something which is second nature by the time of the test.

The good driving instructor might also have made awareness of other road users an integral part of the learner's driving by using the technique of making the trainee give a running commentary on the road, traffic, etc. around him as he drives, as is done by trainers for the Advanced Driving Test. This is both good training and allows for assessment of performance at the same time.

The training for the driving test leaves us, therefore, with knowledge we refuse to use and other knowledge and skills which have become ingrained by careful training.

The trainer will give a great deal of feedback because he will be informally assessing the trainee's progress the whole time and using that assessment to improve the learner-driver's performance. He may decide to have some apparently more formal points of assessment such as "Now we will do an emergency stop just as you would in the test." (See above) Remember, however, that although the trainer will report on this in such terms as "That would not have passed the test" or "That was excellent. That would easily pass." only the final or 'real' assessment counts in the eyes of the trainee. It is the trainer who is getting just as much as the trainee out of this mid-point, informal assessment.

The good driving instructor will break down the various skills of driving which are required into certain groupings even though the ability to drive a car well is a combination of skills with complex interrelationships. There are such sub-skills, as they are called, as changing gear, reversing, doing a 'three-point' turn, coming up to a road junction correctly, etc. He may decide that, as a check-list for himself to monitor learner progress, and as a motivator for the learner, who will be given recognisable success at regular and frequent intervals, he will do a mini-test on each of these skills after say a couple of training sessions concentrating on that particular skill.

Despite the old-wives' tales, the test is criterion referenced. The examiners do not have to have their quota of failures. The trainer has to treat the test as purely objective in order to get as 'correct' a performance as possible out of his trainee. However, there is some subjectivity because, though it may be possible to define with some accuracy the standard expected for the setting-off routine, a hill-start, and reversing round a corner, there is still room for examiner judgement and this is certainly true where he has to assess 'consideration for other road users'. It is also true that only by having a set form to the question and one acceptable reply can subjectivity be eradicated from the section of the test on 'knowledge of the Highway Code'.

You might question the validity of the driving test and therefore the programme leading up to it because of a lack of congruence between driving as most of us experience it and what is missing from the test. Most obvious are the lack of an assessment of motorway driving, night-time driving, and a specific test of parking in a confined space. However, a distinction is now drawn between the test for automatic and manual gearboxes, a recognition that different skills are required and therefore taught and tested.

You might also question whether the form of questioning on the Highway Code is testing recall rather than understanding and that if this is so whether the 'canny' trainer trains for the former rather than the latter.

You will no doubt be able to reflect on other aspects of the training for driving as an assessment problem, but turn this now to your own situation by using the following checkpoint.

▰▰▰

Put yourself in the position of an outside (external) examiner testing and assessing your trainees who have followed a specific training course in your firm.

Consider the checklist of skills, knowledge and attitudes you would want to see displayed which you prepared for Unit One Component Two. Thinking of the way we have just looked at the driving test are there any additions you want to make or parts you would now leave out? Do you want to have some assessment of all these items?

In the driving test you do not have to achieve perfection in each item; perfection is not the criterion; that is not the standard required. There are acceptable levels of performance below this.

Below is the start of an example checklist based on the driving test. Add to your own assessment checklist the levels of performance you would judge the individual assessment items on. That is, for each skill, item(s) of knowledge, or attitude which you test, provide headings such as 'good', 'acceptable', 'poor'. (Or your own headings for the levels of performance.)

As a preparation for future Components and Units in this Package consider also how many 'poor' and 'unacceptable's you can allow or which items might be allowed to fall below 'acceptable' and which not.

	GOOD	ACCEPTABLE	POOR	UNACCEPTABLE
Gear changing.				
Use of mirror.				
Emergency stop.				
Consideration for other road users.				
Knowledge of the Highway Code.				

Component 3:

Planning an Assessment Scheme

Key Words

 Assessment scheme/plan; assessment programme; topics; outcomes; knowledge; application; attitudes; skill; grid; columns; rows; cells; weighting; tests.

Entry requirements

Before commencing this Component, you should be familiar with the concepts of aims and objectives, job descriptions, levels of learning outcomes (e.g. knowledge, application, skills).

Introduction

Within an overall assessment programme (ideas about which have been considered in the previous Component) we will need to develop schemes for assessing specified areas of competence and achievement. The assessment programme is the overall plan or strategy; the assessment schemes represent the next stage, leading on to the development of actual tests. We are therefore engaged in the intermediate stage of working from the general outline towards the detailed assessment instruments.

Assessment schemes are also sometimes called assessment plans or assessment/test specifications — or even test plans! To avoid confusion we will stick to the term assessment scheme, although any of the other expressions are virtually interchangeable with it.

Planning an assessment scheme
What to cover?

The 'point of departure' is the area of the course/subject matter (and the corresponding section of the assessment programme) which **you choose** as an appropriate 'unit' for assessment. Again this will depend on the extent of the overall programme and the degree to which you intend to break it down at this stage.

In order to develop the assessment scheme, you will need to collect together all the available information e.g. course aims and objectives, job description (if appropriate), syllabus, scheme of work/course timetable. Having done this, you should then identify, for the chosen unit,

a) the various subject matter TOPICS (or headings) which need to be assessed, and

b) the types and levels of LEARNING OUTCOMES or ABILITIES which need to be assessed (e.g. knowledge, comprehension, application, attitude, practical skill). You will need to consider the topics one by one in order to identify and list these various outcomes.

In order to clarify this procedure, let's look at a simple example — it's probably easier to do it this way than continue to talk in rather abstract terms!

The Process of Assessment and Evaluation

Let us imagine you are concerned with a short training course on "Using the Telephone". The topics/headings you have identified as needing to be assessed are shown down the left-hand side of the following table. **Taking each one in turn**, you decide the level(s) of outcomes/abilities you feel will need to be assessed, (building up the list of outcomes as necessary as you go along). You could end up at this stage with something like this:

TABLE 1

OUTCOMES / TOPICS	Knowledge	Application	Skills & Affective Behaviour
Services available	YES	NO	NO
Using Directories	YES	NO	NO
Lists of Telephone Numbers	YES	NO	NO
Costs	YES	NO	NO
Calls via Operator	YES	NO*	NO
Direct Dialling	YES	NO*	NO
Making a Call	YES	YES	YES
Receiving a Call	YES	YES	YES

* Tested under 'Making a Call'

The Grid

You should now prepare a more formal two-dimensional grid as follows:

a) Label the head of each COLUMN with one type of learning OUTCOME.

b) Enter the TOPICS down the rows on the left-hand side.

c) Add a blank COLUMN at the right-hand side and a blank ROW across the bottom (for entering row and column totals).

At this stage, your grid would look like this, with all the individual CELLS blank:

TABLE 2   COLUMNS

OUTCOMES / TOPICS	KNOWLEDGE	APPLICATION	SKILL	
TOPIC A				
TOPIC B		(CELLS)		
TOPIC C				
TOPIC D				

R O W S

Enter an arbitrary TOTAL POSSIBLE SCORE (normally this will be 100 for convenience, or possibly 1,000 for a large area of assessment) in the bottom right-hand corner cell. Indicate those cells which were given a 'NO' in your rough table (as not requiring assessment) by entering zeros.

Carefully consider the **relative** importance of the various TOPICS and OUTCOMES and decide on the 'weighting' to be given to each one.

(NOTE Only you — and your colleagues — can decide these relative weightings).

The corresponding figures (normally these will be percentages) are then entered in the right-hand column and bottom row — in pencil at this stage, as you will almost certainly want to alter them as you proceed! Check that these figures add up to the correct total. Your grid should then look something like this:

TABLE 3   COLUMNS

OUTCOMES / TOPICS	KNOWLEDGE	APPLICATION	SKILL	
TOPIC A			0	15
TOPIC B		(CELLS)		25
TOPIC C	0			30
TOPIC D	0			30
	20	30	50	100

(ROWS)

You will see that 50% of the total score has been allocated to assessment at the skill level, and that topics C and D carry 60% of the total score.

Then you should consider each topic in turn in relation to the various outcomes, and decide on how the total score for that TOPIC (ROW total) should be allocated among the outcomes. Simultaneously consider the allocation of the total score for each OUTCOME (COLUMN total) among the topics. You will realise, of course, that these figures are based on your personal judgement as to the (relative) weighting each one should have.

Enter the corresponding figures in the cells as you go along — still in pencil!

Your grid should now look something like this:

TABLE 4   COLUMNS

OUTCOMES / TOPICS	KNOWLEDGE	APPLICATION	SKILL	
TOPIC A	10	5	0	15
TOPIC B	10	5	10	25
TOPIC C	0	10	20	30
TOPIC D	0	10	20	30
	20	30	50	100

(ROWS)

53

In this very simple example, it has been decided that:
a) topic A only needs to be assessed at the knowledge and application levels
b) topic B needs to be assessed at all three levels
c) topics C and D need not be assessed at the knowledge level
d) 40% of the total marks are allocated to testing topics C and D at the skill level.

You may like to go back and suggest appropriate percentage figures for the example in Table 1. There is no 'right' answer — partly because, without fuller information, the interpretation of the bare topic headings is bound to be somewhat speculative.

Having constructed the grid, and agreed the relative weightings (which can now probably be written-in more permanently!), the next step would be to decide on the appropriate assessment procedures. In the above example (Table 4), it may be appropriate to decide that assessment of topics A and B at the knowledge, and possibly application, levels could be undertaken using an objective (e.g. multiple-choice) or short answer test. The skill level of topic D may, however, require assessment by means of a practical test, which would then be allocated 20% of the total possible marks.

Finally, you should prepare or select these appropriate assessment devices (tests, case studies, questionnaires etc.) based on the assessment scheme. For example, the objective test for topics A and B will need to give equal weighting to the two topics, and the total possible score should be based on the percentage figures in the individual cells in the scheme, i.e. 30%. This could probably be conveniently covered by a thirty-item test, if time allows.

NB it would be quite usual, at this stage, to develop separate assessment schemes for those sub-sections which can be covered by a single test, using an appropriate figure for the total score for that test (entered in the bottom right-hand corner cell). This will be referred to later on in Component 3 of Study Unit 3 of this Package.

Practical examples

Having explained these procedures, it is probably a good idea to have a look at a number of specific examples — in order to appreciate the advantages of being systematic in the planning of assessment schemes.

Example 1
OUTCOMES

Let us imagine that you have been made responsible for preparing an assessment scheme for the section of an Industrial Catering Training Course covering food preparation and cooking. It has already been decided that assessment will be based on a practical task, namely the preparation of a main course (e.g. a goulash) for six people. The necessary resources and raw materials will be provided.

The TOPICS (job elements in this case) start with selection and preparation of ingredients and end with cleaning and putting away of equipment.

▨▨▨ Checkpoint

Try to write down the OUTCOMES which you think will need to be assessed, and which therefore should be entered at the top of the assessment scheme. There's no harm in looking at this as an outsider — you should be able to think of a number of suitable outcomes for assessment!

Well, one 'expert' came up with the following:
1. *Knowledge and Comprehension (e.g. quantities required, choice of tools, size of individual pieces of ingredients, choice of suitable utensils, cooking temperatures)*
2. *Perception and Dynamics (e.g. judging condition of ingredients, weighing, handling, tasting)*
3. *Speed and Economy (e.g. speed of operating, utilisation of foodstuffs, minimum wastage)*
4. *Quality of product (e.g. appearance, taste, quantity, temperature)*

"It looks good, it tastes good . . . . . ."

In the case of a practical task like this, it is probably unnecessary to itemise knowledge and comprehension separately, as long as one is aware of the danger of over-testing at the knowledge level — always the easiest one to assess and mark.

Items 2 and 3 could probably be combined under "Skill", provided you are aware of the different features of 'skilled performance' in a case like this.

Quality of product is an interesting one. It will require subjective assessment, but the reliability of assessment can be improved by using a suitable checklist or maybe a scale (e.g. from 0-25 marks, where points at 5 mark intervals along the scale are defined clearly). The assessor would also have to decide whether to elicit the trainee's opinion about the product, and assess that!

You will see that in a situation such as this, quality control is an essential part of the assessment scheme, in addition to the more normal outcomes of trainee achievement and performance.

Example 2

The following topics form part of a training course for secretary/receptionists in a large organisation. Decide on the appropriate outcomes, and then draw up an assessment scheme, assuming a total score of 100.

Company Procedures. Office Routine. Filing System. Correspondence. Appointments Diary. Telephone. Visitors.

Without having much more detail of the content which will be covered under each topic, it is obviously difficult to be very precise, but I hope you agree with me that the outcomes which will need to be assessed include KNOWLEDGE (recognition/recall of factual information), APPLICATION of knowledge (or similar heading), ATTITUDE (or similar heading, to include general approach and relationship with others), and probably SKILL.

Don't worry if your scheme differs from the following — you will see that in the absence of detailed information the process of allocating weightings appears very subjective. However, the discipline of having to make this type of relative comparison, and weighing up the importance to be attached to each cell, should help to clarify the whole process of planning and preparing appropriate assessment procedures.

TABLE 5

OUTCOMES / TOPICS	KNOWLEDGE	APPLICATION	ATTITUDE	SKILL	
COMPANY PROCED'S	10	0	0	0	10
OFFICE ROUTINE	10	5	0	0	15
FILING SYSTEM	5	5	0	0	10
CORRES-PONDENCE	5	10	5	0	20
APP'T DIARY	0	10	0	0	10
TELEPHONE	0	5	10	5	20
VISITORS	0	5	10	0	15
	30	40	25	5	100

Now you should try to produce an assessment scheme for a suitable set of topics from a training course with which you are familiar.

You may find it useful to see some different 'sets' of outcomes which have been used by various people to cover the range of items which may need to be assessed:

Different outcomes

Types of Knowledge:
1 Factual Knowledge.
2 Comprehension (of principles).
3 Application (of procedures, techniques to a novel situation).
4 Analysis/Evaluation.
Knowledge, Relationships, Procedures.
Knowledge, Interpretation, Problem Solving.
Affective Behaviour (involving feelings and attitudes)
Practical Ability, Technique, Skill.
Physical, Social and Cognitive Skills.

Component 4:

Implementing the Programme or Scheme — Practical Problems

Key Words

 Cooperation; involvement; communication; performance; improvement; individualisation; individual strengths/weaknesses/differences; planning; implementation; resources; procedures; arrangements; operating.

Introduction

Implementing an assessment programme or scheme involves getting the cooperation of all those involved, so that you can actually start functioning.

Checkpoint

List as many individuals or groups as you can whose cooperation you need in your own training role.

The list you have just made is bound to be personal and closely related to your own situation. This is as it should be, as this Unit has moved away from the generality of Unit 1 and we are trying to focus more and more on our own specific situation. Nevertheless, I'm sure that you will have included one or two of the following:

1. *colleagues — other people in your firm with a training role like yours*
2. *trainees*
3. *your boss in the training context (manager, training officer etc)*
4. *management in general*
5. *outside agencies (professional associations, examining bodies etc)*

Writing the sort of list we have just made is quite important, even if it's only a sort of check-list of who "needs to know" in our own organisation.

If it's a matter of trying to convince people about any **changes** you may have in mind, then a list or perhaps a diagram, showing the links in the communication chain, is going to be vital. You'll probably have to win the goodwill and approval and even the active involvement of many other people or groups. How you do this and the way in which you present your case may well determine the success or otherwise of your scheme.

Putting people in the picture

(a) How people view assessment

If ever you intend to change something in your training programme, it's probable that the change will affect other people in some way. It depends on how big a change you have in mind. But if you are going to change anything about the way you **assess**, you'll **certainly** need to let others know, probably all those listed in my checkpoint answer, but with the trainees right at the top of the list! For most trainees, and for many other people, assessment can loom larger than anything else in a course.

"Assessment can loom very large."

Management is interested in assessment because it provides some measure of how successful the training has been. Management will certainly notice quickly if a change in the pattern of assessment leads to an improvement or deterioration in performance.

Colleagues who also train may often see assessment as some kind of public measure of their own competence. Their trainees' performance reflects, in some way, their own performance. So they may not be happy if a change in **your** methods of assessment appears to discriminate in any way in favour of **your** own trainees.

Any outside body, such as a validating agency for a professional or technical qualification, will certainly look askance at changes in assessment patterns within the training context unless these have been fully discussed and approved.

So, whenever we talk of **changes** in assessment, whether in our own relatively small scale training courses or in the context of national examinations, there is always a lively interest in exactly what is involved. Assessment is a key issue in both training and in education and almost everyone has an interest in it.

Because assessment seems so important to so many people, one might think that all those involved in a particular training programme would always have a very clear knowledge and understanding of what the assessment programme was like and how it fitted into the whole scheme of assessment, how much weight was given to one part, as against another part of the assessment. But this is probably not the case!

Obviously **the trainee** will very quickly notice if the assessment does not give him the opportunity to show that he can do something, or if it does not test what he has learned, or if what had seemed to be a key point in the training seems to have been totally ignored in

assessment. But your own **detailed** understanding of the **structure** of your programme or scheme of assessment will almost certainly not be shared by your trainees or by the other interested groups or individuals we have mentioned. You will always know **much more** than anyone else about how **your** course and its associated programmes and schemes of assessment actually work. It is fatal to assume otherwise. If you want people to understand **exactly** what you are doing and why you are doing it, how the assessment relates to the objectives and content of the training, how a balance of types of assessment is achieved, the whole detail of the scheme, you will have to work very hard to put your message across.

(b) The trainee — the key person

We have just noted once again the trainee's key interest in his own assessment. In Component 2 of this Unit, **trainee involvement** was also a major consideration. If an assessment programme is to work, our trainees must have the opportunity actually **to discuss** with us how the assessment works and this should be done right at the beginning of the programme.

▰▰▰▰

From memory, list as many key words or phrases as you can which relate to what trainees need to know about assessment before the training starts. (It may help you if you actually make a list of **questions**).

1. *How **important** is the assessment?*
2. *What are the **criteria?***
3. *What **kinds** of test?*
4. *Will **practice tests** be given?*
5. *Will there be **informal** as well as **formal** assessment?*
6. *What kind of **feedback** will be provided as the course proceeds?*
7. *What will be the **timetable** of assessment? (how frequent will it be?)*
8. *Will there be **time to make use of feedback** for **improvement or performance?***
9. *Will there be **time to prepare for any final assessment?***
10. *Will there be **continuous assessment?***

*These are just some of the questions which will need to be dealt with in order to put our trainees in the picture regarding the assessment of the course. Our first concern must be with helping them to understand and appreciate what is involved in the assessment of **their** course.*

___

(c) How can we put our trainees in the picture?

Putting people in the picture is often, ideally, a **one-to-one** process. If you are involved in training just a few people, it's worth spending time with each individual, making sure he or she understands what the assessment is designed to do and exactly what it will be like. Assessment should never be an end of course threat, something frightening, an unknown quantity, concerned more with catching people out rather than in finding out what they actually know or can do. In fact, sometimes the assurance of **confidentiality** may help in the implementation of assessment and its acceptance by individuals. In a one-to-one situation we can present assessment as non-threatening and even helpful. It can be a quite personal way of telling us how **well** we are doing, as the course proceeds. Some forms of assessment can even be seen by trainees as an exciting opportunity.

For example, continuous assessment or an on-going 'project' involving practical work, can offer the opportunity for coaching and feedback which is so often not there if one is not taking part in a course or undergoing training.

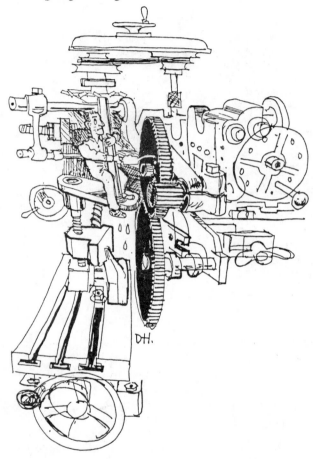

"An ongoing project involving practical work . . ."

However, very often, the one-to-one method of presenting the assessment programme or explaining the scheme is not possible. It is just too time consuming if there are large numbers of trainees.

What ways, other than one-to-one, can you think of to get across to trainees a clear picture of what we intend in assessment?

Probably you thought of:
1. group discussion or question and answer
2. written explanation
— and possibly,
3. other media (audio tape, tape/slide, videotape)
4. a combination of methods

Let's look at each of these ideas in more detail.

1. **Groups** can be useful because other people in the group sometimes come up with questions which we might never have thought of. Or we can often see from other people's questions that our worries are shared by them too. We may actually decide that we are not as stupid as we thought! Other people may be struggling too!

   But groups can sometimes seem threatening. Perhaps everyone appears much cleverer than we are, or more experienced or confident. Being in a group can sometimes be inhibiting. Individuals may hold back questions or contributions through shyness.

2. **Written explanations** are difficult to formulate clearly. They often seem impersonal. A comprehensive explanation may be too long and complex at this early stage and just frighten people or put them off. On the other hand, something which is too sketchy may lead to misunderstanding or uncertainty.

3. **Other media** such as tape/slide or audio or video tape may be a good compromise, offering the possibility of an almost one-to-one approach. I can talk to you on tape as if I were there. I can perhaps **sound** more reassuring than the printed word would be. I can also build in the possibility of your replying to my questions and raising questions yourself, using the same audio-tape. On video or slide I can illustrate what I'm saying. With all these media the trainee can work privately or with others, as he or she prefers.

4. **— or a combination of methods?**

   A combination of methods may be a good compromise – a sort of information package which offers some interaction and individuality.

"Examples . . . may be very reassuring . . ."

Whichever method or methods we use, **examples of assessment** will be very helpful, in written form, or real objects, or a display or exhibition, the products of the assessment of other trainees. Particularly if assessment includes something which trainees might consider to be very threatening or alarming, for example, a videotaped recording of a simulation, or having to give a short speech or 'lecture', examples on audio or videotape of the sort of thing that others have done may be very reassuring, particularly if they are not all perfect. If we can give trainees a clear picture of what they are required to do, assessment will not seem too frightening, but just a logical and necessary part of the training process.

Our trainee is an individual — but how do other trainers see him?

In the final Component of Unit 1, we concluded that it was very important to think about assessment and evaluation in relation to the end product — what trainees in general should be able to do as a result of the training — but that it was also an important quality of the good trainer to see each trainee as an individual.

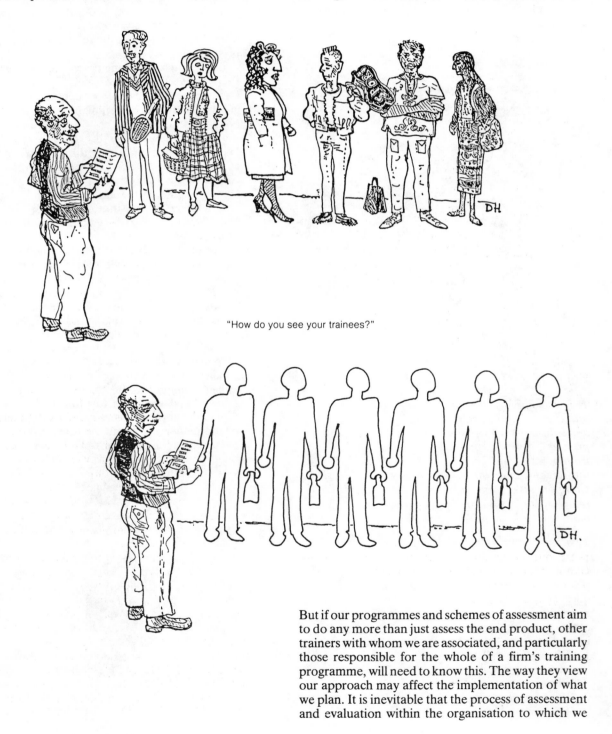

"How do you see your trainees?"

But if our programmes and schemes of assessment aim to do any more than just assess the end product, other trainers with whom we are associated, and particularly those responsible for the whole of a firm's training programme, will need to know this. The way they view our approach may affect the implementation of what we plan. It is inevitable that the process of assessment and evaluation within the organisation to which we belong will involve decisions about just how individualised our training can or should be. Certainly, individualisation brings with it many problems.

▰▰▰

Make three columns and list issues which one might face when considering implementing a system of assessment which aims to take account of individual differences in trainees. List alternative points of view and implications, as they strike you. Look at my example first and continue with point 3 onwards — or start again from 1 if you don't like what I have done!

Issue	Alternative point(s) of view	Implications
1. Any assessment programme should enable us to take account of a trainee's existing strengths (what he can do already).	If a trainee is already strong in a particular area, he'll be able to progress more quickly through the course anyway, so why worry?	Pretesting or no pretesting?
2. The scores in any particular section of a training course should tell us all we need to know.	Figures on their own don't mean much. In fact, they can be very misleading indeed.	Needs careful thought (but Component 5 will help a lot!)
3. etc		

Figure 7

This checkpoint exercise is to help you to clear your mind, using your existing knowledge; also to speculate and suggest for yourself possible solutions to a difficult problem. It is an opportunity to focus on your own training situation. There are no answers provided, but the remainder of this Component and the final two Components of this Unit will encourage you, I hope, to return to this last Checkpoint and the list you have made, and to change it or to add to it from time to time.

To conclude this brief section on the importance of taking into account other trainers' attitudes and possible approaches, here is a rather random list of questions which trainers thinking about implementing an assessment programme might raise. This may even cause you to return to the last Checkpoint **immediately** and to start thinking all over again!

1. "Does taking into account individual differences on entry mean that we need to think about individual differences at the end of the training too?"
2. "If we **are** concerned about individuals in a course of training, how can we 'pick up' the difficulties and anxieties of particular trainees on our courses? Does our programme allow for this?"
3. "If an individual needs to spend extra time on part of the course in order to master it, how can we reward him for this effort? Does our programme build in measures which provide feedback along the way and which tell the trainee how well he's doing and help him to self evaluate?"
4. "Aren't many 'new' types of assessment which purport to pick up individual strengths and weaknesses just too time-consuming and expensive to be worth while?"

I have thought it important to spend quite some time on this one aspect — the consideration of the possibility of an individualised approach to our assessment procedures — because it illustrates quite well just how complex a task it may be to implement **any** scheme. In fact, we could have looked at some other aspect in detail and found that, there too, things might not have turned out to be as straightforward as they at first appeared. Careful planning and a clear understanding of the issues are always essential if acceptance and efficient implementation are to take place.

Implementation — the difficulties of employing unconventional methods of assessment

I have suggested that pressure to employ traditional methods of assessment may be very strong. Everybody is familiar with the sort of scheme which involves the kinds of test we all met at school — for example an essay question. Familiarity gives many a feeling of confidence — trainees, trainers, and those who will take notice of the results, such as employers. Assessment which employs traditional methods is regarded as respectable, but this can often lead to surprising illogicalities such as the assessment of quite practically orientated training by a formal, written examination. Equally, an assessment programme which involves a broader range of methods of assessment may be regarded with suspicion and be considered to be lacking in rigour. Any kind of informal or unusual assessment may be difficult for all concerned to accept, because it doesn't conform to traditional expectations of what 'proper' assessment is about.

Random observation by CCTV — acceptable or unacceptable as a method of assessment?

You are convinced that an assessment programme should involve planning to test the **range** of knowledge, skills and attitudes you have defined as outcomes of your training (see Component 2). You have planned a scheme of assessment which you feel is really comprehensive (bearing in mind the lessons of Component 3). You are now faced with convincing a senior person within your organisation that the way assessment of a particular unit of a training course on which you teach is too limited and is therefore unsatisfactory. In the words of Component 1, it lacks 'congruence'.

Without proposing details of new, alternative techniques of assessment (wait for Unit 3!), try to muster some of the more general arguments contained in this Unit so far, in order to support your more comprehensive programme and scheme and to ensure that the decision is made to implement it.

1. *Using just one kind of assessment may well mean that we are failing to test what we need to test. (A written test may test recall — knowledge of facts — but not skills and attitudes.)*

2. *We may rate as poor a person who doesn't perform well in a written test, but who has other over-riding qualities which the firm would value highly.*

3. *A range of assessment procedures gives several dimensions to the evaluator, whereas a single mark, or even a list of marks, may be very misleading.*

4. *Some forms of assessment are a useful part of the learning process (for example, in projects or other types of continuous assessment).*

5. *If the only test we give is at the end of a course, we won't be able to assess the trainee's progress and we won't know anything about the effect of the training programme on the individual. It may even be difficult to evaluate the training course itself.*

6. *If we don't assess trainees as the course proceeds, we won't be able to pick up individual difficulties at all easily and thus help people to give of their best.*

7. *Frequent shorter term assessment will provide feedback for the trainee and for us as trainers. The trainee will know how well he is doing (motivation).*

8. *The trainee should learn to monitor his own performance. A good assessment programme, properly presented to the trainee at the beginning of the course will help him to do this. He knows where he's going and some of the ways to check whether he's getting there.*

*Most of these points will be there in your list, I expect. Almost certainly they will be differently expressed, but that doesn't matter at all. Just pick out the key words or phrases and note those you haven't covered. The most important thing of all is that we need a **range** of evidence to use in evaluation. An approach which uses just one method of assessment won't really help anyone, employer, trainer or trainee.*

Implementation — the practicalities

This Component has raised a number of key issues to the implementation of a scheme or programme of assessment and there has been a particular concentration on effectively communicating to other people the idea of changing methods or patterns of assessment. You may feel, though, that we have, so far, neglected a number of obvious but vital aspects of implementation. It is now appropriate to note a few of these, simply to alert us that to ignore such practical aspects of implementation could be disastrous.

(a) Resources

Implementing a scheme or programme is costly in terms of resources.

List as many of the areas of expenditure which immediately strike you.

I'm sure that you will have included many of the following. The sort of thing we need to consider here includes, for example:

1. **Time** — *of personnel involved e.g. 'experts' (designing, marking etc)*
   printers ⎫
   typists ⎬ *production*
   other workers (collation, despatch etc)

2. **Space** — *for storage of print materials, preparation and collation, space for extra personnel.*

3. **Equipment** — *general office equipment print/reprographic equipment other media (e.g. video, audio etc) computer equipment*

4. **Training** — *personnel involved may have to be trained.*

(b) Procedures

Guidelines will be necessary for those intending to offer trainees for assessment under any new scheme.

A trainer about to embark on a new scheme of assessment will be likely to ask at least some of the following questions:

How will the assessment be conducted?

Is there a sample or specimen test?

What will the weighting of particular parts of a test be?

Who will conduct the test?

What is the responsibility, if any, of the individual trainer?

Who will mark the test?

What about certification?

Does the trainee get a formal certificate?

What is the feedback to those who have been assessed?

Is there any arrangement for cross accreditation? (i.e. a 'pass' here being credited towards another similar training qualification).

This aspect of implementation, the practical business of communicating procedures, may be as vital to the success of the scheme as the actual scheme itself.

(c) Arrangements

Linked to procedures are the arrangements that have to be made. Clearly the complexity of such arrangements will depend on the complexity of the scheme itself, and here it is only necessary to illustrate this obvious but important point with one or two examples:

(1) **Physical arrangements**

Is it necessary to organise a special room or area for the test?

Is it necessary to lay out particular equipment?

If the test is administered and marked by the trainer, is there a need to arrange for recording devices, so that moderation can take place, for example, video recordings of tests which demand the achievement of a particular level of skill?

(2) **Arrangements involving personnel**

Can the test be conducted in the place of work or must the trainee attend elsewhere?

Is it necessary to arrange for a moderator, perhaps another trainer, to observe the test?

etc.

(d) Operating the scheme

The ongoing implications of implementing a new scheme should not be ignored. To operate the scheme effectively may involve, amongst other things:

Establishing effective methods of record keeping.

Providing on-going training for the trainers who will operate the scheme.

Possibly even providing new training materials to enable trainees to meet new objectives implicit in the new scheme of assessment.

This section of the Component has given just a few examples of the practicalities to be considered when implementing a programme of assessment.

List for yourself the examples which seem best to suit your situation. Add more of your own if you can.

Conclusion

This Component opened with the observation that implementing a scheme involves getting the cooperation of all concerned. We have seen that whether the considerations are related to attitudes to assessment or to the practicalities of arrangements and costs, a wide range of people will certainly be involved.

The key question for all is 'has the training programme worked?' The employer is clearly interested in the end product. The assessment scheme or programme enables us to find out about how successful the training has been.

This Component has emphasised the importance of the individual trainee in the business of training for improvement. Good assessment schemes tend to involve the trainee actively and directly and don't just provide feedback to management.

Many firms these days see the importance of matching jobs to people and developing jobs round **individual strengths**. The need for careful planning and the recognition of the clear role of assessment and evaluation as a crucial part of this process of helping individuals to learn, to identify their own strengths and weaknesses, to self-evaluate, and to improve their own performance, are the key messages of this Package.

So, although the emphasis of this present Component has been on the individual trainee, we are clear that schemes and programmes must be accepted by **all** those interested in the training, but they should also accept that the **individual** is of crucial importance. Our assessment should therefore provide answers to such questions as:

How well suited are the trainee's abilities to the particular job for which he is being trained?

How suitable is he as a candidate for further training, bearing in mind the strengths and weaknesses which our range of assessment measures indicates?

The practical problem posed by broadly-based assessment is that it **will** throw up individual differences, strengths, weaknesses — so we must plan a trainee's progress through programmes geared to his needs and ability. Though this may seem to be obvious

and good — and the purpose of this Component has been to convince you of this! — it is much more complicated and difficult to achieve than a system of assessment which is only concerned with a few dimensions or which merely aims to grade trainees by the marks they get in a particular area.

An exploration in detail of the range of methods and techniques available to trainers who are concerned about encouraging individuals to achieve their full potential is the particular concern of the two Units which follow this one, but the next Component in this Unit is concerned with the data that we collect when we assess, how to make sense of the result of an assessment procedure in order to make evaluation possible. We shall look at this last process in Component 6, at the end of this Unit.

Component 5

Collecting and Using the Data

Key Words

 Marks; scores; data; individual/group; comparing scores; range; statistic; rank/rank order; describing a set of scores; average; mean; spread; distribution; deviation; standard deviation.

Introduction

One immediate outcome resulting from the production and implementation of a programme/ scheme of assessment is the **acquisition of information (data) relating to the performance** of individual trainees and sometimes groups.

This information may take different forms, such as

a) a simple 'count' of the **number of times** something happened or an event occurred, e.g. mistakes in a typing exercise, damaged/wasted components, goals scored, 'Yes' or 'No' answers, passes/failures, trainees fainting in a practical first aid test;

b) attempts at ordering or **ranking** the outcomes, e.g. first, second etc. in a race to finish a task, numbers ticking each box of a five-point scale from 'strongly agree' to 'strongly disagree' with a given statement, judging entries in a livestock competition, arranging a set of projects from best to worst on a global assessment;

c) attempts to improve on b) by using a numerical scale of some sort to give a **score** or **mark** to each individual's attempt thereby enabling comparisons to be made using the scale), e.g. most examinations and tests, intelligence tests, quizzes.

In this Component we are going to concentrate on (c) above, as this represents the most usual and useful outcome resulting from assessment procedures. In any case, (a) and (b) give very obvious results which require little elaboration.

What we are therefore going to look at is how to make sense of such numerical data, i.e. how can we simplify and **put together** the results of any assessment procedure in order to facilitate analysis and comparisons.

Let us begin with a simple example, where an individual trainee has completed a written 'test' of some sort and obtained a score.

Individual scores

Let us say that Jim has taken the test and obtained a score of 60.

What does this tell us? Not a lot, really!

▰▰▰▰ Checkpoint

Try to think of two or three questions that you could ask, in order to find out more information about the test and Jim's score.

We might start by asking "Out of what?" If the answer is, say, 100, then we would say Jim has got 60%, whereas if it was out of 80 then the score of 60 represents 75%

Even this computed figure might be slightly misleading, as 60 out of 80 is not **strictly** *equivalent to 75 out of 100 (e.g. 6 out of 10 is often referred as to 60% which is not really correct). Assuming, however, that it was out of 100, what exactly does 60 out of 100 tell us?*

Was it really 6 out of 10 multiplied up, or was it 60 individual marks out of a possible 100 maximum?

Was Jim unable to answer the other 40%, did he answer them wrongly — or did he just run out of time (or energy)?

If Bill also got 60, it should be noted that his 'mix' of marks may not have been the same as Jim's, anyway.

Consider these results, obtained on ten items of a multiple-choice test by four trainees, Jim, Bill, Shirley and Karen. "R" means right answer given.

TABLE 1

ITEM	JIM	BILL	SHIRLEY	KAREN
1	R		R	
2	R			R
3	R		R	
4	R			R
5	R	R	R	R
6	R	R	R	R
7		R	R	
8		R		R
9		R	R	
10		R		R
TOTAL	6	6	6	6

This simple table shows that four people who all apparently obtained the same score of **6 out of 10** had each built up that score very differently.

I hope you are beginning to see that in starting to

examine the data resulting from administering some test or assessment device, nothing is as simple as it might seem to be at first glance.

So far, we have found out that Jim got 60 out of 100. On its own, this doesn't tell us very much — unless it has been previously decided, say, that 50 is a minimum pass mark, in which case Jim has 'passed' reasonably comfortably.

What we are more likely to want to know about is how Jim's score **compares** with other people's individual scores.

Now the scores obtained by individuals on a particular test are usually referred to as **RAW** scores (in the sense that they haven't been processed or 'cooked' in any way). Let us assume that eighteen other people have taken the same test as Jim and Bill, and that the collection of raw scores is as follows:

48 72 29 75 70 39 52 57 61 46
60 49 55 51 63 64 53 58 60 68

Provided that the total number of scores is not too great, we can easily 'scan' these raw scores by eye and get a general impression of their relative values. Check to see that the highest score is 75 and the lowest 29. This **RANGE** from highest to lowest (75−29 = 46) is a useful piece of information (a STATISTIC), but in this case it is misleading. What is the next lowest score to 29? It is 39, ten higher, whereas the next highest score to 75 is 72, a difference of only three. We must not, of course, ignore or attempt to discard the score of 29 because it doesn't seem to 'fit', but we should note that it is very untypical — compared to the other 19 scores. (Don't start jumping to conclusions about it!.)

Even with 20 individual raw scores it is going to be useful to put them into some sort of order — to make it easier to compare them and take in the overall pattern. Let us re-arrange them from highest to lowest (do it yourself if you feel it would help you, or at least check to see that you agree with the figures):

75 72 70 68 64 63 61 60 60 58
57 55 53 52 51 49 48 46 39 29

(Note: One way is to cross out each score on the original list as you transfer it to the new one.)

I think you will agree that it is now much easier to scan the array of scores and appreciate the general arrangement.

A possible danger is in tending to forget that the two scores of 60 are not necessarily identical, as we saw earlier. Numbers have a strange fascination for most people and often blind us to what they really represent!

The picture can be made a little clearer by arranging the scores vertically, and possibly by putting the RANKINGS alongside, i.e. arranging the scores in RANK ORDER.

TABLE 2

RANK	SCORE
1	75
2	72
3	70
4	68
5	64
6	63
7	61
8=	60
8=	60
10	58
11	57
12	55
13	53
14	52
15	51
16	49
17	48
18	46
19	39
20	29

This highlights the top and bottom scores, and also the middle of the table, where a number of scores seem to be clustering around the low sixties to high fifties.

You may have noticed that **we have gone a long way towards getting a good appreciation of this set of scores**, and seeing where any individual score lies in relation to the others — **without doing any calculation** other than comparing individual scores one with another. In many cases, where a group of individuals have taken a test as part of an assessment scheme, this is as far as you will need to go in making the results easy to examine.

To summarise so far:

You might like to make your own summary before reading on. It will help to consolidate what you have learned so far.

A Individual results need to be looked at carefully — they are not always quite what they seem.
B It may be useful to draw a grid of marks (as in Table 1) based on each question or item, to highlight similarities and differences and facilitate other detailed comparisons (for example do we need items 5 and 6 if everyone is getting them right?).
C The overall RANGE of a set of raw scores (highest to lowest) may be useful information, but beware the exceptionally high or low score.
D Arranging raw scores into descending 'rank order' makes it much easier to see where particular scores lie in relation to the overall pattern.
E Figures can't lie, but are easily open to misinterpretation!

Decisions about whether a score of, say, 60 represents a 'satisfactory' or 'pass' standard will be dealt with elsewhere in this Package, particularly in relation to norm-referenced or criterion-referenced performance.

Sets of scores

In addition to seeing where individual scores lie in relation to other scores within a group, we may want to
a) compare sets of scores on different tests (e.g. a written test on theory against a practical test of skill or applied knowledge),

Q A carburettor is a device for
a) controlling the flow of petrol to the petrol pump
b) preventing the engine from overheating
c) mixing petrol and air in the correct proportions
d) pumping petrol/air mixture into the engine

b) compare different groups of trainees taking the same test (e.g. different groups undergoing the same assessment programme/scheme).

Arraying one set of scores alongside another will be of limited value,

a) because the amount of information to be processed mentally will be excessive, and
b) cross-comparison of individual scores is difficult and not very helpful. Even comparing the ranges is not going to be all that useful.

What we need now is an acceptable standardised way of **describing** a set of scores, which at the same time simplifies the resulting amount of information.

In order to do this we will need to **combine** the individual scores in some way (so that each score is taken into account and contributes to the results) in order to produce two figures which give an indication of

a) an **average** score, and
b) the **spread** or distribution of scores around that average.

The two most commonly used figures or STATISTICS to DESCRIBE a set of scores are the mean and standard deviation.

The Mean

This is simply the arithmetical mean or average, obtained by adding all the scores together and dividing by the total number of scores. In Table 2 it is

$$\frac{75+72+70+\ldots+39+29}{20} = \frac{1130}{20} = 56.5$$

Note that this is a **computed** figure — no-one actually obtained a score of 56.5, in the same way that there is no 'average' family actually having, say, 1.8 children!

Again, this is as far as you may want to go in comparing two sets of scores (provided the ranges and distributions look much the same).

Distribution or Spread

However, let us assume that you wish to compare the following two sets of scores obtained by Groups A and B:—

TABLE 3

GROUP A	GROUP B
70	62
62	60
57	57
53	53
48	50
40	48
330	330

The means are the same (55), but it is obvious by inspection that there is a much wider spread in Group A's scores than in Group B's. In this case, as each set of scores is symmetrical above and below the mean, it would probably be sufficient to look at the ranges (70 to 40 and 62 to 48) for the purpose of making comparisons. However, if we wish to be more exact in making such comparisons, we would need to calculate some figure (as with the mean) which takes into account the amount by which each and every score differs or DEVIATES from the average (i.e. the mean) score.

Standard deviation

The best figure to quote is the STANDARD DEVIATION, because it is based on the squares of each score's deviation from the mean, thus giving more 'weight' to extreme scores. Many pocket calculators include a procedure for calculating the standard deviation (as well as the mean) when a set of scores is entered one by one. I suggest that if you need to compare sets of scores you should buy, beg or borrow (but not steal!) such a calculator.

As a matter of interest the two sets of scores in Table 3 have standard deviations of roughly 10 and 5 respectively, indicating the much greater spread in Group A's scores.

As a rough guide, provided we have a reasonably large set of scores which follow the normal pattern (where most scores cluster around the average and the number of extreme scores is relatively low), then the standard deviation is about one-sixth of the range of scores (highest minus lowest).

Approximately two-thirds of the scores can be expected to lie within one standard deviation either side of the mean.

For example, if test results give a mean score of 50 and a standard deviation of 10, the range is probably about 60 (80 to 20) and two-thirds of the scores will lie between 60 and 40.

To summarise

In order to simplify a large set of individual scores, or to compare two or more sets of scores, we need to
a) ensure that every score counts, and
b) find some way of indicating
   i) an average score,
   ii) the spread or distribution within each set of scores.

The mean and standard deviation are two statistics which meet these requirements.

In many cases, once we have calculated these figures, the individual scores can be filed away, since the mean and standard deviation are sufficient to describe the **general** pattern of a set of scores. For example:

Group A Number = 20   Mean = 50   Standard Deviation = 7
Group B Number = 30   Mean = 60   Standard Deviation = 10

gives us sufficient information for most purposes, PROVIDED THAT WE DO NOT LOSE SIGHT OF WHERE IT ALL STARTED FROM i.e. that 'Jim got 60'.

In the next Component we will start to look more closely at the ways in which we can make decisions based on the information resulting from collecting and processing the data resulting from assessment.

In the meantime, you should now feel confident that you can:
a) arrange a set of scores in rank order and note where any score lies in relation to the others,
b) give the range,
c) work out the mean,
d) give two reasons* why the standard deviation is the preferred way of expressing the spread or distribution.
* 1 Every score contributes to its value.
  2 It is based on the squares of the amounts by which each score deviates from the mean.

Component 6:

Evaluating the Results — A Summary of the Process

Key Words

 Evaluation; improvement; planning; constraints; description; judgement; intentions; observations; conditions; activities; results; organising information; outcomes.

Introduction

In Component 6 of Unit 1 we agreed that Evaluation was not necessarily a large-scale, grand affair to do only with national training projects or huge organisations. It could be and should be the stock-in-trade of the individual front-line trainer dealing, day-to-day, with individual trainees. The concern should be with using the results of assessment:

1. to improve training,
2. to improve training materials,
3. to improve the provision of information about the results of the training, so that . . .
4. decision making may be improved.

We are very clear that evaluation and assessment are by no means the same thing — even if they are often spoken of in almost the same breath and used side by side on the printed page. Both, however, involve a whole range of activities. Indeed, a problem for evaluators could be having **too much** assessment information. One might have so much information that one became totally over-loaded, making it difficult to interpret the data usefully. Or perhaps the information might be incorrectly focussed and therefore of little value.

The Components in this present Unit have looked at ways of **planning** the process of assessment and evaluation and the emphasis in Components 1-5 has been on assessment. This final Component focusses on Evaluation — making sense of the evidence, using the results to decide what to do next. In looking at assessment we have also been involved in making decisions. We have considered the importance of assessment, its timing and the forms it may take. We have asked questions about who it is for. We have made suggestions for the design of schemes and programmes of assessment and we have thought about the constraints that may operate in doing this. Component 5 focussed on collecting and using the data of assessment — making sense of the marks. Now, in Component 6, we look at the results of assessment in all its forms and ask questions about ordering them and interpreting them. This final component of Unit 2 tends, therefore, to ask the 'So what?' and 'What next?' sort of question, rather like Component 6 in Unit 1 did.

The process

When looking back on a process, there is considerable value in considering what it was one had set out to do in the first place — our original objectives or intentions. It's also very clear that we can't interpret

the results of assessment without knowing something about the conditions under which assessment was carried out, (for example the constraints and other influences were identified in Component 4) and considering what actually happened, the transactions and activities which were the focus of assessment. Results alone can be misleading — at worst, just a list of numbers.

---

*Stake, R. E., Introduction in Tyler, R. W. *et al Basic Principles of Curriculum Evaluation,* Rand McNally, 1967

Making use of the results

"A full evaluation results in a story . . . it tells what happened. It reveals perceptions and judgements that different groups and individuals hold — obtained, I hope, by objective means. It tells of merit and shortcomings . . . It may offer generalizations for the guidance of subsequent . . . programmes.

. . . two main kinds of data are collected:

1. objective **descriptions** of goals, environments, personnel, method and content, and outcomes.
2. personal **judgements** as to the quality and appropriateness of those goals etc."

(From the American expert, Bob Stake*, quoted in Derek Rowntree's *Educational Technology in Curriculum Development* (1974) (Second edition (1982) Harper and Row).

I suggest we use Stake's approach to help us with our own thinking about the problems which this Component raises. Michael Eraut of Sussex University has presented Stake's approach in the form of a matrix which many evaluators have found to be very helpful. It makes clear, in a sort of check-off form, the range of evidence available and which we may need to consider when we evaluate training — or more precisely when we are thinking about making sense of the material of evaluation, the assessment results and evidence. It will help us, I hope, to organise this material and to tell 'a story'.

You may now find it helpful to browse quickly through the rest of this Component, and then return to study it in detail. At first sight, some sections may appear to be a bit off-putting and even bewildering until you read on a good way. I think, however, that if you persevere, this final Component will help to pull together the lessons of the whole Unit.

Organising data

	Descriptive Data		Judgemental Data	
	Intentions	Observations	Standards	Judgements
Conditions				
Activities and Transactions				
Results				

Figure 8

Matrix for Organising Evaluation Data, adapted from Stake (1967) by Dr Michael Eraut (University of Sussex).

How does this matrix help us to organise our information? Let us consider what we already know. In this Package we have already thought quite a lot about evaluation. In an early Checkpoint in the final Component of Unit 1, we listed a number of key points, culled from that Unit and which related to Evaluation.

▰▰▰ Checkpoint

I won't ask you to do this again now unless you think it would help you, but if you would like to, try to recall as many of those key points as you can, perhaps just jotting down single key words or short phrases before you move on to the list below. (You'll see that I have emphasised some of the key words to help you check.)

Evaluation is about **using the information** *of assessment to make* **judgements**.

Evaluation tries to demonstrate the **effects of** *training — to show* **what actually happened**.

Evaluation is concerned about **the real situation**. *(etc. — I'm sure you will have listed more. See Unit 1 Component 6 if you need more help here.)*

Eraut's presentation of Stake's model can help us considerably to organise these thoughts in a useful way. We know what the intended outcomes (objectives) were and we may have available to us lots of information relating to the assessment, including, perhaps, unintended outcomes — but how can we order this information so that we can make sense of it, so that we and others can use it to make judgements which we hope will lead to improvement in training and performance?

▰▰▰

Look back to the matrix and see how the words in bold print in the answer to the previous Checkpoint fit the plan. Let's just focus on Descriptive Data and consider the Observations column only. Try to link your key words (or mine) to the words used in the left hand column of the matrix.

Using my words from the previous Checkpoint, I produce these links
the real situation — *Conditions*
what actually happened – *Activities/transactions*
information — *Results*

The matrix

A. Descriptive Data
1) The **INTENTIONS** column helps us to consider what was planned by the trainer.
a) **Conditions** — those conditions we had in mind when we designed the training — the context for assessment and evaluation and all the influences and constraints which we perceive as influencing our own situation. If we are considering **change**, this might well include:
(1) a view of what **has been** the context up till now, for example how the trainer **had organised** his assessment programme.

(2) a picture of what trainees' and other peoples' expectations of assessment **had been,** up till now; what their previous experience had led them to expect from assessment.
b) **Activities/transactions.** As trainers, we plan activities which are appropriate to the learning we wish to take place and, in the context of assessment, activities which will enable us to observe what is going on.
c) **The Results** we plan are, in fact, intended outcomes (objectives) — what we hope the training will enable trainees to do.

Applying the Matrix in a real situation
At this point, before moving on to Judgemental Data, it will probably be helpful to try to fill out the Framework by applying a real-life example to it.

Once again, we'll just look at a small part of the Stake model but I hope this will convince you that it really does help us to organise our information to help us with the business of evaluation.

Let us take a short description of an actual course, and relate it to the **Intentions** column. (Don't worry about the letters in brackets at the end of each paragraph, for the moment.)

A course in Communication Skills
A large national firm whose training programme is predominantly technically orientated decides to include an element which aims to develop communication skills in trainees, as most will have face-to-face dealings with the general public. (A)

Above all, the particular unit aims to help trainees to develop the ability to communicate orally and to use language effectively. (B)

"Communicating orally and using language effectively . . ."

The 'communicative studies' unit is the only non-technical unit in the range of **distance learning** courses offered by the organisation to its employees all over the country. (C)

We are concerned now with the assessment and evaluation of such a course and not directly with course design, content etc., so it wouldn't be surprising if we were tempted to turn immediately to the section at the back of the unit entitled Assessment Analysis or to the section at the front on Assessment. However, our matrix reminds us that we should adopt a wider perspective and so we turn first to descriptive data. (D)

Briefly, the course includes print material bound in a loose-leaf, hard-backed file. There are two Topics - "Communication and Organisation in the Firm" and "Science Technology and Society". We'll just consider the first of these. In Topic 1, there are sections on Formal Organisation of the Firm; Communication; Informal Organisation; Business Objectives and Goals of the Firm; and a Case Study. An audio cassette forms part of the materials and this enables students to hear the authors talking about the course and introducing themselves and it also includes interviews, 'lectures' etc., to support the written material. (E)

As with our own course materials (TTP), the student is helped through the course by activities and self-assessed 'checkpoints', but there are also various formal assessment points. These include 'homework' assignments and tests, at certain specified points in the course and an end of course test and project. There are also back-up tutorials to discuss problems with a tutor and to meet other students and to compare experiences. (F)

General aims are clearly stated. There is a list of learning outcomes. Topic areas have lists of general and specific objectives. The specific objectives indicate the kind of activity required of the student. The most frequently used word, defining student abilities is "Describes . . ." (for example, Describes characteristics of formal and informal communication within a firm . . .). (G)

An Assessment Analysis provides a key to an assessment specification or scheme. For Topic 1, we note that Motor Skills have 0% and Intellectual Skills 100% weighting. The latter category is divided as follows: Information (32%), Comprehension (32%), Application (12%), and 'Invention' (12%). etc etc (H)

You will recognise that we are beginning to build up a very useful range of information relating to the **Intentions** of the course designers, and in particular, with reference to assessment and evaluation.

▰▰▰

Go back through the **description** of the course which I have started in the example above. Try to decide on the guiding or 'organising' word from **the matrix** which helped me to begin to tell the evaluative story, as it relates to the **Intentions** of the authors.* I suggest

---

*Although based on a real course, my description is too brief and inaccurate for me to attribute it to the original. It should therefore be regarded purely as an example, useful to us at this moment as partial illustration only, a sort of fiction based on fact.

you make a copy of the Descriptive Data sections of the Matrix (left hand part of Figure 8). Then write in the Intentions column the appropriate letters which refer to the paragraphs above. For example, Paragraph G clearly refers to results, so put it in that slot.

Each paragraph is identified by a letter in brackets.

Organising word	Intentions
Conditions	C
Activities/ Transactions	E, F, G
Results	A, B, G

Conditions
C. The mode is distance learning. The constraints here are obvious, particularly for a course in Communication which claims to develop ability in oral as well as written skills.

Activities/Transactions
E, F, G. All these paragraphs tell us something about how the student will work.

Results
A, B, G. Here the focus is on what the authors hope the course will enable students to do.

Note: D indicates that we should try to focus clearly on description in this section — the whole point of using the matrix is to help us to organise our material clearly — but in H, we move to the Standards/Judgemental area!

Now we turn to the second part of the Descriptive Data — **OBSERVATIONS.**

2) OBSERVATIONS

We can't take our example from the last Checkpoint further, into **Observations**, of course, although it may have struck you that this aspect is particularly difficult in a distance learning course anyway!

However, I hope you are convinced from the **Intentions** example, that evaluative judgements should not be made just on **Results**, but that **Conditions** and **Transactions** will both tell their own important story.

It is also worth reiterating that mismatches between **Intentions** and **Observations** may be interesting, not just because they may reveal inadequacies which may need to be put right but also because very often they reveal unintended outcomes.

What the Stake model doesn't do is to remind us to take note of our **Sources** of data — **whose Intentions and Observations?** The **Intentions** will probably include those of the course designers, the trainer and the student. The observations, in this case, may be much more limited — perhaps very much **student orientated**, because of the nature of the **Conditions**.

B. Judgemental Data

When we turn to Judgemental Data, the value of the matrix as an 'organiser' is even more apparent. It's all too easy to turn first to scores in tests, to lists of marks, when we use the results of assessment for evaluation. But we have already agreed in Unit 1 and again in earlier Components of the present Unit that there is more to the business of evaluation than this. So when we consider Judgemental Data, we'll be thinking once again of the three areas, Activities, Transactions and Results. Judgements are likely to be based on Standards which depend on the values of those who are judging — the particular point of view that they hold. (We have already noted in Unit 1 that value questions can be a very powerful factor in decision making and that the very **Selection** of assessment data may reflect values.) Research has shown that it's likely that individuals within a group **observing the same events** will 'see' different things; sometimes their observations even differ so much that it's impossible to believe that they have been observing the same event! Even more so, then, when it comes to **Judgements** and **Standards**. Judging the **Results** of the parts of the course we have just been looking at (Communication Skills) may well depend on a particular frame of reference, reflected, perhaps, by questions like this

> How happy were we in the first place about a course which was concerned, at least to some extent with oral communication, being taught by distance learning?

We might take this further and blame the **Conditions** (the distance learning mode) for the lack of provision for **oral interaction** between student and tutor or student and others as part of the assessment of a course on Communication. The **Activities** and **Transactions** seem to confirm the emphasis on the written medium which is clearly there in the methods chosen for assessment. On the other hand, our judgements may be so very firmly based on our own experience of what assessment is about (see Component 6 of Unit 1) that, despite objectives and even the Course title, we cannot really bring ourselves to see assessment other than in traditional terms, such as written performance.

One of the advantages of Stake's model is that it does force us to consider **all** of these perspectives. The model also fits very well with our previous argument that evaluation need not be seen as a grand-scale, almost mysterious activity.

> . . ."in day-to-day training, it's likely to be a tool of the trade, involving a range of simple, common-sense techniques — opinions, impressions, judgements, as well as more objective methods" (Component 6 Unit 1).

In effect, all the **Intentions, Observations, Standards** and **Judgements** could be collected quite informally. Their value is that they provide an overall **perspective** which the matrix helps us to draw clearly.

This helps us to decide how best to view the **formally** gathered evidence, in effect how to make sense of assessment information, so that we can decide what to do next.

 ### Tutor Seen Work

Do you feel that the procedure we have just worked through is rather too complex? This putting of information into categories is all very well as a sort of clever exercise, but how can we actually use the product obtained? What does it tell us?

The main thing, I think, is that it can be used very simply as a check list. It reminds us to adopt a number of perspectives and not just the most obvious ones.

If you have a course which you are considering or are involved in at the moment (even this one, if you like!) try first of all listing at random the obvious assessment data which are available to you and which should be considered in any evaluation. Then place these alongside the Matrix and see whether there are important perspectives which you have missed.

(If you wish, you can send this exercise to your Tutor.)

Conclusion

In this final Component we have reviewed much of our thinking about the process of assessment and evaluation, not I hope by just repeating material from the preceding five Components and the previous Unit, although I have consciously looked back to this, but more through attempting to solve the problem of making sense of the information we collect, by suggesting an organising strategy which is flexible and adaptable, a sort of check-list for the do-it-yourself evaluator that we all must be. Our aim is to look systematically at **our** situation and to make decisions, based, as best we can, on all the information to which we can have access.

The purpose of all this effort is, above all, to achieve an improvement in our training or at the very least to keep an on-going check on how well the materials (and we ourselves) are doing.

The first two Units in this Package have been, in a large sense, introductory, defining the area of assessment and evaluation and outlining the process. The Units which follow are extremely practical and tightly focussed and we hope that you'll now feel ready to tackle them, recognising the value of the methodologies of assessment proposed in Units 3 and 4 and the important (perhaps the **most** important) skill, self-assessment, which is the subject of Unit 5. In Units 6 and 7 we will have the opportunity to take our understanding of assessment and evaluation to a higher level, thus fulfilling one of the aims of the Training Technology Programme, that there should be progression within each Component, each Unit and each package.

You may well feel that we have only scraped the surface in our investigation of the nature of evaluation in Units 1 and 2, the emphasis has certainly been on assessment. The final Unit of the Package will deal with evaluation in detail.

We hope that you may have found Units 1 and 2 a helpful introduction or a useful revision of the subject, stimulating enough to encourage you to press on into the Package and thought-provoking enough to help you to see applications to your own training situation.

Objectives for Study Unit 2

On completion of this Unit the student will:

* Accept that the way a course is assessed must be related to its objectives;
* Be aware of the purposes of formative and summative evaluation;
* Value the idea of 'stages' in assessment;
* Be able to list ways in which assessment during a training programme might be of value to the trainee;
* Be aware of the role of pre-testing within a training programme;
* Be able to list factors to be considered in drawing up an 'assessment timetable' for a training programme;
* Be able to draw up a check list of levels of performance in sub-skills contributing to a general skill acquired in training;
* Be able to draw up a check list of levels of performance;
* Be able to identify outcomes in a given context;
* Be able to differentiate between outcomes related to knowledge, application, skills and attitudes within a given context;
* Be able to draw up an assessment scheme related to his own situation;
* Be able to list key individuals/groups who are likely to be interested in the implementation of a programme of assessment;
* Be aware of the importance of the details of the assessment scheme to the individual trainee;
* Be able to list ways in which trainees may be informed of the details and purposes of assessment;
* Be aware of some of the problems of implementing schemes of assessment which aim to take account of individual differences;
* Be able to list several arguments for adopting a comprehensive, wide ranging programme of assessment;
* Be able to list important practical issues relating to the implementation of a scheme, a programme of assessment in his own organisation;
* Be able (1) to arrange a set of scores in rank order and note where any score lies in relation to the others
  (2) give the range
  (3) work out the mean
  (4) give two reasons why the standard deviation is the preferred way of expressing the spread of distribution
* Accept that assessment information, to be useful, must be organised systematically;
* Value the idea that a key function of assessment is to enable individuals to improve their performance;
* Be able to list at least 3 important purposes of evaluation.

Acknowledgements are due to Harper and Row (Publishers) for permission to use material from Rowntree, D. *Educational Technology in Curriculum Development* (Second Edition 1982).

Study Unit 3

Methods, Techniques and Instruments (1)

Component 1:

What am I Assessing?

Key Words

 Job description; objectives; knowledge; skills; attitudes.

Introduction

This is the first of two units which will help you to decide on what tests and assessment procedures are appropriate for your training programme. You will also be given guidance on test construction.

The nature of the job — job description

From Study Units One and Two of this package you will know that it is important to:

a. say what the trainee will be able to do — **specify your objectives.**

b. decide how **well** you can expect the trainee to perform.

Before you can do either of those things, you have to produce a job description, because it is only then that you can begin to make decisions about the kind of assessment which will be suitable.

Of course you cannot be expected to be an expert in or even familiar with all the skills and processes you are required to assess.

What is the solution?

Get help from someone who is an expert:

* a foreman
* a supervisor
* an experienced worker

You may be lucky and have a shop or works manual which describe what each worker in the organisation is expected to do.

Stage 1 Writing a JOB DESCRIPTION

▨▨▨ Checkpoint

Most jobs seem to be fairly simple until you break them down into all their components. Many of these are taken for granted or forgotten. Even a works manual may describe a job in very general terms and ignore crucial operations, techniques and knowledge.

In order to check what you know already have a go at writing a job description for a job with which you are familiar.

Did you find that easy?
Did you include enough detail?
Have you included **everything** *the worker should be able to do? Is the order important?*
Did you include such things as:
* *Fire precautions*
* *Safety regulations*
* *Employment rights and health and welfare policy*
* *Communications within the company?*
These are things all employees need to know.

Here is my attempt to describe the job of a sales assistant in a shoe shop.
* *selling technique*
* *measuring feet and fitting*
* *cash handling*
* *stock control*
* *stocking shelves and display*
* *answering the telephone*
* *knowledge of fire regulations and security.*

Take a critical look at what has been included. Can you spot any glaring omissions?

Yes I am sure that you can spot a number of gaps in the above description of what might be expected of any shop assistant.

Stage 2 Writing OBJECTIVES for our assessment

A general job description is an essential first stage, but it is too vague and general to be of much use when you come to assess the quality or effectiveness of training.

Returning to my example, it describes what a sales assistant does, but it will not help you to make **judgements** about the particular techniques involved.

Let's take one of the features of the job description already outlined — "selling technique". It is a very complex activity, but can be broken down into objectives which can be tested. Here is an attempt:
Selling technique.
a. Before you begin the selling. Ability to:
   (i) recognise ways in which customers signal for help.
   (ii) greet a customer.
b. Opening a sale. Ability to establish customer needs.

c. Making recommendations. Ability to:
   (i) present features of products.
   (ii) note benefits of products.
d. Handling selling hurdles. Ability to:
   (i) overcome customer resistance.
   (ii) overcome out of stock situation.
   (iii) handle customer complaints.
e. Ability to clinch the sale.
f. Ability to promote link selling i.e. selling of related products (e.g. shoe laces, polish, stockings).

Now that you have a clear idea of what the job involves, it is easier to devise a way to assess when the trainee needs help and further guidance.

Have a go at breaking the job of answering the telephone into its component parts.

Answering the telephone.
The trainee should demonstrate the ability to:
a. greet caller and identify branch and department
b.
c.
d.

Check. Did you include:
* *Give information clearly*
* *Take detailed messages and make clear notes*
* *Handle complaints*
* *Maintain a friendly and courteous manner*
* *Sign off.*

Stage 3 How to categorise objectives
Once you have a clear idea of what the job involves we are in a better position to devise tests to assess the effectiveness of training. However there is another stage in the process. You have to say what **kind** of objective is being tested.

There are many kinds of tests and assessment procedures available and it will be impossible to identify and select the ones suitable for your purposes until you have done this.

Can you recall the following categories from Unit 1 Component 2?

Knowledge
Skills
Attitudes

Write down in a few words a brief description of each.

Check: Skills — what people do
Knowledge — what people know
Attitudes — How people react or approach their work.

The following are examples of activities and procedures in which **knowledge** is the important feature.

Knowledge

* Storage procedures in the stockroom
* Disposal regulations for 'out of life' foods
* Reporting and recording of accidents
* Fault recognition in an industrial process
* Fire regulations and procedures
* Invoicing procedures

Here the trainee should be able to write down or tell you the relevant information to demonstrate that he **knows** the procedure or regulation.

You should recall from Unit 1 Component 2 that objectives which require knowledge or understanding are written in a form which will lead to assessment.

Examples of **inadequate** objectives requiring knowledge or understanding.

* Knows laboratory procedures.
* Understands ordering procedures.
* Is acquainted with fire regulations.
* Is familiar with fault finding strategies.

Why are these **un**helpful as a starting point for assessment?

Have you noted that:
* *They do not say what the learner will be able to DO at the end of training. The words 'know', 'understand', 'acquainted with' and 'familiar with' will not lead you directly to the evidence you need to collect.*
* *What is needed are words which will lead you to a way of testing the trainee's knowledge.*

Example: The trainee is able to:
* **Identify** *the form numbers required for the despatch of merchandise.*
* **Distinguish** *between type faces in printing.*
* **Name** *the parts of a circuit diagram.*

* **List** *the faults likely to occur when using a cassette recorder for computer storage.*
* **Describe** *what aid you would give someone who has sustained chemical burns.*
* **Construct** *a sales chart.*
* **Explain** *the company policy on shrinkage.*

Why is this list better than the last?
Why are the underlined words important?

This list says what the learner should be able to DO and these words will make it easy to select an appropriate test.

Skills

Testing SKILLS is rather different from testing what people should KNOW. Before we begin it is useful to divide skills into two:

Performance Skills

Social and Communication Skills

Performance Skills
These are concerned with:
* **Hand eye coordination and dexterity** e.g. driving, machine operation, craft skill, sorting.
* **Perceptual skills** e.g. fault finding in quality control.
* **Technical** e.g. ability to follow laboratory routines.

Assessment should be concerned with the trainee's ability to **perform** the tasks described in the objectives. Here are some examples of objectives related to performance skills.
Ability to:
* Position a fork lift truck for correct lifting
* Measure chest, bust and hips
* Change a printing roller
* Locate a microchip under a binocular microscope
* Rethread a shuttle on a sewing machine
However, there is no mention of the **speed** or **level** of accuracy required. If the **standard** of performance is important this should be included in the statement of objectives. It gives a clear guide to you when planning appropriate assessment.
Examples:
* The ability to locate process faults with 95% accuracy.
* The ability to stitch 50 buttonholes in 20 minutes with less than a 1% rejection rate.
* The ability to group blood samples with 100% accuracy using the standard procedures.

Social and Communication Skills
These are concerned with:
* The ability to respond appropriately in social situations e.g. selling, negotiating.
* The ability to listen, speak and write clearly and effectively.
Although these are more difficult to write as objectives it is still important to know what is being assessed.
Examples: The trainee should be able to:
* Write legibly
* Spell correctly
* Speak clearly
* Greet customers using the correct form of address
* Respond to complaints politely.
As you can see, the standard of performance is very difficult, if not impossible, to specify. This is one of those areas in which it is most sensible to resort to subjective assessment measures (see Unit 4 of this package).

Attitudes
The most difficult category to recognise is **attitudes**. It is concerned with the way a trainee responds to customers, supervisors, colleagues, and the job itself. Here are some examples:
* Co-operation — outlook towards work, supervision and fellow workers
* Timekeeping and attendance
* Courtesy in customer relations
* Alertness

How successful are you at categorising activities and procedures?

Knowledge, skill or attitude?

Below is a series of activities or procedures. Decide how you would categorise each — put
  K — for knowledge
  S — for skills
  A — for attitude
a. Explain how sizes, colours and styles are replaced according to sales
b. Demonstrate how to use the pricing gun
c. Explain the liaison between stockroom and sales floor staff
d. Adjust lathe for polishing
e. Show how merchandise should be packed
f. Handle customer queries
g. Take initiative in the absence of the supervisor
h. Transplant lettuce seedlings
i. Accept responsibility

CHECK
How did you do?
Here are the answers. Check your responses
  Knowledge — a. c.
  Skills — b. d. e. h.
  Attitudes — g. i.

It is not **always** clear in which category to place a particular job. You will note that 'f' does not appear in the answers. This is because either
a. the task is not sufficiently specific
b. the task could fit more than one category.

Handling customer queries could demand clear **knowledge** of products but could also require particular **attitudes** to customer relations as well as **social skills**.

Conclusion

You should now be able to:
1. write a job description
2. transform the job description into objectives
3. categorise activities and procedures as:
   knowledge
   skills
   or attitudes.

Component 2:

What Kinds of Tests are Available? An Overview

Key Words

 Informal/Standardised tests; individual/group tests; objective; subjective; multiple choice; multiple response; sequencing; matching; recall; completion; logs; diaries; interview; profiles; observation; simulations.

Introduction
At the end of the Component you should be able to:
a. recognise objective and subjective test items
b. identify the range of tests and assessment procedures available.

Types of test and test items 1 (Objective/Subjective)
Once you have decided on:
* the nature of the job;
* the precise components of the job you need to assess (objectives);
* divided these into knowledge, skills and attitudes;
only then can you start to select the most appropriate method of assessment.

What kinds of test will be suitable?
Informal or Standardised Tests?
* Informal tests are those constructed by the trainer. While you may regard this as a chore, these tests can be made to fit your particular needs. There are commercially produced standardised tests for some areas of commerce and industry, but they only rarely seem to match exactly what is wanted.

* Standardised tests are designed by test experts and are subjected to rigorous statistical analysis. These are usually commercially produced.

Individual or Group Tests?
As you work through the unit, you will see that some tests are administered on a one-to-one basis (e.g. fork-lift truck driving test) while others can be administered to a group of individuals (e.g. most paper and pencil tests).

Objective or Subjective Tests?
As this is a key decision you will have to make in either the selection or construction of your tests, the overview which follows in this component attempts to group them as subjective or objective. Such a grouping is useful to recognise the limitations and strengths of the tests.

Objective tests
What is an objective test?
An objective test consists of a number of items the responses to which are all precisely predetermined. The term 'item' is used rather than 'question' because although some items may be in the form of questions, others may not.

▰▰▰ Checkpoint

Using your knowledge from previous units outline the advantages and disadvantages of objective and subjective tests.

Answer:
Well constructed **objective** *tests are more valid, more reliable, easier to score and easier to administer than subjective forms of assessment.*
Subjective *tests, although requiring the assessor to make judgements, enable greater flexibility in their construction and conduct. Nevertheless, even here objectives must be explicit and standards of performance stated whenever possible.*

Objective items

Here are some examples of objective items:
Example 1.
What immediate First Aid Treatment should you give yourself if your skin comes into contact with acid or caustic material?
  (i) Flush immediately with plenty of water
  (ii) Wipe off with a dry cloth
  (iii) Apply some type of neutraliser
  (iv) Ignore the contact because it is probably harmless
Example 2.
  (i) What are your responsibilities under the Health and Safety at Work Act 1974?
Example 3.
Circle the letter on the answer sheet which represents the correct answer.
If mechanical trouble develops in the fork lift truck during the shift, the driver should:
A. Park truck immediately and try to get another truck to finish shift.
B. Report it to an authorized person right away.
C. Make the truck last until the end of the shift, if possible.
D. Find out what is wrong and try to fix it to keep truck operating.
The items are 'objective' — there is only one **correct** response in each case. Whoever marks the test will come up with the same score.

Subjective tests
What is a subjective test?

Miss Heavy Engineering

Here the responses to the questions are more difficult to predict precisely.
  These tests are also more difficult to score because:
  (i) the quality of a trainee's response has to be judged by the assessor.
  (ii) the mark will therefore depend upon the individual assessor's judgement.
Here are some examples of subjective test items.
Example 1.
A customer has brought an item of merchandise back to you which he presumes to be faulty.
  How would you handle the situation?

Example 2.

Present the operator with two situations which will require machine controls to be operated to avoid damage or effect an improvement (simulation). Assessor should look for order of operation and level of skill demonstrated.

Example 3.

What parts of your job do you like least and why?

▰▰▰

Place the last three examples in order starting with the least subjective and ending with the most subjective. Give reasons for your order.

Check 1. Example 1
     2. Example 2
     3. Example 3

Reasons.
1. Example 1 appears to be very subjective but it is likely that the trainee will have been given a number of ground rules for dealing with customer complaints. The assessor will have a reasonable, if not exact, idea of what to expect and in what order.
2. Example 2 would seem to be 'objective' in that there will be a predictable sequence of machine operation. However, because there is an unspecified element of skill in the process, it is probably more subjective than example 1.
3. Example 3 is completely open-ended. It is almost impossible to predict, and there are no right or wrong answers.

▰▰▰

Are you now able to spot the difference between subjective and objective test items? Here is a list of six items from various tests. Say which items are:

a) Objective

b) Subjective

1. What type of portable fire extinguisher should never be used on an electrical fire?
   (i) CO_2
   (ii) Dry chemical
   (iii) Water type
   (iv) Vaporizing liquid
2. On which form do you enter defective merchandise?
3. Write a list of the qualities required in a quality control worker on a production line.
4. Put the following operations in the correct sequence:
   Engage cutting tool
   Switch on machine
   Lower safety guard
   Check machine speed
   Adjust angle of cutting edge
5. What factors must you consider before re-ordering stock?
6. What is meant by sales promotion?

Check: Objective items: 1. 2. 4. 5.
       Subjective items: 3. 6.

Types of tests and test items 2.

A. You will have realised already there are several ways in which to ask questions or get the information you require to test particular characteristics of the trainee and his level of competence.

B. Apart from the division into 'objective' and 'subjective' there are further sub categories.

The remaining components of this unit will be devoted to those tests and items which are considered to be objective and the whole of Unit 4 will tell you how to construct tests which are subjective.

Meanwhile here is the range of possibilities. At this stage it is only important for you to **recognise** the type of items illustrated.

Objective test items: an overview

1. Multiple Choice

From a list of possible answers to a question the trainee is required to select one.

Example:

A customer has returned to your branch with a toaster which he purchased less than a week ago. Would you:

a) apologise and exchange the toaster immediately.

b) apologise and examine the toaster to find out the fault and then take appropriate action.

c) apologise for the inconvenience and give the customer a refund.

d) apologise for the inconvenience and ask the customer if she is prepared to accept goods to the value of the toaster.

2. Multiple Response

This consists of an incomplete statement followed by several responses which are suggested answers to complete the sentence. Such items differ from multiple choice in that there may be **one** or **more** correct responses.

Example: 'Over printing' may be caused by:

a. Uneven tension in the paper

b. Dirty rollers

c. Fluctuations in roller speed

d. Wet storage

e. Misaligned rollers

3. Sequencing

These items test the trainee's ability to list information or a process in the correct sequence.

Example: which is the correct order of seniority in the store?

a. Manager, supervisor, assistant manager, departmental manager.

b. Supervisor, assistant manager, departmental manager, manager.

c. Manager, assistant manager, departmental manager, supervisor.

d. Departmental manager, manager, supervisor, assistant manager.

4. Matching

This is another variety of a multiple choice item. The trainee is presented with two lists and is required to make the correct link between an entry in list A with one in list B.

Example: Various transactions are listed in list A and forms in list B. Place the letter corresponding to the form in the space next to the transaction for which it is required.

List A	List B
1. Refund to customer	(a) D72
2. Defective stock	(b) E20
3. Stock transfer	(c) D17
4. Textile reorder	(d) E11
	(e) N4
	(f) M62

5. True/False (Or Yes/No)

The trainee is presented with a statement that is true or false and is asked to underline which answer he considers correct.

Example:

True/False The term shrinkage in retailing refers to losses due to theft or damage.

6. Simple Recall/Completion

These are common items which demand the recall of a fact.

Example:

Question type: What is the colour of the neutral wire in an electric cable?

Completion type: The colour of the live wire in an electric cable is . . .

7. Check Lists/Rating Scales

These can be objective or subjective. They are particularly useful for practical competence tests and on-the-job assessments.

Example:

Here are some items from one form of checklist used for assessing the practical competence of fork lift truck drivers.

Faults

1. Travels with forks/load too high/low
2. Fails to position mast correctly for travelling
3. Fails to release brake when travelling
4. Accelerates or brakes erratically
5. etc.

Example:

Here is an example of a rating scale commonly used in appraisal forms for sales floor staff.

Service	Very good	Good	Satis-factory	Unsatis-factory
Attitudes to selling General helpfulness to customer Dealing with customer problems and complaints				

From what you know about objective and subjective items, comment on the last two examples.

Check: Have you noted that in the check list the trainer is making a judgement which is based on a simple observation? There is one correct procedure on each manoeuvre. The rating scale however demands a **subjective** *assessment about the level of competence.*

Recap — Objective Tests

At this stage you are only required to recognise the range of objective test items available. The problem of test construction will be covered in some detail in later components of this unit.

Here is a list of the objective items reviewed.

* Multiple Choice
* Multiple Response
* Sequencing
* Matching
* True/False
* Recall/Completion
* Check Lists and Rating Scales

Subjective tests

You will realise by now that the distinction objective/subjective is sometimes difficult to maintain. While there are cases where overlap is evident, the following methods of assessment are usually categorized as subjective. This is because the assessor is required to judge the quality of the performance, answer, product or attitude.

1. Essays

You will not need reminding that this is the most used form of assessment in school examinations, but there are occasions in industry when essays can also serve a useful purpose.

The distinctive features of the essay question are:
* No one answer is correct

* The answers vary in quality and correctness
* The trainee has the opportunity to recall and organise his ideas.

2. Logs and Diaries

A very useful device for continuous assessment is the log or diary. It is of particular value for apprentices and trainees who are expected to include in their training programmes experience of a wide range of skills and techniques.

A log or diary serves to:

* Check that a technique or skill has been covered
* Provide the learner with an opportunity to describe the techniques involved e.g. a laboratory process
* Allow the trainee to comment on the quality or effectiveness of the instruction.

3. Oral Questioning

This is frequently used in training to provide informal feedback on the success of instruction and the level of understanding. The advantage is that its effect is immediate.

Oral questioning may also be used on a more formal basis as a variation of the essay question. It can even be used by the trainer to help assign grades. Some benefits of oral questioning:

* It permits detailed probing by the examiner
* Candidates can ask for clarification of the question
* Errors in thinking can be diagnosed
* Trainees with poor literary skills can succeed.

4. Interviews

This is one of the means of assessing the suitability of trainees/employees for roles within the organisation. If properly structured it serves a variety of purposes:

* Assessing the attitudes, aspirations and commitments of the trainee
* Explaining company policy and options available
* Assessing knowledge as in oral questioning.

It is therefore a useful two-way process for gaining and providing information.

5. Profiles

This is rather different from most of the other techniques which have been outlined in that it is not strictly a form of assessment. It might be better described as a multi-faceted means of **recording** a learner's skills, capabilities, experiences and achievements. Such a device both encourages and supports a great variety of assessment techniques.

The range of achievements and qualities for which profiles are suitable:

* Communication skills
* Numerical skills
* Planning, problem solving, learning, creative thinking

* Manipulative skills
* Attitudes

Profiles can also be used for self assessment of the trainee.

6. Appraisal Forms

Appraisal forms have been used for many years and usually consist of a check list of qualities against which the assessor grades from 'very good' to 'unsatisfactory'. In many respects it is a crude version of a profile.

7. Observation

There are many important features of a trainee's performance which can only be assessed by direct observation. There is a whole range of techniques available.

* Anecdotal records i.e. a descriptive account of what the apprentice or salesman does
* By checklist or rating scale where the assessor notes when particular procedures occur or at what standard.

8. Simulations

Simulation describes the context rather than the precise assessment methods adopted. The trainer tries to reproduce conditions, situations or problems which are as close to reality as possible. He has then to find a means of assessing the learner's ability to respond. The classic example is the flight simulator in aircrew training.

Which of the 'subjective' assessment methods do you think would be suitable for the following.
a. A comprehensive record of all the skills and qualities of a trainee
b. A trainee's aspirations in the company
c. A trainee's ability to placate an angry customer
d. The diagnosis of a mechanical fault
e. The satisfactory completion of a series of laboratory procedures.

ANSWERS
a. Profiles
b. Interview and oral questioning
c. Observation (on the job or simulated)
d. Observation (on the job or simulated), oral questioning or essay
e. Log or diary.

A further classification

While the division of tests into objective or subjective is necessary to understand the nature and validity of the assessment a further classification may be helpful in test selection.

Method of Administration	Subjective	Objective
Written	Essays	Standardised tests
	Logs and diaries	Multiple choice
	Profiles	Sequencing
		Matching
		True/False
		Recall/Completion
	Rating Scales	Check lists
Oral	Oral questioning	Oral questioning
	Interviews	
Practical	Observation	Observation
	Simulations	Simulation

Note: A number of tests can be placed in more than one column depending upon the precise nature of the test items.

Component 3:

How to Write an Objective Test: an Introduction

Key Words

 Objectives; systematic approach, Bloom's *Taxonomy of Educational Objectives*; skills/abilities; test-scheme specification; specification table; 'weights'.

You are now ready to make a more concentrated study of objective tests i.e. those containing such as recall/completion and multiple-choice items. In particular, you will make a closer examination of the advantages to be gained from personally constructed objective tests and will learn how to set about planning and writing them.

Objective tests in assessment

You already know something about objective tests and the forms taken by test items. It would now be useful for you to determine how much you understand about the advantages to be gained from using them.

▰▰▰ Checkpoint

List what you think are the advantages to be gained from using objective tests and then check your points with those which I have made. You may have thought of points additional to those which I made.

Answers
Advantages to be gained from using objective tests:
  1. *The marking is consistent regardless of who is marking the test.*
  2. *They are quick to mark.*
  3. *They are efficient in assessing a wide range of knowledge.*
  4. *If written with skill, more than mere facts can be tested. For example, comprehension of material and the application of knowledge to solve problems can be tested.*

5. *They discourage question spotting for examinations.*
6. *Answers are restricted by the questions asked so that the tester can assess exactly what he wishes to assess.*
7. *There is less chance of certain candidates being lucky in that the 'right' questions came up in the examination.*
8. *Rapid feedback in the form of knowledge of results is provided for both learner and trainer.*
9. *They encourage the learner to acquire a solid basis of factual matter.*
10. *Scoring is not influenced by the 'halo effect' produced by a candidate's ability in written expression.*

Now these advantages apply to objective tests in general, commercially produced tests included, but there are even more advantages to be gained from tests which you yourself have constructed.

Can you suggest what some of these advantages might be? Write down a few of those which immediately spring to mind.

Advantages to be gained from using personally constructed tests
It seems to me that the following are relevant.
1. *There will be a closer match between the test and your needs than would have been the case with a commercially produced test.*
2. *They would provide an on-going evaluation of the students and their progress.*
3. *You can make the tests as long or short as you consider appropriate, thus providing the specific information which you require.*
4. *You can decide on the levels of difficulty of the test items, thus making the test appropriate for your particular students.*
5. *You can set the time limits for testing.*
Of course, many see disadvantages in objective testing as compared with, for instance, assessing by means of essay-type tests.

What do you think are the drawbacks? List a few and compare your list with mine.

Common objections are that objective tests:
1. *Encourage cramming of facts rather than understanding them and using them;*

2. *Demand totally right or totally wrong answers, thus preventing credit being given for partly right answers;*

3. *Provide little opportunity for self expression, development of argument and expansion of answers;*
4. *Take too long to construct.*

There may be some truth in all of these objections and it must be accepted that planning and writing objective tests is a skilled and time-consuming business. It is certain that a systematic approach must be employed and we will now see how we can do this.

A systematic approach

Here are a few questions that the test constructor must ask himself before he begins the task of actually writing the test items. As you read them, try to think of possible answers.

1. What is to be assessed?

2. How will the trainer ensure that the completed test truly reflects the content that is to be tested? For example, are the right number of appropriate questions being asked about the various sections of the content?

3. What form will the test items take? Will they be, for example, true/false, completion, multiple-choice? How will the trainer-constructor decide which are the most appropriate for his purposes?

4. How can the trainer be sure that the items which he has written are doing the job that he intends they should do?

5. How can the trainer be sure that the test as a whole is doing a good job?

6. How can the marking of the test be accomplished?

Below is a table which summarises ways in which these questions may be effectively answered. Don't be discouraged by the fact that the terms may be new to you and may seem rather complex. You will be learning about them in a progressive, systematic manner. The first two problems will be dealt with in this component, the next (form of test items) in Component 4, and the last three in Component 5.

Before reading them, cover up the 'Solutions' column and try to answer the questions yourself. How close can you come to what is written?

Problems of test construction

PROBLEM	SOLUTION
1. What is to be assessed?	Define the objectives of the teaching and learning, hence the testing. (You already know something about objectives.)
2. How will the completed test reflect the content of the teaching, learning and testing?	Plan a test-scheme specification in the form of a specification table. This makes use of your stated objectives and also of different levels of questions.
3. What form will the test items take?	You will decide after you have considered the strengths and weaknesses of the various kinds of items and which are the appropriate ones for your purposes.
4. How can the trainer be sure items are doing the job that he has intended?	He must carry out an **item analysis**. This means finding out something about the **difficulty** levels of the test items and also about how effective they are in discriminating between the most able and the least able students.
5. How can you be sure that the test as a whole is doing a good job?	Following your **item analysis** you will be better able to produce a final, balanced test.
6. How can the marking best be accomplished?	You will have to consider whether you should **correct for guessing** and whether you could conveniently produce a marking key to speed up the process.

Now to look at the problems in detail.

1. What is to be assessed?

This may be decided by defining the objectives of the teaching, learning and testing.

Consequently in Component 1 you learned about classifying objectives in terms of knowledge, skills and attitudes and this is a generally accepted way of looking at them.

However, there is another useful way of categorising them and this is concerned with defining them in terms of the **level** of skills and abilities which are to be tested.

Here's an example taken from the field of electrical engineering. A trainer may decide that his test, in addition to testing his apprentices' learning of electrical regulations, should also discover the extent to which they can **apply** their knowledge in practice.

In this case, the two skills to be measured are:
i. the factual recall of the regulations;
ii. the application of the regulations to practical situations.

It is possible to construct a test to measure both these skills but the trainer will have to decide which skill is the more important. If he thinks that they are equally important, he will allocate half of the test items to each. On the other hand, if he considers that factual recall is twice as important as application of regulations, he will devote two-thirds of the items to factual recall and one-third to application. This is called 'weighting' and in this case we are assuming that all the items themselves are equally weighted.

▰▰▰

If all items were weighted equally, what would be the proportions of items to be included in the test if he considered:

(a) factual recall to be three times as important as application of regulations?
(b) factual recall to be only a third as important as application of regulations?

Answers
(a) factual recall 75%/application 25%
(b) factual recall 25%/application 75%

Levels of skills/abilities

Let's now take a closer look at the different levels of skill and abilities to be tested.

The City and Guilds of London has instructed its test constructors to take into consideration three different skills, these being:
i. Knowledge (of factual recall) (a category you met in Component 1)
ii. Comprehension (of principles)
iii. Application (of procedures, techniques, etc.)

Can you suggest examples of how a test can assess these different skills with regard to the field of electrical regulations?

I think that you would agree that the test items would require the apprentice to:
i. correctly recall factual material;
ii. demonstrate that he understood the meaning of that factual material;
iii. show that he could apply his knowledge and understanding in practical situations.

How could these ideas be applied to sections from your own sphere of interest? Can you think of a few examples?

Weighting

The kinds of skills and abilities may be extended still further and it is also possible to allocate 'weights' to the various categories so as to reflect more correctly the preferred emphasis of the trainer.

For example, an examination board might suggest the following arrangement as a guide for their constructors of objective tests:

Skill/ability	'Weight'	
i. Knowledge	35%	(What is it?)
ii. Comprehension	30%	(What does it mean?)
iii. Application	20%	(How can I use it?)
iv. Evaluation	15%	(How good is it?)

Do you see how the demands of the different kinds of skills/abilities to be tested become increasingly more demanding?

Did you note how the relative 'weights' progressively decrease in this case? What is the intention underlying this particular statement of 'weights'?

It seems to me that the board considers that testing of knowledge should take precedence and that the higher level skills should carry progressively less emphasis, thus giving opportunities for students of all abilities to achieve success but giving the more able the chance to gain high marks.

Bloom's Taxonomy of Educational Objectives

Most classifications of abilities and skills are based on the work of Professor B. S. Bloom of Chicago University. He set out his *Taxonomy of Educational Objectives* and it is from this that the following list of major areas of educational testing are taken. Also contained in the table are suggestions for appropriate words which might be used when the activities are being defined or when test items are being set.

LEVELS IN THE TAXONOMY	APPROPRIATE WORDS
i. Knowledge	recall, define, explain, identify, describe, state
ii. Comprehension	give in your own words, illustrate, rephrase, translate, deduce, predict
iii. Application	calculate, apply, transfer, classify, categorise
iv. Analysis	classify, analyse, categorise, discriminate between, distinguish
v. Synthesis	relate, unite, organise, derive, conclude
vi. Evaluation	compare, contrast, argue, appraise, judge

Although it would be possible, it is not suggested that a test constructor should use all these levels in all his tests. He would decide which categories were relevant to his particular purpose and would limit his selection of items accordingly. His test specification, in the form of a specification table, sometimes called a test blueprint, would then be tailor-made for his own purposes.

2. How will the completed test reflect the content of the teaching, learning and consequential testing?

This may be done by making a test-scheme specification in the form of a specification table.

Note: An introduction to the preparation of our **overall** assessment scheme was given in Component 3 of Study Unit 2 of this Package. Here we are concerned with a similar task, but narrowed down to the production of a specification table for an objective (written) test.

'Let's get the mixture right'

Let's see how this may be done by taking into consideration the objectives (different categories of skills/abilities), e.g. Knowledge, Comprehension, Application, etc. and the content of the learning to be tested. Here's an example. Suppose a trainer wishes to assess how much an apprentice has learned about aspects of a motor car engine. He could divide the learning content into four sections comprising 'the carburettor', 'the alternator', 'the radiator' and 'spark plugs' — a rather simplistic example but one which will suit our purpose.

He might then decide to test two categories of ability, factual recall (Knowledge) and Application of Knowledge. His next decision is to state the relative importance of the two abilities. Let's say that he decides that he wishes to test these abilities in the ratio of 60% factual recall and 40% application of knowledge. He may now begin to construct a specification table, as it appears below.

Writing a Specification Table
Step 1

Section of content to be tested	Skills/abilities to be tested			
	Factual recall	%	Application of Knowledge	%
Carburettor		60		40
Alternator		60		40
Radiator		60		40
Spark plugs		60		40

Step 2

After taking into account the limitations set by available time for testing and coverage of the content, the trainer then decides on the number of questions to be set. Let's suppose that he decides that 60 questions are enough for his purpose and that they should be evenly divided between sections. This would mean that each section of the content would require 15 questions. He would now add another column to his specification table, this would give the total number of questions to be allocated to each section, i.e. 15.

The numbers in brackets refer to the numbers of questions resulting from dividing the 15 questions in each section in the proportions decided for each of the skill/abilities categories that is 60% to factual recall (9) and 40% to application of knowledge (6). The completed table appears below.

Specification table

Section of content to be tested	Skills/abilities to be tested				Number of questions
	Factual recall	%	Application of Knowledge	%	
Carburettor	(9)	60	(6)	40	15
Alternator	(9)	60	(6)	40	15
Radiator	(9)	60	(6)	40	15
Spark plugs	(9)	60	(6)	40	15
Total Questions	(36)		(24)		60

Step 3

The trainer will now have prepared a test-scheme specification to suit his own particular purposes, his next task being to write the questions according to the plan, that is so that 15 questions cover the section devoted to 'the carburettor', 9 of which demand factual recall, the remaining 6 being directed towards application of knowledge.

You will note that this scheme could be used to plan specifications to suit many different requirements. For instance, the numbers of questions allocated to the different sections of content could be changed as could the proportion of questions related to the different skills/abilities. Such changes would result in different numbers of questions to be planned to assess attainment in sections of content in their relationship to skills/abilities. Any such adjustments would be made after the trainer had considered the particular group to be tested, the skills/abilities he wished to test and their related needs, the sections of content to be covered and the length of test required.

Complete a specification table to comply with the following requirements.

i. Sections of content
   (a) opening a sale
   (b) sales technique
   (c) advising on terms of purchase
   (d) closing a sale
   the items will be equally divided between the sections.
ii. Skill/abilities and weight
   (a) factual recall   75%
   (b) application of knowledge   25%
iii. Total number of questions:
   80 to be allocated equally to sections of content.
Check your findings with the table below:

Answer
Specification table (test-scheme specification)

Section of content to be tested	Skills/Abilities to be tested				Numbers of questions
	Factual recall	%	Application of knowledge	%	
Opening a sale	(15)	75	(5)	25	20
Sales technique	(15)	75	(5)	25	20
Advice on purchase terms	(15)	75	(5)	25	20
Closing the sale	(15)	75	(5)	25	20
Total questions	(60)		(20)		80

Further developments

It may have occurred to you that increasingly complex specifications could be drawn up to suit more diverse requirements.

For instance a trainer might wish to:
i. test a wider variety of skills/abilities;
   (This would call for a further breaking down of the relative 'weights' given to each skill/ability)
ii. vary the 'weights' attached to each section of the content to be tested. (This would call for different number of questions to be allocated to each section of content and consequently to each skill/abilities section of content in the table).

Before we look at an example, write down the skills/abilities which are derived from Bloom's Taxonomy.

Answer
Skills/abilities derived from Bloom's Taxonomy
   i. *Knowledge*
   ii. *Comprehension*
   iii. *Application*
   iv. *Analysis*
   v. *Synthesis*
   vi. *Evaluation*

The trainer could include in his planning any or all of these categories depending upon the level of ability of his students, thus perhaps leading towards a more complex scheme.

Here's another example taken from the field of automotive engineering. Our aim will be to construct a specification table from the details below.

Test specification

A   Four sections of content

		Relative weights
(a)	transmission	10%
(b)	ignition	20%
(c)	fuel system	30%
(d)	braking system	40%

B   Skills/abilities

	Relative weights
(i) Factual Knowledge	10%
(ii) Comprehension of Knowledge	10%
(iii) Application of Knowledge	20%
(iv) Analysis	30%
(v) Evaluation	30%

C   Total number of items to be set: 100

Here is the resulting table.
Check the procedure and resulting figures.

Specification table

Sections of Content		Skills/abilities to be tested					Number of items per section
	%	Factual Knowl. 10%	Comprehension of Knowledge 10%	Application of Knowledge 20%	Analysis 30%	Evaluation 30%	
(a) Transmission	10	1	1	2	3	3	10
(b) Ignition	20	2	2	4	6	6	20
(c) Fuel system	30	3	3	6	9	9	30
(d) Braking system	40	4	4	8	12	12	40
Total Items	100	10	10	20	30	30	100

You will find working in the following order to be an effective way of tackling the job.

i.   Complete the final column (total number of items per section) paying attention to the 'weights' in the "Sections of Content" column and the planned total number of items in this case 100.

ii.   Starting with the top row, fill in the rows which are concerned with the number of questions allocated to each "Section of Content" in relation to the various "Skills/abilities" and the 'weights' attached to them.
For example look at the "Transmission" row.
10 items have been allocated altogether (10% of 100)
 1 item has been allocated to 'Factual Knowledge' (10% of 10)

1 item has been allocated to "Comprehension of Knowledge" (10% of 10)

2 items have been allocated to "Application of Knowledge" (20% of 10)

3 items have been allocated to "Analysis" (30% of 10)

3 items have been allocated to "Evaluation" (30% of 10)

The remaining rows can now be completed. In fact, the task becomes easier as it progresses because it is easy to use cross-referencing to insert the required numbers.

Now construct your own specification table which satisfies the following requirements. The example is taken from the field of building.

Test specification

A. Five sections of content   "Weights"
- (a) composition of materials   25%
- (b) practical techniques   10%
- (c) behaviour patterns of materials   15%
- (d) measurement   30%
- (e) general ideas   20%

B. Skills/abilities
- i. Factual Knowledge   20%
- ii. Comprehension of Knowledge   40%
- iii. Application of Knowledge   20%
- iv. Analysis   20%

C. Total number of items to be set: 100

How did you get on?
How does your table compare with mine? Here it is.

Sections of Content	%	Factual Knowledge 20%	Comprehension of Knowledge 40%	Application of Knowledge 20%	Analysis 20%	Number of items per section
Composition	25	5	10	5	5	25
Techniques	10	2	4	2	2	10
Behaviour patterns	15	3	6	3	3	15
Measurement	30	6	12	6	6	30
Ideas	20	4	8	4	4	20
Total items	100	20	40	20	20	100

Naturally, not all specifications would include the convenient, easily computed figures which you have dealt with in the examples, but now that you have learned the principles of construction, you will be able to apply them in any situation. Sometimes you may find that you will have to compromise by rounding off numbers to complete the table. In such cases, you merely use your own judgement.

Examine the following example. You will note that estimation is very much used in deciding the cell values.

Sections of content	%	Factual Knowledge 23%	Comprehension of Knowledge 46%	Application of Knowledge 15%	Analysis 16%	Number of items per section
Materials	26	6	12	4	4	26
Techniques	11	3	6	1	1	11
Characteristics	14	3	6	2	3	14
Measurement	28	6	12	5	5	28
Ideas	21	5	10	3	3	21
	100	23	46	15	16	100

Having worked carefully through this component, you will have learned a great deal more about objective tests. Besides knowing about the advantages to be gained from using them, particularly from using self-constructed tests, you will also be able to plan an effective test bearing in mind the various kinds of skills and abilities which you might wish to test and also the number of questions to be allocated to each section of the content to be tested.

You are now ready to learn how to write different kinds of objective test items.

After completing this Component you will be able to:
1. State some of the advantages gained from using objective tests;
2. State some of the advantages gained from using the trainer-constructed tests;
3. State some of the objections to objective tests;
4. List objectives in terms of skills/abilities in terms of Bloom's *Taxonomy of Educational Objectives*;
5. Discriminate between the various levels of skills/abilities;
6. Prepare a Specificaton Table (Test-scheme specification).

Topics to be considered in Components 4 and 5 will include:
1. The various kinds of objective test items;
2. How to write effective test items;
3. How to identify 'good' and 'bad' questions.

Component 4:

How to Write an Objective Test: Types of Test Items

Key Words

Types of items; construction; choice; recall; completion; alternative response; matching; context dependent; statement/reason; skills/abilities; laboratory/workshop.

Now that you know how to plan an objective test specification, the next step is to have a look at:
— the various types of test questions (usually called **test items**) which you could include in your test;
— the strengths and weaknesses of these items so that you will know which will best suit your purposes;
— how test items can test the different levels of skills and abilities which you learnt about in Component 3.

It would be greatly to your advantage if you would write an item relevant to your own sphere of interest after I have described each type. Also, it would increase your understanding if you attempted the items given as examples.

Types of test items

Test items are generally of two main types, those in which the candidate must:
  a) **construct** an answer for himself (a **construction** type),
or b) **choose** an answer from several possible answers (a **choice** type).

Here is a summary of the various kinds of test items which are commonly used.

a) Candidate **constructs** an answer (CONSTRUCTION type)	b) Candidate **chooses** an answer (CHOICE type)

1. SHORT ANSWER OR COMPLETION
   i. formula, single word, symbol
   ii. multiple words or phrases
	3. ALTERNATIVE RESPONSE
	   i. true/false, yes/no
	   ii. multiple choice (varied and possibly the most frequently used).

2. CONTEXT FOCUSSED (May also be **choice** type)	4. MATCHING 5. CONTEXT FOCUSSED (May also be **construction** type)

Construction

Choice

Here are a few examples:

1. Short answer or completion

i. Formula, single word or symbol

Question type which requires in the answer a single word, symbol or formula.

a) What is the name of the capital city of Spain?

b) Who invented the telephone?

What kinds of skills/abilities are being tested? Can you remember what you learned in Component 3? You'll agree that these items require only **recall of factual knowledge.**

What about this one?

c) If I share £45 equally between 5 apprentices, how much would each get?

What kind of skill/ability is being tested by this item? To answer the item, the candidate must **apply his knowledge** of multiplication tables and division. Therefore it calls for **application**, the third level skill/ability.

Here are a few items of a different type.

ii. Multiple words or phrases

a) the chemical symbol for water is . . . .

b) If $x + 7 = 11$, $x = $ . . . .

c) If you discover a burst water pipe in your house, your first action would be to ....

d) Draw a circle with a radius of 5 cm.

Look at ii. (a), (b), (c) and (d) above, noting the different kinds of answers required.

They all require **completion** by means of answers **constructed** by the respondent, i.e. (a) a symbol, (b) a symbol (digit), (c) number of words, (d) a figure (a circle).

Which different levels of skills/abilities are tested by (a), (b), (c) and (d)?

You'll probably agree that part ii (a) requires only **factual recall** but the others call for **application** of knowledge.

In what situations do you think that the short answer completion type of item could be used with advantage?

You'll perhaps agree that they could be useful in:

— cases where only a single correct answer is required;

— mathematics and science where computation as well as knowledge may be tested;

— cases where knowledge of technical terms, symbols, definitions, and formulae need to be tested.

You can see that more than mere **factual recall** may be tested.

Some would criticise these items because:

— they may encourage mere rote learning, that is learning facts parrot-fashion without necessarily understanding them.

— they may be restricted to testing only the lower levels of skills/abilities, i.e. **factual recall, comprehension and application**.

— it is easy to ask ambiguous questions,

e.g. (a) Where are the Victoria Falls?

What answer is required? Zambesi River? Africa? Livingstone? Zimbabwe/Zambia?

(b) Drake sailed against the Spanish Armada in In what? 1588? a ship? a fleet? a suit of armour?

It is obvious that the onus rests with the test writer who must make his requirements crystal clear.

▨▨▨ Checkpoint

Write a few test items of each type, short answer and completion, concerning your own sphere of interest. Try to include both **recall** and **application** types of items.

Examine your items carefully.
  Have you written items which:
(a) *include both* **question** *type and* **completion** *items in which the answers are* **constructed** *by the respondent?*
(b) *are clearly expressed and call for one answer and one answer only?*
(c) *examine different levels of skills/ability?*

_____

Now to the next type of item.

2. Context focussed type

These items usually test **comprehension or application.**
Here's an example which makes use of a graph.

The graph below shows the daily midday temperatures recorded during one week.

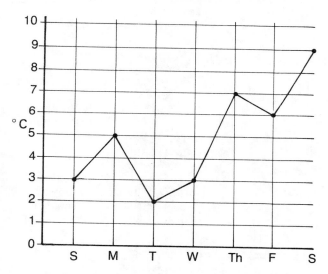

a) The lowest temperature was recorded on ....
b) The highest temperature was recorded on ....
c) The difference between the highest and lowest temperatures is:
  (1) 6 C
  (2) 7 C
  (3) 4 C
  (4) 5 C

  Tick the right answer.

who needs to be told its cold anyway

▨▨▨

Here are a few items to check your understanding of CONTEXT FOCUSSED items.
(i)   the levels of abilities/skills which are tested above are:
      (a) ....
      (b) ....
      (c) ....
(ii) Earlier you were told that CONTEXT FOCUSSED items could be either **construction** or **choice** types.
      In the example about temperatures:
      (a) is a .... type
      (b) is a .... type
      (c) is a .... type
(iii) In Part (ii) above, the basic level of ability tested is ....

_____

(i)   *It seems that Parts (a) and (b) test* **comprehension** *of the graph while Part (c) calls for a modest degree of* **application**.
(ii) *(a) construction*
      (b) construction
      (c) choice
(iii) *Comprehension (You might be able to make a case for higher levels).*

_____

Another type of CONTEXT FOCUSSED item is the 'reading' type which makes use of a paragraph of writing and a series of questions of either **construction** or **choice** items which usually require **comprehension** or **application** of the materials. However, with ingenuity, it is possible to test higher levels of skills/abilities.

3. Alternative response types
i. True/False, Yes/No

The most elementary of these is the kind that requires a choice to be made from only two alternatives, i.e. True/False or Yes/No.

Here are a few examples in which the respondent is asked to underline the correct word:

(a) Lancaster stands on the River Lune   True   False
(b) The square root of 625 is 25   True   False

Did you note that (a) and (b) tested different levels of ability?

(a) required merely **factual recall**;
(b) required **comprehension** and **application**.

The Yes/No format is useful in the asssessment of opinions and attitudes, e.g.

(a) I believe that the death penalty should be retained for certain crimes.   Yes   No
(b) I enjoy watching sport on television.   Yes   No

Here is an example of a **cluster** type of item.
    To answer this, the respondent must answer several parts which are based on the same introductory stimulus.

The mean of a set of scores is:
(a) the same as the average   True   False
(b) calculated by dividing the sum of the scores by the number of scores   True   False
(c) the score of the person exactly half-way down the rank order   True   False

What do you see as being:
(a) the advantage of the True/False, Yes/No and Cluster type items?
(b) their disadvantages.

You might have included some of the following:
(a) **Advantages**
   — *They can be marked very quickly.*
   — *A great deal of material can be covered relatively quickly.*
   — *If they are prepared thoughtfully, they can test comprehension as well as simple recall.*

(b) **Disadvantages**
   — *Usually they test only low level abilities.*
   — *Guessing is a problem.*
   — *Considerable time is needed to prepare items.*
(It is true that a person who knows nothing about the material is likely to score about 50% by merely guessing. In Component 5 we will consider this problem.)

---

ii. Multiple choice type

This is probably the most common type and there are various kinds of items within this category, all of which require a **choice** to be made from several alternative responses.

   Let's look at a few examples.

(a) Which of the following is the world's longest river?
   A   Nile
   B   Amazon
   C   Mississippi
   D   Zambesi

You will note that only **one** answer is correct. Therefore this could be called the **single response** type of item. Mere factual recall is required here but higher abilities could be tested with thoughtful preparation of items.

'BEST ANSWER' TYPE

Here's another kind of item:

(b) What was generally considered to be the **main** reason for the introduction of the comprehensive education system?

   A   to satisfy political principles

B to solve the problems of falling numbers of children in secondary schools.

C to equalize educational opportunities for all children.

D to provide a more efficient education system.

The intention underlying this kind of item is that the "best answer" should be chosen from a few apparently reasonable responses. This means that each possible answer has to be considered in turn. Do you think that this means that higher levels of ability, e.g. analysis and synthesis, and evaluation too, are tested? You'll probably agree that it does.

STEM COMPLETION

And yet another kind:

(c) If I invested £10,000 in building society shares which paid interest at $12\frac{1}{2}$% per annum, after one year the amount of interest received would be:

A £125 B £1,250 C £675 D £125.50

This may be called a stem completion type. (The stem is the first part of the item — that part which asks the question.) What kind of skill/ability is being tested here? Would you agree that it is application? The respondent is certainly asked to apply what he knows to a particular situation.

Sometimes the respondent is asked to underline more than one response. Here's an example:

(d) Which of the following are thought to be factors involved in heart disease?

A smoking
B high blood pressure
C intake of surplus vitamins
D high cholesterol level in the blood
E stress

This is called a **multiple response** type and it is evident that this particular item tests factual recall, but it may be used to test higher levels of ability.

It could also be adapted to ask which came first/most important or came last/least important.

It is also possible to prepare a **negative multiple response** item.

For example:

Which of the following are **not** examples of alkalis?

A caustic soda
B vinegar
C chalk
D diluted sulphuric acid

Many test constructors dislike using negatives because they think that they complicate questions unnecessarily.

ALTERNATIVES COMPLETION

Another kind of multiple choice item is the **alternatives completion** type. This requires the respondent to be more active and it is particularly useful with mathematical problems.

Example: (e) The full cost of a lawnmower is £45 but a discount of 10% is allowed for a cash sale. If you paid cash how much would you be charged?

A £40
B £41.50
C £39.50
D £40.50

This obviously tests **application** of knowledge since the candidate is required to apply his knowledge percentages, etc.

STATEMENT AND REASON

The last kind of multiple choice item is a more sophisticated type which requires the respondent to relate a **statement** and a **reason**. Either of these may be correct or either may be incorrect and to get the question right, the candidate must first identify the truth or otherwise of the two parts and then relate them in a particular way. In fact, he is required to choose the correct response from the following:

A Both the **statement** and the **reason** are correct and the **statement** is correctly explained by the **reason**.

B Both the **statement** and the **reason** are correct but the **statement** is **not** correctly explained by the **reason**.

C The **statement** is **not** correctly explained by the **reason** because the **statement** is correct and the **reason** is incorrect.

D The **statement** is incorrect but the **reason** is correct.

E Both **statement** and **reason** are incorrect.

You might think that this is all very complicated, but an example should help to make it clear.

(f)

STATEMENT	REASON
BECAUSE	
Salt which is frequently spread on icy main roads in winter helps to melt ice.	The freezing point of brine (salt and water) is higher than the freezing point of water alone.

Which of the alternatives from A, B, C, D or E would you choose in this case?

C would be the correct response because the **statement** is correct but it is **not** correctly explained by the **reason**.

Which response would you choose in this case?

STATEMENT	REASON
	BECAUSE
Salt which is frequently spread on icy main roads in winter helps to melt the ice	The freezing point of brine (salt and water) is lower than the freezing point of water alone.

Yes, A is right because both statement and reason are correct and the second correctly explains the first.

You can imagine that lists of such statements and reasons could be used to provide a substantial and challenging question.

Which levels of skill/abilities do you think that this kind of item is capable of testing? It can certainly test a person's powers of analysis.

To check on your understanding of the items, write one of each type related to your interests.

Make a list of the **six** kinds of multiple choice item which we have considered in this section, and beside each type, briefly note what the respondent is required to do.

Answer

TYPES	RESPONDENT'S ACTION
(a) Single response	*Underline only one response*
(b) Best answer	*Underline the 'best answer' only*
(c) Item completion	*Underline the response which correctly completes the item*
(d) Multiple response	*Underline all correct responses (Or negative responses if it is a 'negative' item)*
(e) Alternatives completion	*Underline the correct alternative*
(f) Statement/Reason	*Establish the relationship between a statement and reason and choose the right response.*

4. Matching type

You might decide that this is just another kind of multiple choice item. Here's an example:

> (a) Various motor car companies are listed in column A and models of cars in column B.
>
> Place the number corresponding to the car companies next to the model which each makes.
>
> | A | B |
> |---|---|
> | 1. British Leyland | A. Orion |
> | 2. General Motors | B. Nova |
> | 3. Ford | C. Metro |
> | 4. Fiat | D. Fuego |
> | 5. Renault | E. Sunny |
> | 6. Datsun | F. Uno |

This kind of item is useful for learning which involves simple relationships of the 'what', 'who', 'when', 'where' type. You will have noted that it is a **choice** type which tests simple **factual recall** in the example above, but a carefully thought out item could test higher abilities than this, e.g. List A might contain a list of mathematical relationships, e.g. 12 × 17, 59 × 3, 154 + 35, and List B the answers in random order.

Write a **matching** item to test a section from your work interest

Laboratory/workshop tests

Objective tests can be useful in assessing, for example, an apprentice's management and correct ordering of operations required to produce a particular article or to operate a piece of equipment or machinery. This type of test might begin with diagrams or pictures of the equipment or machinery and a statement of the end product or intention. Following this would be a series of test items, most likely multiple choice items, which would trace a logical sequence between the preparatory work and the final result.

You will be able to imagine a similar application to laboratory experiments. Try an example for yourself from your own line of work.

List, under the headings CONSTRUCTION and CHOICE, the various kinds of items which may be used in objective tests. There are **five** main categories, several of which may be sub-divided.

Answer

CONSTRUCTION	CHOICE
1. SHORT ANSWER OR COMPLETION *i. symbol, single word formula* *ii. multiple words or phrases*	*3. ALTERNATIVE RESPONSE* *i. true/false, yes/no* *ii. multiple choice (various)*
2. CONTEXT FOCUSSED *(may also be **choice** type)*	*4. MATCHING* *5. CONTEXT FOCUSSED* *(may also be **construction** type)*

(You may have included further details)

Now that you have completed this Component you will be able to:
1. Describe types of items which you could use in objective tests;
2. List the advantages and disadvantages of each type of test;
3. State appropriate uses of the different kinds of items;
4. Identify levels of skills/abilities tested by the various items.

In Component 5 you will learn how to write effective test items and how to manage and modify tests where necessary.

Useful References

You may find more detailed development of these ideas in:

Rust, W. B. (1973). *Objective Testing in Education and Training,* Pitman Publishing.
Satterly, D. (1981). *Assessment in Schools,* Basil Blackwell, Oxford.

Component 5:

How to Write an Objective Test: Effective Items and Item Analysis

---

Key Words

 Specific; accuracy; ambiguous; stem; key; distractor; response; timing; item analysis; difficulty; facility; High group; Low group; discrimination; index; reject; retain; correction for guessing.

You are already able to:
— plan a test specification, taking into account the various levels of skills/abilities to be tested;
— describe the different kinds of items which are used in objective tests;
— state the uses, advantages and disadvantages of the various types of items.

The next steps are to ensure that you can:
— write effective test items of various kinds;
— plan a test in terms of the time a candidate will take to complete it;
— carry out an item analysis i.e.
 (a) establish the difficulty levels of the items;
 (b) identify the items' power to discriminate between high and low achievers;
— deal with the problems caused by a candidate's guessing the answers to alternative response items.

You will then be ready to write objective tests, examine their effectiveness and make the necessary modifications to make them more effective in the light of your findings.

Short answer/completion types

Let's take a critical look at a few test items, beginning with **Questions/Completion** types. As you read them be on the look-out for faulty expression.

1. Where is Nelson's Column?
2. What is the length of the hypotenuse of a right-angled triangle with adjacent sides measuring 7 cm and 9 cm?

3. Francis Chichester sailed round the world in ....
4. The .... of a circle is calculated by using the formula πd.
5. When .... is poured on to .... , ... is given off and may be collected in a ....

What did you make of them?

You will probably decide that they are all unsatisfactory for the following reasons:

1. The question is not sufficiently specific. Two appropriate answers readily spring to mind — either London or Trafalgar Square. You may be able to think of additional answers.
2. The question is not sufficiently precise in that it does not indicate the degree of accuracy required in the answer. Is the answer to be correct to one, two, three or more decimal places?
3. What is required here? A date? 'Gypsy Moth'? A sailing boat? Once again there is need for specificity.
4. This is clumsy because the reader may have forgotten the requirement by the time he has read the item.
5. If you are a mind reader you may be able to answer this question. It is an extreme example but it demonstrates how including too many blanks can produce an ambiguous item.

▰▰▰ Checkpoint

Rewrite items 1-5 above in a satisfactory, unambiguous manner.

Answers:
You might have written them along these lines. Check your items against the criticisms of the original items.

1. *In which city is Nelson's Column? (or something equally specific)*
2. *If the other adjacent sides of a right-angled triangle measure 7 cm and 9 cm, what is the length of the hypotenuse? Give your answer correct to two decimal places.*
3. *The name of the boat in which Francis Chichester sailed round the world was .... (or some other clear requirement)*
4. *The formula π d is used for calculating the ...... of a circle.*
   or To calculate the circumference of a circle we use the formula.................................
5. *When hydrochloric acid is added to zinc, ... is given off. (Another item could be produced to ask how it is collected.)*

False/true items

Now look for faults in the following **True/False** items.

6. Few members of Parliament would support the re-introduction of capital punishment True False
7. It is not true that Mario Andretti did not win the World Motor Racing Championship in 1981   True False
8. The Ford Sierra is equally as good as the Vauxhall Cavalier   True False

What are your criticisms?

Perhaps you will agree that:

6. This is insufficiently precise. The word 'few' is too open to personal interpretation.
7. This is an extreme example of a weak item. But you've most likely got the idea! There are far too many negatives mixed up in it.
8. This item is also lacking in precision because it calls for a personal judgement. Not everyone would agree with either answer. You must use this kind of item only when your statement is without doubt either true or false.

▰▰▰

Modify items 6-8 so that they make better sense.

Answers

6. *According to recent information, the numbers of Members of Parliament who would support the re-introduction of capital punishment would be .... True/False (In fact, unless it was based upon recent concrete evidence, this would not be a satisfactory item for various reasons).*
7. *Mario Andretti won the World Motor Racing Championship in 1981   True/False*
8. *(A question here would have to refer to something specific, e.g. The engine of a Vauxhall Cavalier 1600 develops more brake horsepower than the engine of a Ford Sierra 1600),   True/False*

Multiple choice items

You'll probably agree that **multiple choice** items are the most difficult to write.

So that you'll be better able to understand what is presented later in this Component, let's first examine the structure of this kind of item.

There are **three** main parts:

(a) **the stem**

This contains the question which is asked.

(b) **the key**

This is the correct answer and it is one of the possible responses.

(c) **the distractors**

These are the remaining incorrect responses.

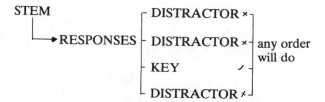

To illustrate these terms here's an example taken from Component 4:

What was generally considered to be the **main** reason for the introduction of the comprehensive education system?

A. to satisfy political principles   DISTRACTOR   STEM

B. to solve the problem of falling numbers of children in secondary schools   DISTRACTOR

C. to equalise educational opportunities for all children   KEY   RESPONSES

D. to provide a more efficient, economic educational system   DISTRACTOR

Do you see how the different parts are named?
Can you find any faults in the following example?

In an objective test, a multiple choice item may not be necessarily restricted to only either True/False or Yes/No items, but also may appropriately include the kind of multiple choice item which presents an instruction and a kind of question in the first part of the item called the stem, and also perhaps four or five responses, one called the key and the others the distractors, all of them together called responses. In the commonly occurring case of this kind of multiple choice item, the purpose underlying the inclusion of the key:

A. is to provide the right answer which is possible to the question being presented.

B. is to provide a plausible alternative to the answer.

C. is to provide the additional material which helps the respondent to answer the question.

D. provides the distractor.

E. none of these.

What did you make of this item?
If your first reaction was to think that the faults have been deliberately emphasised to the extent that they become ridiculous, you'd be right, but there are important points to be made.
Those which immediately occur are that:

(a) the stem is far too long, and confusing. Only the necessary minimum of words should be used;

(b) the verbal expression is poor;

(c) the item would take too long to answer. There is too much reading to be done in return for very little;

(d) the (misplaced) information given in the stem would allow the patient reader to answer the question without his having prior knowledge of the topic;

(e) the responses are of unequal lengths. Such responses might mislead the testee. In any case, over-long responses complicate the item;

(f) in view of what was included in the stem, the responses were not equally plausible;

(g) the phrase 'is to provide' which appears in each response would have been better placed in the stem. Better still, the stem write 'The key of a multiple choice item' followed by appropriate short responses. The test writer should aim for clarity and economy.

111

(h) the response 'None of these' suggests that the test writer can't think of plausible alternatives and it may attract the respondent's attention if he doesn't know the answer. Sometimes he may choose 'None of these' when it is the correct answer but when he doesn't know the correct one, e.g. in an item requiring computation.

Here's an elementary example of this:

9. $12\frac{1}{2}\%$ of £500 is:

    A. £62 B. £60 C. £57.50 D. £64 E. None of these

The correct answer is not included in the alternatives and the testee who underlined 'None of these' would score a mark whether he knew the answer or not.

Here are a few additional important points about writing multiple choice items.

— Alternative responses should be parallel with each other and grammatically consistent with the stem.
— The same wording should not be used in both the stem and the key since common expression would provide a clue to the correct answer.
— The correct option should be randomly placed throughout the tests, i.e. placed by chance in possible positions. This could be achieved by drawing numbers out of a hat.
— Four or five responses have been found to be satisfactory. The problem is to find plausible alternatives, but the larger number of alternatives, the less the influence of guessing.
— Responses should be completely independent of each other. Here's an example of an unsatisfactory item in which this is not the case.

10. Out of 40,000 people who watched the football match, 3,600 did not pay for admission. What percentage did not pay?

    A. over 5%   C. over 8%
    B. over 10%   D. over 3%

The correct answer is 9% but this is not included. The nearest alternative is C but A and D are also correct. It would be difficult **not** to score a mark in an item like this.

— Distractors must appear to be right but there must be no doubt about the only correct answer, the key.
— The key should resemble the distractors in form and should be unambiguous.

A great deal of information has been presented to you. Now see whether you can apply it.

Write one multiple choice item, each to test a person's knowledge of (a) a stem, (b) a key, and (c) a distractor, i.e. three altogether.

Answer
Something like this would be satisfactory
(a) The stem of an objective test item:
    A. gives the right answer;
    B. contains the question;
    C. leads the respondent astray;
    D. tests the respondent's knowledge.
(b) and (c), concerning the key and a distractor respectively, might contain similar responses. The important point is that they should be plausible and clearly expressed.

Context focussed items

What do you think of this?
Can you see any weaknesses in it?
11. The graph below shows the output of a factory for the years 1983-5

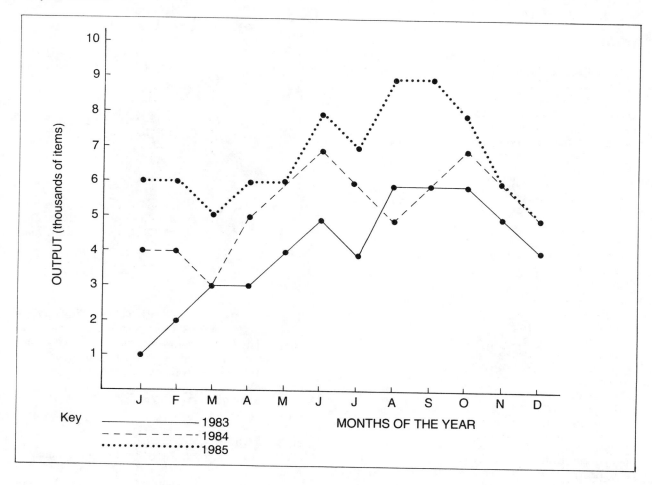

All items below refer to the year 1984
(a) The lowest output occurred in the month of ....
(b) The highest output occurred in the month of .....
(c) The difference between the highest and lowest outputs is:
   A. 1,000 items
   B. 3,000 items
   C. 5,000 items
   D. 6,000 items
   E. None of these

You'll probably agree that serious weaknesses are that:
— the graph contains irrelevant information. If the completion items refer to 1984 only, there is no need to include data about 1983 and 1985.
— the irrelevant data make the graph confusing.
— the correct response, 4,000 items, is not included in the alternatives but there is no certainty that the respondent who opts for E has worked out the right answer even though he'll be credited with a mark.

Are you satisfied with the items themselves?

Most likely you'll agree that they are clearly expressed but that they would have been better if the correct response, the key, had been included. Some would object to the lack of independence of the items. Note that they are all related to each other.

List the changes you would make to Item 11 to turn it into a satisfactory item.

Answer
The graph would be drawn with the data for 1983 and 1985 excluded. The responses would preferably include the correct response (key) – 4,000 items.

We have now carefully examined weaknesses which might occur in objective test items and how items may be improved. You will have noted that clarity of expression, precision and exclusion of ambiguity are essential, particularly in the writing of multiple choice items. Looking back to Component 3, you must always remember the different levels of skills abilities which may be tested by such items.

Timing a test

Have you any ideas about the number of items you should include to give a test which would take a preferred time to complete? How long do you think it takes the average respondent to complete an item?

What about the different times taken to complete items of various kinds? It's obvious that a short **answer/completion** item would be answered more quickly than a **statement/reason** item and you might think it difficult to reconcile these differences.

In fact, it is usually found that the average candidate will deal with the item of average difficulty in the average time of one minute. By 'item of average difficulty' we mean the kind of item which would be challenging, but which would be answered successfully by about 60% of the candidates. This means that the average candidate will deal with thirty items in about half an hour.

The idea of 'the item of average difficulty' is important. Not only is it the most useful because it is appropriate for the majority of candidates in a group, but each mark should be as easily gained or be as difficult to gain as any other since each item scores one mark only.

It is to the question of item difficulty that we now turn our attention.

Item difficulty

We've already commented on the importance of including items of average difficulty in our tests, but there are other reasons why we should know how our items measure up to this idea. For instance, we might want to include items which will stretch the most able or we might think it appropriate to begin a test with less difficult questions which will encourage the less able but which would get progressively more difficult.

The measure we need to determine for each item is the DIFFICULTY INDEX.

How then are we to determine a DIFFICULTY INDEX?

The answer is . . . very easily. Look at the example below.

1. Ten apprentices took an objective test and their answers to the first item were as follows:
   Peter, David, John, Paul and Donald got it right. (5)
   Ian, Jim, Joe, Eric and George got it wrong. (5)
   The DIFFICULTY INDEX is $\dfrac{\text{Right}}{\text{N}} \times 100\%$

   'Right' is the number who get the item right.
   N is the total number of students who took the test.
   Now back to our example —
   In this case, the **difficulty index**
   is
   $$\frac{5}{10} \times 100\% = 50\%$$

2. Their answers to the second item were as follows:
Peter and Paul got it right.
The rest either got it wrong or did not do it.
What is the difficulty index?
Let's apply the formula.
Difficulty index is

$$\frac{\text{Right}}{\text{N}} \times 100\% = \frac{2}{10} \times 100\% = 20\%$$

Difficulty index 20%

What is the relationship between the **difficulty index** and the difficulty of the item?

When 5 apprentices got the right answer, the **difficulty index** was 50%

When 2 apprentices got the right answer, the **difficulty index** was 20%

Therefore, as the item gets easier, the **difficulty index** increases — which all seems rather odd.

In practice it has been found that the difficulty index of a satisfactory item will fall between 40% and 60%. We would usually like to include questions that we would be pretty sure that everyone could answer thus providing encouragement and a logical arrangement of such a test would be to present the items in order of increasing difficulty. A knowledge of the difficulty indexes of all items would allow us to construct a test with these features.

Sometimes the term FACILITY INDEX (denoted F) is used instead of difficulty index.

20 apprentices completed an objective test and 5 of them got a particular item right.
(a) What was the **difficulty index** (facility index F) of that item?
(b) What decision would you be likely to take on the item?

Answer
(a) The difficulty index is 25%
(b) You would most likely omit the item in a future test on the grounds that it was too difficult.

On the other hand, if you wished to include difficult items in order to stretch the most able, you might retain it.

(Before any truly valid decision was reached, you would have to consider the DISCRIMINAT-ION INDEX also.) (See later material).

The two occasions on which you would be likely to calculate difficulty indexes (facility indexes) are:
(a) when you are in the fortunate situation of being able to try out your items with people similar to those for whom your test is intended.
(b) after you have administered the test and are considering modifications to make it more effective the next time you used it.
You will note the intention in both cases is to **improve** the test by retaining, rewriting, excluding or re-ordering certain items.

When calculating the difficulty index, we would expect students who got the item right to be in the top part of the group and, although this is usually the case, it does not always happen. We would need to know whether the more able members of the group were getting the more difficult items right and the less able were getting them wrong.

Another way of putting it is that we would like to find out whether the items were capable of **discriminating** between the more and less able members of the group. We would need to find the DISCRIMINATION INDEX of each item.

When we find the DIFFICULTY INDEX (FACILITY INDEX) and DISCRIMINATION INDEX of each item, we are said to be carrying out an item analysis.

Finding a discrimination index

You will agree that one of the important functions of a test is that it should help us to identify those who are high achievers and those who are not, that is we should be able to **discriminate** between them.

It follows that we need to know whether the individual items which we have included in our tests are doing this job effectively. **This means that we must compare those people who score high marks on the test as a whole with those who score low marks to see how successful or unsuccessful they were with individual items.**

Let's return to the group whose scores we used to find the Difficulty Index of an item.

Here are their total scores on an objective test: (marks out of 50)

Peter 47, David 39, John 42, Donald 34, Ian 38, Jim 32, Joe 24, Eric 27, George 17.

Our first job is to arrange them in rank order, that is from the highest scorer to the lowest. In the next column we indicate how they fared with the first item of the test.

Rank	Total Score	Item 1	
1. Peter	47	Right	HIGH GROUP
2. John	42	Right	(4 got it
3. David	39	Right	right)
4. Ian	38	Wrong	
5. Paul	35	Right	
6. Donald	34	Right	LOW GROUP
7. Jim	32	Wrong	(1 got it
8. Eric	27	Wrong	right)
9. Joe	24	Wrong	
10. George	17	Wrong	

See how they are divided equally into a HIGH and a LOW group?

We are now ready to apply the formula which will give us the DISCRIMINATION INDEX.

The formula is $\dfrac{H-L}{N}$ where:

H is the number of students who got the answer right in the HIGH group

L is the number of students who got the answer right in the LOW group

N is the number of students in each group, that is, half the total number of students.

Let's apply our figures to the formula.

DISCRIMINATION INDEX is

$$\frac{H-L}{N} = \frac{4-1}{5} = \frac{3}{5} = 0.6$$

A test constructor would consider that this item discriminates well.

▨▨

(a) Find the DISCRIMINATION INDEX for Item 2 (see details on page 115)
(b) What would be your decision on this item?
Remember that only Peter and Paul got the answer right. Both are in the 'High' group.
The rest either got it wrong or did not do it.
Remember that you must take into account only the **right** answers.

Answer
(a) The DISCRIMINATION INDEX is
$$\frac{H-L}{N} = \frac{2-0}{5} = \frac{2}{5} = 0.4$$

This would be considered an acceptable item because it discriminates satisfactorily.
(b) If the Difficulty Index also proved satisfactory, you would retain this item.

Here's a bit of mental arithmetic for you.
(a) when the same group of ten did item 3, all the HIGH group got it right and all the LOW group got it wrong.
What is the DISCRIMINATION INDEX of Item 3? Here's the formula again as a reminder.
Discrimination Index is $\frac{H-L}{N}$

What's your answer?
Here's the calculation $\frac{H-L}{5} = \frac{5-0}{5} = 1$

This index of 1 indicates that the item has discriminated perfectly between the high and the low scorers.
(b) When they completed Item 4, the results were very odd because all the HIGH group got it wrong and all the LOW group got it right.
What is the DISCRIMINATION INDEX in this case?
Do you agree that the DISCRIMINATION INDEX is −1?
If not, re-work your calculation.

These two examples allow you to arrive at basic and important conclusions.
1. A DISCRIMINATION INDEX of an item will always fall between −1 and +1.
2. An item which favours the LOW group gives a negative result.
3. An item which favours the HIGH group gives a positive result.
What do you think a Discrimination Index of 0 signifies?
Yes, it means that the item fails to discriminate at all between the high scorers and the low scorers. This means that as an instrument for discrimination it is **useless**.

Discrimination Indexes and decisions

What decisions should we take once we have found a Discrimination Index for each item in our test?
Here are a few generally accepted principles:
1. It is quite safe to accept an item with a Discrimination Index of +0.3 and above.
2. An item with a Discrimination Index above +0.4 discriminates well.
3. Items which yield indexes below +0.3 are of doubtful value and if an item has an index below +0.2 it should be discarded without fail. Of course, this means that all items with negative indexes should be discarded.

Time analysis

Discrimination index and difficulty index (Facility index)

Earlier we said that carrying out an ITEM ANALYSIS of a test meant that we would examine each item in turn to compute its Difficulty Index and its Discrimination Index. In order that we may make the best decisions about an item, we must consider both measures together. Let's consider the results of the group of 10 apprentices considered earlier. Here they are in the table below. I've inserted the Difficulty Indexes for items 3 and 4. Check them if you like!

Table (a)

	Difficulty (Facility) Index	Discrimination Index	Decision
Item 1	50%	+0.6	?
Item 2	20%	+0.4	?
Item 3	50%	+1	?
Item 4	50%	−1	?

Examine Table (a) and say whether you would include the items in your revised test. Give your reasons for the decisions you take.

Answer
Do you agree with these?

Item	Decision	Reason
1.	Retain	*Difficulty level satisfactory Good discrimination.*
2.	Retain	*A difficult item to test the most able. (depending on purpose) Discrimination quite good*
	Reject	*Too difficult for purpose*
3.	Retain	*Difficulty level satisfactory. Discrimination perfect.*
4.	Reject	*Discrimination negatively perfect*

Here are the measures for items 5, 6, 7, 8, and 9

Table (b)

	Difficulty (Facility) Index	Discrimination Index	Decision
Item 5	60%	+0.4	?
Item 6	20%	+0.2	?
Item 7	40%	+0.3	?
Item 8	80%	+0.3	?
Item 9	60%	−0.4	?

What would be your decisions about the items in Table (b)? Give your reasons for retaining or rejecting the items.

Answer
Are you in agreement with these?

Item	Decision	Reason
5.	Retain	*Difficulty satisfactory Discrimination good*
6.	Reject	*Too difficult Discrimination poor*
7.	Retain (Borderline case)	*Difficulty fairly satisfactory Discrimination satisfactory*
8.	Retain (Borderline case)	*Very easy item Discrimination satisfactory*
9.	Reject	*Negative discrimination, therefore unsatisfactory*

Item analysis with large groups

Most of our calculations have been concerned with a group of 10 apprentices and we could divide these easily into halves to form a High group and a Low group. The common practice adopted by examination boards who deal with very large numbers is to arrange in rank order and then take about the top 27% as the High group and the bottom 27% as the Low group. Using this procedure, in the case of 1,000 students, they would be ranked in order of scores from high to low and the top 270 would form the High group and the bottom 270 would form the Low group.

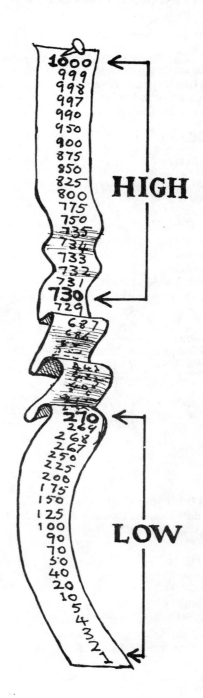

The formula used to determine the Discrimination Index (D) for each item could then be worked out as below.

Discrimination Index (D) $= \dfrac{N_H - N_L}{N}$

Where N_H is the number obtaining the right answer out of the top 27% of students;

N_L is the number obtaining the right answer out of the bottom 27% of students;

N is the number in each of the top and bottom group i.e. 27% of all students.

Taking the top and bottom 27% also simplifies the calculation of the Difficulty Index (Facility Index F)).

In this case, the Facility Index (F) is $\dfrac{N_H + N_L}{2N} \times 100\%$

You will see that 2N denotes all the students whose marks are being used, that is the combined number of the High and Low groups.

In practice, it has been found valid to use anywhere between the top and bottom 25% to $33\frac{1}{3}\%$

100 students completed an objective test and were ranked in order of their scores from highest to lowest. Discrimination Indexes and Facility Indexes were then calculated for each item using the top 27% and the bottom 27% as the High and Low groups respectively. 19 of the High group and 10 of the Low group obtained the right answer to one of the items.
(a) What was the Discrimination Index (D) of the item?
(b) What was the Facility Index (F) of the item? Give your answer correct to the nearest whole number.

Answer
(a) Discrimination Index (D) is +0.33
$$\frac{N_H - N_L}{N} = \frac{19 - 10}{27} = \frac{9}{27} = 0.33$$

(b) Facility Index (F) is 54%
$$\frac{N_H + N_L}{2N} \times 100 = \frac{19 + 10}{54} \times 100 = \frac{29}{54} \times 100$$
$$= 53.7$$

Correction for guessing

We now turn our attention to measures which may be taken to take into account the guessing which can affect the true scores obtained on objective tests. By the law of probability, a candidate completing a test which contained only True/False items would obtain half marks by merely guessing the answers. If the test contained multiple choice items each having four responses, he could obtain 25% of the marks by mere guesswork.

If we intended to correct scores for guessing, we would first have to tell the candidates **not to guess**. We would do this because items left unanswered are not taken into account when correcting scores for guessing.

The formula which we would apply is:

Score $= R - \left(\dfrac{W}{N - 1} \right)$

Score is the candidate's final score;
R = the 'raw' (original) scores of 'right' responses;
W = the number of 'wrong' responses;
N = the number of responses following the stem.

As noted earlier, unanswered questions are not included in the calculation.

You will readily understand that the calculation would become most complex if items of differing response sizes were included, e.g. some with two, some with four, others with five. If three different sizes were used, three different calculations would have to be made for each candidate.

Not everyone favours correcting for guessing. It has been found that it does very little to alter the existing rank order and not to generally affect the effectiveness of the test.

Taking into account what you learned in Components 3 and 4 you will now be able to:
— plan a test specification in the form of a specification table; taking into account the various levels of skills/abilities to be tested;
— describe the different kinds of items which are used in objective tests.
— state the uses, advantages and disadvantages of the various types of items;
— identify the different parts of objective test items, i.e. stem, key, distractors;

— write satisfactory test items of the kinds specified in Component 4;
— estimate the number of items necessary to provide a test to be completed in a given time;
— produce an item analysis of a test, i.e. calculate difficulty (facility) indexes and discrimination indexes for each item;
— make desirable revisions of tests on the basis of your item analysis;
— apply the correction for guessing formula.

In all, you will be able to demonstrate that you are familiar with the essential elements of objective test construction so that you are in a position to write, manage and revise objective tests.

For further detailed treatment of these topics, see
Rust, W. B. (1973) *Objective Testing in Education and Training,* Pitman Publishing
Satterly, D. (1981) *Assessment in Schools,* Basil Blackwell

Component 6:

Checklists and Rating Scales

Key Words

 Checklist; rating scales; skill and procedures; attitudes; work habits; numerical scales; graphic scales; continuum; halo effect; generosity error; severity error; central tendency error.

INTRODUCTION

At the end of the component you should be able to:
1. Recognise what kind of skills, procedures, products and attitudes can be assessed by this method.
2. Break these qualities down into units which can be measured.
3. Devise appropriate rating scales or check lists.
4. List the advantages and disadvantages of checklists and rating scales.

Checklists and rating scales

are probably one of the most widely used methods of assessment.
a. They can be constructed to assess skills, procedures, attitudes, work habits or products.
b. They can be used for objective or subjective assessments.
c. A single mark on a test or exam does not provide specific information which may be needed for **diagnosing** a trainee's strengths and weaknesses. A check list or rating scale can provide this detail.

Where do you begin?

1. Job description

As with all assessment you need to be sure what it is that is to be assessed. This means drawing up a job description and breaking this down into objectives. (Refer to Unit 3 Component 1).

2. What kind of objectives can be assessed by checklists and rating scales?

Skills and procedures:
a. Mechanical e.g process operation, driving.
b. Technical e.g. performing laboratory experiments.
c. Manual e.g. sorting, manipulating.
d. Social e.g. communicating, negotiating, customer relations.

Work habits:
e.g. initiative, persistence.

Products:
e.g. aesthetic, technical, accuracy of items produced.

Social attitudes:
e.g. relationships, reaction to criticism.

▰▰▰ Checkpoint

Classify each of the following qualities by placing the appropriate letter at the end of the list. There is only one answer for each category.

Objectives
A Punctuality
B Machine fault analysis
C Helpfulness to colleagues
D Lathe operation
E A window display
F Pricking out plants
G Calming an irate customer

121

ANSWER

SKILLS AND a. Mechanical
PROCEDURES b. Technical
c. Manual
d. Social
e. Work habits
f. Products
g. Social attitudes

Answer: The order is D.B.F.G.A.E.C.

As you can see, a wide range of behaviour can be assessed by check lists or rating scales, but KNOWLEDGE is better tested by other means. Consequently, once you have decided upon the nature of the task a decision can be made about the suitability of these measures.

Which of the following would best be assessed by the use of checklists or rating scales?
a. The ability to park a fork lift truck.
b. The laboratory analysis of water samples.
c. The Safety at Work Regulations.
d. Organising the despatch of merchandise.
e. The attitudes desirable in a sales supervisor.

With the exception of 'C' all could be assessed by checklist or rating scale. 'C' is the subject of KNOWLEDGE and therefore easier to check by some form of pencil and paper test.

Construction of a checklist

Checklists demand a "Yes-No" judgement. It is basically a method of recording whether:
a. a characteristic is present or absent;
b. action was taken or not taken.
They are especially useful in evaluating those performance skills that can be divided into a series of clearly defined specific actions.

Example: Checklist for correct parking of a fork lift truck.
1. Parked in a safe position
2. Controls at neutral
3. Parking brake set
4. Forks in fully lowered position
5. Mast tilted slightly forward
6. Power shut off
7. Ignition key withdrawn

As you can see, each specific action desired in the operation is listed in order. To help your assessment and diagnosis, you can add those actions which represent **common errors** if they are limited in number and can be clearly identified.

Example: Part of a checklist for using a microscope. This example includes a common error (i.e. item 3)
1. Takes slide
2. Wipes slide with lens paper
3. Wipes slide with finger
4. Places drop of culture on slide
5. Takes cover glass and wipes with lens paper
6. . . . etc.

Products can also be assessed as well as skill performance. If there is a tangible end product which the trainee is required to produce note the characteristics it should possess.

Caution: A checklist should only be used if the trainer simply wishes to check whether each characteristic is present or absent. If **quality** is more precisely indicated by noting the **degree** to which each characteristic is present then a RATING SCALE should be used instead (see later).

Write a checklist that would be useful for evaluating a business letter.

Specimen Answer:

Correct reference
Correct forms of address
Layout/presentation
Clarity of information
Sequencing of information
Correct spelling
Correct grammar/punctuation

Attitudes: A checklist can serve as a convenient method of recording evidence of growth towards desirable personal characteristics.

Example:
1. Courteous to others
2. Enjoys working with others
3. Accepts help and advice willingly
4. Gives encouragement to others
5. Shares ideas and materials

This is another case where it may not be sufficient to rate merely whether the trainee exhibits the attitudes, but the degree or frequency. If this is the case, a RATING SCALE would be more appropriate.

Construction of rating scales

Similarity with checklists
Rating scales are not very different from checklists in that they too consist of a list of characteristics or qualities about which you wish to make a judgement.

Differences from checklists
Rating scales allow **finer** judgements to be made in that they:
* permit a numerical score to be given;
* have a scale which can be used for judging:
   the **relative quality** of work;
   the **degree** to which the behaviour or attitude is evident;
   the **frequency** of behaviour.

Types of Rating Scales
Rating scales may take specific forms but the majority belong to either:
1. Numerical Rating Scale
2. Graphic Rating Scale

1. NUMERICAL RATING SCALE
This is one of the simplest. The rater ticks or circles the number to indicate the **degree** to which the characteristic is present. Each of the numbers is given a verbal description which remains constant. A key is always given.
Example:
Directions: Indicate the degree to which the trainee performed. The numbers represent the following values:
5 - outstanding
4 - above average
3 - average
2 - below average
1 - unsatisfactory
1. To what extent did he exhibit skill in the use of:
   a. Layout and measuring tools?   1 2 3 4 5
   b. Cutting edge tools?   1 2 3 4 5
   c. Boring and drilling tools?   1 2 3 4 5
2. Did he select the proper tools for the job?   1 2 3 4 5
3. Did he use the tools properly?   1 2 3 4 5

The numerical rating scale is useful when the qualities to be assessed can be classified into a limited number of categories. One disadvantage is that the numbers are only vaguely defined. Consequently variation will occur in the interpretation and application of the scale. The range 1-5 used in the example is arbitrary, but it is recommended that more than ten should be avoided, as such fine discriminations are too difficult to make.

2. GRAPHIC RATING SCALES
The graphic rating scale is similar to the numerical rating in that the tester is required to assign a value to a particular characteristic. The difference is that the ratings are made in graphic form e.g. by placing an 'x' anywhere along a continuum. Consequently the rater is not confined to any particular point, but can record anywhere between points.
Examples:
Directions: Below is a list of characteristics that are descriptive of the trainee during training. Please rate the trainee for each characteristic along the continuum. You may use the points between the scale values. Place an 'X' at the appropriate place along the continuum.

How enthusiastic was the trainee during training?

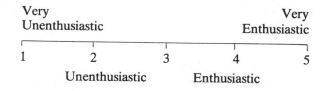

How attentive was the trainee in training sessions?

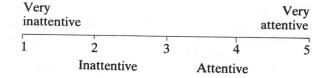

Here is a slightly different form which does not include a numerical scale. The directions would be the same as for the example above.

To what extent does the trainee participate in discussions?

Never participates	Participates as much as other group members	Participates more than other group members

Some common errors in rating scales

a. Ambiguity of the scale itself.
b. The rater's personality and judgement.
c. The opportunities for adequate observation.

a. Ambiguity

This occurs when the rater is uncertain as to what **qualities** he is being asked to rate. For example two managers rating a sales assistant on 'confidence' may be scoring quite different characteristics. To one a high 'confidence' rating may have been interpreted as 'over assertiveness' by another.

The frame of reference may also prove to be ambiguous. The trainee is to be marked against what standard? Is his performance 'Excellent' 'Good' 'Average' etc. compared with an experienced operator or someone who has had limited practice?

b. The rater's personality and judgement

Excellent

(i) The halo effect. This occurs when a rater's general impression or feelings about a person influences his judgement. If attitudes are favourable towards a candidate he is likely to be marked high, but low if attitudes are unfavourable.

(ii) Generosity/Severity/Central Tendency Errors. Raters who favour the high end of the continuum are committing the **generosity error.** Occurring less frequently is the **severity error** where the lower end of the scale is favoured. A third type of

response is called the **central tendency error** used by those who avoid using the extremes of the scale and who rate everybody as about 'average'.

c. Opportunity for observation

When judging skills, procedures or products the ratings are usually made during or immediately after a period of directed observation. Evaluating personal and social characteristics is quite a different process in which ratings are made at periodic intervals as a summing up. Consequently these tend to be more casual and reflect personal bias.

Characteristics of an effective rating scale

a. Rating scales should reflect the **objectives**. So decide what you want the trainee to be able to do, what attitudes or qualities you want him to possess or what you want him to produce.
b. Characteristics should be directly **observable**.
c. Characteristics and points on the scale should be clearly defined.
d. Between three and seven rating positions should be provided and raters should be permitted to use intermediate positions on the scale.
e. Raters should be encouraged to omit sections where they feel unqualified to judge.

When can checklists and rating scales be used?

a. At the selection of trainees.
b. During training as each skill or set of procedures has been achieved.
c. On the job during the performance of an operation.
d. During simulation exercises.
e. As a periodic appraisal of skills, products, work habits or attitudes.

Trainee participation

It is sometimes useful for the trainee to rate himself and then compare his rating with that of his instructor. This can be useful for:

a. Acquainting the trainee with the objectives to be achieved and the level of performance required.
b. Helping the trainee to recognise his progress.
c. Providing more effective diagnosis of strengths and weaknesses.
d. Helping the trainer to gain insight into the ways in which the trainee is learning.

////

1. Prepare a checklist for assessing the ability to perform a three-point turn when driving a car. Would a rating scale be better?
2. For which of the following would a checklist be appropriate:
   a. replacing a fuse on a 13 amp plug;
   b. assessing the ability to diagnose faults in a car which has broken down;
   c. communication skills required by a secretary;
   d. the laws governing termination of employment.
3. What is the halo effect?

4. Write a numerical rating scale for some of the qualities you would wish to develop in a sales supervisor.
5. Write a graphic rating scale for two work habits desirable in any employee.

Answers
1. *Are you certain that the manoeuvres are in the correct order? A checklist is better than a rating scale because you cannot rate many of the procedures e.g. the handbrake is either off or it isn't. However, each item should be performed to a satisfactory standard before it receives a tick.*
2. *'a' and 'b' can both be assessed by a checklist. There are easily defined procedures and an approximate order. 'c' could not be assessed by a checklist because the* **level** *of performance is important. 'd' requires complex knowledge so would have to be tested in some other way.*
3. *This occurs when the rater's feelings towards the trainee influences the score given.*
4. *Example: 1. Very good*
   2. Good
   3. Average
   4. Satisfactory
   5. Unsatisfactory
   Ability to work under pressure 1 2 3 4 5
   Ability to plan ahead/priorities 1 2 3 4 5
   Ability to establish good
   personal relationships   1 2 3 4 5
5. *Example:*
   To what extent is she able to work unsupervised?

Never   Rarely   Occasionally   Frequently   Totally

Review of Unit 3

How much of the unit have you understood? To help you to check and at the same time review the material, a series of questions will be asked which cover the main points from each component. If you are unable to answer the questions return to the relevant section in the text and try again.

Answers may be found at the end of this component.

COMPONENT 1
1. You have been asked to assess a trainee's competence. What is your starting point?
2. How can you categorise objectives?
3. Which of these categories would you apply to each of the following objectives:
   a. The ability to describe the appropriate use of 'Yours sincerely' in correspondence.
   b. The ability to reverse a heavy goods vehicle in a straight line for 25 metres.
   c. Willingness to accept responsibility for the training of juniors.
4. Skills can be divided into two sub-categories. Name them and say which would apply to the following activities:
   a. The ability to greet a customer.
   b. The ability to adjust a circular saw.

COMPONENT 2
1. Outline the two main differences between objective and subjective tests.
2. List the following methods of assessment under the headings 'Objective' and 'Subjective'
   Essays
   Multiple choice questions
   Sequencing questions
   Logs
   Interviews
   Rating scales
   Recall/completing questions

COMPONENT 3
1. List some of the drawbacks of objective tests.
2. List the following levels of Bloom's *Taxonomy of Educational Objectives* in their correct order, beginning with Knowledge.
   — Knowledge, analysis, synthesis, comprehension, application, evaluation.
3. Construct a specification table which satisfies the following requirements:

A CONTENT	WEIGHT
Packaging & Labelling	10%
Textile care labels	10%
Merchandise layouts and moves	30%
Stock levels	20%
Salesfloor documentation	30%

B SKILLS/ABILITIES |
---|---
Knows terms and facts | 10%
Understands principles | 30%
Application of principles | 40%
Analysis of information & principles | 20%

C Total number of items to be set | 100

COMPONENT 4
1. Below (i-v) is a series of questions. Match each question with one of the following TYPES:
   a. Multiple choice
   b. Alternative response (true/false)
   c. Short answer/completion
   d. Matching
   e. Sequencing
   (i) What is the name of the device which regulates the fuel and air mixture in a petrol engine?
   (ii) Customer theft is an example of shrinkage   True False
   (iii) Various bodies may be found in list A and initials in list B. Place the appropriate letter next to the number.

LIST A	LIST B
1. Employers in Industry	N.H.S.
2. Health	C.B.I.
3. Social Security	T.U.C.
4. Unions	D.H.S.S.

   (iv) 'Pinking' in a petrol engine is caused by:
   a. an electrical fault.
   b. water in the petrol.
   c. petrol of an unsuitable octane rating.
   d. dirty plugs.

(v) Place in the correct order of seniority
   Brigadier
   Colonel
   Lieutenant
   Major
   Captain
   Field Marshal
   General

2. All the above questions are of the factual/recall type. What are the disadvantages of questions of this type?

COMPONENT 5

1. State why the following question is unsatisfactory.
   Women are more likely to make better process workers than men   True False

2. State the three main parts of a multiple choice question.

3. Work out the difficulty index for a question for which there were 15 right anwers and 35 wrong answers.

4. Here is a set of results from a test. Organise these so that you can work out the discrimination index for the test item (individual responses given).

NAME	SCORE	Item X
Ian	40	Wrong
Paul	37	Right
Peter	49	Right
Jim	34	Wrong
George	19	Wrong
David	41	Right
Donald	36	Right
Eric	26	Wrong
Joe	26	Wrong
John	42	Right

5. Would you retain the item on the above question? give your reasons.

COMPONENT 6

1. Which of the following would **not** be suitable for assessment by a check list:
   a. Ability to change a wheel on a truck.
   b. A trainee's reaction to advice.
   c. The ability to test the acidity of soils.
   d. The ability to extract relevant information from a graph.

2. In what circumstances would it be better to use a rating scale rather than a check list?

3. What are the three common errors likely to occur on a rating scale?
4. What do we call the influence an assessor's feeling (about a trainee) may have on his judgement?

ANSWERS
COMPONENT 1

1. Write a job description and refine this into objectives.
2. Knowledge
   Skills
   Attitudes
3. a. Knowledge
   b. Skill
   c. Attitudes
4. Social and communication skills (a)
   Performance skills (b)

COMPONENT 2

1. a. Subjective tests contain items/questions to which there is only one correct response and which are easy to mark.
   b. Objective tests contain items/questions to which there is only one correct response and which are easy to mark.
2. **Objective** Multiple choice questions
                 Sequencing questions
                 Recall/completion questions
   Subjective Essays
                  Logs
                  Interviews
                  Rating Scales (could also appear under objective)

COMPONENT 3

1. a. They encourage cramming of facts rather than understanding.
   b. No credit can be given for partially right answers.
   c. They provide little opportunity for self expression, development of an argument or novel solutions.
   d. They take too long to construct.
2. Knowledge
   Comprehension
   Application
   Analysis
   Synthesis
   Evaluation

SKILLS/ABILITIES TESTED						
CONTENT	%	Knows facts & terms	Understands Principles	Application of Principles	Analysis of Information & Principles	No. of Items/Section
		10%	30%	40%	20%	
Packaging & Labelling	10	1	3	4	2	10
Textile Care Labelling	10	1	3	4	2	10
Merchandise Layouts & Moves	30	3	9	12	6	30
Stock Levels	20	2	6	8	4	20
Salesfloor Documentation	30	3	9	12	6	30
Total items per section	10	10	30	40	20	100

COMPONENT 4
1. a. (iv)
   b. (ii)
   c. (i)
   d. (iii)
   e. (v)
2. They are likely to encourage rote learning with little understanding. They may be restricted to testing only the lower levels of skills and abilities.

COMPONENT 5
1. Opinions are of little objective value. 'Better' in what way and at which process?
2. Stem, Key, Distractors
3. 30%
4.

RANK	SCORE	ITEM	
1. Peter	49	Right	
2. John	42	Right	
3. David	41	Right	
4. Ian	40	Wrong	High Group
5. Paul	37	Right	(4 Right)

6. Donald	36	Right	
7. Jim	34	Wrong	
8. Eric	29	Right	Low Group
9. Joe	26	Wrong	(2 Right)
10. George	19	Wrong	

Discrimination Index $= \dfrac{H - L}{N} = \dfrac{4 - 2}{10} = 0.2$

COMPONENT 6
1. (d) This is concerned with the recall of factual information and its application and is therefore better tested by one of the pencil and paper (objective) tests.
2. Where the level or standard of performance is required.
3. (a) Ambiguity of the scale.
   (b) The rater's personality and judgement.
   (c) The opportunities for adequate observation.
4. The halo effect.

 Tutor Seen Work

1. Write a job description for one of your trainees and translate it into a series of training objectives.
2. Decide on the range of alternatives open to you for assessing each objective or group of objectives. These need only be stated in terms of the type of test. Detailed questions are not required.
3. Outline the advantages and shortcomings of each alternative.

Study Unit 4

Methods, Techniques and Instruments (2)

Component 1:

Essays and Structured Questions

Key Words

 Subjective; control; sampling; reliability; essay; open-ended; restricted; structured; questions; marking; analytical; impressionistic.

In Components 3, 4 and 5 of Unit 3 you learned a great deal about objective tests and objective testing, one kind of written assessment. We will now take a look at other forms of written tests, this time tests of a more **subjective** nature. These are the open-ended essay, restricted essay and structured question.

Checkpoint

First of all, let's review some of the material you learned earlier. Write a sentence to answer each question and check it before moving on to the next question. You will find the answers at the end of this section.

Control of content, subjectivity and reliability

1. How would you explain the connection between objectives and the purpose of assessment?
2. How effective is an objective test in testing whether objectives have been achieved?
3. How effective is the objective test in covering a large number of objectives which you wish to test?
4. If you constructed an objective test to assess what a candidate had learned over a long period of time, would you be able to cover every single piece of the learning content?
5. To what extent is the trainer in control of the sampling of content when he writes his own objective test?

6. If the trainer is fully in control of the sampling of the objectives, the kind of questions asked, and the form of answers, how does this affect the marking of the test?

Answers
1. *You'll agree that the purpose of assessment is to find out whether the learning objectives which you defined in the first place have been achieved.*
2. *The majority of people would say that this kind of test is a most effective way of doing this, particularly when factual material is being tested.*
3. *You will remember that one of the advantages of the objective test is that a large number of objectives can be tested. If you construct your own test, you can cover all the objectives in which you are interested, deciding how many and what type of questions to ask about each of them. You can also ask questions at the kind of level of thinking which you think is necessary. Remember Bloom's Taxonomy?*
4. *Almost certainly not. You will most likely agree that even though the objective test can test a great deal of learning content, you would have to choose to test what you think are the most important points. When we have to select which parts we wish to test, we say that we are **sampling** the content.*
5. *You will agree that he is fully in control. He chooses which questions he wishes to ask, the form of the question (e.g. short answer, multiple choice, etc.) and the level of the questions. The candidate has no say in the matter. He can do no more than answer*

the questions set, giving his answers in exactly the way the trainer has planned. He has no control at all over either the sampling of the objectives or the way he answers the questions.

6. *You will remember that one of the advantages of the objective test, is that the marking can also be considered to be objective, that is there is only one right answer to each question and the marker is not required to make any decisions which depend on his own opinions, that is to use his **subjective** judgement. The marking is **objective**, in that the final marks would be the same no matter **who** did the marking, **when** it was done or **how many times** it was done. Another way of expressing this is to say that the marking is highly **reliable**.*

To summarize, delete one alternative in each of the following statements:

With regard to objective tests:

a) they are highly effective/ineffective in testing whether objectives have been achieved.

b) they are effective/ineffective in covering a large number of objectives.

c) sampling of content to be tested is fully under the control of the trainer/learner.

d) form of answers to questions is fully under the control of the trainer/learner.

e) the marking is objective/subjective.

f) the marking is reliable/unreliable.

Answers

a) *effective*	d) *trainer*
b) *effective*	e) *objective*
c) *trainer*	f) *reliable*

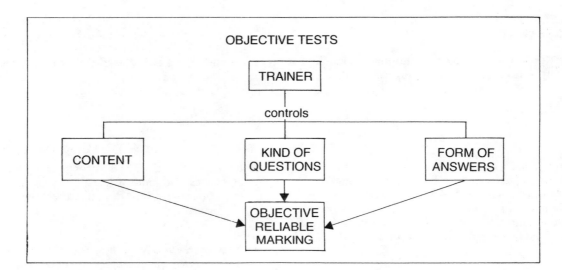

Essays

We are now going to have a look at what is probably the most commonly used kind of written assessment — **essays**. There are two main types:

a) the open-ended essay.

b) the restricted essay.

Open-ended essay

Whether the trainer sets the occasional essay or sets a few essay titles for a formal examination, he is able to use only a few questions to sample the learning content. The learner is then required to select what he thinks are relevant pieces of knowledge from his learning content and organize them into an effective answer to the question. In fact, control of sampling of content is, in a way, being passed to the learner. What is more, the learner uses the facts he knows to answer the question in the way he chooses.

Consider the following:

1. How will this affect the trainer's marking of the essays?

You'll agree that because he is not fully in control of the selection of the content, the trainer will have to use his own personal judgement about the relevance of the content chosen by the learner and how he has used it. The marking will be **subjective.**

2. How will this affect the reliability of the marking? Well, we're all human, and our judgements can be affected by all sorts of factors — the way we feel, our personal attitudes, tiredness, etc — and it is well known that our grading of essays can be unreliable. Later we will consider ways to try to overcome this unreliability.

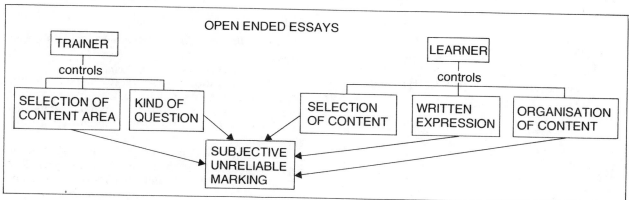

OPEN ENDED ESSAYS

Now I think this is worth 45 ... or 50 ... or 52 or perhaps 57!!

Levels of questions

One factor which influences the level of subjectivity of our marking is the type of essay question we set. Let's think back to the levels of possible questions as suggested by Bloom's *Taxonomy of Educational Objectives.* A lower-order question might call for simple recall and description, e.g.

Describe the operation of an internal combustion engine.

In order to answer this question, the successful learner will use a number of required facts which will also be in the mind of the trainer who will be able to be quite objective about his assessment. On the other hand his assessment could be affected to some extent by the fluency of the expression, handwriting style and spelling, hence leading to some degree of subjectivity.

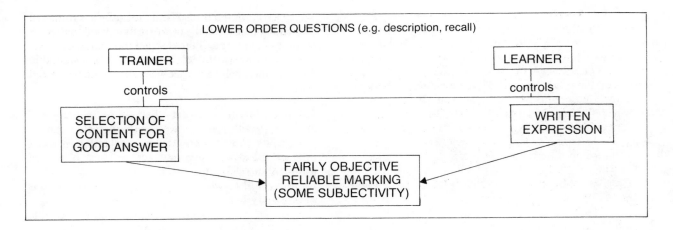

LOWER ORDER QUESTIONS (e.g. description, recall)

TRAINER — controls — SELECTION OF CONTENT FOR GOOD ANSWER

LEARNER — controls — WRITTEN EXPRESSION

FAIRLY OBJECTIVE RELIABLE MARKING (SOME SUBJECTIVITY)

That's worth almost full marks. He's included all the main points.

Write an essay title relating to your own area of interest which is at the simple recall, descriptive level.

Would it be possible to list the facts which should be included? Would you find the essay fairly easy to mark?

Here's a question which calls for thinking of a higher level, for analysis, synthesis and evaluation. *How true is it that the internal combustion engine is a health hazard?*

Justify your answer.

3. Write a question at this level relating to your own field. Would you be able to list all the content necessary to answer the question? Would you find it a straightforward task to mark the answer to the question?

You will note that although you have chosen the general content area, the learner is at liberty to select from his knowledge of it only that material which suits the case he personally wishes to argue. He may even include something which is either forgotten or unknown to the trainer or legitimately may not use material which the trainer thinks is important or take a perfectly justifiable view which does not agree with yours. In addition, the facts and ideas will have to be organized into an effective argument, thus requiring the learner to engage in thinking of an advanced nature.

How will this affect the marking?

You'll most likely agree that in the case of the lower order question the trainer's assessment could be fairly objective and reliable but that when marking the higher-order question, he would be necessarily more subjective, therefore unreliable in his marking.

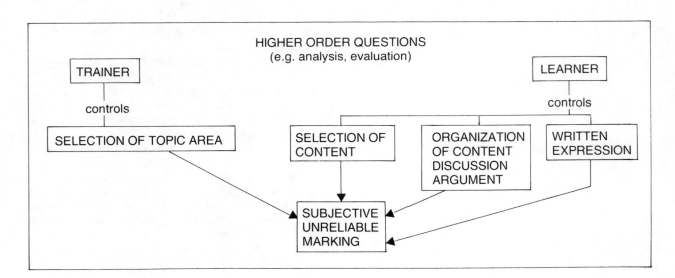

HIGHER ORDER QUESTIONS
(e.g. analysis, evaluation)

TRAINER — controls — SELECTION OF TOPIC AREA

LEARNER — controls — SELECTION OF CONTENT | ORGANIZATION OF CONTENT DISCUSSION ARGUMENT | WRITTEN EXPRESSION

SUBJECTIVE UNRELIABLE MARKING

Generally speaking, the more open-ended the essay title, and the more it challenges the learner's ability and imagination, the more subjective the marking is likely to be. On the other hand the more the guidance given in the question, the more focussed and limited its requirements, the more objective the marking.

A type of essay which does allow a considerable amount of guidance is what we may call the **restricted essay**.

Restricted essays

Here's an example of a restricted essay title.

Describe the working of the following parts of an internal combustion engine:
a) the carburettor,
b) the cooling system,
c) the fuel pump.

Do you see how limits have been placed on possible answers? This means that the trainer has retained a greater control over the sampling of content and, although the learner has still been given some opportunity to organise his own answers, scope for the sampling of content has been reduced. The reliability of the marking will have been increased to some extent.

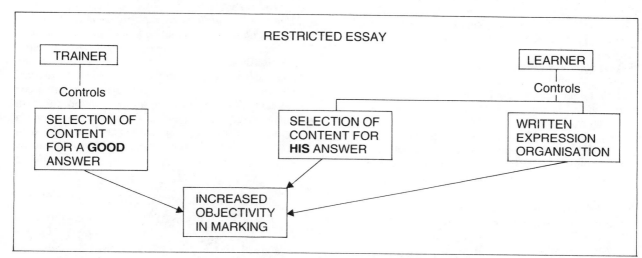

4. Write an example from your own field.

Is the question well focussed on definite aspects, thus limiting the learner's sampling opportunities? Would you find it fairly easy to assess in a relatively objective way?

The example (of a restricted essay title) above is a merely descriptive item.

5. Can you suggest a restricted essay question which calls for a higher level answer?

Remember that you could require the candidate to comprehend, apply, analyse, synthesise or evaluate.

Here's an example which calls for a higher level answer.

Of the various kinds of
a) carburettors
b) cooling systems and
c) fuel pumps
found in internal combustion engines, which do you consider the most efficient? Justify your answers.

Perhaps you wrote something similar.

Length of essays

Another way of restricting the answer to an essay is to limit its length, at the same time focussing it on particular material.

Look at this:

Write 250 words about the operation of a carburettor in an internal combustion engine.
a) In what ways are possible answers restricted?
b) Who is in control of the sampling of content?
c) How reliable will the marking be when compared with the marking reliability of an open-ended essay?

a) You will have noted that both the content and the length of answers have been restricted.
b) The trainer is still in control to a large degree even though he has transferred some responsibility to the learner.
c) The marking is likely to be more reliable than that of more extensive open-ended essays because of the deliberate restrictions in terms of length, subject matter and level of question.

Preparing essay titles

At first sight, this seems to be an easy exercise, but it must be done with great care.

Factors to be borne in mind are:
a) fair and effective sampling of the learning content;
b) clear, unambiguous wording;
c) level of questions (the abilities of the learners must be considered as well as your own requirements);
d) time limits (of particular importance in examinations, but they might interfere with the opportunities for the most able);
e) appropriateness of open-ended or restricted types;
f) possibilities for challenging candidates with high level questions.
(perhaps testing of mere factual material is better left to objective testing);

Prepare a few essay questions.

Now check them against (a), (b), (c), (e) and (f) above. Are you satisfied with them?

Advantages of essay-type tests

Can you list what you think are some of the advantages of essays? Write a few quick notes before comparing them with the notes below.

You will not have written in the same words, but may have included the sense of the advantages listed below.

Many would agree that some of the advantages are that they:
a) go beyond mere factual material and challenge the candidates ability to select and integrate his material in presenting a cogent argument, thus assessing higher intellectual abilities;
b) are easily and quickly constructed;
c) are thought to encourage good study habits in that more than mere memory of facts is required to produce a good answer;
d) give scope for the more able to express themselves more fully.

Disadvantages of essay-type tests

Write a list of the disadvantages of essay-type tests and then check it with the points made below.

Among the disadvantages commonly noted are:
a) they favour the verbally fluent;
b) marking is subjective, thus leading to low reliability;
c) they cannot cover all the learning content very efficiently;
d) in timed examinations, lack of time may not allow a candidate to display all his knowledge on a subject.

Examinations

With regard to timed examinations, what is expected of a candidate must be carefully related to time made available. An examination should not be a test of handwriting speed. Many would say that the trainer's opportunity for assessing learning is limited because he can only sample the material and abilities to be tested.

Another criticism of examinations, is that success depends too much on luck in spotting the right areas for revision and that those with good memories for information are rewarded too highly. For these reasons, the introduction to examinations of **structured questions** has been recommended by many trainers.

Structured questions

Important features of the structured question are that the tasks set during assessment should match the activities engaged in during the learning period and also be related to planned future activities. There are many possibilities for this kind of question, but basic to all of them is the setting of a particular situation and calling for the learner's response to that situation.

The basic form of the structured question is as follows:

a) Information is presented in some form. It could be a form of written material, pictures, diagrams, graphs, equipment, resource material, artefacts, objects.

b) The information may be presented in several sections with questions following each section.

c) Structured questions are then set. These are usually in the form of objective-type items or short restricted essays, but could be in the form of longer more open-ended essays. They might require the candidate to respond graphically.

d) Responses are written on the question paper itself. This means that the amount of space left for written answers gives some guidance about the length of response required.

e) The level of thought required to answer the questions rises as the candidate proceeds through them, that is from the recall/descriptive to the evaluative type.

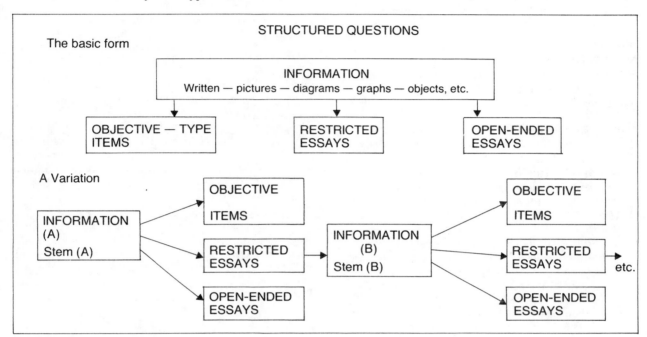

How reliable do you think the marking of structured questions is likely to be when compared with the marking of objective tests, open-ended essays and restricted essays? Justify your answer.

Following on our earlier discussions about control of the sampling of objectives etc. you will probably have decided, in order of marking reliability, from the most to the least reliable, as follows:

a) *Objective tests because the trainer is in full control of the sampling.*

b) *Structured questions because the trainer has almost total control of the sampling. A precise marking scheme may be prepared.*

c) *Restricted essays because the candidate's attention is focussed to some extent.*

d) *Open-ended essays because even though the trainer can choose the essay titles, he is not in control of the material and the approach taken by the learner.*

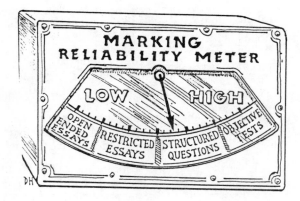

You will note that control of sampling of the content passes progressively from the trainer to the candidate, thus making marking progressively more subjective and less reliable.

Writing structured questions
They are not easy to devise but the following hints will be of value.

a) Always be on the lookout for material which would be useful for the purpose, e.g. appropriate written passages, pictures, diagrams, tape-recordings, objects, films, slides, graphs, in fact, any appropriate resource material.

b) Carefully examine the source material you present, commonly called the stem (a term you will remember), from both your own and the candidate's point of view so that you can be satisfied that it is generally appropriate to the skills and abilities you wish to be used in dealing with it.

c) Make sure that your sequencing of items is appropriate, that is that they proceed from the relatively easy to the more difficult and that there is a logical development of the content itself.

d) As far as possible, think of the answers which you require before framing the questions. Of course this will not be so easily accomplished with freely written essay-type answers.

e) As you write the questions, write a marking scheme. Of course, you might have to revise this when you have seen the candidates' answers.

f) Include no more than eight sub-questions, each dealing with no more than four points to which marks may be allocated.

g) Ensure that you have left sufficient room for answers to be written and make provision for the candidate who requires additional space. On the other hand, you must not encourage lengthy, wide-ranging, irrelevant discussions since this would lead to lack of objectivity in the marking.

h) Inform the candidate of the marks to be gained by answering each item and try to make these equal to the main points you expect to be included in each answer.

i) Ensure that all sub-questions are independent of each other, that is that the answer to a question is not dependent upon the answers to preceding questions.

j) Allow a reasonable time for the candidate to answer all parts, bearing in mind that he will need more time to complete essay-type questions than he will to do the more objective type.

Insert ticks and crosses in the cells to summarize your learning. A tick means a positive and a cross a negative response. Use up to three of either in each cell to indicate the strength of each response.

Comparisons and contrasts
Objective test, structured questions and essays

	Objective tests	Structured questions	Essays	
			Restricted	Open-ended
Trainer's control of content sampling				
Candidate's control of content sampling				
Candidate's freedom in responding				
Ease of marking				
Objectivity of marking				
Reliability of marking				
Efficiency in assessing factual knowledge				
Efficiency in assessing more than factual knowledge				
Efficiency in testing higher level thinking				
Influence on acquisition of solid subject matter				
Favours the verbally fluent				
Content coverage in relation to time limits				

Your responses may vary in detail from those appearing below but it is likely that the general pattern of responses will be in agreement so that general trends may be discerned. You will note that strengths and weaknesses in one aspect have their corresponding effects in others.

	Objective tests	Structured questions	Essays Restricted	Essays Open-ended
Trainer's control of content sampling	√√√	√√	√√	√
Candidate's control of content sampling	×××	√	√	√√
Candidate's freedom in responding	×××	√	√	√√
Ease of marking	√√√	√√	√	××
Objectivity of marking	√√√	√√	×	××
Reliability of marking	√√√	√	×	××
Efficiency in assessing factual knowledge	√√√	√√	√	×
Efficiency in assessing more than factual knowledge	√	√√	√√	√√√
Efficiency in testing higher level thinking	√	√√	√√	√√√
Influence on acquisition of solid subject matter	√√√	√√	√√	√
Favours the verbally fluent	××	√	√√	√√√
Content coverage in relation to time limits	√√√	√	××	×××

Do you see the progressive trends appearing in the table as you look from left to right? Also note the relationships appearing vertically.

We will now move on to the problem of marking essays.

Marking

We have seen that the marking of essays presents problems of various kinds and we will now consider ways of coping with these.

The two basic methods for marking essays of both kinds i.e. restricted and open-ended, are:
a) analytic marking
b) impressionistic marking

Analytic Marking

This is aimed at making the marking more objective but you will note that subjectivity still plays its part in the choosing of items for the checklist of content and in taking into account the relative importance of factual knowledge included and material included by the student which has not been thought of by the trainer. However, two markers using the same checklist are likely to award fairly similar marks and grades for essays, thus demonstrating an improvement in reliability.

A BASIC METHOD

a) After carefully analysing the question and deciding upon the points required to produce the ideal answer, the trainer lists these and allocates marks to them according to their relative importance. A notional award of marks is usually made for general presentation. The maximum possible marks should conform to a required total, e.g. 100 if percentages are to be used.

b) When marking the essay he then allocates the appropriate marks as he notes and checks off the points made in the essay.
c) At his discretion, he may award marks for material included by the student but which don't appear on the checklist.
d) The trainer may award a mark for general presentation.
e) The trainer arrives at the final mark for the essay and transforms it into a grade if necessary.

a. Write an essay title relevant to your area of work.
b. Analyse the requirements for the ideal answer and construct a relevant checklist.
c. Award marks to the various points and also a mark for general presentation. The essay is to be marked out of 50.

A possible format:

Essay title		Mark
Main points for ideal answer		
1.		
2.		
3. etc		
Other relevant points not included by trainer (Discretionary award)		
General presentation		
	Total /50 Grade	

— Have you included all the required relevant points?
— Have you correctly weighted the marks according to the importance of the points or have you decided on equivalent marks?
— Is the mark for general presentation reasonable?
— Does the total of marks come to 50?

AN ANALYTIC/IMPRESSIONISTIC SCHEME

This method attempts to improve reliability of marking by analysing the main features of an essay. These include things like the subject matter included, ability to organise and use material to develop an argument which answers the question, general presentation and language skills. In this case, the student's selection of relevant material is assessed as a whole, the trainer bearing in mind what he considers to be necessary for a good answer to the question.

The marker prepares a marking scheme as follows:
a) He lists those points which he thinks are essential to a good answer. These might include choice of

content, development of arguments, fluency of expression, language use etc.

b) He then allocates marks to each item as he thinks appropriate. This requires the weighting of marks allocated to each point.

Example:

Marks (1 to 5) are allocated for each point and multiplied by the weighting factor. Sub-totals are summed to give the final score.

1 = inferior;   2 = below-average;   3 = average;
4 = above average; 5 = superior

	Mark (out of 5)	Weighting	Weighted mark
a) Selection of relevant subject matter		×4	
Logical development of argument		×4	
Originality of approach		×4	_____
			Sub total
b) Structure and style		×2	
General expression		×2	_____
			Sub total
c) Punctuation		×1	
Legibility		×1	
Spelling		×1	
Syntax		×1	_____
			Sub total
		Total %	

Note that the awarding of all marks is subject to impressionistic marking but that an attempt to be analytic has also been made, thus aiming at increased objectivity.

You might like to try out the scheme with essays produced by your trainees, but in any case, use it to calculate the total percentage marks from an imaginary essay so that you can be sure you know how to use it. Try it with (a) marks which are generally below average and (b) marks which are generally above average. Your final marks are likely to be about (a) 40 and (b) 80. You may think that using a marking scheme takes considerable time and you would be right. However it does help to focus the marker's mind and to help him to make comparisons in a relatively objective manner. In practice you would most likely be much less concerned with sections (b) and (c) than with section (a) in the scheme above.

Alternatively, the trainer may wish to mark according to the more frequent practice of impressionistic marking.

Impressionistic marking

After gaining a general impression of the essay as a whole, the marker awards the grade or mark. Time is usually an important factor since marked essays should be returned to their writers as soon as possible — preferably with some meaningful comment as well as a grade or mark — and deadlines are always set for the marking of examinations.

For impressionistic marking we would follow the procedure below.

a) Mark only one question at a time.

b) After reading them for the first time, select a specimen answer from the set of essays to illustrate each grade, e.g. A B C D E F (or equivalent numerical values, e.g. 70+, 60-69, 50-59, 40-49, 35-39, below 35). Obviously, you might not have essays to illustrate **all** grades, particularly A and F. You will have to decide which grade or mark represents a 'Fail'.

A	B	C	D	E	F

c) Rapidly read through the remainder and grade them by placing them on the appropriate piles. Finer judgements may be made at this time by ordering by merit in the piles. If both marks and grades are required, many find it best to allocate marks when orders of merit have been decided in the various grade piles.

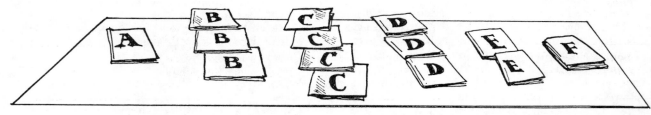

d) Let a second reader mark the essays, preferably marking 'blind', that is without his knowing the marks given by the first marker.
   Second marker repeats steps (a), (b) and (c)

e) Resolve significant discrepancies in marks by means of a third independent marker, perhaps one designated as senior examiner.

f) If necessary and practicable, refer the scripts to a moderating panel. This is usually done if comparisons need to be made of assessments from different institutions, but in practice the procedure ends at any one of steps (c), (d) or (e).

Unless you purposefully set out to spread out the marks you award, you will probably find that they will not be as widely spread as those resulting from analytic marking. In fact, markers normally use only a limited part of the possible numerical scale, with a tendency for marks to cluster round 50-59 in the case of a percentage scale with very few marks indeed at the extremes. Every attempt should be made to spread out marks so that students displaying high ability are to be rewarded.

With regard to the relative merits of analytical and impressionistic marking, in practice it has been found that there is general agreement when essays are ranked in order of merit. It is the marker's responsibility to choose what is best for his purposes.

Write a few comments in the table.

Marking methods	Analytic	Impressionistic
Time taken		
Subjectivity/Objectivity		
Reliability		
How to improve reliability		
Problems in awarding grades and marks		
Other problems		
Your personal preference with justification		

You might have written something like this

Marking methods	Analytic	Impressionistic
Time taken	Expensive. Takes longer than impressionistic	Still substantial
Subjectivity/ Objectivity	Attempts to improve objectivity but still subjective basically	Generally subjective
Reliability	Perhaps a little more reliable than impressionistic	Lacking in reliability
How to improve reliability	Use second independent marker or moderating panel	As for analytical
Problems in awarding marks and grades	Deciding on marks in the marking scheme. Finding totals expensive in time.	Finding specimens for each grade. Using the whole range of marks.
Other Problems	Consulting the marking schedule. Interferes with marking. Excessive time	Subjectivity. Time consuming
Your personal preference with justification	You might have written something about using the techniques according to the requirements as you see them.	

You now know a great deal about written forms of assessment — about objective tests, two kinds of essay and structured questions.

How would you decide which kind to use if you thought that some sort of written assessment was appropriate?

After considering the advantages and disadvantages of the various techniques and your particular purpose you would make your choice.

Generally speaking, since you would aim at giving your students as wide a learning experience as possible, you would also need to use a wide range of assessment techniques - would need to match the assessment techniques with the learning experiences. It follows that you should use as many assessment procedures as is possible in your particular situation.

Choosing the form of written assessment:

Ask yourself:
1. What do I already know about my trainees, their knowledge and abilities?
2. What do I wish to know about them now?
3. **What** have they been learning?
4. **How** have they been learning it?
5. Which form (or forms) of written assessment will best suit my purpose?

Having completed this component, you should now be able to:

1. explain the relationship between the reliability of the marking of objective tests, essays and structured questions and control of content sampling;
2. describe open-ended essays, restricted essays and structured questions;
3. compare the strengths and weaknesses of objective tests, essays and structured questions;
4. prepare effective essay questions and structured questions;
5. explain analytical and impressionistic marking;
6. make an informed choice of written assessment methods for your own purposes.

Component 2:

Selection and Testing I: Attainment, Special Aptitudes and General Ability

---

Key Words

 Selection; attainment; general ability; intelligence; special aptitudes; levels of human ability; trainability.

Having looked at objective and essay-type tests in earlier Components, we are now going to examine other kinds of tests, in particular published tests used in selecting trainees who have applied for certain work roles or training courses.

What is the purpose of the kinds of tests studied earlier?

You'll agree that besides helping to check on the effectiveness of the training methods, the main purpose is to check whether our objectives have been achieved, whether the trainee has learned the material. To put it another way, we are attempting to assess the trainee's **attainment**.

In testing for attainment, the trainer is basically interested in the material he has been teaching in a restricted training sequence but sometimes he would be interested in attainment in a much wider sense, particularly when **selecting** applicants for particular jobs or for training courses.

When we think about attainment in this sense, we mean the applicant's general educational level, existing knowledge, skills and experience.

How could you find out something about these attributes at the start of the selection procedure for a particular role?

You will almost certainly have decided that the applicant's completed application form will provide much of the information about his attainment.

What kind of information could be collected about an applicant's:
a) general educational attainment?
b) specific technical/commercial attainment?
c) other relevant experience?

a) The usual measures of general educational attainment are grades gained in the CSE and GCE examinations. In the future the General Certificate of Secondary Education will take the place of these. Obviously use is being made of test results here.

b) Attainment in more specific examinations, for example City and Guilds and BTEC, would be appropriate as would commercial and professional qualifications. Again, the results of testing are being considered.

c) Information about apprenticeship and other experience would provide the other useful information about attainment, part of which might have originated in test results.

If further immediate evidence is required, published tests of attainment in, for example, Mathematics and English may be administered. These are readily available from companies like the National Foundation for Educational Research (NFER) — Nelson.

After a short list of candidates has been selected, the usual next stage in the selection procedure is an interview during which further details about an applicant's attainment can be discovered.

▨ Checkpoint

Suppose you wished to select applicants for either particular training or a specific post in your sphere of interest. List aspects of attainment which you would prefer the candidate to have.

Of course, all employment and training roles have their special requirements, but all would give attention to general educational attainment, e.g. GCE, CSE, GCSE, more specific qualification, e.g. City and Guilds, commercial and industrial qualifications, and apprenticeship and other experience. Did you refer to all of these?

Testing and Selection

We've seen how information about **attainment** can help us to make the right decisions in selection for various purposes and we could make use of test results. What else would a trainer like to know about an applicant? Jot down a few points.

Compare what you have written with aspects first listed by Alec Rodger in 1930 in his Seven Point Plan published in 1952. Although written so long ago, it is still influential among many people who have to make selection decisions. He believed that the following were important and few would argue with his list.

1. Physical makeup, including health and physique.
2. Attainments.
3. General intelligence.
4. Special aptitudes.
5. Interests.
6. Disposition, that is his acceptability to others and his ability to influence.
7. Circumstances, including domestic circumstances.

How did your list compare with this one? Which of these aspects of an applicant's knowledge, skills and attributes would be fairly easily and readily assessed by the trainer?

You'll probably agree that physical makeup, attainment, interests and circumstances are pretty much open to investigation. Disposition too, although a somewhat more problematical area, could be assessed by means of interview, references and others who know the applicant. It is valuable to know that it is possible to use published tests to assess attributes like attitudes, interests and personality.

However assessing general intelligence and special aptitudes is not so straight-forward. When we talk about general intelligence, we are referring to general intellectual ability which may underlie all our mental functioning. Special aptitudes are more specialised capacities, for instance aptitudes for music, verbal fluency, mechanical tasks, manual dexterity, drawing, etc. These are much more difficult to assess since they cannot be identified and observed directly.

We might be able to get an impression of an applicant's general ability while talking to him but such impressions are notoriously unreliable because we might be misled by his confident manner, verbal fluency and physical appearance. This lack of reliability is even more pronounced when we are trying to compare one candidate with another or attempting to discover how he stands in comparison with the population at large.

The position is similar with special aptitudes. Although we might be able to discover relevant information through inquiry, this is likely to be insufficiently detailed and reliable for our purposes.

It is when the more hidden attributes are being assessed that pencil and paper or performance tests are used and the most reliable way is to use reputable published tests. There is no doubt that such tests can provide additional evidence but they need careful handling and results must only be used in conjunction with other evidence. As noted earlier, special aptitude tests may also include performance tests designed to test skills such as manual dexterity, sorting skills, oral fluency, etc. can provide additional evidence but they need careful handling and results must only be used in conjunction with other evidence.

Complete the table below

Assessment and Selection

To be assessed:	Means of assessment
Attainment	
Physical makeup	
Disposition	
Circumstances	
General ability	
Interests	
Special Aptitude	

Perhaps you included some of the ideas appearing below.

Assessment and Selection

To be assessed	Means of assessment
Attainment	Knowledge of GCE, CSE, GCSE for general educational attainment. City and Guilds, BTEC & commercial and industrial qualifications. Apprenticeship and other relevant experience. (Application form/interview).
Physical makeup	Medical examination. Application form/interview. Leisure/sporting activities
Disposition	References. Observation in group situation. Interview (Personality tests are also available)
Circumstances	Application form/interview
General ability	Published test
Interests	Application form/interview
Special aptitude	Reputable published tests. Standard performance test, e.g. manual dexterity.

Attainment and special aptitudes

Let's take a look at the relationship between attainment, and special aptitudes. When we do this we are moving into a somewhat controversial area, but we won't involve ourselves in theoretical argument but rather take a more general, pragmatic view.

Write down your definitions of:
1. attainment;
2. special aptitude.

1. We have seen already that attainment refers to a person's general educational or more specialized commercial, professional or technical achievements through apprenticeship or other activity. In short, it refers to measures of his existing knowledge and skills.

2. Special aptitudes relate to a person's particular capabilities to learn to perform certain tasks or to succeed in specific areas of activity. For instance, one person might exhibit capabilities to perform well on a musical instrument, another to succeed in writing, others to understand the workings of and to work with engines.

Can you see any relationship between attainment and special aptitudes? Do you think there may be any difficulties in discriminating between them?

You'll most likely agree that the person who has shown high **attainment** in handling common tools as a result of his experience is likely to score well in a special aptitude test of manual dexterity also or the individual who has achieved high GCE grades in Mathematics will most likely do well on a special aptitude test which assesses his capability to succeed in some sort of activity involving numerical ability. Clearly attainment can influence assessment of special aptitudes. Looking at the other side of the coin, how do you think that special aptitude for number work might affect attainment in Mathematics?

You'll agree that if special aptitudes mean anything at all, attainment must be affected always granted that the person has been given the opportunity to gain the necessary mathematics **experience**.

Unfortunately this doesn't always happen and we all know cases where young people, particularly during their school years, have been directed along the wrong paths as a result of either unsatisfactory methods of selection, poor teaching or failure to identify general ability and special aptitudes.

Well, your results don't show you have a particular aptitude for nuclear physics. What has been your experience in this field?

The problem set by this 'chicken and egg' situation is that it's really impossible to produce tests which measure **only** special aptitudes or **only** attainment. Consequently, the trainer must give results their due consideration and always treat them with caution. We'll see that we will find similar difficulties when considering general ability. On the other hand, it is worth remembering that there are special aptitudes like co-ordination, and reaction times which may be less linked to attainment but even when assessing these the question of individual experience remains.

Suppose you wished to assess a trainee's special aptitude for verbal reasoning and you administered an appropriate test.
a) On what would his success depend?
b) How could you account for the failure of another trainee?

You'll agree that:
a) Success will depend on both the trainee's special aptitude but also on his previous successful experience. We'll see later how his general ability will also be influential.

b) His failure might be a result of lack of aptitude but to some extent it might also reflect lack of opportunity to learn through poor teaching or through relevant experience.

Now try to apply the same ideas to the following exercise. Complete the table below. You have six ticks to share between columns (2) and (3) to signify whether the measures in column (1) are assessments of Attainment or Special Aptitude. The number of ticks allocated signifies the strength of your choices. The first is done for you as an example.

Examination/ experience (1)	Attainment (2)	Special aptitude (3)	Reason for choice (4)
CSE	√√√√	√√	Measures general educational attainment. Although basically attainment, special aptitude in certain areas would be signified
GCE 'O' Level			
"GCE 'A' Level			
Degree			
Professional qualification			
City and Guilds examination			
Apprenticeship			

You'll conclude that this is a problematic area but these ideas do help to highlight some of the problems which must be borne in mind when selecting for particular work roles or training courses on the basis of tests of attainment and special aptitude.

You probably found it a difficult exercise. There are no completely right or wrong answers but you might have come to similar conclusions as the following:

Examination/ experience (1)	Attainment (2)	Special aptitude (3)	Reason for choice (4)
CSE	√√√√	√√	Measures general educational attainment. Although basically attainment, special aptitude in certain areas would be signified
GCE 'O' Level	√√√√	√√	As for CSE
GCE 'A' Level	√√√	√√√	A more subject-specialised examination thus reflecting both attainment and suitability for higher education in specific fields of study.
Degree	√√	√√√√	Even more specialized than 'A' level. Reflects both successful attainment and suitability for particular employment.
Professional qualification	√√	√√√√	As for degree
City and Guilds examination	√√	√√√√	Likely to be in a specialized area, therefore also pointing to aptitude
Apprenticeship	√√	√√√√	Successful specialized attainment points to special aptitude also.

The diagram below helps to illustrate the relationship. The shaded area signifies the 'grey' area where attainment and special aptitude are indistinguishable from each other because each may affect the other.

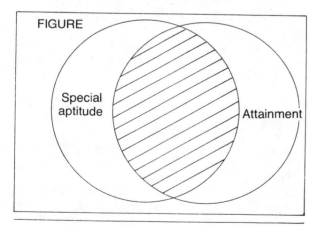

FIGURE

General Intelligence (General ability)

We'll now take a look at the highly controversial often confused area of general intelligence. A particular work role may call for a particular level of general intelligence, often called **general ability.** For instance, we would expect that higher general intelligence would be required for high level managerial work than routine repetitive shop floor practices. We have already seen that a reputable test must be used for selection purposes to assess this.

Now that you understand what is meant by attainment and special aptitude, try to define general intelligence (**general ability).**

If you had difficulty in arriving at a definition, it would not be surprising. There is no one generally accepted definition but the majority would agree that it is to do with the ability to reason, or general mental ability which many believe underlies all our intellectual functioning but it is not possible to arrive at a definition in terms of which it can be measured. This is a crucial point. If there are difficulties of defining intelligence, how do you think that will affect the contents of intelligence tests written by various people? You will probably have concluded that the content of the test reflect the writer's own view of intelligence and this indeed is what happens. They do have one thing in common in that they all try to measure the ability to reason — with words, numbers and symbols. A person with high measured general intelligence would be able to reason very powerfully without previous experience of a particular problem. It follows that if a certain level of reasoning ability is required for a job or a training course it is best assessed by means of a reputable published test.

Here are a few examples of the kind of items used in tests of general ability. Note that they are concerned with **words, numbers** and **symbols.** Such items as these would appear in children's tests but they will serve to illustrate the point.

Underline the right word:
Chicken is to hen as calf is to (bull sheep cockerel cow ram)

Write the next number:
1 9 18 28 39 —

Underline the figure which is most unlike the other four:

△   ▢   ▢   ▱   ⬭

Caution
Intelligence test scores can broadly indicate the level of a person's general intellectual ability but this measured intelligence must never be considered a **cause** of success or failure. Results must be interpreted with caution and always in conjunction with other evidence.

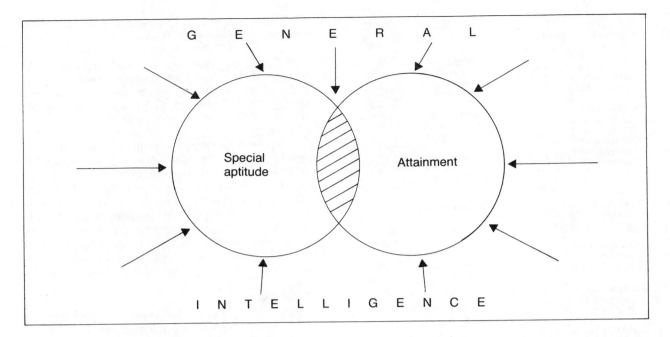

The difference between British and American views provide the most significant example of how different views of intelligence have affected the kind of test produced.

Historically, British psychologists have supported the idea of 'general intelligence', one general ability which underlies all intellectual functioning. Consequently, their intelligence tests — verbal, numerical and spatial — have been intended to produce a single final measure — a number called the **Intelligence Quotient**, usually referred to as I.Q. — which indicates a person's general intellectual ability.

Generally speaking on any intelligence test, a person of average intelligence would always be expected to achieve an I.Q. of 100. In fact about two-thirds of all people would be expected to score betwen I.Q. 85 and I.Q. 115.

What proportions of people would you expect to have I.Q.s of
a) over 115?
b) under 85?

You've no doubt arrived at the answer one-sixth in each case. The scoring of intelligence tests is always so arranged as to give these **standardised** scores which enable us to gain an immediate impression of general intellectual status when we hear an I.Q. figure.

Examples of such tests are the AH2/AH3, AH4, AH5 and the AH6 about which more will be said in the next component.

The traditional American view is that intelligence comprises a number of separate independent abilities, the result of this being the production of separate tests which are intended to measure different aspects of a person's intellectual ability.

Here's an example of this.

As a result of his research, a notable American psychologist called Thurstone concluded that intelligence was comprised of a number of independent abilities which he called Primary Mental Abilities.

Look at the table below. It shows how the Differential Aptitude Tests, a well-known series of separate tests which originated in the United States about 30 years ago, but which are now widely used in this country in modified form, reflect this theoretical approach.

Thurstone's Primary Mental Abilities	Differential Aptitude tests
Space factor (S) (linked with mechanical ability and the ability to visualise flat or solid objects)	Space Relations Test
	Mechanical Reasoning Test
Number ability (N) (with numerical exercises)	Numerical Ability Test
Verbal comprehension (V) (dealing with ideas expressed in words)	Verbal Reasoning Test
	Spelling
Word fluency (W) (ability to think of words at a rapid rate)	Language Usage
Induction factor (discovering principles from a number of examples)	Abstract Reasoning Test
Deduction factor (applying given principles to solve problems)	
Flexibility and speed of closure: (ability to interpret instructions and to readily get to the root of a problem)	Clerical Speed and Accuracy Test. (covers clerical and office skills)
Rote memory (M)	

Do you see how they are related?

The advantage of tests like these is that they may be used separately in any combination. This means that a user can choose tests appropriate for selection for particular occupational roles. You'll not be surprised to hear that the value of being able to choose tests to measure different abilities has been generally recognised and this has led to greater dependence on such tests as the Differential Aptitudes Tests (DAT).

It is also possible to combine scores from these separate tests to give measures of more general abilities.

Which tests would you consider appropriate for applicants for occupations with which you are concerned? General ability tests? Differential Aptitude Tests? If DAT, which ones in particular?

Special Aptitudes

We have been referring to the Differential **Aptitude** Tests during our discussion of general ability and this might have puzzled you. It does help to point out that there is no completely distinct division between the general ability and special aptitude. In fact it seems that the writers of the Differential Aptitude Tests have included tests which are aimed at measuring both general ability and more specific abilities and aptitudes.

Let's see if you can discriminate between special aptitude and general ability. Write your definitions of
a) General ability (general intelligence)
b) Special aptitudes.

a) *General ability, often referred to as general intelligence, is the ability to reason and is thought to be involved in all our intellectual abilities and activity.*
b) *A special aptitude refers to a person's capacity to learn to perform certain tasks or to succeed in specific areas of activity.*

Listed below are the subtests comprising the Differential Aptitudes Tests which you met earlier. In the National Foundation for Educational Research (NFER) — Nelson Catalogue of Occupational Tests, Training Courses and Consultancy Services 1986, these subtests are separated and listed under the headings **General Ability** and **Specific Abilities/Aptitudes**.

In the table below, place a tick in the column which you think will signify agreement with the NFER-Nelson classification.

DAT subtests	General Ability	Specific Abilities/Aptitudes
Verbal Reasoning		
Abstract Reasoning		
Clerical Speed and Accuracy		
Spelling		
Language Usage		
Numerical Ability		
Mechanical Reasoning		
Space Relations		

149

NFER-Nelson categorize as follows;

DAT subtests	General Ability	Specific Abilities/ Aptitudes
Verbal Reasoning	√	
Abstract Reasoning	√	
Clerical Speed and Accuracy		√
Spelling		√
Language Usage		√
Numerical Ability	√	
Mechanical Reasoning		√
Space Relations		√

You probably got the general pattern right but if you didn't, think about how you can account for your differences in your table.

Can you think of any special aptitudes for particular jobs which might be difficult, perhaps impossible to measure?

You might have thought of many examples, but here are a few. It would be difficult to test for special aptitudes needed by prospective counter assistants and sales representatives, in fact any job involving human relationships. Most jobs require specific training and it might not be possible to define all the required aptitudes but it is usually accepted that certain aptitudes are required for training in specific skills and activities.

General Ability and Special Aptitudes

Let's see if we can clarify our ideas about the relationship between general ability and special aptitudes.

Do you think that special aptitudes depend upon general reasoning ability?

It's likely that many have some connection with it and that some may depend on it to a great extent. For instance aptitude for working with words, numbers or diagrammatic material is likely to depend on general ability, but selection for a job in which working with numbers is highly important would be better served by a test of numerical ability than by using a test of general intelligence.

In high level occupations, logical reasoning would be important and it would be valuable to test this during the selection procedure. At the technician level, more elementary and basic ideas and processes would be more appropriately assessed.

Theory and Practice

It is now generally agreed that theories of intelligence and special aptitudes cannot provide a complete and satisfactory guide for assessment which would be accepted by everyone. The vast majority would take the pragmatic view and not involve any particular theory of mental ability. The most important point is that the special abilities and special aptitudes required for particular jobs or training are specified in some manner and are then assessed.

In Column (1) below are listed features which might be considered important for selection purposes. Place ticks in Columns (2), (3) and (4) as appropriate to show most accurately what aspects of an applicant are being studied. In Column (5) write a word or two, e.g. 'test', 'application form', 'interview' etc. to show how the necessary information could be acquired.

Feature (1)	Attainment (2)	Special aptitude (3)	General ability (4)	Source of Information (5)
'O' level Maths Grade B				
A 3-year apprenticeship				
Verbal Reasoning				
Clerical speed and accuracy				
Abstract reasoning				
3 years working on a farm				
Numerical ability				
Language usage				
Mechanical reasoning				
Manual dexterity				
B.Sc. (Hons) Chemistry				

Check your responses with those below. If yours differ in some respects it will serve to underline the relatively undefined divisions between attainment, special aptitudes and general ability. Could you justify all the choices you made?

Feature (1)	Attainment (2)	Special aptitude (3)	General ability (4)	Source of Information (5)
'O' level Maths Grade B	√			Application form/interview
A 3-year apprenticeship	√			As above
Verbal Reasoning			√	Test
Clerical speed and accuracy		√		Test
Abstract reasoning			√	Test
3 years working on a farm	√			Application form/interview
Numerical ability			√	Test
Language usage		√		Test
Mechanical reasoning		√		Test
Manual dexterity		√		Test
B.Sc. (Hons) Chemistry	√			Application form/interview

A classification of human abilities

When we considered special aptitudes and general ability, it was implied that we were looking at abilities on two levels, general ability being at the higher level since it was thought that it could influence special aptitudes. Generally speaking, the higher a person's general ability, the higher the special aptitude. If we expand on this, and also drawing loosely on theory to assist us, we should be able to arrive at a logical structure of human abilities. This should help us to clarify our overall ideas about what we are trying to test. Let's take a couple of examples to illustrate our ideas.

1. A glassblower uses a special tool to nip off threads of molten glass. We can say that the ability involved here is specific to his particular job.
2. A motor car exhaust system fitter uses a dolly to ensure that the pipe he is fitting is quite circular before joining it to another pipe. We might say that the ability to do this is specific to his job.
3. A newspaper editor marks copy to convey certain instructions or needs for modification. This ability is specific to his job.
4. A trainer completes his trainees' record sheets.

Can you allocate abilities 1, 2, 3 and 4 to more inclusive categories of special aptitudes? Choose from manual dexterity, verbal fluency, numerical aptitude, spatial aptitude. You'll most likely agree that 1 and 2 could be related to manual dexterity and that 3 and 4 are more concerned with verbal fluency or verbal comprehension.

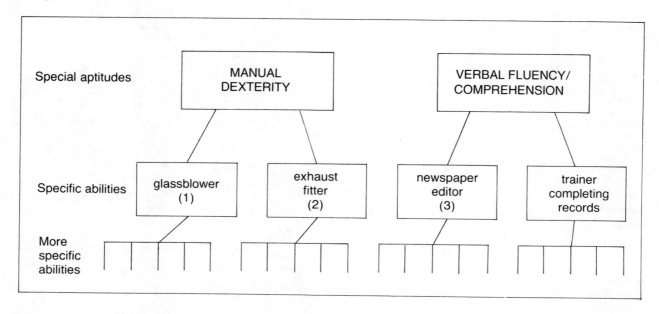

We have now identified a second level of ability, that of special aptitudes. A list of these would include verbal fluency, mechanical aptitude, spatial aptitude, numerical aptitude, verbal comprehension, manual dexterity, musical aptitude and abstract reasoning.

Can you see any way of grouping these into two more inclusive categories? Give it a try and think of a name for each category. Rawlings (1985) calls these categories scholastic or verbal education ability and the other 'technical ability'. Did you decide on something similar?

List the special aptitudes noted above under the headings to which they belong.

Scholastic or verbal educational ability	Technical ability

How does your answer compare with this?

Scholastic or verbal education ability	Technical ability
verbal fluency numerical aptitude verbal comprehension musical aptitude	mechanical aptitude spatial aptitude manual dexterity abstract reasoning

Let's see how our classification looks now. The figure below gives some idea.

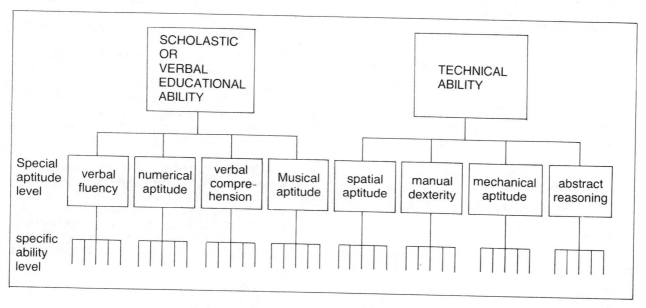

If a careers adviser knew something about a person's performance in these very general areas, he could more confidently guide him towards an occupation in either the technical/scientific or the non-technical/commercial area. People usually have more strength in one or other of these. If a person scores highly in both areas it could be said that he had high general ability.

Draw a diagram to illustrate the various levels of human abilities.

There is no single way of doing this but anything which shows the overall classification in terms of its various levels would be appropriate.

Here's an example

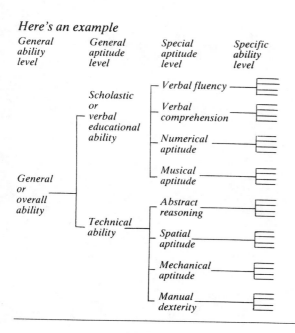

Trainability testing

It would help to round off the picture if we were now examine another kind of test which is useful for selection purposes — the trainability test. We could say that it is a kind of aptitude test which attempts to assess a person's capabilities and capacities at a more specific level than the usual special aptitudes test.

Here are a few examples of trainability tests.

1. A prospective bricklayer would be taught how to build a small section of a brick wall and would then be asked to do the same job himself.
2. An applicant wishing to train as a fork lift truck operator, after being shown the basic controls which he would then operate, would then be asked to complete a few basic manoeuvres.
3. After he had been taught to make a simple straight weld in a steel plate, the applicant would complete the exercise, being allowed several attempts at the job. Then, after instruction he would similarly make a circular weld.

In each of these cases the applicant's performance would be assessed by means of observation and by the quality of the final job or operation.

If you related this level of testing to the classification of human ability framework which you completed earlier, where do you think that trainability testing would fit as a selection test?

It is more specific than the special aptitude test already discussed because it requires an applicant to perform skills and operations which are near to the job for which he wishes to train. In a way, it strings together several of the skills and pieces of knowledge specific to the particular occupation. We could say then that it belongs somewhere between the special aptitude and specific skill levels.

Could you suggest a trainability test appropriate for a job in your sphere of interest?

You will now know something about the classification of human abilities and will now appreciate how tests of general ability and special aptitude can provide evidence which would otherwise be unavailable to the trainer or careers officer interested in selection for particular occupations. In addition, you will understand how information about attainment, some of which comes from test procedures can also be taken into account to assist in making the correct selection decisions. You will also appreciate the usefulness of trainability tests.

Having completed this Component, you should be able to:

1. justify the use of tests in selection procedures;
2. define attainment, special aptitude and general ability;
3. discriminate between British and American views of general intelligence;
4. describe the Differential Aptitudes Test;
5. discriminate between tests of attainment, special aptitude and general ability;
6. describe trainability tests;
7. construct a hierarchical framework showing levels of human abilities.

Further reading

NFER-Nelson have published a most informative collection of relevant books in their Personnel Library series. They are quite short and are highly recommended. They are:

Bolton, G. M. (1983) *Testing in Selection Decisions.*
Bolton reviews the case for testing in the selection process, identifies tests for special attributes and lists the names and addresses of test suppliers.

Downs, S. (1985) *Testing Trainability.*
Downs discusses trainability testing, gives examples of trainability tests and gives information about trainability tests available.

Rodger, A. (1952) *The Seven Point Plan* and
Rawling, K. (1985) *New Perspectives Fifty Years On.*
The Rodger plan for selection written over 30 years ago is reprinted and Rawlings reviews it in the light of recent ideas, updating it where appropriate.

In Component 3 we will look at selection of tests, testing, procedures, interpretation of results and sources of tests.

Component 3:

Selection and Testing II: Selection of Tests and Interpretation of Results

---

Key Words

 Standardisation; reliability; validity; norm-referenced; criterion-referenced; normal distribution; mean; standard deviation; standard error; percentile; grade; selection; occupational tests; battery.

Having studied Component 2, you will understand what we are talking about when we refer to attainment, special aptitudes and general ability, their importance in selecting personnel for either jobs or training courses and how they are best assessed by using tests.

We're now going to take a close look at the nature of the tests themselves, the crucial importance of interpretation of results, the training of test users and how we can most effectively choose the right tests for our purposes.

Criterion-referenced and norm-referenced testing

To begin, let's return for a moment to the objective-type and essay-type testing which we considered earlier.

Here's the same question which was asked at the beginning of the last Component.

What is the main purpose of the kinds of tests studied earlier?

The answer is still the same!

The main purpose is to check whether our objectives have been achieved, whether the trainee has learned the material. We might add to this statement a specification of the level of success which will satisfy us, e.g. 75%, 90% correct — a 'passing mark' in fact. Another name for this kind of testing is **criterion referenced** testing. As this has been dealt with elsewhere in Package 4, we'll spend no more time on it than is necessary for our purposes.

What we're really interested in here is the level of a trainee's mastery of the material presented with regard to a specified criterion of performance. Our intention wouldn't really be to compare his performance with other members of the group of which he might be a member, even though we could do this if we so wished.

Suppose you received the following details of the test results of a trainee new to you.

English Language 65%
Mathematics   70%
Mechanics   63%

What conclusion would you draw from such scores?

You'll agree that they'd mean very little to you because you'd need more information before you could attempt to evaluate the trainee's performance satisfactorily.

What else would you need to know?

You'd certainly need to know something about:
1. the levels of difficulty of the tests themselves;
2. the content of the tests;
3. the levels of abilities of the other trainees in the group who took the tests;
4. the average scores in the various tests;
5. the range of scores gained in the tests.

Although these details would help you to make a more considered judgement, the scores would be of limited value because you could still only compare the scores with those achieved by the small group to which the trainee belonged. You would still have no idea of the trainee's standing in the population at large.

When we compare a person's score with the scores achieved by others in the group, we are moving towards **norm-referenced** testing of a very limited kind, but when we use reputable published tests of attainment, general ability and special aptitudes, we are using norm-referenced tests of a particularly general kind. By using these tests, we are able to compare a trainee's score with the scores achieved on the same test by a very large number, typically thousands, of similar people. A trainee's scores on tests like these are **standardised** scores which are of great value when we are assessing attainment, general ability and special abilities for selection purposes.

▨▨▨ Checkpoint

Before we turn our attention to the question of standardised tests, complete the following table. Work on a separate sheet of paper.

Criterion-referenced and norm-referenced tests

	Criterion-referenced assessment	Norm-referenced assessment
Purpose		
Meaning of score		1. **Unstandardised small group tests** 2. **Standardised tests**

You might have written something which has similar meaning to the answers below:

	Criterion-referenced assessment	*Norm-referenced assessment*
Purpose	*To check on a trainee's mastery of the material learned relative to a specified criterion.*	*To compare a trainee's achievement with other members of the group.*
Meaning of score	*An assessment of the trainee's level of mastery of the material relative to a specified criterion with no attempt to compare with scores of others.*	*1.* **Unstandardised small group tests** *Shows trainee's standing relative to the small group to which he belongs.* *2.* **Standardised tests** *Shows the trainees standing relative to thousands of other similar people.*

The Construction of Standardised Tests

To help you to make sense of scores from standardised tests, we'll examine some of the basic ideas about them. Let's first of all see how a standardised test is typically constructed. Standardised tests of attainment and special aptitude would follow a similar pattern but we'll use the example of a test of general ability.

The following steps would usually be taken:

1. The target population would be identified. For example, the NFER AH4 Group Test of General Intelligence was designed for use with a very wide age range, in fact from 10 years of age to adult.

2. A large number of appropriate questions arrived at covering the areas listed in the specification would be drafted. In the case of a test of general ability, you'll remember that they would most likely be concerned with verbal reasoning, numerical reasoning and spatial reasoning. The test specification would deal with this. Remember that you met the idea of test specification in Unit 3.

3. The questions would then be tried out with groups representative of the target population at whom the test is aimed.

4. An item analysis would then be completed. You will already know something about this process since we dealt with it in Unit 3. You'll probably remember that the intention would be to identify unsuitable questions, for instance those which failed to discriminate between high and low achievers and those which were too easy or too difficult. Do you remember the Difficulty Index (or Facility Index) and the Discrimination Index and what they stand for?

    You're right if you decided that weak questions would be discarded and the satisfactory questions retained for further testing and item analysis. Trials would continue until an appropriately balanced number of questions had been collected.

5. The final test would then be administered to a very large, balanced, sample representative of the target population. In the case of AH4 Group Test of General Intelligence, a sample ranging from children aged 10 to adults would need to be tested. The scores obtained are called **raw scores** and it is once scores like these are available that the real process of standardisation can take place.

▰▰▰

Detail the probable steps to be taken in producing a numerical test suitable for the selection of apprentices and factory workers.

The procedure followed would likely follow the pattern below.

1. *The target population would be identified. An appropriate age range would be 16 years — adult, incidentally the range adopted by the Personnel Tests for Industry (Numerical and Verbal) published by National Foundation for Educational Research — Nelson. (NFER-Nelson) is 15 years to adult but you will appreciate that these tests were most likely standardised when the school leaving age was 15.*

2. *After carefully examining the specification of the numerical needs of apprentices and factory workers, a large number of questions would be drafted.*

3. *These questions would be tried out with appropriate groups, perhaps actual apprentices and factory workers as well as representatives who are of the type likely to seek such employment. These groups would range from age 15 years to adulthood.*

4. *An item analysis, aimed at rejecting unsatisfactory questions and retaining discriminating questions at the appropriate levels of difficulty, would then be completed.*

5. *Further trials would be completed until such time as a final test appropriate in terms of content and length was constructed.*

6. *This test would then be administered to a sample comprising a large number of subjects representative of the target population. The* **raw scores** *from this testing procedure would then be used for purposes of standardisation.*

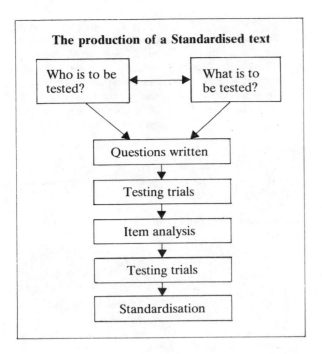

The production of a Standardised text

Who is to be tested? ↔ What is to be tested?

↓ ↓

Questions written

↓

Testing trials

↓

Item analysis

↓

Testing trials

↓

Standardisation

Standardisation

What is your understanding of the term 'standardisation'?

You probably had ideas about providing some sort of common basis, bringing some sort of basic order to otherwise confusing data. In effect this is one of the main intentions of the test standardisation process.

Earlier you met the problem of trying to make sense of a list of percentage marks gained by a trainee new to you. We decided that information in that form would be of very little use in absolute terms because you would know nothing about

1. the levels of difficulty of the tests;
2. the content of the tests;
3. the abilities of the other trainees who took the tests;
4. the average scores in the various tests;
5. the range of scores gained in the tests.

Can you see how several of these factors would have been dealt with when a standardised test was being constructed?

Certainly points 1-3 above would have been resolved in the early part of the test construction and you'll see that the rest of the standardisation procedure is intended to deal with points 4 and 5. We would then be able to confidently compare a person's test score with the scores of other similar subjects, in other words to make the score meaningful for us.

Since there are many complex technical concepts and statistical procedures involved in standardising tests, we will confine ourselves to the basic ideas which will enable you to meaningfully interpret test scores.

As a straightforward illustration, we'll have a look at the particular system frequently used in standardising intelligence tests, tests of general ability.

You must have met the term IQ (Intelligence Quotient). If so, you'll probably know that the IQ of the average person is 100 and this is the average, or **mean** which is set as a basis for the standardisation of

the raw scores obtained from the final testing noted earlier, each year group being dealt with in turn. For instance, in standardising an intelligence test for children, the scores of each year group, i.e. the seven year olds, the eight year olds, the nine year olds, etc., would each receive separate attention. (NB If you are unfamiliar with statistical techniques, then you might like to work through, or at least refer to, Components 3-5 of Study Unit 6 of this Package. These Components deal in a general way with the processing of numerical results obtained from assessment.)

With the help of statistical techniques, the standardisation proceeds as follows:

1. The average (**mean**) is set at 100 so that the average raw score (the actual average score on the test) becomes 100 as a standardised score.

2. The range of raw scores gained by the year group is converted to spread between 40 and 160, that is **60** marks below the mean and 60 above it. This is in accordance with what is called the **curve of normal distribution** which we will examine later.

   In the case we are taking as an example there would be four divisions of 15 points above the mean and four of 15 points below the mean. Each of these divisions is called a **standard deviation**. The **standard deviation** is a measure of the **spread of the marks** and the raw scores, regardless of their initial spread, are made to fit into this preconceived pattern.

3. When all the scores have been converted to standardised scores, in this case with a **mean** of 100 and standard deviation of 15, a table of **norms** is drawn up. This allows raw scores to be quickly converted to standardised scores and tables of norms are included in the test manuals which are always provided with published standardised tests.

Let's take a closer look at the curve of normal distribution which is used as the basis for standardisation procedures. It is assumed that all human abilities are distributed among the general population according to the properties of this curve. Remember that the raw scores from each year group are treated separately and converted to fit this pattern.

It looks like this

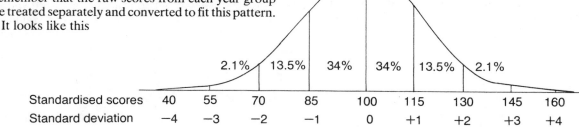

Standardised scores	40	55	70	85	100	115	130	145	160
Standard deviation	−4	−3	−2	−1	0	+1	+2	+3	+4

The rounded percentages in the various standard deviation units are the proportions of each year group population who will score between certain marks.

We can see that the majority will score near the mean. In fact, 68.26% of scores will fall between 85 and 115 (within 1 SD either side of the mean) and 27.08% will fall between 70 and 85 and 115 to 130.

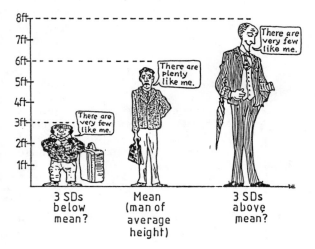

What are your definitions of the following?
(a) the mean of a set of scores
(b) the standard deviation of a set of scores
(c) standardisation of scores
(d) the curve of normal distribution.

You might have answered as below.
(a) The mean is another name for the average of a set of scores.
(b) The standard deviation (SD) of a set of scores is a measure of the spread of scores.
(c) The standardisation of scores takes place when a set of raw scores are converted to standardised scores determined according to some pre-arranged pattern. (In our example, the standardisation is based on the curve of normal distribution as a basis with a mean of 100 and SD of 15.)

(d) The curve of normal distribution provides the basis for the standardisation of scores and it is assumed that all human attributes are distributed among the population at large according to its properties.

Use the rounded figures appearing in the illustration of the normal curve appearing above to answer these questions.

What proportions of the population at large would you expect to score:
(a) between 100 and 130?
(b) between 115 and 145?
(c) over 130?

Answers
(a) 47.5% (34% + 13.5%)
(b) 15.6% (13.5% + 2.1%)
(c) 15.6%
(d) 0.4%

Note that our example is concerned with an intelligence test and that knowledge of the properties of the normal curve enables us to predict the distribution of IQs among the general population. Another way of looking at this is that we can assess a person's standing in the general population with regard to intelligence if we know his IQ. For instance, we would estimate that a person scoring 100 would be scoring higher than a little less than 50% of the population. To use another example, a little more than only 2% of people would be placed higher than a person scoring IQ 130.

Using these ideas we can convert standardised scores into what are called **percentiles**. In fact, the norms for the AH4 Group Test of General Intelligence mentioned earlier are given in three forms: grades, **percentiles** and standardised scores (in this case called T scores which are based on a mean of 50 and a standard deviation of 10).

A percentile indicates the percentage scoring below and including a particular score. For instance, a standardised score of 140 would be given a percentile ranking of 99.7, a standardised score 100 would become percentile 51.3 and 85 would become percentile 16.7. Look at the diagram of the normal curve and relate these figures to it. Percentile rankings are indicated in various ways. For instance a percentile ranking of 70 (indicating a score as good as or better than 70% of the population) might be written as a PR of 70 or P70 or 70%ile.

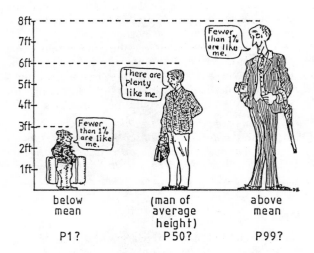

<table>
<tr><td>below
mean</td><td>(man of
average
height)</td><td>above
mean</td></tr>
<tr><td>P1?</td><td>P50?</td><td>P99?</td></tr>
</table>

Here are a few standardised scores and their related percentile rankings. Complete the table.

Standardised score	Percentile	Percentage scoring same as or lower than standardised score	Percentage scoring higher than standardised score
140	99.7		
130	97.9		
100	51.3		
75	5.1		

Answer

Standardised Score	Percentile	Percentage scoring same as or lower than standardised score	Percentage scoring higher than standardised score
140	*99.7*	*99.7%*	*0.3%*
130	*97.9*	*97.9%*	*2.1%*
100	*51.3*	*51.3%*	*49.7%*
75	*5.1*	*5.1%*	*94.9%*

Comparison of scores

Suppose you were interested in considering together a trainee's scores on a number of different tests, for example tests of general ability, numerical ability, language ability and abstract reasoning. What advantages would be gained if all scores had been standardised in the same way, let's say with a mean of 100 and SD of 15?

You'll be able to see that the immediate advantages would be that:
(a) the trainee's standing in each ability relative to the general population could be quickly established;
(b) the standardisation process would have converted the score to a common scale so that they would be immediately interrelated;

(c) finally, the scores would have immediate meaning for you so that you could use the scores to make informed decisions.

It is important to note that the standardising of scores to a mean of 100 and standard deviation of 15, although frequently met is only one pattern which may be used. Standardised norms may be constructed using different means and SDs, for example in the AH4 as indicated earlier, and sometimes raw scores are standardised to yield grades, again as happens with the AH4 Group Test of General Intelligence.

However, the principles of the curve of normal distribution, those concerned with mean, SD and proportions of scores occurring within SD units apply in all cases.

Test constructors use their personal preferences to choose whichever method suits their purposes.

look at Compoment 5 of SU6, but you should find what appears here enough for your immediate understanding.

All correlation coefficients range from −1 to +1.

A perfect relationship, perfect correlation, would be expressed by a coefficient of +1, but since no test is perfect, reliability coefficients never achieve that perfect measure.

Given the coefficients of two tests, how would you decide which was the most reliable — which test was likely to be least affected by chance factors?

You'll have concluded that the general rule is that the nearer the reliability coefficient approaches 1, the more reliable the test. Tests authors frequently claim a reliability coefficient as high as 0.95 and above for their tests and these would be considered most reliable.

The testing situation may be a source of error.

Reliability

You will appreciate that performance on any test cannot be measured with complete accuracy because certain factors interfere with the process. No test would yield the same results on different occasions.

What do you think are the factors which are likely to contribute to errors in testing?

Can you group them under broad headings?

You'll probably agree that there are three main sources of error, these being:

(a) the test itself (expression, content etc)

(b) the testing situation (tester, heat, cold, noise, lighting etc)

(c) the person taking the test (attitude, general well-being, personality, chance learning, etc)

All these contribute to error in the score and if you examine the manual of a reputable test you will always find reference to the **reliability** of the test.

This reliability is usually quantified by a **reliability coefficient**, a certain kind of **correlation coefficient**. For further details of the concept of correlation, have a

Standard Error of Measurement (SEₘ)

Finding that a test boasted a high reliability coefficient might help you to decide to use that test, but you would not be able to use that index of reliability directly to help you to take into account possible errors in any actual scores obtained by your trainees when taking the test in scores which you would need to do when interpreting scores.

The statistic used to help you to interpret such scores, and reach more accurate conclusions about likely errors in them is the **standard error of measurement (SEₘ)** which is calculated from the reliability coefficient and the standard deviation of the scores. The SEₘ of a reputable standardised test is always noted in the manual.

The use of the SEₘ is based on probability arising from the curve of normal distribution met earlier but it is sufficient for you to understand certain general rules which will help you to interpret scores more accurately.

Although you would never be able to state a true test score with complete confidence, the SEm would help you to calculate a range of scores within which the true score would be likely to occur and would enable you to express the degree of confidence with which you could reach your conclusion.

Look at the diagram below. You'll recognise it and its properties but this time we are considering the SEm (which is a type of SD) instead of the usual SD met earlier. You'll see that the underlying principles remain the same.

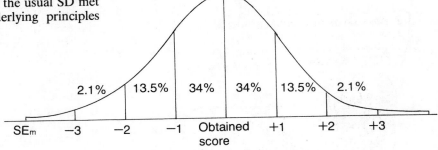

This illustrates that 68% of true scores are likely to be within 1 SEm of the obtained score, 95% within 2 SEm and 99 within 3 SEm of the mean.

Let's take an (unlikely) example.

100 people obtained a score of 98 on a test with an SEm calculated as 5. We could conclude that 68 of them would have true scores between 93 and 103 (1 SEm either side of the obtained score), 95 would have true scores between 88 and 108 (2 SEm either side of the obtained score).

How many would have true scores between 83 and 113?

You'll no doubt have arrived at the answer 99 because the range 83-113 relates to 3 SEm on either side of the obtained score.

Here's another way of interpreting scores. When we are considering the score of an individual it is acceptable to conclude that there is a 68% chance of the true score occurring within 1 SEm, a 95% chance of

its being within 2 SEm and a 99% chance of its being within 3 SEm of the obtained score.

Here's yet another way of looking at it.

If a trainee obtained a score of 103 on a test with an SEm of 4, we would be wrong on only 5 occasions in a 100 if we concluded that his true score lay between 95 and 111 (within 2 SEm of the obtained score).

You'll see that by considering the possible true scores round an obtained score we are able to appreciate the error associated with a test.

You'll agree also that it is vital that we take these ideas into consideration when we are dealing with borderline cases. But more of that later.

▰▰▰

Appearing below are details of scores obtained by individuals on various tests. The SEm given for each test.

Complete the table.

The first is done for you.

Obtained score	SEm of the test	True score range	SEm distance from obtained score	% chance of true score occurring
96	4	88-104	2 SEm	95%
107	5		1 SEm	
	6	74-86		
		80-88		95%
76	3			99%
109	2		2 SEm	
116	4			95%

Obtained score	SE$_m$ of the test	True score range	SE$_m$ distance from obtained score	% chance of true score occurring
96	4	88-104	2 SE$_m$	95%
107	5	102-112	1 SE$_m$	68%
80	6	74-86	1 SE$_m$	68%
84	2	80-88	2 SE$_m$	95%
76	3	67-85	3 SE$_m$	99%
109	2	105-113	2 SE$_m$	95%
116	4	108-124	2 SE$_m$	95%

Let's review what we have considered so far.

We have looked at:

(a) the difficulties involved in interpreting scores obtained on unstandardised tests;

(b) criterion-referenced and norm-referenced testing;

(c) construction of standardised tests;

(d) means and standard deviations;

(e) the curve of normal distribution and the standardisation of raw scores;

(f) reliability and reliability coefficients;

(g) standard error of measurement SE$_m$;

(h) approximating true scores.

Before we leave our general discussion of standardised tests, and remember that they may be tests of attainment, general ability and special attitudes (and also of interests, attitudes and personality which we haven't dealt with which follow similar patterns), there is one other concept to be considered and that is the idea of **validity**.

Suppose an author constructs a test of numerical reasoning. How can he be sure that his test in fact assesses numerical reasoning ability — and not, for instance, basic attainment, reading comprehension or mechanical arithmetic? In other words, how can he be sure that his test is **valid**?

Validity

A **valid** test measures what it is intended to measure, and the manual of a reputable test usually contains details about the validity of the test and how evidence of validity was collected.

In the test we are considering, high correlations with other established tests of numerical reasoning could provide appropriate evidence and this method is frequently used.

When using a standardised test to help in selection decisions, you would be interested in a particular kind of validity called the **predictive validity** of the test. For example, you would be using a particular aptitude test because you considered that the scores obtained by individuals would help to predict future success in engineering. You will sometimes find an index of predictive validity associated with a test. It will be expressed in the form of a correlation coefficient so that the nearer to 1 the index, the higher the predictive validity. However you will need no reminding that in selection procedures it would be most unusual to use only one predictor, e.g. a score on an aptitude test. You will remember that using tests is only one aspect of the selection process.

A test of general ability considered suitable for the selection of apprentices has norms expressed as T scores (mean 50, SD 10). The reliability coefficient is 0.95 and the SE_m is 3. The test is adminstered to 1000 16 years olds of very wide-range ability.

1. Estimate the number who are likely to score:
(a) between 40 and 50
(b) between 50 and 70
(c) between 40 and 60
(d) less than 30
(e) more than 70.
2. Listed below are the scores obtained by five individuals on the same test. Estimate the ranges within which their true scores have a 95% chance of occurring.

Obtained	True score range
A 49	
B 54	
C 46	
D 37	
E 60	

Answers

1. *(a) 340 (About 34% would score between 40 and 50 — 1 SD below the mean)*
   (b) 475 (34% + 13.5% — 2 SDs above the mean)
   (c) 680 (34% + 34% — 1 SD either side of the mean)
   (d) 25 (about 2.5% beyond 2 SD below the mean)
   (e) 4 (Using the rounded figures in the figure given earlier, only 0.4% would score beyond 3 SD below the mean).

2.

Obtained	True score range
A 49	43-55
B 54	48-60
C 46	40-52
D 37	31-43
E 60	54-66

If they have a 95% chance of occurring, they must be within 2 SE_m of the obtained score.

NB See how the ranges overlap even though the obtained scores appear to vary considerably. This underlines the need for careful interpretation, particularly in borderline cases. It also points to the necessity of gathering evidence from many sources before decisions are made.

Use of tests

By now you will understand that specially designed standardised tests are sophisticated testing instruments and that you would require considerable knowledge and skill before you could administer them and interpret results correctly. You will understand basic ideas concerned with test construction, the nature of the tests themselves and factors to be considered when interpreting results. You would certainly be able to make some sense of reported results but, unless you have had specialised training, would not be able to obtain every kind of test from reputable suppliers for your personal use. In fact, the system in Britain is controlled by the British Psychological Society which provides guidance on test use and also monitors practice. Reputable test suppliers accordingly apply certain restrictions with regard to which tests they will sell to particular people.

According to BPS recommendations, the tests are categorised and prospective test users themselves are placed in related categories so that the test supplier immediately knows whether an applicant is sufficiently qualified to be supplied with the test which is being requested. For instance, NFER-Nelson uses a numerical system which helps them to relate immediately prospective users and related tests.

The table below will give you a general idea of the existing situation.

Prospective user	General requirements.
Qualified teacher in schools and colleges.	Qualifications are normally sufficient for use of tests of educational aptitude and attainment. Further training and experience needed for the use of more complex tests
Training and personnel staff in the occupational sector.	Training courses are organised at various levels for those without basic qualifications. Tests may be administered under the supervision of an already qualified user.
Graduate psychologists recognised by BPS.	Qualifications are usually sufficient to enable them to purchase the majority of tests but specific training is required before more complex tests can be used.

Can you see where you fit into the scheme of things? You would have to contact a test supplier, for example NFER-Nelson, for clarification of your own standing. Taking NFER-Nelson as an example since they are perhaps the major test supplier in Britain, if you consult their *Catalogue of Occupational Tests, Training Courses and Consultancy Services 1986,* you'll find details of tests available, training courses dealing with, to name a few, test administration, occupational testing, personality assessment, vocational guidance and engineering selection testing, and also of consultancy services offered. You would also find guidance on the selection of tests for various purposes, and we will use this information as an example of the application of the kinds of tests you now know something about, that is tests of general ability, special aptitudes and attainment. You will remember that it's not possible to clearly discriminate between the influence of attainment and special aptitude, the most important point being that all relevant facets of a trainee's ability should have been considered.

Choice of Tests

The first thing you would do at the start of the process of selecting future trainees would be to define the objectives of your selection and your choice of tests would depend upon these objectives. NFER-Nelson suggest a range of tests of relevant abilities, aptitudes and personality appropriate for selection in areas as diverse as managerial, industrial, computer processing, general office personnel, sales personnel, supervisory and vocational guidance and counselling, each area being considered under separate headings.

If you consult their catalogue, under each heading

you would find a list of suggested tests of general ability, specific abilities/aptitudes and personality.

Let's take an example to illustrate the procedure.

Suppose you were selecting general office personnel and, as part of the procedure, you wished to use standardised tests to assess appropriate abilities and aptitudes. In what kinds of abilities and aptitudes would you be interested? How does your list compare with the guide from the NFER—Nelson catalogue?

Their guide is divided into three sections headed General Ability, Specific Abilities/Aptitudes and Personality and under each heading are listed a number of appropriate tests. For instance the General Ability section includes a number of tests of general ability and also tests of verbal reasoning and numerical ability. Tests under the Specific Abilities/Aptitudes heading are listed tests of general clerical ability (speed and accuracy, numerical ability and verbal facility), spelling, language and other tests of speed and accuracy. Two different personality tests are suggested also.

Did you include these abilities in your proposals?

After the introduction, the test user is then given detailed summaries of each of the suggested tests, details about age, ranges, time taken, content, normative data, administration, costs of manual, booklets, answer sheets, etc., in fact all those details which would enable the prospective user to make an informed choice.

Test batteries

The suggested tests of Verbal Reasoning, Numerical Ability, Clerical Speed and Accuracy, Spelling and Language Usage are of particular interest because they form part of a **multiple aptitude battery**, namely the Differential Aptitude Tests which are available in two forms, Form V and form W. Each contains eight sub-tests, Form W allowing them to be administered separately according to the preferences of the user.

These **test batteries**, the National Institute of Industrial Psychology (NIIP), Engineering Selection Test Battery being another example, allows the user to construct a candidate's profile of relevant abilities, thus providing much valuable information. When interpreting the results, knowledge of reliability, standard error of measurement and norms in their various forms would be applied.

You could learn a great deal about testing procedures and the numerous tests available for selection purposes by examining catalogues of occupational tests like the NFER-Nelson example used here. Other suppliers of tests include Educational and Test Services, Science Research Associates, Hodder and Stoughton Educational and Saville and Holdsworth Ltd.

This concludes your introduction to standardised tests of general ability and special aptitude. You will now know something about their construction, standardisation procedures, factors to be taken into account when interpreting results, training opportunities, selecting appropriate tests and their sources. Since use of standardised tests has much to contribute to making valid selection decisions, it is important that all trainers and personnel staff should have a general knowledge of them and that many should gain that experience and receive that training which would enable them to fully participate in testing procedures.

Having completed this Component you should be able to:
1. discriminate between criterion-referenced and norm-referenced testing;
2. describe the construction of standardised tests;
3. explain standardisation of scores and the construction of norms in the form of scores, percentiles and grades;
4. define and apply the concepts of mean, standard deviation, reliability, standard error of measurement (SE$_m$) and validity;
5. describe restrictions placed on the use of tests;
6. describe methods of selecting appropriate tests;
7. explain the uses of a test battery.

Further reading

The books recommended in Component 2 are also useful with regard to the material presented here. In addition the *NFER-Nelson Catalogue of Occupational Tests, Training Courses and Consultancy Services, 1986* provides a great deal of useful information. Similar catalogues from other suppliers are also useful sources of information.

Component 4:

Profiles: Introduction

Key Words

 Profile; summative; formative; norm-referenced; catalytic; criterion-referenced; ipsative assessment; descriptors.

This is the first of two Components on trainee profiles. In this one you will be introduced to their nature, advantages, and construction. The next Component will deal with the variety of formats available, self evaluation, the administration and problems associated with this form of assessment and recording.

What is a profile?

It is a means of saying what is known about a trainee which can either replace or supplement conventional assessment procedures.

There is no precise definition which would satisfy all areas of education or industrial training but a profile has the following characteristics.

It is a record of the trainee's
    achievements
    experiences
    assessments
    skills
    personal qualities

It is not in itself a new form of assessment but a means of **recording** information. Having said that, the act of formally recording such diverse information may well encourage a greater variety of assessment techniques covering a wider range of experiences and skills than those normally invoked in traditional tests and examinations.

You will have a clearer idea of the nature of profiles and what they have to offer when you have worked through the many examples which follow, both in this Component and Component 5.

▨▨▨ Checkpoint

Make a list of what you consider to be the limitations of traditional methods of assessment.

Limitations of traditional methods of assessment

* *Traditional methods are often crude and simplistic in that the assessment is in the form of a single mark or grade which attempts to describe a whole range of skills or knowledge. This can give a distorted impression of what the trainee has achieved.*
* *Traditional methods only attempt to assess and record a limited view of the trainee while ignoring many important characteristics.*
* *Traditional methods give the learner little or no information about how and why they are being assessed in a particular way.*
* *Traditional methods view trainees as passive objects of assessment with no opportunities provided for taking responsibility for their own development and learning.*
* *Traditional methods are rarely in the form of comprehensive accounts of either interim or terminal assessment which can be of use to monitor the trainee's progress or suggest changes in the training programme.*

Formative *(or diagnostic) assessment, on the other hand, is inward-looking and is largely concerned with generating information about the learner's performance* **during** *the course of training. This information should be of benefit both to the trainer and the trainee by acknowledging success to aid motivation and by diagnosing weakness for remedial action.*

How can profiles help?

Can you recall from previous units the difference between FORMATIVE and SUMMATIVE assessments?

Summative *Assessment is outward-looking and is mainly in the form of a short* **terminal** *statement about a trainee for an external user such as an employer or selector. It is often directed towards grading trainees and sorting them into appropriate pigeon holes for employment or further training. As it is, by definition, produced at the end of a course, it cannot give the instructor or learner any feedback that can affect the performance.*

Profiles may be constructed to fulfil both purposes. That is they can:
1. Sum up a trainee at the end of his course or training programme (Summative).
2. Help a trainee get the best from his course during training (Formative).
3. There is a third important category. Profiles can be used for CATALYTIC purposes to bring about change in training programmes and the methods of assessment employed. On-going diagnostic assessment may consequently result in improvements in the learning and teaching processes.

Practical advantages – resulting from the above:

1. Dialogue is more likely to be established between the trainer and his trainee.
2. Records and reports are more likely to be meaningful for both employers and young people in training.
3. Quality control of training programmes is likely to be more effective.
4. The reporting process is personalised. Even the simplest profile differentiates the learner from others who share the same total but 'add' up differently from him.
5. There are experiences, attainments and qualities which are worth recording which cannot be represented by conventional methods of assessment.
6. Some other forms of assessment can dominate (even determine) what is taught and the methods of training. Profiles can be designed to match the precise nature and sequence of learning and assessment.
7. Profiles can provide a record of what has been achieved at any point on a course.
8. Profiles can avoid damaging comparisons.
9. Profiles can provide a guide to what still needs to be learned. The training programme is therefore made more explicit to the learner.
10. A profile can provide a focus for guidance and counselling.
11. Profiles provide the motivation and continuous feedback which is a feature of continuous assessment.

From the list of advantages above:
1. Outline the ways in which the **trainer** is likely to benefit from the introduction of profiles.
2. Outline the ways in which the **trainee** is likely to benefit from the introduction of profiles.
3. Consider how the **course programme** might be improved by the introduction of profiles.

1. The trainer will:
Be able to avoid making damaging comparisons with other trainees.
Have clear and continuous information about the trainee's progress.
Be able to include a wider range of skills, experiences and qualities unreported in more traditional assessments.
2. The trainee will:
Receive more detailed information about progress and achievements which should aid motivation.
Receive clearer guidance on what needs to be learned.
Feel that he is a partner in the enterprise and not merely the object of assessment.

3. The course programme should be more effective because:
It is under continuous review.
*Assessment does not **dominate** course design as in more traditional assessment.*
A wider variety of assessment can be included.

What can be included?

The answer is — practically anything that will aid learning and provide useful information about the learner.

Types of information:
* Experiences e.g. tasks complete, courses followed;
* Records of mental abilities, e.g. numeracy, literacy, problem solving;
* Descriptions of physical skills, attributes and dispositions e.g. dexterity, appearance, practical skills;
* Personal qualities e.g. initiative, leadership;
* Motivation e.g. interests, ambitions.

As you can see there is virtually no limit to what **might** be included. What **should** be included will depend upon:

What the information is for and for **Whom** it is intended.

What comparisons are to be made?

What is the difference between criterion — referenced and norm-referenced assessment? (You will have encountered these terms on several occasions in previous units on assessment).

In NORM-referenced assessment trainee performance is measured against that of other trainees allowing a simple ranking system which may require only a single number or letter to indicate position within the group.

CRITERION-referenced assessment on the other hand measures students against external criteria and aims at a predetermined level of competence.

Categorise each of the following statements as norm-referenced, or ipsative.
1. John has an IQ of 123.
2. Andy can do 50 press ups.
3. Ann can swim 500 yards.
4. Beryl is the best typist in the pool.
5. Beryl can type at a speed of 50 words per minute.
6. Ian is becoming more punctual.
7. Frank has reduced his error rate by 50%

Norm-referenced 1. 4.
Criterion-referenced 2. 3. 5.
Ipsative 6. 7.

Many, though by no means all, profiles involve criterion-referenced rather than norm-referenced assessment. Why do you think this is so?

*As norm referencing is concerned with comparisons between members of a group there is a tendency to emphasise high and low scores — success and failure. The majority will be awarded middle rank grades and no one learns what the trainee can actually **do**.*

Ipsative assessment

This is a third possible category of assessment IPSATIVE — whereby trainees are judged against **their own** previous performance. In this case the criteria will be adjusted or revised constantly as the learner improves.

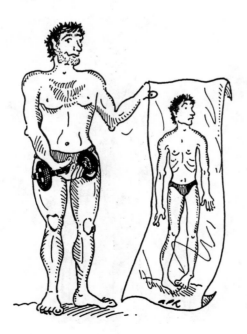

Review

At this point it is worth reviewing what you know about profiles.

Why are they more flexible and comprehensive than traditional methods?

What kinds of information can be included?

What is meant by the word catalytic?

Why are criterion referenced assessments more likely to predominate in a profile than norm referenced?

How to design a trainee profile
Objectives

The first step is clearly to design the training programme, since until such decisions have been made, it will not be possible to make statements about what might be achieved. You will remember from earlier units that this begins with a job analysis and description followed by the formulation of objectives. From these it should be relatively easy to produce clear statements of achievements.

Categories of achievement and experience

You will find that it helps to categorise or group these statements of achievements. Most profiles have some elements in common and many designed for young people in the transition from school to work contain the following grouping of achievements:

Communications, including writing and interpersonal skills.

Numerical skills, especially in applications such as measuring, ordering and estimating.

Planning and problem solving, including the ability to study, learn and think creatively.

Manipulative abilities.

The ability to operate in, or manipulate the environments in which the individual finds himself. (Source FEU (1982) Profiles)

These categories may prove to be a useful starting point when you attempt to group the achievements appropriate to your training programme.

The City and Guilds of London Institute have, after several evaluation exercises, refined slightly different categories of basic abilities in vocational preparation (City and Guilds, 365 Vocational Preparation (General)).

From the City and Guilds categories:
Communication
Practical and numerical
Social
Decision making
Decide under which of these headings to place the following subgroups of abilities:
Talking and listening
Safety
Using equipment
Working in a group
Planning
Reading
Writing
Numeracy
Accepting responsibility
Obtaining information
Using signs and diagnosis
Computer appreciation
Coping

Here is a little help:
Five of them should be grouped under **Communication**
Three of them should be grouped under **Practical and Numerical**
Two of them should be grouped under **Social**
Three of them should be grouped under **Decision Making**

COMMUNICATION	Talking and Listening Reading Writing Using signs and diagrams Computer Appreciation

PRACTICAL & NUMERICAL	Safety Using Equipment Numeracy

SOCIAL	Working in a group Accepting Responsibilities

DECISION MAKING	Planning Obtaining Information Coping

Profiles can be constructed using a wide range of formats and these will be introduced in the next Component of this unit. The most common involve the construction of a check list. Of these two basic profile designs have emerged. The first is a straightforward list of trainee competencies demonstrated during a course and assessed by a variety of means.

Example: (items taken from the RSA certificate of Vocational Preparation — Clerical)

The candidate has demonstrated competence in:

Handling Mail
Parcelling, addressing, weighing, stamping, sorting and distributing mail;
Use of franking machine;
Duplicating and copying;
Use of carbons, ink duplicators and copiers and hand collation,
Use of a spirit duplicator,
Use of electrical and heavy-duty staplers.

Descriptors

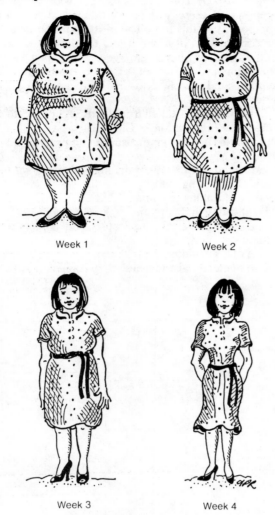

Week 1   Week 2

Week 3   Week 4

Weight Watchers

This however, is relatively crude. A more sophisticated version would include items which could be assessed at any point in a course. Once the common core skills have been identified, as in the City and Guilds 365 — Vocational Preparation course, DESCRIPTORS on the profile are written to set criteria. In this particular example they are written to represent five levels of attainment. This is because the profile is intended to be used formatively and record progression through the skills.

Example of descriptors from City and Guilds 365 (Basic level)

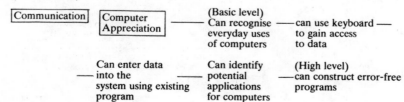

Each level of attainment describes clearly what is required of a trainee and caters for the different points at which he enters the course.

Organise the following descriptors in order from Basic Level to High Level.

Practical and Numerical — Using Equipment

A. Can select and use suitable equipment and materials for the job without help.
B. Can set up and use equipment to produce work to standard.
C. Can use equipment safely to perform simple tasks under guidance.
D. Can use equipment safely to perform a sequence of tasks after demonstration.
E. Can identify and remedy common faults in equipment

Basic Level				High Level
C	D	A	B	E

It is worth taking a look at a good example of a complete grid profile which has been refined over a long period.

Pay particular attention to the categories of achievement and qualities used and the organisation of these into descriptors. Note how each row moves in ascending order of difficulty from 'Basic Level' to 'High Level'. Below each list of descriptors is a horizontal band which can be shaded to indicate the standard achieved at any point in training.

CITY AND GUILDS OF LONDON INSTITUTE
<u>365 VOCATIONAL PREPARATION (GENERAL)</u>
ATTAINMENTS IN BASIC ABILITIES

		(Basic Level)				(High Level)	
COMMUNICATION	TALKING AND LISTENING	Can make sensible replies when spoken to	Can hold conversations and can take messages	Can follow and give simple descriptions and explanations	Can communicate effectively with a range of people in a variety of situations	Can present a logical and effective argument. Can analyse others' arguments	
	READING	Can read words and short phrases	Can read straight-forward messages	Can follow straight-forward instructions and explanations	Can understand a variety of forms of written materials	Can select and judge written materials to support an argument	
	WRITING	Can write words and short phrases	Can write straight-forward messages	Can write straight-forward instructions and explanations	Can write reports describing work done	Can write a critical analysis using a variety of sources	
	USING SIGNS AND DIAGRAMS	Can recognise everyday signs and symbols	Can make use of simple drawings, maps, timetables	Can make use of basic graphs, charts, codes, technical drawings, with help	Can interpret and use basic graphs, charts, technical drawings unaided	Can construct graphs and extract information to support conclusions	
	COMPUTER APPRECIATION	Can recognise everyday uses of computers	Can use keyboard to gain access to data	Can enter data into the system using existing programs	Can identify potential applications for computers	Can construct error free programs	
PRACTICAL & NUMERICAL	SAFETY	Can explain the need for safety rules	Can remember safety instructions	Can spot safety hazards	Can apply safe working practices independently	Can maintain, and suggest improvements to, safety measures	
	USING EQUIPMENT	Can use equipment safely to perform simple tasks under guidance	Can use equipment safely to perform a sequence of tasks after demonstration	Can select and use suitable equipment and materials for the job, without help	Can set up and use equipment to produce work to standard	Can identify and remedy common faults in equipment	
	NUMERACY	Can count objects	Can solve problems by adding and subtracting	Can solve problems by multiplying and dividing	Can calculate ratios, percentages and proportions	Can use algebraic formulae	
SOCIAL	WORKING IN A GROUP	Can cooperate with others when asked	Can work with other members of the group to achieve common aims	Can understand own position and results of own actions within a group	Can be an active and decisive member of a group	Can adopt a variety of roles in a group	
	ACCEPTING RESPONSIBILITY	Can follow instructions for simple tasks and carry them out under guidance	Can follow instructions for simple tasks and carry them out independently	Can follow a series of instructions and carry them out independently	Can perform a variety of tasks effectively given minimum guidance	Can assume responsibility for delegated tasks and take initiative	
DECISION MAKING	PLANNING	Can identify the sequence of steps in everyday tasks, with prompting	Can describe the sequence of steps in a routine task, after demonstration	Can choose from given alternatives the best way of tackling a task	Can modify/extend given plans/routines to meet changed circumstances	Can create new plans/routines from scratch	
	OBTAINING INFORMATION	Can ask for needed information	Can find needed information, with guidance	Can use standard sources of information	Can extract and assemble information from several given sources	Can show initiative in seeking and gathering information from a wide variety of sources	
	COPING	Can cope with everyday activities with help	Can cope with everyday problems Seeks help if needed	Can cope with changes in familiar routines	Can cope with unexpected or unusual situations	Can help others to solve problems	

Objectives for this component

Having completed this Component, you should be able to:

1. Recognise the advantages of profiling over traditional methods.
2. Demonstrate how the trainee can benefit from profiling.
3. Outline what information can be included in a profile.
4. Categorise achievements.
5. Write descriptors of a trainee's achievements.

The next component will outline the variety of profile formats available and consider self assessment as an alternative.

Bibliography

Goacher, B. (1983), *Recording Achievement at 16+*, Schools Council.

F.E.U. (1982), *Profiles*, F.E. Curriculum Review and Development Unit.

Law Bill (1984), *Uses and Abuses of Profiling*, Harper Educational.

Acknowledgements

We are grateful to the following for their permission to use examples of profile material:

Further Education Curriculum Review and Development Unit.

City and Guilds of London Institute.

Component 5:

Profiles: Formats, Self Evaluation, Administration

Key Words

 Self evaluation; grade referencing; criterion referencing; trainee centred reviewing; norm referencing.

In the last Component of this Unit you were introduced to the nature of profiles and their advantages as well as the early stages of their design. This Component will consider the variety of formats available in the construction of profiles and look at self evaluation as an alternative (or complementary) strategy in this kind of assessment and record keeping. Finally an attempt will be made to evaluate profiling methods and the problems of administration.

Formats

What follows is a variety of examples from a number of sources to illustrate some of the techniques you may wish to consider. As each case is presented, try to identify what its purpose might be as well as its limitations.

Grade referencing (Estimates on a scale)

There are many forms of these where an attempt is made to estimate a trainee's competence or other qualities on a scale. All scales contain a 'descriptor' but they differ in the way grades are defined.

Methods, Techniques and Instruments (2)

Example 1.
Graded scale in which two poles are defined:

	1	2	3	4	5	
2. Uses mathematics without difficulty a) Carries out basic arithmetical operations with ease. b) Has no problems with fractions and decimals						2. Prefers to avoid situations involving mathematics. a) Has difficulty with basic arithmetic. b) Has difficulty with mathematics involving fractions and decimals.
3. Develops manipulative skills quickly a) Able to use basic workshop tools/laboratory equipment b) Produces clear drawings/sketches						3. Takes a lot of practice to develop manipulative skills a) Has difficulty in using workshop tools/laboratory equipment b) Has difficulty in producing clear drawings/sketches
4. Methodical						4. Haphazard in approach to problems

(Source: Technical Education Council)

These items are taken from a profile statement for a course in technician studies and represent some of the basic skills. The profile is in the form of two opposite statements with the position of the trainee between these two extremes being indicated on a five-point scale.

Example 2.
Graded scale in which only one pole is defined:

Perfection
1-5 miles

Unit General Objectives for the student are that he:	NA	3	2	1
A. Safety hazards 1. Identifies the hazards in a workshop environment. 2. Knows the appropriate procedure in the event of workshop accidents. 3. Knows the importance of safe electrical working in protecting life and property. 4. Knows procedures when persons are in electrical danger.				
B. Hand and Machine Processes 5. Selects hand tools for given tasks. 6. Performs working out exercises on plane surfaces such as marking out profiles. 7. Uses simple measuring equipment. 8. Carries out basic sheet metal operations, etc.				

(Source: Technical Education Council)

These items are taken from the same profile as Example 1 above, but the grading technique is different. Here an entry of × in NA means not yet assessed, 3 means needs more practice, 2 the student has shown basic competence and 1 the student has shown a high degree of competence.

Checkpoint

1. What criticism might be levelled at both the scales above?
2. Why do you think that only four or five points have been used instead of say, ten?
3. How could I check the reliability of the descriptors and scales I have adopted?

1. *It could be argued that the levels of performance and the nature of the experiences being assessed are imprecise and subjective.*
2. *Usually four to seven points are used on a scale because it is difficult to achieve greater accuracy by employing more categories or grades.*
3. *Once the profile has been designed it is sensible to check with a number of users that:*
* *the descriptors convey the same meaning for everyone;*
* *it is possible to obtain a clear and consistent picture of performance from the scales employed.*

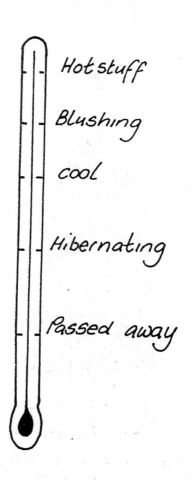

Hot stuff

Blushing

cool

Hibernating

Passed away

Example 3. Graded scales with each point defined

	A	B	C	D
CONDUCT	Always polite & well behaved	Usually polite & well behaved	Generally acceptable, occasional lapses	General conduct not satisfactory
ATTITUDE TO WORK	Always keen interested & industrious	Interested & trying to improve	Accepts all tasks & performs adequately	Lack of interest and enthusiasm

Items taken from a MSC profile of employment characteristics. Here is the same technique but using a different format.

PUNCTUALITY		
A		Always on time
B		Late only with good reason
C		Shows some lack of dependability
D		Regularly late
E		Invariably late

Norm referencing

This type of profile design is rarely used. It attempts to measure the performance of the trainee with a known group. He is placed near the top middle or bottom of that group. This can be noted in a number of ways e.g.

A	Top 5%
B	Above average
C	Average
D	Below average
E	Bottom 5%

or

	A	awarded to 10% of group
	B	awarded to 20% of group
	C	awarded to 40% of group
	D	awarded to 20% of group
	E	awarded to 10% of group

The grades can be applied to whatever skills appear on a profile.

Criterion referenced profiles

This type of profile attempts to describe what the trainee has done (or can do) and perhaps other qualities. No comparisons are made with others in the group and levels of performance should be explicit.

Example 1. Criterion Referenced Check List.

SKILLS DEALING WITH PEOPLE / TASK AND DATE							
A1 Establish working relationships with individuals							
A2 Establish working relationships as a member of a group							
A3 Relay given information orally to an individual							
A4 Relay given information orally to a group		The tutor ticks the box in which the student has demonstrated this skill in a particular assignment.					
A5 Ask questions in order to gain information for a specific purpose							
A6 Make and carry out arrangements (in accordance with a stated goal)							
etc.							

These are a few items from The Royal Society of Arts Practical Communication Skills section. The tutor ticks the box in which the student has demonstrated this skill in a particular assignment.

Example 2. Criterion Referenced Grid.
The criteria are arranged in order of difficulty. In this respect they resemble a scale. The example selected is of particular interest to trainers as it reproduces the Instructional Skills section of the Joint City and Guilds/MSC profile for the Supervision/Instruction Award.

While the criteria are difficult to define (and time consuming) they should be a more accurate description of the trainee's abilities.

PROFILE — INSTRUCTION SKILLS

Name: Phil Woodward

Objectives The trainee instructor/ supervisor should be able to:	Profile Grade			Tutor's Observations
	1	2	3	
1. Identify and select appropriate instruction methods and plans for instructing individuals and/or small groups	Identification and selection is restricted in most cases — limited grasp of methods available.	Identification and selection is correct in most cases — some lack of variety.	Identification and selection is correct in all cases	
Mark present status				
2. Make effective use of available resources for updating his own knowledge, and preparing instructing/ learning materials.	Makes only partial use of available resources and even then in a limited way.	Makes use of easily available resources, without seeking further afield.	Makes full and effective use of all resources for planning and preparation	
Mark present status				
3. Select and use appropriate resources including audio-visual materials, effectively in a range of instructing/ learning situations.	Uses learning aids and resources in a very limited way.	Makes use of available resources, but uses limited creativity.	Uses resources and aid to the fullest effect in the learning situation.	
Mark present status				

What follows is a series of items from profiles. Attempt to identify which format is being used from the following categories:

Graded scale with one pole defined
Graded scale with each point defined
Criterion referenced grid

1.

	BASIC LEVEL				HIGH LEVEL
WORKING IN A GROUP	Can co-operate with others when asked.	Can work with other members of the group to achieve common aims.	Can understand own position and results of own actions within a group.	Can be an active and decisive member of a group.	Can adopt a variety of roles in a group.

2.

	Excellent	Very Good	Below Average	Poor
1. Selection of appropriate tools				
2. Safe use of simple tools				
3. Co-ordination of hands				
4. Use of power tools				

3.

COOPERATIVENESS AND DEPENDABILITY		
A		Exceptionally cooperative and dependable
B		Very helpful and dependable
C		Works well with others and is reasonably dependable
D		Not much cooperation and some doubts as to dependability
E		Is difficult and can be a source of friction: Not reliable

1. Criterion referenced grid
2. Graded scale with one pole defined
3. Graded scale with each point defined.

Which of these are norm referenced and which are criterion referenced?

They are all criterion referenced in that they do not attempt to compare the trainee with other individuals or groups.

Administration

Timing: when should profiles be completed?
In most training, assessment is a continuous, ongoing process integrated with the teaching/learning activities. If it is to provide a useful guide to the needs of the learner, it should ideally involve the trainee in dialogue about progress made. Several profile formats provide for an assessment on entry to the programme as individuals vary in their initial level of competence. The regularity of assessment will depend upon the nature of the timing and the profile adopted.

Revision: Should profiles be fixed or open to revision?

The best training programmes are those which can be adapted to the needs of trainees. This revision can often be facilitated by assessment and recording methods which are both formative and summative. Similarly profile descriptors and performance criteria should constantly be open to revision. Users should be required to comment on problems and difficulties they encounter in administration and changes made. Trainees themselves should also be encouraged to

comment on the levels of performance expected and suggest possible revisions.

Who? Who should be involved in the completion of profiles.

It has already been suggested above that trainees should be involved as well as their instructors. This has several obvious advantages.

* The learner should be aware of what he has already achieved and what is still required.
* The programme is made clear and schedules of training can be negotiated.
* Completion of the profile with the trainee can provide a focus for guidance and counselling.
* The learner feels that he has some control over his own learning. Consequently motivation should be improved.

Assessors should accept that others may hold quite different opinions about a trainee's progress and performance. Consequently second opinions should be sought from colleagues particularly where assessments are particularly subjective e.g. as in personal qualities.

What are the disadvantages?

The advantages of profiling over traditional methods of assessment have already been stated. What then of the drawbacks? Some trainers are critical because they claim that:

* Grid style profiling lacks validity and reliability;

* Broad descriptions of skills and crude grades are open to casual judgements;
* It is just another process of attaching labels to learners rather than helping the learning process;
* The learning steps prescribed by grid style profiles are often too large and arbitrary;
* There is insufficient involvement of the trainee in his own learning and development.

To help you to make judgements about your present assessment practice the Scottish Vocational Preparation Unit has prepared a useful check list. If you have no assessment programme, check it against the City and Guilds 365 Vocational Preparation grid in the last component (Unit 4 Component 4).

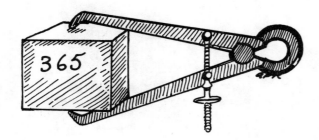

COURSE ASSESSMENT (Source: Scottish Vocational Preparation Unit)

Check these assessment issues against your present practice.

Tick the first box if the statement more or less fits your present situation.

Tick the second box if you think the statement **should** be a focus for your assessment policies or practices.

Create an agenda for developing assessment within your courses.

	Present Situation (tick)	Future Focus (tick)
assessment based on individual needs	☐	☐
allows appraisal of skills on entry to course	☐	☐
offers realistic and progressive targets	☐	☐
contributes to self-knowledge of trainees	☐	☐
based on idea of 'typical' clientele	☐	☐
positively assesses what students can do	☐	☐
fails set proportion of trainees	☐	☐
labels deficiencies	☐	☐
gives clear description of course activities	☐	☐
gives clear description of individual performances	☐	☐
realistic testing of skills/competencies	☐	☐
flexible and quick feedback	☐	☐
motivates trainees	☐	☐
helps course evaluation	☐	☐
has flexible procedures	☐	☐
offers course/individual contracts	☐	☐
allows learners say in assessment methods	☐	☐
uses peer assessment	☐	☐
avoids 1-4, A-D grading	☐	☐
uses consensus (tutor/learner) grades	☐	☐
uses non-teacher judges of competence/recorders of activities	☐	☐
learner control of records/reports	☐	☐
learner control of administration of records	☐	☐
use of checklists to analyse learning needs and activities	☐	☐
course goals and assessment methods match each other	☐	☐
assessment addresses too many audiences	☐	☐
assessment values well-balanced	☐	☐
good balance of life and vocational elements	☐	☐
assessment mainly learner-centred	☐	☐
assessment mainly employer-centred	☐	☐
assessment mainly sponsor-centred	☐	☐

Self assessment (trainee centred reviewing T.C.R.)

This represents a whole range of assessment strategies in which the trainee is central. They can be used in isolation, but are more effectively used in conjunction with traditional as well as profiling techniques. In general the trainee is encouraged to make statements about his:

    past experience
    present experiences
    future aspirations
    feelings and needs

WHY? By asking simple questions of himself such as:

The **trainee** is able to:
1. Make sense of his experiences
2. Recognise his own strengths and weaknesses
3. Take a measure of responsibility for his own learning
4. Monitor his own progress
5. Develop a sense of responsibility

and it helps **trainers** to:
1. Identify individual needs (and possibly renegotiate objectives)
2. Make better judgements about a trainee's progress
3. Supplement other forms of assessment and records
4. Motivate his trainees.

▰▰▰

1. Outline three disadvantages of grid profiles.
2. What kind of information would you expect to collect in a T.C.R.?

1. a. Can lack validity and reliability
b. Descriptions of performance often broad and crude and lead to casual judgements
c. Appending labels does not help the learner
d. Learning steps often arbitrary and too large
e. Too little involvement of the learner in his own learning
2. First of all have you remembered that TCR means Trainee Centred Reviewing? TCR seeks to find out what the learner thinks about what he has experienced, what he is doing now, what he wants to achieve in the future and how he feels about it.

HOW? While dialogue between the trainee and his supervisor forms an important part of Trainee Centred Reviewing (TCR) other systematic forms of recording are important.
> e.g. Diaries
> Logs and timesheets. Personal questionnaires and checklists
> Reviews and reports of experience

Diaries

Personal diaries, because they are not prescribed by headings or check lists, can reveal a great deal about the progress, feelings and attitudes of the trainee. However because of this lack of direction some may be inhibited from revealing what they might regard as irrelevant information. There will also be some for whom literacy is a problem. Consequently it may be better to turn to a more structured format.

Logs and timesheets
Here there is a clearer indication of what should be recorded.

Example 1 — Timesheet

Timesheet   Week No.

DAY		TASK OR PRODUCT	MATERIALS INVOLVED	SKILLS AND TECHNIQUES INVOLVED	TIME TAKEN (hours)	GENERAL COMMENTS
MONDAY	AM					
	PM					
TUESDAY	AM					
	PM					
WEDNESDAY	AM					
	PM					
THURSDAY	AM					
	PM					
FRIDAY	AM					
	PM					

Source: Pearce *et al* (1981)
While this is a valuable record of experience, only in the 'general comments' column is there space for evaluating the tasks.

Example 2 — Log

WEEKLY/DAILY RECORD

Week number.............

1.   What new jobs have you done this week?
2.   What new skills have you learned?
3.   How did you learn these?
4.   What did you find easiest to do and why?
5.   What did you find hardest to do and why?
6.   What tools, equipment, machinery have you used this week?

Questionnaires and checklists

Here are two examples using a questionnaire format.

Example 1 – Questionnaire

Personal Assessment Form   Name

                                  Department

This form is to help you to think about your experience in this department and to think about how the things you have learned can help you in your future career.

1. List the jobs you have learned about in this department ....
2. What skills have you gained while in this department? ....
3. What has been best about working in this department? ....
4. What has been difficult about working in this department? ...
5. How will working in this department help you in any future jobs you may have? ....

If you have any further comments to make about your experience so far please make them below.

Source: Pearce *et al* (1981)

Example 2 — Questionnaire

Trainee Self Review weekly Report
WEEK DATE:
What did you most enjoy at work last week? ....
Why?...
What did you least enjoy at work last week?.........................
Why?...
Did you do any new jobs last week? ....
What were they? ....
Did you learn any new skills last week? ....
What were they?..
How was your time-keeping last week? ....
Did you learn anything about health and safety last week?........
What was it?...
What did you do on day release last week? ....
How did these things help you?.................................
My suggestions for improving (state training programme) are: ...
Have you any new objectives? ....

Source: Pearce *et al* (1981)

Both examples illustrate how factual information about the nature of the task has been combined with self assessments and evaluation. Many of the questions are 'open' thus allowing the trainee to include any issues he considers to be important.

Example 3 – Checklist

TRAINEE SELF REVIEW: GOALS (OBJECTIVES)
Which of the following would you say are reasons why you came to (name of organisation) or are goals (objectives) which you would like to achieve while on the scheme.

PERSONAL
To get to know myself better.
To like myself more.
To become more confident.
To become more self disciplined.
To know more about what I want to do with my life.
To get better at making decisions.
To get better at reading and writing.
To manage my money better.
To learn how to manage a home.
To learn more about personal health and hygiene, contraception etc.
To get on better with other people.
To understand other people more.
To communicate with others more.
To trust others more.
To make new friends.
WORK
To get to know the sort of job I would like.
To know the sort of job that would suit me.
To want to get a job more.
To want to go to work more.
To enjoy work more.
To get on better with the people whom I work with.
To work better with teams of "groups" of people.
To know where I can find out about jobs available.
To learn how to write letters of application.
To learn how to fill in application forms.
To become better in interviews.
To become safer at work.
To learn special skills in shop work or warehouse work.
LEISURE
To know the range of spare time activities open to me.
To know where these can be done, how much they would cost me.
To know about possible holiday opportunities.
To know how to arrange holidays.
To make better use of my leisure time.
To make better use of my holidays.
OTHER ISSUES
To know more about:
Law and the Police.
Rights and responsibilities.
Race relations.
Politics and government.
Current affairs.
How companies work.
Public and private industry.
Trade Unions.
Rights at work.

Is there anything else you would like to learn about while you are a trainee?

Source: Pearce *et al* (1981)

In this case the list is a series of objectives to which the trainee is asked to respond by ticking those with which he identifies. It is obviously a good basis for follow up by the supervisor in counselling/guidance sessions.

Reviews and reports of experience

These can take the form of an essay in which the trainee writes freely of his experience, achievements and feelings. However, many find this a daunting task.

A simple way to help is to provide a series of uncompleted sentences (stems) which the trainee is asked to complete.

Examples of some useful "stems"

My job is ....

I am responsible to...

The thing I like most about the training programme is
....

The thing I dislike most about the training programme is...

I like working with ....because.....................

I am having problems with ....

I am most successful at..

I have benefitted most from ....

Administration

* Self assessment requires time specifically set aside for supervisor to discuss progress with their trainees.

* Good personal relationships are essential if the process is to be effective. This means acceptance of the trainee in terms of his own values and aspirations.

* Trainees should be encouraged to reflect on their experiences and identify their own needs.

* The actual recording should be done in a notebook or on cards to be inserted into a loose-leaf file.

Which of the self-assessment procedures could you use for each of the following purposes:

1. What tasks have been completed and when.
2. What particular difficulties the trainee has experienced with fellow workers.
3. Future aspirations.
4. Attitudes to a particular unit of the training programme.

As you can see, several different procedures can be adopted in most cases.
1. Log, timesheet, diary
2. Questionnaire, Review (using "stems")
3. Check list, questionnaire, reviews (using "stems")
4. Questionnaire, comments on log, reviews (using "stems")

Summary

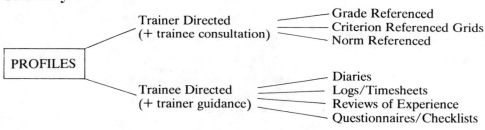

Objectives

Having completed this Component, you should now be able to:

1. Recognise the variety of formats used for grid profiles.
2. Outline the advantages and disadvantages of this form of profiling.
3. Outline the administrative procedures with respect to when assessments should be made and by whom.
4. Be aware of the place of self assessment (trainee centred reviewing) in the compilation of profiles, and its advantages.
5. Recognise the procedures available in TCR.

NOTE: More detailed advice on self-assessments may be found in Study Unit 5 of this Package.

Bibliography

FEU (1982) *Profiles*, FE Curriculum Review and Developing Unit.

Law Bill (1984) *Uses and Abuses of Profiling*, Harper Educational.

Pearce, B. *(et al)* (1981) *Trainee Centred Reviewing*, CCDU Leeds University.

Scottish Vocational Preparation Unit (1982) *Assessment in Youth Training — Made to Measure*, SVPU.

Acknowledgements

We are grateful to the following for their permission to use examples of profiles and trainee centred review materials:

   CCDU Leeds University
   Further Education Curriculum Review and Development Unit
   Royal Society of Arts
   School Council
   Scottish Vocational Preparation Unit

Component 6:

Interviewing

Key Words

 Selection interview; appraisal interview; job profile; person profile; open questions; closed questions; leading questions; reflecting back questions.

NOTE: No checkpoints have been included in the text. They may be found on the accompanying audio-cassette which you should play after completing the Component.

Introduction

An Interview is probably the most common form of assessment used in making critical judgements about people for employment, training and promotion. The problem is that it can be the least valid and reliable. It is often a 'seat of the pants' affair performed by trainers and managers who are lulled by habit because they have done it so many times before. Confessing that you are an inadequate interviewer is about as likely as admitting that you are a poor driver. Rarely is training given and early mistakes are repeated because there is no one to evaluate the techniques employed. In spite of the fact that such faith is placed in interviews, they are at worst "off the cuff" events which are unfair to the candidates involved.

Interviewing is a high level skill which requires training, thought and practice.

Selection or appraisal?

As far as we are concerned interviews are used for two main purposes.

Selection

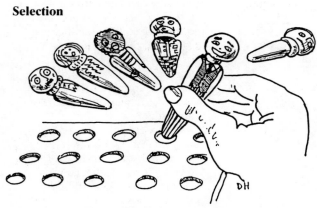

To get the right recruits for training

To match people to jobs.

Appraisal

To assess progress

Review the effectiveness of training

Negotiate future action

As these two types of interview are quite different in their purpose, preparation and conduct, they will be considered separately.

The selection inverview — The process

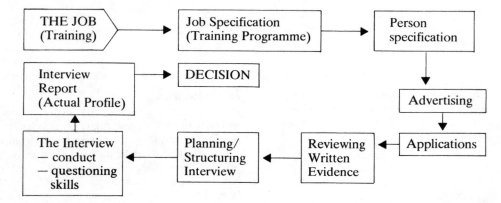

Although the selection interview is only **one part** of the decision-making process it is frequently assumed to be the most important. Whether this is justified or not, every attempt should be made to make it as valid and reliable as is humanly possible. You should also realise that an interview provides a candidate with an opportunity to assess your organisation before he makes **his** decision. Many good prospects are lost because the occasion fails to inform, impress or attract those who have other options.

Job specification (or job profile)

As with practically every method of assessment the starting point is to take a look at the job (or training programme) and try to define the different elements it demands. Too often we start by trying to specify the kind of **person** we are looking for. That should be the second step.

A job specification requires an analysis of:
* Activities
* Responsibilities
* Conditions
* Training needed

Activities:	Main purpose of the department Essential features of the job Occasional/possible features of the job
Responsibilities:	To whom? What responsibility is carried upwards? For whom? What responsibility is carried downwards? For what? e.g. machinery, accounts, stocktaking
Conditions:	Salary, career, structure, hours of work, holidays.
Training:	Phasing of training Knowledge of skills involved Assessment and evaluation of training.

Example: Secretary for Sales Department.

Activities:	Required to maintain telephone contact with sales representatives, process orders and invoices. Shorthand — 100 w.p.m. Typing — 50 w.p.m. Reception Filing — Storage and retrieval of customer details Word processing.
Responsibilities:	Responsible to area sales manager. Responsible for training and supervision of office junior.
Conditions:	£6,500 p.a. with annual increments (3 × £250) 38 hour week. 20 days annual holiday + bank holidays.
Training:	On-job training in word processing and invoice/accounting systems used.

Person specification (or ideal person profile)

Now you are in a position to translate this into the kind of **person** you want. This should result in an 'ideal' person specification clear to everyone involved in selection.

You may find it useful to use some system which divides a person into relevant qualities.

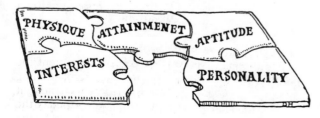

Here is one suggestion which can be adapted to your particular needs.

Physique:	What physical capacities does the job require? Is normal good health required or could a handicapped or disabled person carry out the job? Does the job involve particular strengths, endurance, mobility? Are better than average standards of hearing or eye sight important?
Attainment:	What background **knowledge** is called for? Should a minimal educational standard be set (e.g. GCE 'O' level Maths, English, Physics). What **skills** should the applicants possess (e.g. level of spoken English, typing speed)?
Aptitudes:	**Mental** — this refers to the candidates capacity to learn. **Special** — this is concerned with any particular aptitude for acquiring specialist skills e.g. mechanical, technical, craft.
Interests and motivation:	What kind of interests will the job satisfy e.g. to work with people, computers, to create? In other words, what kind of motivation does the activity require?
Personality:	What particular personality characteristics are called for? Does the job require one to meet people or work in relative isolation? Does it demand independence, responsiblity, initiative, drive, enthusiasm, patience, sensitivity, tough mindedness, resilience? There are scores of words which could be used to describe the disposition of the person most likely to do the job successfully.
Circumstances:	While this refers to the opportunities and conditions of employment it also includes housing, travel and family implications (e.g. periods of separation).

One thing you should remember — **be realistic**. You are not trying to employ the archangel Gabriel. A useful strategy is to distinguish between what is ESSENTIAL and what is only DESIRABLE. Perhaps there should also be a third category CONTRA-INDICATIONS i.e. those characteristics which would be unsuitable in a candidate. Some applicants may be too highly qualified, ambitious or articulate to fit into the organisation and their prescribed role within it.

Advertising — applications

Once the person specification has been drawn up you should consider how potential applicants can be reached. Although it is an important step in the process, it is outside the scope of the Component.

Letters and forms of application will provide you with much of the information you require to decide on which candidates are likely to match the "ideal" person specification.

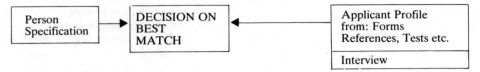

Person Specification	→	DECISION ON BEST MATCH	←	Applicant Profile from: Forms References, Tests etc.
				Interview

Preparing for the interview
REVIEW OF EVIDENCE.

The first step in preparing for the interview is to short-list the applicants by putting together what written evidence is available and the person specification. Apart from application forms and references you may also have results from tests or simulation exercises. From this information you will be able to discover some aspects of the applicant's profile which match your requirements. You should note any gaps, doubts and possible difficulties.

THE INTERVIEW AGENDA (or PLAN)

Having eliminated candidates who are obviously unsuitable the interview agenda can be drawn up. Of course the interviewer should be prepared to be flexible and follow up issues which were unforseen, but in the interests of efficiency a formal structure will provide order and make sure that you don't miss anything. What is more you need to make the best use of the limited time available.

There are several plans which have been used successfully in the past, but as you will see from the examples, they are just different routes to the same place.

Plan 1. Direct questions on the candidate's
   PAST: Education, early life, past jobs and relevant experience.
   PRESENT: Current job, attitudes, abilities, judgements, circumstances.
   FUTURE: Aspirations, career objectives
   CURRENT JOB technical aspects
                human aspects
   PAST JOBS   Selected items
   EDUCATION & TRAINING
   PERSONAL & DOMESTIC TOPICS

Plan 2. This follows the pattern of the person specification outlined earlier.
   PHYSIQUE
   ATTAINMENTS
   APTITUDES
   INTERESTS AND MOTIVATION
   PERSONALITY
   PERSONAL CIRCUMSTANCES

Whatever plan you decide to adopt, a reasonable period should be reserved towards the end of every interview for the **candidate** to put questions about the job and conditions of employment.

Having worked out the agenda it is worth listing:
* Key questions you will put to every candidate
* Questions you will put to particular candidates to fill in gaps or explore beyond the written evidence available.

Questioning technique will be covered later under 'The Interview'

PREPARING THE ENVIRONMENT

An interview is a stressful occasion in which every effort should be made to generate a calm atmosphere. You will not gain a true picture of the candidates if they find the situation intimidating. It will help if:
* They are courteously received.
* You give the whole of your attention to the interview. Try to avoid interruptions (e.g. telephone).
* You try to be punctual and stick to the agreed timetable.
* Seating arrangements are given thought. They can either intimidate or produce a relaxed atmosphere. Creating barriers between the parties, like a large desk and a battery of telephones, should be avoided. Easy chairs arranged at a comfortable angle to each other are less likely to inhibit relaxed dialogue.

Arrange the seating so that the candidate is not at a psychological disadvantage.

The interview
CONDUCTING THE INTERVIEW

ONE TO ONE. The focus will be on the one to one situation rather than the panel or board interview as it is generally considered to be less intimidating. Some candidates may cope more easily with a board but this may not be relevant to the job. If more than one opinion is required sequential interviews can be arranged with different interviewers.

OPENING. Allow time for the candidate to become familiar with his surroundings. A warm welcome and sensitivity to his feelings of apprehension will help to establish a rapport within which the real work can be done. Enquiries about the journey or some mutual interest will help the applicant to relax and warm up before launching into the main business. You might then lead in by outlining the form the interview will take.

QUESTIONING

Some general rules:
* Be a good listener. Smiles of encouragement and a friendly gaze show that you are interested.
* Don't talk too much. You are there to discover what you can about the applicant not to lecture.
* Make sure the questions and answers stick to what is relevant.
* Although you should try to keep to the plan you have prepared, follow up leads presented by the candidate.

TYPES OF QUESTIONS

What kind of questions are you going to ask the candidates? Many interviewers make the mistake of slipping into a pattern of 'closed' or 'leading' questions. These are questions which produce simple yes/no responses or simple factual information. Although they have limitations they are useful for providing a clarifying factual detail.

Examples of **closed** and **leading** questions:
"How long did you spend on your Youth Training Scheme?" is a **closed** question.
"Am I correct in thinking that you enjoyed the experience" is a **leading** question.
Questions which give the applicant an opportunity to reveal more of himself are **open** questions. They usually include words like 'why', 'how', 'compare', 'explain', 'what', 'tell me about'.

Examples of **Open** Questions.
"Why did you prefer to work in the typing pool?"
"Explain the difference between the marketing policy of the two organisations."
"How did you come to hear of our training programme?"
"Tell me about your interest in computers."

Some questions require the candidate to **reflect back** on what he has said to enlarge on his answer and enable you to probe for information or attitudes. The skill is to listen carefully and select significant cues.

Examples of **Reflecting back** questions:
"What in particular did you find unhelpful in the management structure?"
"You said that you had been treated unfairly. Tell me about it."
"Can you say why you found the task difficult?"

The diagram below summaries the main categories of questions with examples, suggested uses and limitations.

TYPES OF QUESTIONS

Type of Question	Example	Use	Limitations
OPEN ENDED	"Why did you decide to take that job?"	To open up an area for discussion without biasing the response	Will invite a talkative applicant to give a long speech
REFLECTING BACK	"You mentioned the rewards, tell me about them"	To probe something that has been said which seems worth exploring further	Takes time and may lose the thread of previous discussion
CLOSED	"Did you start the job on 1st September?"	To clarify a factual detail or give a nervous person an easy question to answer	May not produce any material of value for later discussion
LEADING	"You took the job because it had more responsibility — am I right?"	To indicate an aspect that interests the interviewer or to save time	Gives clues about the bias of the interviewer and is unlikely to obtain a true or full answer

(Bolton, G. M. (1983) *Interviewing for Selection Decisions*, NFER-Nelson).

NON-VERBAL COMMUNICATIONS

The Interviewer: A skilled interviewer gives the right signals at the right time. He should avoid scowls or glances at his watch which imply criticism and impatience, whereas eye to eye contact and encouraging nods and smiles convey interest and support. Too much time spent on note taking may suggest detachment as well as preventing you from concentrating on the applicants' responses.

The Applicant: What the applicant has to say is only part of the picture from which you will be making judgements. Whether you are conscious of it or not, you will be drawing inferences from the following non-verbal cues:

Appearance: e.g. dress, build
Touching behaviour: e.g. handshake
Body language: e.g. gesture, posture, eye contact and hand movement

This will present you with a problem because, while it is possible to pay too much attention to non-verbal behaviour, it can be useful. Non-verbal expressions are difficult to disguise and may therefore be the most reliable indication of feelings and attitudes.

Prejudices — Examine yours. Although it is impossible to suppress personal preferences when judging others, it is at least worth trying to analyse your attitudes on such things as dress, the opposite sex, ethnic and cultural minorities, regional accents.

Having examined his prejudices a good interviewer can then allow for them in the interpretation of the assessment data.

CLOSING THE INTERVIEW

After you have worked your way through your plan, applicants should have an opportunity of asking questions. It is then important to summarise and outline the next step e.g. approximately how long it will take to come to a decision and how will he be informed. The interviewee should finally be thanked warmly for applying and attending.

Making your decisions

Too many interviewers make up their minds on impressions from the interview alone. If you have taken the trouble to produce an **Ideal Person Profile** it needs to be matched against the **Actual Profiles** of applicants who were interviewed.

The actual profiles will already contain the information from the review of written evidence received earlier (e.g. application form, references). They can now be supplemented from the notes taken at interview. You may just wish to make notes against the headings, used for the Ideal Personal Profile e.g.

Physique
Attainment
Aptitudes
Interest and Motivation
Personality
Circumstances

Alternatively you may wish to adopt a numerical rating scale which attempts to assess how well a person matches the specification.

Example: (from Bolton, G. M. (1983))

5 = Fully matches the part of the specification with no doubts at all
4 = Matches very well with only slight discrepancies in minor respects
3 = Matches fairly well but has weaknesses in a few respects
2 = Matches in some respects but there are important omissions
1 = Does not match specification.

The following represents an assessment of applicants X, Y & Z by means of references, application forms, simulation exercises as well as interview.

Examine your prejudices

DISPLAY OF DATA FOR DECISION-TAKING

	X	Y	Z
PHYSICAL MAKE UP Essential: Fit, no allergies, aged 17-23. Smart, groomed, fluent in reaction to public Desirable: Aged 19-21, good diction	5	4	4 Health needs investigation
ATTAINMENTS Essential: 2 'A' levels, 5 'O' levels including Maths & English Desirable: Responsibility at school, work experience in service industry	3 subjects not suitable	4 More academic than needed	5
GENERAL INTELLIGENCE Essential: Think clearly and quickly Desirable: Creative and flexible Contra-indication: Not an 'intellectual'	5	3 Lacking in ideas	5
SPECIAL APTITUDES Essential: Generally numerate, responsive to people Desirable: Effective written and oral communication for general business	5 Quick in response	2½ Inappropriate humour	4 Communicates well, given time
INTERESTS Essential: Wants variety and responsibility relating to people Contra-indication: High salary aims	5	2	4 No interest in variety
DISPOSITION Essential: Can earn respect and cope with crises Desirable: Honest and consistent with people	5	1 Responds aggressively to crisis	4 Doubts about ability to lead
CIRCUMSTANCES Essential: Able to relocate with no hindrance Desirable: Driving licence	5	4	4 Health might limit relocation
	33	20½	30

It would be foolish to assume that the candidate with the highest total should automatically be appointed. This may be the case if an acceptable minimum standard has been achieved in each attribute, but one significant weakness may rule out someone who is suitable in every other respect, e.g. a person who fails to meet the health requirements. On careful examination it may emerge that the highest scorer does not necessarily have the most suitable blend of abilities.

Validation

Once a decision has been made there is a tendency to assume that the selection process has finished when in fact there are two further steps;

1. The submission of a report for the guidance of trainers and departmental heads responsible for induction. This might suggest what remedial action could be taken for weakness or indicate particular programmes of training.

2. Testing the validity of the selection process. How effective are the predictions made by the recruiters? You should make frequent checks on those you have recruited for employment or training to find out if they have lived up to your expectations. Should you be making frequent errors of judgement you will need to review the strategies adopted.

Summary

Check that you:

* are clear about the job and the person you want to employ
* structure the interview
* review written evidence
* prepare the physical environment
* enable the candidate to relax
* don't talk too much, listen and pick up leads.
* think about the type of questions you will use
* try to be objective and avoid your prejudices
* write a report
* test your judgements against the future performance of those you have selected

The appraisal interview

Although many of the principles of good selection interview technique hold good for the appraisal interview, there are several differences as this form of assessment is used to judge the performance of those already in employment.

Purpose?

EVALUATE PERFORMANCE

1. How is the employee/trainee doing?

2. Does he meet the required standards of performance?

3. Are relationships with superiors and subordinates satisfactory?

IMPROVE PERFORMANCE

1. Provide support, counselling and training.

2. Improve commitment and motivation.

3. Provide career guidance.

4. Improve co-operation and team work.

What is expected?

As with any other form of assessment, appraisal must be conducted against the background of the job description and the required standards of performance. Advice on this has already been given in the section on recruitment interviewing and in several Components of Package 4.

Guidelines for effective appraisal

✱ If the main purpose is to improve a person's effectiveness at work, it should involve DIALOGUE. Only the supervisor or immediate superior will have sufficient knowledge of the employee and the job to do the appraisal.

✱ Both parties need to PREPARE for the interview as off-the-cuff judgements are rarely of value. It will help if each has a set of guidelines well in advance of the meeting. Below are examples:

APPRAISEE'S PREPARATION FORM

BEFORE THINKING ABOUT THE POINTS BELOW
READ YOUR JOB DESCRIPTION AND
CONSIDER POINTS RAISED AT YOUR LAST
APPRAISAL.

1. PREPARE FOR THE MEETING.
   Read your job description.
   If you have been appraised before have you
   achieved the aims set?
   Outline any problems you have encountered in
   the past year.
   What could have been done better?
   What training do you need?
   Do you enjoy your job? What in particular?
   What parts do you find easy, difficult, boring,
   interesting?
   Think about the future. What do you want to do?
   Become?

2. AT THE MEETING.
   Try to come to an agreement with your
   supervisor about:
   How well you have done since the last
   appraisal.
   Plans to improve your performance.
   Aims for next year.
   Realistic hopes for your future.

APPRAISER'S PREPARATION FORM
APPRAISEE'S NAME_____

BEFORE COMPLETING THE FORM READ THE
APPRAISEE'S JOB DESCRIPTION AND
CONSIDER POINTS RAISED AT HIS LAST
APPRAISAL.

1. Note points from last appraisal and action taken.
2. List main tasks.
3. Which have been performed well and why?
4. Which parts of the job have not been carried out
   well and why?
5. What potential does the appraisee have for
   further development?
6. What targets have you set for the coming year?
7. What training is necessary? How can this be
   achieved?

At the actual meeting the principles of good selection
interviewing still apply:

* Avoid interruptions and organise the **physical environment** to provide a fairly relaxed atmosphere.

* Be prepared to **listen**. You should be open to ideas different from your own.

* Ask **questions** which will promote discussion e.g. "What extra help will you need to improve?" Avoid questions which provoke 'yes', 'no' responses.

* Write a **report** based on the preparation sheets.

Conclusion

At the end of the interview summarise the main points which should include:
> Praise for work well done,
> What needs to be improved,
> What guidance or training will be given,
> What follow-up is planned.

The whole procedure is more likely to be effective if the meeting can end with positive words of encouragement.

Objectives

Selection Interviewing

You should be able to:

1. Plan a job specification which can be translated into an 'ideal' person profile.
2. Recognise the importance of preparation by:
   Reviewing written evidence
   Planning and structuring the interview in advance.
3. Create the right environment for relaxed dialogue.
4. Structure questions which encourage an applicant to reveal as much of himself as possible.
5. Recognise the importance of producing a comprehensive interview report.

Appraisal Interviewing

You should be able to:

1. Recognise the importance and purpose of the appraisal interview as a method of assessment.
2. Prepare for the interview.
3. Create the right climate for a frank exchange of views.
4. See the importance of agreeing on the positive and negative features of performance and future action.

▟▟▟ Checkpoint

The accompanying audio-cassette tape presents a series of interview situations which you are asked to evaluate using information from this component.

Bibliography

Bolton, G. M. (1983) *Interviewing for Selection Decisions*, NFER-Nelson.
Scott, J. & Rochester, A. (1984) *Effective Management Skills*, Brit. Inst. Management.
Civil Service Dept. (1971) *Job Appraisal Review*, HMSO.
Higham, M. (1979) *The ABC of Interviewing*, IPM.

Acknowledgements

We are grateful to NFER-Nelson for their permission to use material from G. M. Bolton (1983) *Interviewing for Selection Decisions.*

 Tutor seen work

a) Plan a programme for the selection of suitable candidates for appointment to work roles or training in your organisation.
b) Construct a profile which you would find useful in recording a trainee's achievements.

Study Unit 5

Self Evaluation

Component 1:

What is Self Evaluation?

Key Ideas

 Perspectives on the meaning of "training"; establishing criteria; factors in using the evaluation process; identifying the evaluators.

Key Objectives

1. For you to understand the connection between training and evaluation.
2. For you to be able to define self evaluation.
3. For you to be aware of the different factors involved in self-evaluation in a training context.

Introduction

This Study Unit is specifically about self evaluation. That means that there will be a definite focus on the ways in which trainers, trainees and training organisations can evaluate their own performance. In addition to that definite focus there must be an additional factor. Self evaluation raises a number of questions about the actual meaning of "training". Consequently our understanding of the nature of training must also be examined.

During the course of this component you will explore the concept of "training" and will be in a position to understand how the various perspectives on the meaning of "training" effect evaluation.

As you explore the various perspectives on the meaning of "training" it will become clear that "training" in its widest sense actually requires self-evaluation. In other words self evaluation will come to be seen as an essential feature of effective training rather than an optional luxury.

▰▰▰ Checkpoint

We don't seem to have got very far and yet we may already need to pause for thought.

What does the verb "to train" mean to you? Some possible suggestions are listed below. Just put a tick alongside any of the suggestions that you find most reasonable.

to draw on	
to instruct	
to discipline	
to cause to grow in a desired way	
to prepare for performance	
to direct	
to be under drill	

Look at the items that you have ticked.

Try and put them together so that they form a general statement about training.

At this point you should pause a little longer to consider the implications of your statement.

For example, if you have used expressions like "drill" or "discipline" what implications does that have for the work that you actually do?

At this point you may be aware that you are actually entering into the process of self evaluation and we have not yet even defined what we mean by that term.

Defining self evaluation

Evaluation is the process of gathering information about what **is** presently happening and comparing the results of that information-gathering with a view of what **should** be happening. Self evaluation is where the individual establishes for himself how well he is doing in the light of training goals that he understands. That definition of evaluation requires some explanation and in order to focus particular attention on self evaluation three questions must be asked. These questions will take us into considerations about the product and the process of training, ways by which individuals can understand the information they gathered, some thoughts on the conditions necessary for involving individuals in their own evaluation. That definition of evaluation requires some explanation and in order to focus particular attention on self evaluation three questions must be asked.

1. **About what is information being gathered?**
2. **What is involved in having a view of what should be happening?**
3. **Who is evaluating?**

These questions may appear to be a little daunting but really they aren't. If we take each question in turn various points about self evaluation will become clear.

1. About what is information being gathered?

That rather odd question has two broad answers.

The first answer is that the information will be about the achievements/attainments/progress of the trainees. In this sense the trainees can be thought of as being the PRODUCT of training. Training can be thought of as the means of generating a PRODUCT, namely a trained worker.

The second answer is that the information will be about the effectiveness of the training. This answer highlights the idea that training is not simply a matter of generating a product, it is also, in itself, a PROCESS. By PROCESS we are referring to the manner of working with trainees. It refers simply to "what is going on", or to the methods that are used in training.

▨▨▨

To make the idea of PROCESS clearer make a list of the methods used in the training with which you are involved. For example, demonstrations by the trainer, practical practice sessions, written handouts, the use of video, utilisation of the trainees' own experience and so on.

So far we have seen that training is a means of generating a product and it is also a process.

The two distinct aspects of training indicate two different views on the nature of training.

One view is that training is to do with bringing about defined changes in the trainees, with promoting achievement, particularly in the area of knowledge and skills.

The other view is that training is a process which is far more complex, the entire effects of which may not be entirely measurable, may not even appear in the short term and may vary between individual trainees.

At first glance it may seem obvious that what is really required from training is that the trainee should change in some defined way connected with acquiring certain knowledge and skills.

If we can evaluate that change then that is all that needs to be done.

Thus you may say that the trainee should learn to operate a certain type of machine according to the specifications for that machine and adhere to particular safety standards. Further, it should be relatively straightforward for a skilled trainer to evaluate the trainee's competence in these functions. Yet it is not quite as simple as that for two reasons.

(a) Training involves not simply learning how to do something but it also involves evoking a willingness to do that thing. The trainee must also be **willing** to operate the machine according to the specifications set out by the makers of the machine and be **willing** to adhere to the safety standards of which he is aware.

(b) There is a necessary relationship between the training process and the trainee's achievement, the product of the training

We can examine these two areas in more detail.

a) WILLINGNESS

The effectiveness of any training that is offered will be diminished if that training concentrates simply on the acquisition of knowledge and skills. Some attention must also be given to the development of attitudes, of which being willing to exercise the knowledge and skills imparted by the training must be paramount.

How this WILLINGNESS manifests itself in a particular context is, of course, something that will vary from context to context. Some examples of what I mean follow.

A receptionist.
She must be able and willing to use people's names.

Switchboard Operator.
She must be able and willing to speak clearly.

Clerical Assistant.
He must be able and willing to perform routine or even at times boring tasks.

The result is that training is not simply about imparting knowledge and skills. It is also about the development of certain personal qualities that are also essential for the effective performance of the task.

Read through the following list of personal qualities.

"PERSONAL QUALITIES"

1. I am cheerful with people at work.
2. I can get on with a job without supervision once I've been shown.
3. I like to be busy, so I look for useful jobs to do when work is slack.
4. I try to understand other people's points of view.
5. I can turn up on time and keep a good attendance record.
6. I am good at working in a team and doing my fair share.
7. I am willing to do difficult or dirty jobs.
8. I am good at getting on with other people.
9. I am tidy and dress suitably for what I am doing.
10. I can make an extra effort when necessary.
11. I can stick at a job even if I find it a bit boring.
12. I ask questions if necessary to understand what I have to do.
13. I get on with what I am doing without being distracted.
14. I like learning new things.
15. I am willing to work shifts or odd hours.
16. I use common sense and people know they can rely on me.
17. I am good at listening to instructions and getting them right.
18. I have a good general health record.
19. I remember people's names and use them.
20. I don't get upset when I'm told that I've made a mistake.

In the space provided make a note of the qualities that you think are essential in each of the areas of work listed. You can do this simply by writing the appropriate number in the box. Try to limit your choice to a maximum of six.

Garage Mechanic	
Builder's Labourer	
Catering Assistant	
Shop Assistant	

What are the qualities, from the list, that are essential for effectiveness in the area for which you provide training?

Are there any other qualities, which are not listed, which are also essential?

203

REPORT BACK
PERSONAL QUALITIES
The numbers against each worker correspond to the numbers on the original list of qualities. They represent the qualities that we feel are important for each worker. You, of course, may feel differently.

Garage Mechanic	2, 3, 5, 7, 8, 13
Builder's Labourer	1, 2, 5, 6, 12, 18
Catering Assistant	3, 5, 6, 10, 12, 15
Shop Assistant	1, 4, 5, 9, 11, 20

At this stage we should remember that training is more than being concerned with knowledge and skills. It also involves a concern for attitudes and personal qualities.

On this level alone it is important to involve the trainees in their own evaluation of these essential attitudes and qualities. That may be the most accurate form of evaluation that you as trainer have available.

Furthermore, both you and the organisation as a whole will have to seriously question how effective you have been in developing these qualities.

This, therefore is the first of two reasons for saying that training is not merely to do with the promoting of certain knowledge and skills. We can now move on to the second reason.

b) THE RELATIONSHIP BETWEEN THE TRAINEE'S ACHIEVEMENT AND THE TRAINING PROCESS

If we return to our original, rather odd, questions, "What is it that information is being gathered about?" you will remember that one answer was that the information would be about the product of the training namely the achievement of the trainee. The other answer was that the information would be about the process of training.

However, neither answer is complete or satisfactory by itself for three reasons.

1. If we simply collect information about the achievement of the trainee what we in fact obtain has a rather limited use. Such information cannot, for example, be used to make decisions about how to improve achievement unless there is also some reference to the training process.

   For instance, suppose we know that a trainee is not making progress. We know this because we have assessed his achievement. It becomes necessary to find out why there is a lack of progress. Consequently the process of training, the methods of training and the context of the training, must be examined. It might be that something is going wrong with the training, that it is not as efficient as it should be.

2. If we simply collect information about the process of training, again we have something with only a limited value. What sense are we to make of such

information unless we also have information about the level of achievement of the trainees? Only in this way can the information about the process of training be interpreted. Only in this way is it possible to decide whether or not the process of training is appropriate for its task.

3. After making some changes in the training it would be worthwhile to see if they had produced any effect. Indeed, it would be rather foolish not to make such an inquiry. Therefore, again both product and process information are required.

In becoming clear about the two aspects of training we have been able to answer the first question that needs to be asked in order to define SELF EVALUATION.

Evaluation is partly defined as the gathering of information. The information to be gathered will be concerned with both the product and the process of the training.

▰▰▰

1. What is meant by the product of training?
2. What is meant by the process of the training?
3. Give **three** reasons for arguing that information must be gathered about both the product and the process of the training.

REPORT BACK
1. *Think about what your training is for.*
2. *Think about how your training is conducted.*
3. *Your answer should reflect a) a concern for knowledge, skills and qualities and b) a concern for training methods that are actually congruent with the product, reviewing and improving training.*

CONCLUSION

Self evaluation means that information will be gathered about:

* the achievement of the trainees; not just knowledge and skills but also attitudes or qualities.
* the process of the training; the methods, resources and style of the trainer as well as the context of the training namely the training organisation – and that the information will be gathered by the individuals to whom the information refers.

However, there is more to self-evaluation than the gathering of information.

The additional aspects of self evaluation have already been raised in part by the conclusion that has been reached about the gathering of information.

Evaluation is the process of gathering information about what is presently happening and comparing the results of that information-gathering with a view of what should be happening.

Our next task in defining self evaluation is to address the question of "What is involved in having a view of what should be happening?"

2. What is involved in having a view of what should be happening?

A response to this question is partly provided by arguing for the need to collect information about both the product and the process of training.

Having a view of what should be happening is an essential feature of all forms of evaluation. Without such a view no evaluation can occur. So what does "having a view of what should be happening" actually mean? The answer to that question is deceptively simple. It means having criteria for judging success and failure. Six points must be made about having criteria.

(i)

For any sort of endeavour it is possible to identify the criteria by which it is possible to judge performance at that endeavour. With certain sorts of endeavour the criteria for assessing performance can be very specific. Other sorts of endeavour, by their very nature, can only be judged by criteria which are rather general or vague, or even abstract.

Example 1 Specific criteria.
The criteria for judging the performance of someone who is employed as a cutter of sheets of glass can be thought of in specific terms.
Ability to use measuring implements accurately.
Ability to use glass cutting tools.
Ability to lift and carry glass safely.
Ability to store glass in a safe and accessible fashion.

Example 2 General criteria.
We can complicate the example of the glass cutter by adding to the job description the following facts: he is a union representative, the leader of a team of glass cutters and the trainer of novice glass cutters. The criteria by which to judge performance in these additional functions will be far less specific.

In self evaluation the general purpose is to establish for oneself how well one is performing at the particular endeavours with which one is involved. Obviously the criteria for judging how well one is doing will depend upon the nature of the endeavour.

Consequently you as trainers will need to be able to establish criteria by which you can judge your performance as trainers. You will also be instrumental in helping the trainees understand the criteria by which they can judge their performance at whatever it is they are being trained. Finally, you will have a role in establishing and using the criteria by which the training organisation evaluates its effectiveness as a training organisation and also in helping others to establish and use those criteria.

In genuine evaluation it should be possible to distinguish between the information about performance at a particular endeavour and the criteria used for making judgements about that information. Thus information and criteria for evaluating the information are **not** one and the same thing.

The major requirement for making an evaluation is, therefore, that one needs to know a lot about the subject of the evaluation. Without that understanding no criteria can be established and consequently no evaluation can occur.

Think about your own area of training.
Answer the following two questions.
1. How do you gather information about the performance of your trainee?
2. What criteria do you use to make judgements about that information?

(ii)

Having thought about establishing the criteria for making a judgement it is now necessary to reflect upon the obvious idea that the chosen criteria will obviously affect one's understanding of the information. An example will illustrate what I mean.

Example: Imagine a group of trainee studio managers. They are learning to use a piece of recording equipment. The group are sitting so that they have a good view of the demonstrator and the equipment. They can all be seen by the demonstrator who spends most of the time with equipment in front of the trainees. The room is quiet except for the voice of the demonstrator. Training begins with the demonstrator explaining, with the use of a blackboard, what the trainees will be learning. The demonstrator then operates the equipment, indicating the necessary procedures, and sequences that lead to proper operation, the alternatives that are available in case of equipment failure and the dire consequences of incorrect operation of the equipment. After the demonstration the demonstrator dictates the main points for the trainees to note down and remember.

We can apply two different sets of criteria for making sense of that training event. We can think of training in two different ways. One way is to do with the transmission of training and the other is to do with the interpretation of training. The transmission of training is based on the idea that a satisfactory learning experience is that which gives trainees careful explanations of the use of equipment. The interpretation view of training rests on the idea that a satisfactory learning experience is one which provides the trainee with the opportunity to understand what broadcasting involves and the ways in which technical equipment imposes its own parameters on that understanding. The following statements put these two views into real terms.

TRANSMISSION

Trainees should have opportunity to:
listen and pay attention to the trainer

work in an orderly and quiet atmosphere

be given correct information and explanations

keep accurate records of demonstrations

be instructed about the interpretations of the results of demonstrations

INTERPRETATION

Trainees should have opportunity to:
use the equipment themselves

carry out investigations for themselves

discuss ideas with each other

make and record their own observations

interpret observations

make predictions about the equipment

The judgement about the effectiveness of the training event would differ according to whether transmission or interpretation criteria were being used.

(iii)
The criteria that are established to judge performance will actually determine what sorts of information are to be gathered. Our imaginary glass-cutter of a few pages back is no better a glass-cutter because he can drive all the company vans carefully. That particular information becomes relevant only if the glass-cutter also has to deliver the glass to various customers.

What information is gathered is a matter for someone to decide. The evaluation rests upon a judgement about what the evaluation should contain. It is impossible to gather every piece of information and this must be acknowledged. All evaluation is influenced by what is considered to be relevant information as well as what are considered to be the relevant criteria for evaluating that data. These decisions necessarily reflect the values and prejudices of those who make such decisions.

Evaluation is a value laden activity.

In summary, it is important to remember that the criteria identified will influence decisions about which data will be collected. Furthermore, the definition of criteria may serve to clarify just what information is required and provides a rationale for deciding what methods should be used for acquiring it.

(iv)
Defining criteria brings a benefit in its own right, in addition to the production of statements for use in judging the information gathered.

With self evaluation there is the advancing of shared thinking about what the training is about, what the training organisation should be doing and what the roles of the trainers and trainees actually are.

(v)
Policy statements about the criteria used in evaluation must involve the agreement of all the parties concerned in the evaluation. It would be odd (to say

the very least) if a trainee, for example, engaged in the process of self evaluation with regard to his performance and was working with criteria that were at odds with those of the trainer or supervisor. Unfortunately such oddities occur all too frequently. The result of the mismatch of criteria is confusion, leading to frustration, leading to anger. Negotiation is essential in self evaluation.

(vi)
Finally, criteria are not absolute. They must be linked to the process of the development of the training organisation, the trainees and of course yourself, the trainer.

With self-evaluation it is easy to delude oneself about one's own achievements.

Use the ideas contained in this Study Unit so far to make a list of the reasons for this happening.

REPORT BACK
IT IS EASY TO DELUDE ONESELF ABOUT
ONE'S OWN ACHIEVEMENTS.
There are many unfortunate ways in which this can happen.
1. *Appropriate criteria have not been formulated.*
2. *The information about achievement that you have does not meet the requirements of the criteria.*
3. *You are working to a set of criteria which are not shared and may even be disputed by other people.*

At this stage we should stop and review progress to date. If we take a complete view of training it emerges that we are concerned with more than the development of knowledge and skills. We are also concerned with attitudes and personal qualities thus indicating the desirability of self evaluation. Training is also a process. It involves the trainer, the trainees and the organisation. Self evaluation is a means of understanding how well this process is proceeding. Self evaluation also ensures that criteria for making judgements about product and process can be established accurately and fairly. This is important since without these criteria no evaluation of any sort can occur.

3. Who is evaluating?

With self evaluation the whole emphasis is on the capacity of the individual to understand the demands that are being placed upon him and assess his performance in the light of those demands.

In this way evaluation ceases to be a controlling or regulating device and instead becomes a developmental one. Thus the evaluation does not control the individual but allows individuals to take an active part in their own development. This is most important not least because of the notion that being developmental means that this will have implications for the methods employed. The methods must be conducive to the whole point of self evaluation. In other words they cannot be imposed from an outside source.

There are certain key points to be noted:

* with self evaluation the trainer and the trainee must have a good working relationship. How else can they work together?

* performance criteria although difficult to produce are essential and they must be accurate. It is all too easy to confuse performance criteria with personality factors such as "initiative" or "drive". Thus a comment like "I enjoy working the task out", may be an evaluation of something, but it is not an evaluation of performance. Similarly "reliable worker" is simply too vague. This is not to say that there is no place for allowing the individual to reflect on what he feels he is doing.

* criteria for success must either originate from the individual or at least be understood and accepted by the individual. They will probably have to be negotiated between trainees, training organisations and people like yourselves if they are to be effective and make sense.

* self evaluation must provide continuing feedback into the larger questions of training policy and development. With self evaluating this means that the individual has a say in what is going on. This may have enormous consequences for the organisation involved. You might care to ask yourself the question, **"Is the training organisation interested in what I have to say?"** Then there is the question, **"Is the training organisation interested in what the trainees have to say?"**

Ask **yourself** the two questions above.

If we are to make assumptions about performance then we have to be absolutely certain that we understand and share those assumptions. Take a number of key words such as;

    EFFICIENT
    RESPONSIBLE
    SKILLED
    ENTHUSIASTIC
    HOPELESS
    DISRUPTIVE
    TIME-SERVING
    UNMANAGEABLE

Besides each key word write between three and six other words that you associate with the key word.

Repeat the exercise with two or three colleagues. Are their associated words the same as yours? If they are then what assumptions do you share? Are they the same assumptions? If the associated words are different then sort out why they are different.

You should by now have some idea of what self evaluation involves in general terms. You should also be aware of the necessary relationship between training in the broadest sense and self evaluation.

Later in this Study Unit we shall be examining particular aspects of trainer self evaluation, trainee self evaluation and the self evaluating institution.

However, the important question to ask before examining these particular topics is, "Why do it?"

"Why do it?" is the subject of the next Component.

Component 2:

Why Do it?

Key Ideas

 Setting ideas; evaluating personal performance; formative evaluation; establishing worth; training and power; participation; flexibility; creativity and growth; commitment; negotiation; motivation; threat outside/external evaluation

---

Key Objectives

By the end of this Component you will have an understanding of the issues associated with self evaluation and an appreciation of the values of that process.

Having identified what self evaluation is it makes sense in this component to move on to the question of, "Why do it?"

In a sense you have already begun to answer this second question in the first component, **"What is self evaluation?"** In the first component it became apparent that self evaluation is a necessary element of training. We must now take that insight a little further.

Basic Issues

The primary purpose of self evaluation is to enable individuals to plan and control their work better and learn from their mistakes as well as from their successes. It is a way of helping people to perform better. How can this happen?

Self evaluation requires certain things of individuals. If we examine each of these things in turn it should become clear that self evaluation really is a way of helping people to perform better.

1. The individual must be involved in setting the objectives for the endeavour. For objectives you could substitute the words "goals", "aims", "intentions", or "purposes".

   This seems an obvious point yet, strangely, it is one that is often over-looked. Thought of in reverse the point becomes clear. How can anyone evaluate anything, least of all themselves, if they don't know

where they are going or if they do know where they are going but don't want to go there? Key questions therefore are:

* Is the training organisation clear about its purposes and has it allowed other people to be involved in generating those purposes?
* Are the trainers clear about what they are intending to do and are they happy with that intention?
* Do the trainees understand and accept the purpose(s) of the training?

Notice, however, that the point is not simply about understanding the objectives. The point is also about being involved in **setting** them. The full implications of that may take a little time to be absorbed. But the key questions do indicate the significance of that involvement. By involving people in the setting of objectives more is being generated than understanding. What is also happening is that COMMITMENT to those objectives is being generated. People will have a higher degree of MOTIVATION since in a real sense the objectives are their own. They developed them and now can hardly deny them without looking foolish. Yes, I know some people **are** foolish but not the majority, we hope. On the occasions when individuals do deny their objectives new ones must be generated.

The individuals engaged in the endeavour have taken the trouble to work out together what it is that they intend to do. Some sort of NEGOTIATION, even if only at a very low level has occurred. This process has the result of promoting understanding and generating commitment to the endeavour. It is a process that is crucial to effective training. Through it and because of what it does people are helped to perform better.

Self evaluation demands personal involvement because of the twin factors of understanding and motivation. The individual has to understand what is happening and want to find out about his or her progress. They will want to know **for themselves**.

Some of you may baulk at the idea of involving trainees in the setting of objectives. You may accept all that you have read so far but still say, "My trainees couldn't/wouldn't do it", or simply, "It's too impracticable".

Three answers, one for each of those statements, and a general answer occur to me. For the first statement you might care to reflect that if the trainees **can't** do it, it's probably because they don't know enough and such a process is, therefore, a vital learning experience and if they **won't** do it then they are effectively denying themselves a learning experience. Either way, they should. For the second statement I can only urge you to think about what you already do with your trainees. Even things like discussing time schedules, plans for next week, the next step, are a form of negotiation albeit **very** low level and informal. This simply urges you to be a little more structured. Finally, are you involved in setting objectives? Are you included or excluded? How does it feel?

▨▨ Checkpoint

1. Think about the ways in which you involve trainees in setting objectives. Make a list of those ways. Are you happy with your list?
2. What would you need to do to promote more trainee involvement in setting objectives? How many of these things are impossible?

REPORT BACK
Of the things that you have noted as being impossible which are to do with: resources, time, colleagues, the nature of training?

2. Not only must objectives be set but the criteria for judging when those objectives are met must also be made clear and known by everyone involved. The objectives and the criteria for judging the attainment of the objectives are by no means the same thing. I have written at some length about criteria in the first component. Since I don't want to repeat all of that you might at this point care to refer back to the first component and re-read the relevant section.

   Once again it should be said that unless criteria are established no evaluation can take place and unless everyone involved understands the criteria no self evaluation can take place. Understanding the criteria is in itself an important part of learning.

Let's take a frivolous example.

You have as your objective that a particular trainee shall make tea and serve it to all of his workmates. Imagine that the trainee has eight workmates and the tea break lasts for fifteen minutes. All the materials needed to make the tea are at hand. The working environment is a building site on a hot summers day.

What are your criteria for achieving success at the objective?

This is not a complicated exercise but harder than it appears at first sight. Think about it carefully.

REPORT BACK
I don't want to give you precise answers, but your criteria should reflect concerns about the environment in which the task is to be performed, how best to serve that amount of tea in that time, the individual tastes of the tea drinkers and the previous experience of the tea-maker.

3. Self evaluation does not simply require individuals to think about what they are doing ("what sort of a task is this?") and whether they are doing it well ("meeting the criteria"). Further questions are raised:
   * Why are you doing it?
   * Should you be doing something different?
   Thus the questions of the worthwhile (or worthless) nature of the task is approached. Clearly this is of primary benefit to the individuals engaged in self evaluation. Individuals can establish the value of what they are doing.

   Where this worth can be established then that too will help the individual to become more motivated. The work has a point and a purpose and it is valued. Again this leads to more effective performance.

   Of course, if the work does appear to have little purpose and little value then presumably the individual(s) involved ought to change what they are doing. They should be doing something different.

4. Self evaluation, in practical terms, means that individuals and institutions will be reviewing their past and present performance with a view to improving that performance.

It follows, therefore, that self evaluation is primarily intended to influence the individuals and institutions engaged in it. In that sense it is a type of evaluation that is primarily FORMATIVE. Formative evaluation is the constant process of reviewing progress. It is part of the development of the individual or institution. It helps to form that development. Consequently self evaluation is not a single unique occurrence. It does not happen just once, for example at the end of a training progress. (That kind of once only evaluation at the end of a course is known as SUMMATIVE evaluation; it sums-up what has been going on. Self evaluation may contribute to that summing-up but actually self evaluation does far more). Self evaluation occurs time and again and is part of the constant process of involvement in any particular endeavour.

You will notice that because self evaluation means that individuals and institutions will be reviewing their past and present performance with a view to improving that performance it follows that self evaluation is a necessary aspect of reviewing future training and development needs. This relates to the idea contained in the first component whereby training was thought of as not being just about individual PRODUCT but also about PROCESS. Thus self evaluation enables us to think not only about individual achievement but also about what needs to be done to promote further achievement.

5. Self evaluation does not necessarily have to be thought of as a replacement for external or outside evaluation. I am not suggesting that all forms of evaluation by other people or bodies of people should be abandoned in favour of self evaluation. However, self evaluation does provide additional evidence to those who are involved in external evaluation. The results of this are two fold. First, the external evaluation becomes better informed. Second and connectedly, the external evaluation is conducted more fairly.

We are probably all familiar with the situation whereby an external evaluation, be it anything from an interview to an actual written examination and including everything in between, actually fails to locate or unearth the understandings, competencies or achievements of the individual. It can be a very frustrating and, dare I say it, de-motivating experience. Self evaluation helps to act as a corrective against that occurring.

▰▰▰

Make a list of the ways in which self evaluation serves to improve individual performance.

REPORT BACK
Key words are criteria, commitment, performance and motivation.

Participation and training

One of the major themes to emerge so far in connection with self evaluation has been that of "involvement". However, involvement by itself can be thought of in an almost passive sense. What we must stress at this point is that self evaluation requires "active involvement" or PARTICIPATION by all concerned. With self evaluation, concerned individuals will be participating in something which is largely **for them.** For example "setting objectives" is more than simply understanding and agreeing to objectives. It also means developing objectives that are in a very real sense one's own objectives. This is "active involvement" or participation.

Through participation the interests of individuals will be aroused and this is important for the whole concept of training. Little of value will accrue to training organisations unless the interest of both the trainers and the trainees are sufficiently aroused for them to engage in reviewing the training themselves. This demands participation. There are five main reasons for this.

1. Trainers are responsible for the training and welfare of all the trainees in their care. I don't want to make too much of the word "responsibility" but I am sure that for many of you there will be occasions when it all seems "just too much".

It seems to me to be very unfair to have to be expected to live up to that responsibility when the nature of the responsibility is not clear. Understanding the nature of this responsibility must include having and agreeing the criteria by which you are able to judge your own performance as one who is responsible for trainees.

"I knew I was responsible for ensuring that all the trainees took a lunch break but I didn't realise that I had to supply the sandwiches".

Not only is it unfair, it is also a recipe for disaster, particularly in terms of ineffectiveness. The surest way of avoiding the, "I didn't know that I was expected to do that" syndrome is to be actively involved in deciding what "being responsible" means in this context.

2. Trainees also have a responsibility, namely for their own learning. Self evaluation is a way of helping the trainee to assume that responsibility. For the trainee, self evaluation is a way of:
   * monitoring progress
   * understanding the learning
   * deepening the learning experience

This follows from what has already been said. The trainee can understand his or her own progress because he or she will know what counts as progress. Monitoring progress requires the trainee to understand the kind of learning that is necessary (and which has been agreed) and apply that understanding to the task of monitoring. Thus the learning experience is deepened.

The learning experience is also deepened in another way. The kinds of understandings and agreement required by the process of self evaluation place the **ownership** of the learning into the hands of the learner. In other words training is not something that is done to a trainee. The trainee must be a willing participant. The training becomes the property of the trainees. If this does not happen then, as we all know, life just becomes difficult for all involved. As a willing participant one has a responsibility, which cannot really be said of the unwilling or reluctant trainee.

you can't make me be trained. You can't you can't

3. The training organisation as a whole should ensure that the purposes of the training are being achieved and that resources are not only being used but they are being used effectively. In practical terms this means that:

   * strengths and weaknesses in both trainers and trainees will be identified and strategies found for boosting the strengths and eliminating the weaknesses.
   * the balance and structure of the training and the way that it is organised will be reviewed periodically. This is so that as full a picture of problems and constraints can emerge and be dealt with.

4. It should follow that references to the training organisation as a whole includes both trainers and trainees. Both trainers and trainees need to clarify aims and objectives and engage in a regular view of progress.

5. This type of participation will certainly benefit the trainee. However, it should also, under proper circumstances, benefit the trainers. It is ridiculous to expect of trainers everything and all at once. The aspects of participation that are listed here should provide a clear indication of the training needs for trainers themselves. We all have such needs. The clever trick is to identify them and work at ways of having them met. Fortunately, more and more people are recognising these particular training needs so there is every reason for optimism.

Out of the five reasons for promoting participation in the reviewing of training, does any one stand out as being more important than all the rest? Show the list of five reasons to someone else. Compare their answer to that question with your answer.

At this point a word of caution must be raised. For many people it is one thing to read about self evaluation but quite another to actually do and encourage others to do. For many people self evaluation is seen as a THREAT. External evaluation can also be threatening but in a different sort of way. When someone else passes judgement on you if they are particularly insensitive then it can be hurtful. However, a lot of folks can often say, "Well that's just his opinion. What does he know? He only spoke to me for ten minutes". Then the hurt turns to anger. And there is nothing wrong with that happening if those were indeed the circumstances. Self evaluation is different. With self evaluation one is passing judgement on oneself and it is hard to avoid that judgement. Three points may help:
* self evaluation is, or should be, in the control of the individual.
* we tend to be far more critical of ourselves than others would be. This might be particularly apparent among the trainees but it won't be confined to them. Someone could be around to say, "Well, I think that you're being a little hard on yourself". Remember, we live in the kind of society where being "big-headed" or "boastful" is disapproved. Unfortunately, it often means that we tend to feel guilty about genuine pride in genuine achievements. Such pride is not to be confused with being boastful and indeed it is to be encouraged.

* We also live in the kind of society where the opposite of achievement is regarded as failure. We either pass or we don't pass i.e. we fail. However, it is by no means the only perspective that is valid, if indeed it is valid at all. Self evaluation opens up the possibility that learning is occurring even when there is no obvious progress. In order to engage in self evaluation some sort of learning must be going on. Furthermore self evaluation indicates how that learning can be maximised. What might appear to be failure becomes a further learning experience, a further growth point if you like.

▰▰▰

What sorts of skills or attributes do you think you will need as a trainer in order to reduce the threat of self evaluation for your trainees?

Would these skills or attributes have any application in any other context?

Flexibility

Self evaluation permits a degree of flexibility and adaptability that an "objective" or "outsider" external evaluation will lack.

For example:

Training contexts will vary from place to place, even where different places are offering similar or the same training. The context may even change within the same place over a period of time. Training to be a studio manager with the BBC is not the same as it would be with independent radio and even within the BBC the context will change over time. Undergoing training in the winter is not the same as training in the summer. New equipment may have been introduced. But quite apart from that, the actual learning environment has altered. Winter and Summer are,

after all quite different times of the year. People entertain different expectations in the Summer than in the Winter, they may feel different and even dress differently. The coldness or stuffiness or hotness of the room may be significant. External evaluations are not usually able to accommodate such contextual variations. Self evaluation, however, not only can but almost invariably will. Individuals will be responding to the situation in which they actually find themselves.

My example may appear to be small but it is not insignificant. The point is that no two training contexts are exactly the same. The range of variables is immense as the component on the self evaluating institution will indicate. Resources, including facilities, time and personnel, programme content, styles of training, rules and regulations, specific local circumstances and demands are all relevant variables. It is not uncommon to hear both trainers and trainees talking about different training programmes that have the same title and even the same objectives and yet they really are very different programmes because of these variables. External or outside evaluation cannot take these factors into account. Self evaluation not only can, it almost certainly will.

REMEMBER

Outside or external evaluation refers to any sort of evaluation that is imposed from another source. This could be anything from a trainer conducting an interview to an external examination set by an examining body.

Generally speaking, the more thorough an external evaluation becomes, either in order to cover all the variables or to extract the greatest amount of information, the more unwieldy it becomes. Finally, it becomes too long and time consuming and the costs outweigh the benefits. It is possible to conclude, therefore, that in order to be workable there are many aspects of individual growth that external evaluations cannot afford to touch.

Examples of this might be questions like, "How interesting did you find the training?" or, "How difficult was the work you were engaged in?" Any answer must be less than accurate since no criteria have been established by which a judgement may be made. In the end external evaluations become rather arid affairs because without shared criteria the more interesting questions such as "How difficult did you find the training?" cannot sensibly be asked.

Self evaluation and control

The general public have an interest in the effectiveness of training. You will know of the various often expensive initiatives that have been taken. You will have heard of unfavourable comparisons with other countries.

In other words there is some move towards making people responsible for the effectiveness of their endeavours. Whatever you personally feel about that particular point of view it is nevertheless the case that if everyone involved in training is monitoring their own progress then that is a way of maintaining control of that progress and not relinquishing it to someone else, or some other body.

A further issue raised by self evaluation is that of power. All the parties involved in training gain some control over what is going on during that training. This applies to both trainer and trainee. Both are able to contribute something to the design of the training by referring to their own performance. It is an essential result of everyone participating in the evaluation.

Evaluation carried out by other people can often be incorrectly focussed. Such an evaluation may well reflect the interests of those other people. Consequently it may be too involved with the problems that interest them rather than the ones of interest to those directly involved in the training.

Self evaluation allows the control of training to remain in the hands of those involved. If it is only outsiders that have all the information then they also have all the power and can exercise control. However, without any doubt it is the individuals who are involved who are in the best position to know the situation and fully appreciate all the issues which should be the focus of attention. What is more, through the process of negotiation, these issues can be readily understood by all of the involved parties. This does not apply to external evaluation.

Finally, if the result of the evaluation would seem to indicate a need for change in training. For example, then such change is more acceptable if it comes as a result of understandings that are negotiated and mutually agreed by the involved parties, rather than imposed from outside. Self evaluation will convince individuals of the need for change in a way that an external evaluation can never accomplish. The participation of individuals in acknowledging the desirability of change is one more motivating factor. We all like to do things because we think they are valuable. When other people tell us what to do we tend to be distrustful, at least. When individuals accept the need for change for themselves it is more productive.

Read through this Component again. As you do, note down all the "costs" involved in self evaluation, note all the things that count against it for whatever reason. Also note down all the benefits, all the good points.

Compare your two lists.

What conclusions do you draw?

REPORT BACK
The point is not simply to compare the length of the two lists. There should be evidence of improvements in the quality of training where self-evaluation is an established practice.

In the next Component we will consider what self-evaluation will mean for you personally.

Component 3:

Trainee/Supervisor Self Evaluation

Key Ideas

 Features of training; training styles; trainer development; training skills; types of trainer and trainee interactions; approving skills in trainee reinforcement; questioning skills; skills in explaining; and skills keeping the trainees' attention.

Key objectives
1. For you to become aware of and understand the skills that are common to all forms of training.
2. For you to examine certain key skills.
3. For you to gain an understanding of self-evaluation as it applies to you.

The development of the trainer
Training is a term which covers a complex of courses, schemes and activities in a wide variety of settings which are themselves constantly changing. Changes in the trainee population, in training goals, methods and content and in the organisation of training all pose challenges and problems which have to be met and resolved. Commonly individual trainers have had to sort things out for themselves.

However, the task of being a trainer contains certain basic features which are common to all forms of training. Some of these features you will be aware of already.

Basic features of being a trainer:—
— awareness of the effects of the training on the trainees and the ability to maximise the benefits of those effects.
— ability to help other people to become trainers.
— awareness that training is needed.
— willingness to engage in training.
— preparedness to evaluate and improve the training and if necessary replace the training with something better.

— willingness and ability to co-operate with other trainers as appropriate to the running of a particular training programme.
— ability to implement a training programme.
— understanding what training actually involves in any given context.

▨▨▨ Checkpoint
Actually I have been a little naughty. The basic features are developmental. They proceed from one step to the next so that step one is the most basic feature and all the other features follow on in order.

Try to re-arrange the list of basic features so that they are in order. For example in order to **implement a training programme** other things must already have happened and having implemented the programme other things will have to happen.

REPORT BACK
BASIC FEATURES OF BEING A TRAINER
Awareness that training is needed.
Understanding what training actually involves in any given context.
Willingness to engage in training.
Ability to implement a training programme.
Willingness and ability to co-operate with other trainers as appropriate to the running of a particular training programme.
Awareness of the effects of the training on the trainees and the ability to maximise the benefits of those effects.

Ability to help other people to become trainers.
Preparedness to evaluate and improve the training
and if necessary replace the training with something
better.

The basic features that are listed represent what being a trainer means. They are, if you like, criteria for understanding the term "trainer". These features are listed, therefore, because they are a first step in allowing you to enter into the task of self evaluation for yourselves.

However, they are **only** a first step. The key word in each of those features is TRAINING. Just as there are some general features to describe the task of the trainer so also there are some general skills associated with the task of training. So if trainers are people who are involved in training just what does training involve? The task of training in general demands the use of certain skills. These can be described. Before I do describe them please note that I am not defining the concept of training as I did in **Component One — What is self evaluation?** The skills that I am now going to list are those that are necessary to engage in the PROCESS of training and which are needed to generate a PRODUCT.

In order to make things as clear as possible I have arranged the skills involved in training into four groups.

1. **Skill in keeping the trainees' attention.**
   The ability to actually involve the trainees in actually doing something and keeping the trainees interested is an important part of this. It is also important to be able to change the activity when the trainees do appear to be losing interest.

2. **Skill in asking questions.**
   The questions should obviously be interesting as well as relevant and varied. How the questions are delivered should also be considered. Consequently quality of voice and habits of speech are key factors. Repetitive phrases, a flat monotone and an inaudible voice are all to be avoided. Also important would be the use of non-verbal cues such as facial expression and eye contact.

3. **Skill in explaining.**
   Part of this would be the ability to give demonstrations provide examples, and use a variety of teaching aids. The ability to recognise when the trainees are having difficulties in understanding is also part of the skill of providing an explanation. This calls for a degree of sensitivity.

4. **Skill in encouraging appropriate responses.**
   The ability to encourage the trainees in various ways will be one contribution to your understanding of how well you are doing.

With as yet no further details on the four areas of skills to help you are you able to identify any particular strengths that you have?

Each of the four areas listed will be described in detail later in this component.

The features of being a trainer and the skills required for training to occur are common to all forms of training. How these features and skills work out in practice will vary according to what the training is for. I am assuming, of course, that the trainers will be knowledgeable about their own subject.

Specific skills

In this section, I want to focus on the four areas of skills in more detail. After considering each area in turn I will pose a series of questions that will help you to engage in your own self evaluation.

1. Skill in keeping the trainees' attention.

This is arguably the most important skill. Foremost among the means for keeping the trainees' attention are those that are open to and actively involve the trainees in the training. Ideally the training should be "experience-led". This kind of training has a number of key features.

* Personal involvement means that the entire individual is in the learning event.

* The learning is self-initiated in the sense that the sense of discovery and comprehension comes from within.

* The effect of the training is all pervasive in that it makes a difference in the behaviour, the attitudes and perhaps even the personality of the learner.
* It is evaluated by the trainee. The trainee will know whether the training is meeting a need, leading to what the trainee wants to know and illuminating an area of ignorance. The emphasis that I have given to the setting of objectives and the establishment of criteria in **Component Two Why Do It?** is central to experience led training.
* The training moves through a series of steps. First, the trainee is involved in a particular or specific activity. Second, the trainee has to draw out the meaning/purpose/intention of that particular activity. Third, the trainee has to apply that learning possibly in a practical way and/or possibly in a new situation.

Even at the most general level I hope that you can appreciate that telling people how to do something, although sometimes necessary, is rarely as effective as giving them practice in doing it themselves.

Obviously there may be times when the trainees will have to be acquainted with procedures that are routine, or even boring. If it appears that your trainees are losing interest then quickly switch into another activity.

If you **do** have to provide certain explanations, descriptions or even lectures then you will need to be able to use a variety of different sorts of material so that the trainees are using as many of their senses as you can stimulate. Rather than simply relying on the trainees sense of hearing also use their sense of sight by having something to show them. Any other senses should be used as appropriate.

Stimulation is also provided by mixing the kinds of social interactions that involve the trainees:
Trainer with groups of trainees.
Individual trainee with trainer.
Trainee with trainee.
Trainee with small group of trainees (e.g. three or four).
Trainee with whole group of trainees.
Liveliness on your part will also help the trainees to maintain their attention. The way that you move around the training area and position yourself in relation to the training group as a whole as well as individual trainees is important. Gestures both with hands and face are useful aids in making a point. Also useful in making points are the use of key phrases to emphasise the need for attention. Examples of these would be "Now listen carefully to this", "The important point is . . .", "Watch closely . . ." In some ways you are engaged in a theatrical performance and although you don't want to "go over the top", as some bad actors do, neither do you want to be completely lifeless.

SELF EVALUATION CHECKLIST FOR KEEPING THE TRAINEES' ATTENTION
Answer these questions carefully in relation to your last month of training. Refer to them again as soon as possible after your next month of training.
1. How often and in what ways did you actively involve the trainees?
2. What strategy or strategies did you have prepared in case the trainees lost interest?
3. What sorts of resources (picture, diagrams, film, video, items of equipment) did you use? Did you use visual material in a way that required the trainees to **look** in order to obtain information?
4. To what extent did you vary the social interactions of the trainees?
5. To what extent and in what manner did you move around the training area?
6. What typical gestures and attention grabbing phrases did you employ?

Please note that you are not really expected to do all of these things in every single training session.

2. Skill in Asking Questions
There is a saying about asking questions which is useful to keep in mind. "If you ask a question to which you know the trainee has the answer then you are

wasting your time. If you ask a question to which you know the trainee does not have the answer then you are wasting your time". Well, asking questions is one way of testing the knowledge of the trainees. The important point from the saying that I have quoted is that the questions asked must be appropriate for the kind of knowledge being tested. In any case questions have other purposes than testing trainees.

There are different sorts of questions. Indeed some questions are not really questions at all because they neither test nor develop knowledge.

For example:

Rhetorical questions:

These are those questions which you pose with the full intention of answering them yourself. This can be a good device for indicating the importance of a particular point.

Command questions:

Although your utterance is worded as though it was a question it is really an order. "Will you pay attention?"

Other types of questions can usually be divided into lower order questions and higher order questions.

a) Lower order questions.

These are generally "closed" questions in that they usually only have one right answer. e.g. "What colour does acid turn litmus paper?" Questions of this sort are used to test memory and understanding.

b) Higher order questions

These are often "open" questions in that they usually require an element of creativity in order to be answered.

e.g. "You are driving in a car rally. For reasons of space and weight your tool box must measure no more than 18 inches by 18 inches by 36 inches. What essential items would you pack into that tool box?"

Questions of this sort may ask the trainee to:

make inferences
make predictions
solve problems
bring ideas together
make judgements

Good questioning procedures contain a number of elements.

* They must be clear and coherent. They should not be ambiguous or open to misinterpretation. Attention must be paid to voice quality and the use of gestures.
* The pace at which you ask questions should vary. As a general rule you should give short pauses for lower order questions and longer pauses for higher order questions.
* Spread the questions around so that a variety of trainees are involved.
* Give prompts or hints where necessary but not too frequently. Probe or dig particularly with higher order questions.

SELF EVALUATION CHECKLIST FOR ASKING QUESTIONS

Answer these questions carefully in relation to your **last** training session. Refer to them again as soon as possible after your **next** training session.

1. Were your questions usually clearly understood by the trainees?
2. Were your questions usually coherently expressed?
3. Did you use pauses after asking most of your questions?
4. Did you vary the pace at which you asked questions?
5. Did you direct some of your questions at individual trainees?
6. Did you distribute your questions amongst the whole group of trainees?
7. Did you use prompts to help trainees formulate their answers?
8. Did you use probes to help trainees think more deeply about their answers?

---

3. Skill in Explaining

Good explanations **cover the essentials, are brief** and **appeal** to the listener. The key characteristics of such explanations are as follows.

* the main points must be well organised and presented.
* demonstrations, illustrations and examples are appealing, interesting and relevant.
* irrelevancies are eliminated.
* summaries of the main points are provided.
* distractions are avoided.
* clarity is promoted through sensitive questioning and also sensitive listening. As you listen to the trainees comments and responses to your questions you will be able to use those responses and comments to further the training.

SELF EVALUATION CHECKLIST FOR GIVING EXPLANATIONS

Answer the questions carefully in relation to your **last** training session. Refer to them again as soon as possible after your **next** training session.

1. Were your explanations clearly understood by the trainees?
2. Did your explanations appeal to the trainees?
3. Did your explanations cover the essential features?
4. Were the illustrations and examples you used interesting to the trainee?
5. Were the illustrations and examples you used relevant to your explanations?
6. Did you listen carefully to the trainees' responses?
7. Did you clarify their responses, so helping the trainees to gain greater understanding?
8. What did you do to help those trainees who had problems with understanding?

---

4. Skill in Encouraging Appropriate Responses.
At the heart of this skill is the recognition of the importance of developing the trainees' sense of self-esteem or self-worth. Praise, recognition and attention are all ways of promoting this sense of self-esteem. There are both spoken and unspoken ways of doing this. Praise can take the form of a spoken compliment, "Very good". It can also be unspoken, as with a nod or a smile. Obviously it is necessary for you to match the form of praise to the type of situation.

Not just overt praise but also acknowledgement of the trainee's contribution is part of encouraging appropriate responses. Acknowledgement can, of course, be thought of as a form of praise. Acknowledgement means using the trainee's ideas in various ways.

In receiving the trainee's responses you are actually acquiring tools for your own self evaluation.

SELF EVALUATION CHECKLIST FOR ENCOURAGING APPROPRIATE RESPONSES
Answer the questions carefully in relation to your **last** training session. Refer to them again as soon as possible after your **next** training sessions.
1. Did you respond to trainee answers and questions with such words as good, fine, splendid?
2. Did you encourage trainees to participate by using cues such as ah ha, mmmm, m'mm, etc?
3. Did you encourage trainees to participate by using cues such as smiling, nodding your head, writing their answers on the blackboard, looking and listening in a variety of friendly ways?
4. Did you give credit for the correct part of a trainee's answer?
5. Did you link trainees' responses to other trainee responses made earlier in the session?

At this point I think I should add a personal note. If you have worked through the checklists carefully you may be feeling quite pleased with yourself. On the other hand you might be feeling a bit depressed. If you are feeling pleased with yourself then, well done! But don't stop reading. If you are feeling depressed then read on as well. What is being described is really an ideal. You must remember that I am trying to present the very best. In a real training context things can be very different. The Study Units on the **Management of Training** may be of help. Since you have bothered to read this far it might well be the case that your conscientiousness has made you over-critical of your own performance. This is a fairly common occurrence in self evaluation. I urge you to think of the various questions that I have raised as a guide to ideal practice rather than as a critical analysis of you. After all, this is **your** self evaluation. You might not be happy with the criteria.

The trainer's view of trainees
Everything that has been written in this Study Unit so far, although accurate in its own way, lacks one vital dimension. That vital dimension might be thought of as your own personal perspective on that species known as "the trainee". If you have found some difficulty in relating the tasks in this component to your own experience it might be because you have a particular view about the way that trainees actually are. Certainly the responses that you have made to the various questions in this component will be affected by your views, perspectives or assumptions about trainees. If you are genuinely interested in self evaluation then you will have to be alert to the fact that the basis for your self evaluation will be the views that you have of the group that you are training. Your assumptions will colour your perception of the task of training.

Indeed, the way in which the organisation is managed will be based on certain assumptions. One extreme set of assumptions could include the following:

Assumptions A
* The average human being has a natural dislike for work and will avoid it whenever possible.
* It follows that people must be coerced in a variety of ways in order to produce the required effort.
* Most people prefer to be directed, will avoid responsibility, are unambitious and desire security above all else.
* Proper training demands that the trainees conform to the criteria of which the trainer and only the trainer is the custodian.
* The trainer's task is to evaluate and correct the trainee's performance according to those criteria.
* Trainees are uninformed, they know nothing, and are empty vessels waiting to be filled with training.

These assumptions, if you hold them, will to some extent determine the ways in which you act in a training situation. Actually, to be quite honest many people will actually fail to recognise that the items on the list really are just assumptions. Many people will regard these items as self-evident statements of fact. In any event such items can be thought of as forming a frame of reference. That, or any other frame of reference provides the context for self evaluation. If the self evaluation is to have any meaning then that frame of reference should be identified. It is a question of defining the "self" in self evaluation.

You could, of course, hold completely different assumptions, the opposite extreme to the ones given above

Assumptions B

* The expenditure of physical and mental effort at work is as natural as when at play.

* Coercion is only one means for controlling effort. People will exercise self-control in the service of objectives to which they are committed and for which they will be rewarded, particularly if the rewards are associated with self-respect and personal improvement.

* Under proper conditions most people learn to not only accept responsibility but also to seek it.

* Proper training should enable the trainees to formulate their own criteria for success. The trainer's task is to facilitate this, to allow success to occur.

* The trainee already possesses some knowledge, skills or attitudes that are relevant to the training and has the creative capacity to reshape that knowledge and those skills or attitudes.

The first set of assumptions that I listed portrays people as disinclined to make any effort on their own initiatives and capable of little change. The second set of assumptions portrays people as inclined to work at objectives to which they are committed. Clearly if you hold one or the other sets of beliefs then that will affect the self evaluation that occurs.

For example:

1) "Given that they are all disinclined to work I don't think that I did too badly".

2) "I know that they will work like horses when they are motivated. I simply failed to motivate them".

Think of a particular trainee.

Imagine that you agree with Assumption A. Evaluate your performance with that trainee.

Now imagine that you agree with Assumption B. Once again evaluate your performance with that same trainee.

In what way do the evaluations differ?

The Style of the Trainer

I am aware that you are not all the same kinds of people. Different people have different styles of working. Consequently I want to end this component by providing you with the opportunity to evaluate your own styles of working and draw out some practical implications of adopting particular kinds of style for the process of evaluation.

There are a variety of trainer styles and each style has its own strengths and weakness, each carries

different value assumptions and the appropriateness of any one or other style or combination of styles will depend as much as anything on the context in which you operate.

Some of the more commonly found styles can be characterised as follows:—

Authoritarian
— provides a complete and inflexible structure for working.
— expects high work performance.
— bestowal of rewards and punishment is rigidly uniform.
— places a high priority on the completion of the task, productivity takes precedence over the needs of the trainees.
— subordinates are best dealt with through the exercise of power.
— answers are always either right or not right, discussion is discouraged.

Democratic
— participation and feedback from all the individuals affected by a decision is invited.
— fosters a sense of involvement by inviting discussion.
— co-operative working environment is encouraged.
— only assertive when faced with time constraints or "unacceptable" decisions from the trainees.

Facilitating
— assumes that the trainees are generally capable of problem solving, initiative, responsible experimentation; and this is encouraged — work force are generally efficient and capable of getting on with things.
— in evaluating performance he involves the trainees.
— the feelings, values, and perceptions of the individual are regarded as being important.
— functions as a catalyst, **enabling** people to do things for themselves — can be thought of as an enabler.

Please give a one sentence description of each trainer's style listed below and provide an actual example of a situation that you have personally experienced that is appropriate to each.

TRAINER STYLE	DEFINITION	EXAMPLE
Authoritarian		
Democratic		
Facilitating		

You can examine the implications of adopting certain sorts of style by considering some case studies. After a description of a particular situation a number of alternative courses of action will be presented to you. Select the course or courses of action which seem to you to be the most reasonable. In some instances you may have to say, "I'll try this but if it doesn't work I will also have to try that".

Some suggestions as to the most appropriate course(s) of action will appear following the case studies.

Case study 1

For several months the trainees in a large corporation have been dissatisfied with a new trainer. Before the arrival of the new trainer, the department had functioned as a cohesive, effective unit, combining hard work with equal amounts of play and casualness. The new trainer has very strong ideas about the type of environment his trainees should have; as one trainer put it, it resembles a full military operation. No longer are trainees allowed to place personal belongings on the walls or have occasional informal gatherings during working hours. Productivity comes first, with the trainees feelings being considered as an afterthought. Everyone is very upset about the changes in structure, and their dissatisfaction is beginning to show up in their performance. The frustration and anger is now beginning to come to a full boil and the trainees have decided to meet to discuss the situation. As one of the trainees involved, what would you suggest be done to resolve the conflict? Would you:

1. Suggest that a committee be formed to confront the new trainer?
2. Select one individual to represent the committee in confronting the new trainer?
3. Go to a higher level management with documented evidence and state your case?
4. Write an anonymous letter to the trainer?
5. Try to adjust to the situation as best as you possibly can?
6. Get the trainees to sign a petition, and present it to higher level management?
7. Invite the new trainer to the supervisory meeting for discussions?
8. Suggest that a committee be formed to discuss the situation?
9. Quit in protest?
10. Go along with the trainer, but try to make his life difficult?
11. Try to understand his position and support it?

Case study 2

A trainee requests a meeting with you to discuss his recent difficulties in keeping up with the work. As his trainer you are concerned about his well-being and are more than willing to try to assist him in any way possible. Since his past work record has been somewhat patchy you are quite concerned that you may be forced to remove him from the training programme. After sitting down, Mark begins to share with you that he and his fiancée are splitting up and he doesn't know if he can accept the situation. In addition, he admits that he is under tremendous financial stress and has begun drinking more than he should. You tell Mark that you are concerned about both his problems and the work of the programme; that you are worried about his position and don't want

to lose him as a trainee. Suddenly he begins to sob and tell you that he needs your help and doesn't want to lose the training programme. What would you say?

1. "I'm really sorry that you're upset; don't worry about a thing, I'll take care of it".
2. "Why don't you try and get yourself together — it isn't the end of the world".
3. "You must be really going through it".
4. "Things aren't as bad as they seem; you still have work to concentrate on and I know things will get better".
5. "Why don't we talk about this when you're feeling better".
6. "I know you've got serious problems, but if you don't buck your ideas up, I have no choice but to take you off the training scheme".
7. "Mark, I know you can handle anything; all this will pass".
8. "I know just how you feel; I've gone through a lot, too".
9. "If you had come to me sooner, I'm sure things wouldn't have got so bad".
10. "If you had been a little more responsible, perhaps you wouldn't be in this mess".
11. "What options do you think we might have?"
12. "Don't be so childish; it's not the end of the world".

Case study 3

A supervisor of three years' experience is given the additional responsibility of training two new trainees. Delighted at the opportunity to demonstrate her competence as as trainer, Mary meets with the trainees to outline their contractual understanding on their relationship. She tells them that they will be meeting on a weekly basis for the next six months, and if additional time is needed during the breaking-in period, she will be happy to assist. One of the trainees begins functioning effectively from the first day. He is able to grasp instructions and procedures with little difficulty and can be left on his own. But Mary experiences a very different relationship with the second trainee. He requires constant attention and needs continuous clarification of basic material. Mary is initially responsive to his needs, but as time wears on she grows weary of the dependency being formed. She believes in assisting others to become more responsible for their actions on a gradual basis. However, the second trainee has a difficult time in assuming much responsibility although he is able to competently complete any task assigned — as long as she is there to provide the structure for him. She doesn't feel justified in recommending that he be fired, but also finds that her patience is growing thin. How would you cope with this situation?
Would you:

1. Keep providing the structure the trainee obviously needs?
2. Tell the trainee that you will not be able to provide all the support he needs, and that he should start thinking for himself?
3. Ask the other new employee to help him?

4. Try to maintain more distance from the trainee by withdrawing emotionally?
5. Tell the new trainee that you are very concerned that he has become so dependent on you?
6. Begin group supervision with both trainees in hopes that he may get the message through a different type of training process?
7. Decrease the amount of responsibility the trainee has, thereby reducing his constant need for assistance?
8. Set up a limited-access trainer relationship in which he can contact you only during specific hours?
9. Ask for assistance from your supervisor?
10. Attempt to have the new trainee transferred to another department?
11. Suggest he visit the staff psychologist for help with his dependency problem?
12. Try to accept the situation and hope that it will get better as time goes on?

Review of case studies

1. The situation appears to be getting worse as time passes, as opposed to people simply adjusting, which often happens.

   Options 3 and 4 would be an error since the new trainer must be directly confronted in a responsible fashion. As several trainers feel the same way options 8 and 2 are recommended. If the representative presents a coherent and reasonable list of issues and options there is a good chance of a productive result. If the trainer still refuses **then** option 3 becomes reasonable.

What assumptions are being made about the way in which people work most effectively?

What are the general consequences of going on to the next administrative level?

Is this a value conflict?

---

2. Most of the options listed here are either patronising (1, 2, 5, 6, 8, 13) or platitudinous (4, 7, 9, 11)

   The key thing is to listen because individuals in this situation often need to talk without being fearful of being put down. Often during the act of talking the individual will begin to see resolutions appearing. Option 3 provides the individual with the feeling of being listened to. Later, much later option 12 may be employed. However, before that the individual must have an opportunity to fully express their feelings about the situation, otherwise they will still remain a blocking factor.

Should part of your role be assisting individuals with personal problems? If not, how do you stay away from them?

Which response would be most effective if you were in Jim's position?

Where do you draw the line in becoming "too personal" with trainees?

---

3. Attempting to repress one's feelings about a trainee's behaviour will:

   (a) give the trainer ulcers; and (b) not work anyway. The trainer's primary responsibility in this situation is to model responsible behaviour by exercising option 5 — letting the new trainee know that he is concerned that he has become so dependent. From that point it becomes essential that the trainer accurately assess each trainee's strengths and weaknesses and help each individual find an environment that maximizes his talents and capacities. Since this particular trainee can function acceptably in highly structured work areas, option number 10 — attempting to have him transferred to another department — may offer a resolution if the trainee is placed in an environment that will provide the needed structure. Tremendous human resources are often wasted because of the inappropriate placement of manpower. An effective trainer will constantly evaluate the abilities of his trainees, and attempt to place such talents where the trainee can benefit.

How do you foster a sense of greater responsibility in your trainees?

What is the primary purpose of a trainer-trainee relationship?

Each of the three case studies illustrates a different style of being a trainer. There is no such thing as a definitively correct style. All that we can say is that certain styles are more appropriate to the circumstances than other styles. Notice, please, that the key phrase is "more appropriate to the circumstances".

Having said that, under normal circumstances most of us do adopt a predominant style most of the time. The style that you adopt will to a large extent determine the ways in which you work with trainees and the ways in which you allow the trainees to work with each other. This in turn will affect the kind of training that occurs and consequently the nature of self evaluation.

The types of interaction that can occur may be described as follows:
1. Trainer describes, explains, narrates, directs, lectures.
2. Trainer questions.
3. Trainer responds to trainee's response.
4. Trainees respond to trainer's questions.
5. Trainee volunteers information, comments or questions.
6. Trainees involved in an activity.
7. Trainees waste time.
8. Silence.

▰▰▰

Look at the list of interactions.

Describe the kind of atmosphere or climate of training that might be prevailing when

1 and 8 occur together
2 and 4   „   „
2 and 7   „   „
6 and 3   „   „

Suggestions follow.

I hope that you are now more confident about your own self evaluation.

Self evaluation now begins to play an important part in the way that you function. You should now begin to get the information that will help you to modify and improve your style. In this way self evaluation and performance are related.

REPORT BACK

Review of interactions (see the third Checkpoint on page 222)

When 1 and 8 occur together one can imagine a formal, perhaps authoritarian atmosphere.

When 2 and 4 occur together the atmosphere would appear to be fairly structured but democratic.

When 2 and 7 occur together the atmosphere would appear to be laissez-faire, or possibly anarchic.

When 6 and 3 occur together the atmosphere would appear to be facilitative.

facilitator will all be looking, at least in part, for different sorts of things. This Component then should help you to identify your own assumptions and style.

The next task is to help you to convey certain insights to the trainees so that they too can enter into the task of self evaluation.

This is the subject of the next Component.

By now you should be aware of some of the key skills associated with being a trainer. My hope is that you will be able to begin, and continue, your own self evaluation.

You should also be aware of the idea that training in general and self evaluation in particular will be highly affected by the assumptions that you make about training and trainees and by the personal style that you adopt. Thus the authoritarian, the democrat and the

Component 4:

Trainee Self Evaluation

Key Ideas

 Diagnostic and formative evaluation; evaluation as part of the learning experience; motivation; implications for training; involving the trainees in their own evaluation; advantages and disadvantages.

Key Objectives

As a result of working through this component you will have a clear idea of the advantages and disadvantages of encouraging trainee self evaluation. You will also be able to locate the notion of trainee self evaluation against the broader context of training in general. Finally you will have some specific ideas on how to encourage trainee self evaluation.

Advantages

Trainee self evaluation is largely intended to help both the trainee and the trainer to make judgements about how well, or otherwise, the trainee is progressing and to formulate future training needs. To use the technical terms it is a process that is largely DIAGNOSTIC and FORMATIVE. It **forms** part of the constant review of **diagnosis** of the progress that the trainee is making. Trainee self evaluation is intended to help both the trainee and the trainer to become more aware of those areas of training which have been mastered and those which still have to be mastered. (See Component Two of this Study Unit).

Self evaluation is, of course, a process that is going on all the time. We all do it. However, unless it is properly structured and unless we are working towards understood and agreed objectives and criteria it can be a much less useful process than it should be.

And it is a useful process both for the trainees and for yourself.

Most good trainers will be aware of those aspects of the training that are likely to prove difficult. It might be a particular idea that is difficult, or possibly a particular procedure. When that occurs it is recognised that more time has to be devoted to that aspect of the training. By and large we are quite good at identifying particular problem areas. Unfortunately we almost always make mistakes. The mistake is that we assume too much too easily. This happens because we normally ignore what is usually the most sophisticated diagnostic information available, which comes from the trainee's own perceptions. The trainee's own perceptions of whether or not he has attained the skill or mastered the topic or feels good about what is going on is a unique and invaluable source of information.

There are two main advantages in involving the trainees in their own evaluation. The first is that it is in itself a learning experience. Objectives and criteria for success are understood and agreed. The second is that the information generated goes beyond the level of how much progress is being made. It will also include information about how the trainee feels. Since feelings affect performance this too is vital information and information that is most accurately supplied by the trainees themselves. Component One in this Study Unit explores this more personal aspect of training in detail. At this point you might care to look back at Component One and refresh your memory. The main point is that training is more than just making people able to do particular things. People must be both able and willing and that is why attention to the feelings of the trainees is part of your task.

It is most important to remember that self evaluation is, for the trainees, part of their learning. At the very least it provides the trainees with the opportunity to reflect on what they have been doing and arrive at some understanding of how they feel about it all. We can at this point compile a checklist of the advantages of involving trainees in their own evaluation.

* Self evaluation is part of the training. Trainees have the opportunity of understanding the objectives of the training and the criteria by which progress towards those objectives will be measured.
* The effectiveness of the training is increased. By structuring self evaluation into the training programme, difficulties or problems can be quickly identified and particular ways of coping may be found. The approaches to coping with difficulties or problems can be more obviously geared to the needs of the individual trainees since it is they, as individuals, who are presenting the issue.
* Future training needs can be established.
* The very nature of self evaluation with its sharing of objectives and criteria means that there is much more chance of a greater degree of commitment and motivation on the part of the trainees. You may remember that this was one of the arguments in Component Two. At this point you may wish to return to Component Two and re-read the relevant section.
* Self evaluation gives the trainer more accurate information about the trainees and about a wider range of concerns.

Checkpoint

The main advantages of self evaluation have been listed.

Are there any disadvantages that you can think of? You will find that there is one main disadvantage and that is briefly referred to in Component Two.

A further look at that disadvantage and how to overcome it will be provided later in this Component.

Implications for training

At this point I think it would be helpful if I turned things around and placed self evaluation within the context of training as a whole.

Trainees self evaluation has some quite startling implications for the training process. The utilisation of self evaluation as I have described it indicates a particular form or pattern or training. I will outline some of the **typical** features of that pattern and then indicate some of the costs and some of the benefits involved.

* An action or an activity is performed, preferably by the trainee. The effects of that activity are observed. This is the first step in a process whereby information is generated only through the sequencing of the successive steps in the process. What happens **after** this step is more important than the activity itself. For this reason it is important to be sure that the activity itself does not overload the thinking and feeling capabilities of the trainees. The over-loading to which I refer is quite a common feature of the lecture and note-taking approach. In order to observe the effects of the activity you must allow the trainees to share the feelings and insights that accrued as a result of the event.
The results of this individual sharing should be examined by the group in order to establish the patterns, themes, dimensions or insights that have emerged.
* The trainees now have to make generalisations based on the particular circumstances of the activity. From the specific activity a generalised principle emerges. In this way the trainee moves from the activity to the "real world".
Some theoretical/instructional in-put could be made at this point. This could provide a context for the learning or introduce a wider perspective. However, there is a danger that this in-put is not "owned" by the trainees. It can remain something that someone else is telling them.
* The final step in the process requires the trainees to apply the generalisations to actual circumstances. The circumstances need not be the same as those presented in the original activity. In fact the learning is better if the trainees can apply their insights to different working situations or circumstances.

Once again the sharing of conclusions amongst the trainees is an important element at this stage since it is a way of affirming those conclusions. The act of affirmation generally serves to reinforce the trainees' "ownership" of the learning that has taken place.

This pattern of learning has costs and benefits. Among the benefits are:

* The growth of self-assurance. This is largely through having the "ownership" of the learning that has just been described but also because the nature of the process brings people together to share their evaluations.

* Motivation becomes an intrinsic part of the work. Since action occurs at the beginning of the process rather than at the end the personal need for learning exists from the start. It is also a different sort of motivation since the learners are not passive recipients but have to invest themselves in the learning.

* The trainees are "in touch" with the realities being studied.
  The training experience that is most effective is one where the trainee has an experience of what is to be learned, or at least some simulation of that reality. A favourite example of this refers to driving and reading. Most people best learn to drive by driving and not by reading about driving although the latter might be possible. In other words people have the experiences of driving from which generalisations about road safety etc. can be made and actually applied on future occasions, if the instructor is competent. Reading is also an experience but it is an experience of reading, not of driving.

* This pattern of learning means that a much wider range of people can be involved in the learning process than is the case with lectures, for example. Not only is this a pattern which is appropriate for those who are at ease with lectures, it is also appropriate for those who are not. Thus those who are fed up with academic work or disadvantaged by virtue of their lack of mastery of the complex skills demanded by lectures have an alternative pattern of learning with which to become involved.

* Both the academic **and** the emotional aspects of learning are emphasised (both of which are in **reality** part of everyone's learning) as opposed to the artificial and essentially limiting (in terms of participants and scope of learning) emphasis on the academic, factual information orientation.

Among the costs are:

* Objectives have to be stated in general terms ("to examine", "to become aware", to understand" etc.) because this pattern of learning is more of a personal journey and the exact outcomes cannot be specified in advance.

* The need for a long period of time to work the process through.

* Large-scale perspectives are not easily arrived at: a lecture-discussion format would be better for that purpose.

* The learners may know, inductively, what is to be known yet be unable to articulate their knowing. This makes assessment particularly problematic, though by no means impossible. Alternative forms of assessment have to be considered. In that sense self evaluation becomes an essential part of the process.

The characteristics of the pattern of training that I have described are, I am sure, quite familiar to you.

For yourself make a checklist of those characteristics that are already present in your own training programmes.

REPORT BACK
I would be very surprised if you could not relate any of the characteristics that I have described to your own training programmes.

A crucial part of the pattern of training that I have described will be the questions that you ask of the trainees. Look again at the section on questioning in Component 3 of this Study Unit.

How to do it

It is most unlikely that you will be able to make any serious attempt at involving the trainees in self evaluation in any structured or helpful manner unless they have been prepared in a variety of ways. You probably will not be able to walk straight into the room and announce that, "This morning I want each of you to evaluate your own progress to date". A suitable climate or atmosphere must be established. It must not seem an odd thing to do. In order for it to appear to be natural some preparations must be made.

In this section of the Component I want to share with you some ideas on how to prepare your trainees and how to set up a situation whereby self evaluation can occur.

1. Brainstorming
Aim:
To provide an opportunity for trainees to generate a substantial number of ideas, solutions to problems, alternative courses of action from which choices may be made. Since it is part of the methodology of brainstorming that **all** ideas are welcome everyone may join in without fear of failure. This may help to foster a feeling of trust and security in the classroom.

Procedure
A topic is chosen and the trainees have to suggest as many ideas as possible in connection with that topic within a set time limit, e.g. five minutes. With the first few times of use a group that is unfamiliar with this procedure might well be slow to respond.

The topics may cover virtually anything (and brainstorming may therefore be used by virtually any trainer):

* What are the objectives of this programme?
* What are the ways that you can tell you are achieving the objectives of this programme?
* What are the purposes of being involved in a training programme?
* What makes a "good" trainee?
* What are the characteristics of being a good (type of job)?

This exercise can and should be repeated time and time again until the practice of it becomes easier as time goes on.

There are certain rules in brainstorming that should be followed:

1) Under no circumstances should any idea be criticised.
2) The larger the number of ideas the better it is. Quantity, in this instance, comes before quality. From the quantity quality may emerge.
3) Ideas may be used to spark off other ideas. One may build on previous ideas.

4) Even the strangest of ideas should be encouraged for therein lies the possibility of an imaginative or creative solution.
5) Each idea should be recorded (e.g. on a chalkboard) so that trainees can refer to them later.
6) A time limit should be set in advance to encourage rapid responses and to alleviate trainees of the burden of deciding when they have got enough responses.

When the time limit has been reached the trainees could be asked to select one or two or five (etc.) of the "best" responses, in their opinion, for special consideration. In this way this is an ideal exercise for use in generating alternative forms of action, gathering ideas about consequences or as a first step in beginning to negotiate and agree on priorities.

As a follow-up to this exercise the trainees could be asked to join up with a partner in order to focus with each other on particular items they think apply to them. For example, if the trainees have "brainstormed" "What makes a good trainee" the next step could be to ask them to focus on and share with a partner those qualities which they feel that they own. This procedure could be built into a structured conversation. Details of holding a structured conversation will follow shortly. Perhaps you can see that this is a way of involving trainees in a form of self evaluation. It is also an approach into involving trainees in the negotiation aspect of self evaluation.

▰▰▰

Make up for yourself a list of topics that you could ask trainees to brainstorm. Your list should be specific to your own concerns.

2. Coat of Arms
Aim:
This can be thought of as a "fun" activity yet it is one whereby the trainees really are involved in self

evaluation and in thinking about future plans of action.

Procedure:

Each trainee is given a blank sheet of A4 size paper. They are instructed to draw a coat of arms on this paper as shown below.

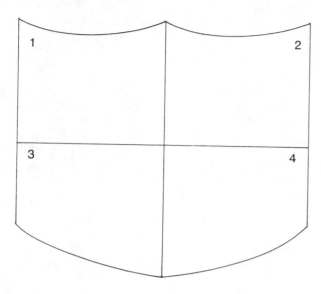

Into each of the compartments the trainees have to draw a symbol to represent the following:

1. My greatest achievement in this training programme.
2. Something in this training programme that I would like to do better.
3. The way that I feel about this training programme at the moment.
4. My ambition.

You can, of course, alter the classification of the various compartments to suit your own requirements.

The various shields can simply be collected in for your own information. Alternatively the trainees can be encouraged to talk to each other and to you about what they have produced. The shields could even be displayed and up-dated periodically. You should tell the trainees what will happen to the shields, or what they are going to have to do with them before actually starting.

Do try this. It will take about thirty minutes. You should receive a lot of useful information.

3. Hierarchy
Aim:

To encourage trainees to exercise their judgement in selecting priorities in training and to make them aware of other people's perspectives.

Procedure:

The trainees are divided into small groups of three or four. Each group is given an envelope containing statements of objectives for the training programme. Each statement of an objective is typed onto a separate slip of paper so that each envelope contains a number of slips of paper. Depending upon the kind of training the actual number of objectives could be as few as six or as many as sixty. The task for the trainees is to work together to identify the major objectives and arrange them in order of priority. The number of major objectives to be selected would obviously vary. Your instruction to the trainees who were considering six objectives could be, "In your envelope there are six pieces of paper. Each piece of paper contains an objective for the training programme. Your task is to select and rank in order of importance the three main objectives." With a larger number of statements obviously more can be selected as priorities. However, I would suggest that the maximum number should be limited to ten otherwise the exercise becomes unwieldy. You should be prepared to allow thirty minutes for this exercise and obviously longer if the trainees actually are having to prioritise as many as ten objectives.

The results of each group's deliberations should be gathered in and displayed. This can be done by simply writing on a chalkboard or some other display surface such as an overhead projector. The display will form the focus of future discussions.

Still in groups the trainees can begin to share their own perceptions of their performance in relation to the displayed objectives. Questions could include:

"What are you happy about?"

"Do you have any anxieties?"

This procedure can be adapted in a variety of ways. For example the statements could be about specific aspects of training.

"Essentials of First Aid".

"The most important things to do with servicing a car".

"Priorities in arranging a playgroup."

Prepare this activity for your own trainees.

Now use it.

4. Diary
Aim:

The diaries, which can be written on a weekly basis, may provide a record of individual activities, feelings and possibly growth.

Procedure:

These are personal records and could contain things which the trainees might be prepared to share with a trusted trainer but not necessarily with other trainees. The various forms of this diary, or types of content, are listed below:

a) A daily record: "What did I do with my time?" "How did I feel about it?"
b) Recording successes: incidents which make a good day.
c) Recording decisions: one is always having to make decisions. The trainees keep a record of their decisions and how they felt about them.
d) Recording possible improvements: how the day/week could have been better.

The trainees may choose any number of the topics listed above to write about.

A number of serious questions might be asked. For example:

Recording decisions:

"How many times did I stick to my decisions?"

"How do I make decisions i.e. did anything influence me?"

"Would I change my decisions with the benefit of hindsight?"

5. Today

Aim:

To encourage trainees to focus on their own feelings and understand something of the feelings of others.

Procedure:

Each trainee is provided with a continuum sheet which they then complete by ticking the appropriate place along the line. Ticks can be placed at **any** point along the line, even between the numbers if that is where people think that the tick really belongs.

Sample Continuum sheet.

Today I feel —

1	2	3	4	5
Strong				Weak

1	2	3	4	5
Hating				Loving

1	2	3	4	5
Happy				Sad

1	2	3	4	5
Worried				Care-free

1	2	3	4	5
Interested				Bored

1	2	3	4	5
Tense				Relaxed

1	2	3	4	5
Brave				Fearful

1	2	3	4	5
Impatient				Patient

1	2	3	4	5
Calm				Turbulent

1	2	3	4	5
Unsuccessful				Successful

Other sheets containing other items could easily be made up by yourself or by the trainees. Since the sheets are meant to focus upon one's feelings at **that moment** then the exercise may be repeated and even incorporated into the trainees diaries.

6. Structured Conversation

Aim:

To provide the trainees with the opportunity to reflect on particular aspects of the training programme and to share their reflections with a partner.

Procedure:

This is a very straightforward process yet it needs to be conducted sensitively. You could easily lead the trainees into areas where they are exposing particular aspects of themselves which normally they would not be prepared to share.

The trainees are arranged in pairs, or at most in groups of three. You then ask them to share with each other their responses to a variety of topics. Choice of those topics will reside with you. It is possible to raise four or five topics at any one time. You should allow approximately five minutes between each topic. This gives each trainee the time to talk about the topic for two minutes or so.

Topics:

What aspects of the training do you particularly enjoy?

Why are you on this training programme?

Are there any things about the training that you find particularly irksome?

What have you found success at?

Is there anything that you feel you need more help at doing?

Suggest some improvements to the training programme that you would like to see.

Would you recommend this training programme to anyone else?

You will have to structure the topics that you raise in such a way so that that they actually follow each other in a logical sequence.

Time should be spent at the end of the session in eliciting responses from the trainees in an open forum.

"How did they feel?" "What were the main points that arose?"

It could lead into a "brainstorming" of particular topics so that there is a basis for the kind of negotiation that is part of self-evaluation.

7. Formal self evaluation

Aim:

You may already do this. Simply it involves using a particular device with the trainees so that they can focus their thinking about an aspect of the training in a more formal fashion. By way of explanation an example of a formal device from a catering course is provided.

Amongst other things it is a way of reminding the trainees of what the course is all about.

The top part of the form, marked Skills and Attitude/Effort although not completed by the trainees will among other things serve the purpose of informing the trainees of some of your criteria for success. They will understand some of the things that you are looking for apart from simply recall of knowledge. A perceptive trainee may well begin to think, "Works well with others? Cares for equipment?, Well do I?"

Aims of Module: To acquire knowledge of nutrition and apply it to the planning and preparation of a meal			
Checklist of objectives	Always	Sometimes	Rarely
SKILLS: Follows instructions Uses full range of equipment Cares for equipment Plans/organises work Solves problems			
ATTITUDE/EFFORT Attentive Willing worker Works well with others Actual work matches ability			
UNDERSTANDING/RECALL OF KNOWLEDGE		YES	NO
Can you give examples of foods rich in: Calcium Protein Vitamin C Vitamin D Iron			
Can you say why the following are important: Calcium Protein Vitamin C Vitamin D Iron			
Do you understand the following terms: balanced diet convenience food junk food attractive presentation			

Write a brief comment on each of the following sentence starters

The amount of effort that I made was ....

Difficulties that I found were..

My interest and enjoyment of the topic was ....

A way of improving the course is...

8. Self evaluation and peer evaluation
Aim:

During this process the trainees working in small groups will be asked to grade themselves and then think carefully about the reasons for their individual grading and this is the learning experience. (See Procedure below).

Reasons must be offered for both the individual and group marks and so superficiality and bias are excluded.

At the same time a number of important social skills are being exercised.

The approach described should help the trainees to understand more clearly the goals they are working towards and at the same time give evidence of their confidence, their willingness and ability to work with others, their honesty, their readiness to accept responsibility and so on.

Finally, the trainees are being encouraged to take responsibility for their own learning.

Procedure
1. The trainees are divided into small groups. Three is an ideal number for this.
2. Each trainee writes about what they have acquired from the training session. In the previous example the trainees could have written something about protein.
3. Each trainee gives him or herself a mark or grade for their written work.
4. Each piece of writing is then considered by the other members of the group.
   The group must reach a consensus "group mark" for each piece of writing.

You will notice that once again negotiation and the shared understanding of criteria are important elements in this.

9. Ending a training session
Aim:

If at the end of an exercise there are still a number of points of learning still unexplained or "left in the air" the value of that exercise will be diminished. Generally speaking more can be gained by the trainee and by the trainer interested in evaluating the session if some definite ending can be reached. This brief exercise is just one way of establishing a definite conclusion.

Procedure:

Unfinished sentence exercises can be a good way of concluding any session. Trainees may be given a specific sentence stem or offered a selection from among a number.

I learned ....

I was pleased that ....

I was displeased that..

I was disappointed that ....

I wonder why..

I wonder whether ....

I hope that...

I believe that...

The responses to these stems may be made verbally by the trainees or presented in some written form, for example in the diaries.

▰▰▰

These are activities of very different sorts from each other. Imagine that you actually are interested in involving the trainees in their self evaluation. You have decided to devote six periods of time between now and the end of the training programme. You are prepared to devote Friday afternoon to reviewing the week's work.

Which six activities out of the nine described will you use to involve the trainees and in which order will you use them?

___

Disadvantages — difficulties and some observations

1. There are three main disadvantages or difficulties with self evaluation. The extent to which trainee self evaluation will really have an impact is likely to depend on how it is arranged and used. Particular impact occurs when the self evaluation becomes an occasion for a helpful and democratic discussion between trainee and trainer.

So involving trainees in an evaluation dialogue is a simple means of providing a wealth of insight into the impact of training, how an individual trainee is coping with that training and its effect on him. In particular it can elicit information which must otherwise remain the exclusive property of the trainee but which may be of vital importance to the trainer in relating to that trainee.

However, one disadvantage or difficulty is that this can seem to be a case of prying into the trainee's own private thoughts.

Yet if you think about it self evaluation is, by definition voluntary (trainees cannot be forced to share their thoughts). It therefore avoids the very serious reservations many people have about any formal evaluation of personal attributes or qualities. It is simple to operate, takes very little time or organisation and is readily incorporated into training. Perhaps most important is the fact that involving trainees in evaluation acknowledges their status as unique, independent and worthwhile individuals. Unquestioned stereotypical views of trainees are quickly demolished. This must be a powerful ally in the training process.

2. Although formal evaluation is logistically difficult for the unaided trainer, for some trainers the solution might be discussion with small groups of trainees about a particular unit of work. Other trainers may prefer to record their impressions from observing the group at work. Another approach is to ask trainees directly for their comments.

Your first reaction to this last suggestion is likely to be apprehension — an apprehension arising from fear of criticisms, and of who might hear these criticisms.

For this reason, in this country, such evaluation has not typically been widespread.

Interestingly enough, in the United States it is quite a different story for, at various levels and even at University level, student's or trainee's evaluations are made public and provide the major basis on which subsequent students or trainees choose their courses. With this rather daunting idea in mind, any suggestion of involving trainees in the assessment process is typically greeted by a howl of opposition. The line most often taken is that trainees, by virtue of being trainees, lack the necessary knowledge and experience needed to evaluate a training programme, far less a trainer. However, this actually misses the main point for in self evaluation the focus of attention is actually the trainee. The comments that are made are about the trainees themselves and the progress that they feel they are making.

3. Self evaluation does not take place in a vacuum. It takes place within a training and working environment. There is no such thing as a "Neutral" or value-free self evaluation. The focus is on oneself but more than that it is on oneself within a particular context. As far as we are concerned the context is the organisation itself.

Different types of organisations have different cultures or styles of operation. It is important for you to be attuned to the overriding culture and style of that organisation. One of the problems/tensions may be where individuals hold different values about the task and who in reality may want to be in an organisation with a different culture, e.g. those who wish to do away with hierarchy in an obviously hierarchical system. This again raises the issue about method because consultation and negotiation will require individuals to make explicit their underlying values and feelings about belonging to a particular organisation.

However, negotiation may be a way of opening up the discussion about ways of changing the organisation if that is deemed to be desirable. Where it is perhaps not deemed to be desirable then the discussion will at least inform you of some of the organisation factors that the trainees perceive as being an influence on their performance.

Reflect back over the content of this Component.

Make for yourself a checklist to show just how many of the ideas and examples of good practice are already in operation in your organisation.

This leads us into the next Component in this Study Unit, which is concerned with institutional self evaluation.

Component 5:

Institutional Self-Evaluation

Key Ideas

 Purposes of institutional self-evaluation, costs and benefits; product and process evaluation; quality; keeping records; personal qualities; communication; listening; solving problems; working as a group; making decisions; institutional ethos; holding meetings; departmental self-evaluation; institutional ideologies: institutional effectiveness.

Key objectives

During the course of this Component you will arrive at an understanding of the purposes of institutional self-evaluation. You will become acquainted with particular areas associated with institutional self-evaluation and become familiar with the check lists and questions that can be raised about those areas. This familiarity is intended to help you to initiate the process of institutional self-evaluation within the context of your own institution.

Institutional self-evaluation has two main purposes. Firstly, it is to improve the training programme. Secondly, it is to promote staff development. In order to achieve these purposes we will have to think of the institution in four different but not completely unconnected ways. These are:

Physical environment

This includes the design and layout of the building or buildings and the type and nature of the facilities that the buildings house.

Aspects of organisation

This focuses on the established routines and expected codes of behaviour, including rules and regulations.

People

Attention must be paid to the members of the instituion at all levels in terms of their background, level of involvement, motives and expectations.

Atmosphere

This arises out of a combination of the first three items, but it is not reducible to those items since as a combination it is the result of the interaction of the members of the institution with each other as influenced by various aspects of the organisation in a particular environment.

▨▨▨ Checkpoint

At this point it would be useful if you could provide a description of your own institution according to the four categories given above. Set yourself a time limit of half-an-hour and with that limit be as thorough as you can. Imagine that you are describing your institution to someone who knows nothing about it. This will provide you with something concrete to think about as this component proceeds.

Before we move on to considering the various aspects of the institution that have just been briefly sketched we should examine some of the intentions and assumptions underpinning institutional self evaluation.

Institutional self-evaluation is primarily aimed at programme improvement and staff development. It can be thought of as a necessary stage in the planning of a training programme where such a programme is viewed as a means to an end, usually the production of a trained individual. In order to engage in programme development it is necessary to specify training goals and select the appropriate training contexts for pursuing those goals.

The opportunities and experiences provided by the training programme will be enhanced if you have a better understanding of the structure and policies of the institution. The analysis of policy decisions should provide information that is relevant to the making of decisions about training.

Self-evaluation allows the institution to determine and produce evidence of the quality of the training it provides. Remember that a compelling reason for espousing self-evaluation is that it encourages organisers and trainers to be committed to the implementation of any recommendations for action that may arise.

There is, of course, more than commitment at stake. Participation in institutional self-evaluation provides trainers with the opportunity to develop professional skills, enlarge perspectives and become better informed about the roles, responsibilities and problems of their colleagues.

As before it has to be recognised that this sort of self-evaluation can be very threatening to all those whose practice is under scrutiny. Consequently procedures have to be devised to protect those who might be vulnerable. These procedures should be made clear to everyone and be accepted as inviolate. It is impossible to be specific about the nature of these procedures since they could vary according to the nature of the organisation and its purposes. However, as a general rule the following procedures would be included:

1. **Impartiality**

   No favouritism should be shown towards particular individuals or aspects of institutional life unless there is a justification for doing so which everyone accepts. In other words it would be wrong to turn the spot-light on selected individuals or areas when in fact the whole institution should be illuminated. Indeed where there are certain areas that are not illuminated it can often turn out to be the case that these are the very areas affecting that which has been targeted.

2. **Co-operation**

   Institutional self-evaluation requires people to work together openly. It is a collaborative venture. This means that a degree of trust is necessary. Responsibility for the venture should be shared.

3. **Accountability**

   This can be the hardest part of all since it acknowledges that the institution is accountable for the quality of its work which in turn points up the accountability of individuals within the institution. Components 3 and 4 of this Study Unit should help various groups of people in their understanding of their roles. This aspect of self-

evaluation should be thought of in terms of it being a learning experience. It should be a feature of the development of individuals rather than any kind of potentially humiliating experience.

Properly handled, however, there are a number of benefits to be gained from institutional self-evaluation

— it would stimulate staff to re-examine their own work and that of their colleagues;
— it would require total staff participation and therefore would act as a means of welding people together;
— it would contribute to the professional development of the staff as a whole and increase the confidence of individual trainers;
— it could help staff to develop a common language for the discussion of training issues.

This is quite important. Unfortunately, no-one can do this task for you in the first instance. Perhaps later on you will be able to persuade other trainers to have a go. Think about the three procedures that I have described - IMPARTIALITY, CO-OPERATION, ACCOUNTABILITY. Think also of your own situation. How in practical terms might these procedures operate? Try to draw up a check list of key tasks.

It is important to recognise that evaluation of the sort envisaged demands the engagement of everyone with the matters in hand as fully as possible.

Considered views, cogently expressed, are what one hopes for. Proposals that take into account likely future trends and possibilities will be valuable as well as ones with more immediate but perhaps short-lived, applicability.

One way into institutional self evaluation is to establish Working Parties to investigate particular aspect of the life of the institution, however, in view of the possibly novel nature of the whole enterprise, and for practical reasons it would be unwise to engage in institutional self-evaluation by starting a large number of Working Parties simultaneously. Among the risks in doing so are:

* that the available expertise will be pulled in too many directions at once.

* that meetings of the various Working Parties become so numerous that they crowd out other important activities.

* that the meeting of Working Parties will be neglected in favour of other activities so that progress is slow and interest wanes.

* as far as possible everyone should be involved for the reasons already given.

In engaging in the evaluation of the various aspects of the institutions work it will often turn out that the work falls into four stages.

* A comprehensive description of the present circumstances/organisational arrangements/ procedures relating to the matter in hand.

* Identification and statement of the strengths of the present arrangements, etc., and/or statement of desirable arrangements.

* Identification and statement of the apparent drawbacks in the present arrangements.
* An attempt to find ways of minimising/eliminating the drawbacks whilst retaining the strengths.

In some areas of study there may be a large degree of understanding of the points at issue. For the majority of issues, however, it is doubtful if that will be the case. For this majority careful progress through the four stages is the approach most likely to lead to improvements of lasting value.

Products and process

In Component One of this Study Unit we saw that evaluation can be thought of in two ways. One way was to think of evaluation in terms of the product of the training and the other way was to think of evaluation in terms of the process of the training.

What do we mean by the product and the process of training and why must both be considered as part of the task of self-evaluation?

Although both the product and the process of training have to be considered in order to obtain a comprehensive evaluation I intend, for the sake of clarity to examine each in turn in the context of institutional self-evaluation.

Product evaluation

Every training organisation has some idea as to what constitutes its effectiveness. To give some system and structure and thereby enable more accurate and objective descriptions of the organisation the following functions are suggested. The evaluation of these functions will be a major feature of the training establishment's own development.

* specifying the goals of the training.
* specifying criteria by which movement towards the goals can be ascertained.
* establishing procedures whereby information about movement towards the goals can be compared with the original plans and intentions about such movement.
* deciding whether the type and rate of movement is acceptable.
* if the type and rate of movement is unacceptable ,then instituting problem-solving procedures for altering the manner of moving towards the goals.
* establishing ways of putting into practice any alterations in the manner of moving towards the goals.

Purely in terms of product the six functions just listed are vital. The institution has to be clear that it is performing those functions if it is to be effective.

The following six items are likely to be the hallmarks of an inefficient institution:

* goals and priorities are vague
* goals are poorly communicated
* the personal goals of the trainers and trainees have little in common with the overall purposes of the institution.

* the institution is not sufficiently sensitive to the external environment, society as a whole.
* the institution is unable to alter its goals to accommodate rapid changes.
* insufficient time is spent on planning for the future.

One general concern that is common to all institutions is a concern for that vague item "quality". Although it might seem to be obvious that the institution would wish to ask questions about the quality of the product. What sorts of questions should these be? Once again it will be true that to a large extent any specific or detailed response to that question will depend very largely on the kind of institution that is being considered. Nevertheless there are some general considerations that will apply to all training establishments. The following checkpoint will provide you with some indication as to the kinds of items that your institution might care to consider.

Evaluating Quality

	DEFINITELY YES			DEFINITELY NO	
	1	2	3	4	5
1. There is a concern for quality in the institution.					
2. Senior Management have a clear policy about quality.					
3. Trainees know that Senior Management have high expectations of them.					
4. Trainees know that trainers have high expectations of them.					
5. There is a common policy on quality control in the institution.					
6. All departments have a concern for quality.					
7. Our trainees are successful in finding employment.					
8. Any trainee's progress can be determined at any time of the year.					
9. The work of this institution compares well with other institutions.					
10. We are successful in achieving our aims and objectives.					
11. This is a very efficient and effective staff.					
12. We make full use of external agencies to monitor our work.					
13. We are proud of our results.					
14. We are proud of the trainees we turn out.					
15. Our neighbourhood reputation is very good.					

One particular aspect of the quality of the product will be the recording of information about the progress of the trainees. Again, irrespective of the kind of training that is taking place or the type of product that is being sought there are some general questions to ask about the institution's policy on keeping records. The checkpoint that follows, therefore, does not seek to ask questions about the progress of the trainees. Instead it is intended as an institutional review of record keeping.

Record Keeping

1. a) What demands are made on sources of recorded information?
   b) What demands on recorded information could not at present be met?
2. Under whose auspices (e.g. individual trainer's departments: Senior Management) is information about trainees stored?
3. a) Who is aware of what information is stored?
   b) Who has access to it?
4. In what locations is information stored?
5. In what respects is stored information about trainees
   a) duplicated
   b) cross-referenced?
6. What arrangements are made to facilitate the access of staff to information?
7. What arrangements are made to protect confidentiality?
8. What techniques are used to ensure that information can be withdrawn from records in a form which is of most use to enquirers? (e.g. is attainment recorded by trainee name, by training group, by sex?)
9. How is information
   a) added to records: b) evaluated:
   c) standardised: d) checked: e) superseded?
10. To what extent is information in records
    a) checked: b) evaluated: c) superseded?

11. To what extent are the systems used for storing information in the institution compatible?
12. What resources of a) time and b) money are devoted to record keeping?
13. Who has an interest in or responsibility for
    a) developing; b) servicing the facility for data handling and storage?

You will recall that in Component One a connection was made between the product and the process of the training. I argued that the acquisition of knowledge and skills on their own was not enough. Such an acquisition would not be a complete form of training. The development of personal qualities is also important. Although the evaluation of personal qualities may well reside primarily with the individual (one argument in favour of self-evaluation) the institution itself must ask questions about its own role in undertaking such an evaluation. The checklist that follows raises questions of the sort that the institution might be asking in order to evaluate and clarify its own position.

Evaluating Personal Qualities

To what extent and for what purpose are the personal attitudes, qualities and behaviour of the trainees evaluated?

How is the information on such evaluations stored?

What limitations are there on the gathering and storing of such information?

How are comparisons made both between trainees and on the same trainee over a period of time?

How are the evaluations of different trainers correlated?

Who has access to such information?

What mechanism is there for reviewing the information so that outdated or incorrect information can be removed?

Process evaluation

We also have to examine the working processes which the institution has implemented in order to arrive at a product. In other words we need to examine the ways in which the institution sets about its task.

Once again some key issues emerge which apply to all training institutions. Remember that process evaluation concerns itself with what happens as the organisation functions since that will help us to understand the effects that the institution produces. Process evaluation must focus, therefore, on the following activities:

1. **Communication.** This means enabling communication between everyone involved in the training to occur. Gripes, requests, reports on progress are part of this process. There are, of course various ways and means of communicating one with another and attention must be given to those sorts of detail. Consequently are people able to ask questions, clarify what they hear and simply listen to each other?

Listening

Listening to other people, really listening, is not quite as easy as we might assume. Look at the following statements and see how many of them apply to you.

When I have something on the tip of my tongue that I want to say I ignore everyone else until I have got it off my chest.

When I can anticipate what the other person has to say I tend to jump in and say it for them.

I value what you have to say because I value you as an individual. I don't particularly listen to people that I don't value.

The longer a person speaks the harder I find it to concentrate.

If an argument develops then I become more interested in winning the argument than in trying to appreciate what the other person is saying.

When I hear misinformation I respond to that rather than the essence of the discussion.

Needless to say these are things that we all do and yet they are all things that cause us to erect barriers to prevent effective listening and hence effective communication.

2. **Solving problems as a group.** Attention should be paid not simply to whether or not groups can solve problems but at the ways in which they are able to work at that task. A key question must be, "How can people work together more effectively?"

Solving problems as a group

What follows are those characteristics which tend to produce poor team work. Please notice that these are overwhelmingly characteristics that should be the concern of the management. Use the scale provided to evaluate your own institution.

	Never	Sometimes	Often
There is conflict between departments.			
People do not work together on common problems.			
People who work together fail to say what they really think.			
Managers from different departments fail to communicate with each other.			
Meetings are unproductive.			
Teams do not deliberately attempt to improve the ways in which they work together.			

More encouragingly it is possible to identify those factors that contribute to the development of a healthy, helpful and effective working group.

The style of leadership (autocratic; persuasive; consultative; democratic) fits both the task and the group.

The task interests the group and they feel competent and willing to deal with it.

The ways of working are consistent with the objectives and are well suited to the group.

The composition and size of group is appropriate to task to be done.

An opportunity is given for unfinished business from previous meetings to be cleared up and members are allowed time to settle into the task.

A clear and acceptable rationale for the task is presented; ground rules are agreed and applied.

There is a clarity of purpose and well-defined routes to its achievement.

Participation is distributed evenly; everyone is involved.

Conflict (if present) is brought out and dealt with and not ignored, brushed aside or allowed to fester.

The trainer leads by example, modelling what he is inviting the trainees to do.

Trust exists within the group; members feel they can say things about themselves without needing to fear that this will be ridiculed, rejected, or used against them subsequently.

The trainer is confident of his or her skills and the content of his or her teaching; he or she presents calmly and is sufficiently relaxed for the trainees to feel the same.

The trainer has the necessary group management skills.

The training session blends serious work with light relief or changes of pace. Humour lightens the sessions and is shared in by the whole group.

Co-operation between group members is the rule rather than the exception.

The trainer's behaviours are clear and open. The trainer is consistent and behaves predictably.

The language that is used during the training is appropriate to the task and the group.

The trainer is sensitive to what the group members are feeling and experiencing and checks out his or her assumptions appropriately.

Some of these factors might appear to you to be more important than others. Think of your institution and the kind of training in which you are involved. Try to arrange the factors listed above in order of importance so that number one is the most important and number eighteen is the least important.

By and large the factors that have been listed are well within the control of the working group itself. There are however other factors which may be outside the control of the group. The following "external" factors are likely to contribute to a good working group atmosphere.

The space available is appropriate to the group size and is used in a way that produces feelings of easiness and closeness.

The work area has pleasant associations for those working in it.

The trainer is readily available.

The group is safe from outside interference and is consequently able to work without interruption.

The work area is warm, airy, and comfortable.

The time of the training event and amount of time available for that event are suitable to all and appropriate to the task.

I am of course referring to the best of all possible worlds. However, the closer the institution can come to attaining the atmosphere in which people can work co-operatively and effectively then the closer it will be coming to maximising its training potential. If the institution is serious about evaluating the product and the process of its training then these are some of the factors that have to be taken into account.

3. **Making decisions.** Decision making is hindered when there is no clear understanding of what is to be achieved. This may be due to the fact that the managers do not have access to all the relevant information, or because adequate criteria have not been developed. Alternatively, it might be the case that too many decisions are made by top management, possibly in response to pressures from outside of the institution. In this case there is a lack of delegation and a wastage of talent.

Making decisions

The following is a checklist of questions which you can use in order to review the decision-making processes in your own institution.

What is the consultative structure used to help arrive at policy decisions?

Are there adequate opportunities for all members of staff to express their views?

What steps do senior staff take outside the formal consultative structure to keep in touch with the views and hopes of their colleagues?

How are decisions recorded and communicated?

What methods are used for making clear who is responsible for seeing that decisions are carried out?

What steps are taken for reviewing the effects of decisions?

Is there a Staff Guide? How often is it reviewed? How is this review conducted? Is the Guide worth the trouble taken to produce it? If not, should it be altered or abolished?

Should trainees have a part to play in the consultative structure? If so do our arrangements work well? How might they be improved?

The ethos of the institution

In this section of this component I intend to look at the institution itself and raise questions about its ethos. By this I mean that I hope to provide you with some tools whereby you can engage with the institution as a whole in order to establish what kind of a place it actually is. What are the characteristics of the institution? What is its disposition?

We can begin this process by examining an area of institutional life which is often taken for granted largely because it is so obvious. The fact that it is an area that is often neglected makes it particularly suitable for our purposes since it can reveal a lot about the nature of the institution. The aspect of institutional life that I am talking about is "The Meeting". The ways in which meetings are conducted can prove to be very illuminating. They can tell us a lot about the nature of the institution. Of course, if there are **never** any meetings then that in itself will tell us something. However, if we assume that meetings do occur then the following checklist of questions might provide further illumination.

Holding meetings
a) **Before the meeting: concepts**
1. How long has the chairperson been considering this agenda?
2. Has this been discussed with senior staff?
3. Is there a group that meets regularly to discuss such matters?
4. Where did the chairperson get the idea for the agenda?
b) **Structure**
5. How were participants prepared? Options include a pre-meeting "paper" or a document circulated? A working party established to consider an issue on the agenda? Informal discussion? Canvassing of opinion? No preparation whatsoever? How were participants notified or informed of the meeting?
6. Was the meeting room prepared in any special way? For example the seating might have been altered, refreshments may have been made available.

7. Are all the participants who will be involved in later implementation actually present?
8. What is the initial tone of the meeting? For example was there a prompt and fluent start or were there a number of late arrivals? The manner by which the agenda was introduced might be significant.

c) **The course of the meeting**
9. How did people participate?
   Did many people participate and who were they? Were there any dominant participants? Did anybody make a record of what was going on?
10. Were there any expressions of commitment or purpose? What sorts of questions were asked? Were they ambiguous or specific?
    Were the comments relevant? Did the participants call for clarity?
    Could the level of interest be gauged? For example did the participants see the agenda as an opportunity to help them to attain professional and/or personal goals or was it seen as threatening?
11. How did the participants react with each other? To whom were comments addressed? To what extent and in what ways were participants controlled? How did participants support each other (e.g. listening, clarifying, reflecting back ideas)? What was the degree of mutual understanding?

d) **Ending the meeting**
12. How did the meeting end?
    Did the meeting end on time?
13. What were the overall impressions?
    Did people seem anxious to leave or did people stay on to talk more?

Departmental Self-evaluation
Individual departments can also ask questions of themselves with a view to developing their effectiveness. The question in the following checkpoint largely suggests a certain desirable state of affairs. A suggested rationale for answering these leading questions in a particular way is provided at the end of this component. Please regard these questions in the first place, however, as indicators of what should be happening within individual departments.

Departmental Self-evaluation

1. Why should communication and consultation within the department be efficient?
   Why should the staff feel effective members of the departmental team?
2. Why should departmental meetings be held?
   Why should minutes be kept?
3. How should it be decided which trainer takes which groups?
4. Who should devise the training programme?
   When should it be revised?
   Why should all members of the Department have copies?
   Why should new trainers receive copies in advance as a matter of course.
5. Why should individual trainers keep regular records of their plans of work?
   At what intervals of time should these be compiled?

Some suggested responses to these questions will be found at the end of this Component.

The ideology of the institution

Institutions have their own distinctive patterns of behaviour, beliefs, history and codes. These may make up the ideology of the institution. This ideology will affect the effectiveness of the institution. Certainly it will provide the context against which the quality of the product is measured, and within which people communicate, solve problems and make decisions.

The institution's ideology can be divided into three orientations: a) Authority, b) Task, c) People. If the institution is serious in its intentions towards self-evaluation then it is important to begin to understand its dominant ideological orientation. As I have indicated such an understanding provides the beginnings of an explanation as to why the institution operates as it does.

The ideology of the institution

Think of your own institution. Give a "3" to the statement that best represents the dominant view in your institution, a "2" to the one which is next closest to your institution's position and a "1" to the least dominant view.

A good trainer is:
a) strong, decisive and firm.
b) egalitarian and capable of being influenced about the proper completion of the task. He will use authority to obtain the resources necessary to complete the task.
c) concerned with the needs of others. His authority is used to provide satisfying work opportunities for the trainees.

A good trainee is:
a) obedient, hard working and loyal to his trainer.
b) motivated to contribute his best to the task and willing to follow others who have greater ability.
c) interested in developing his potential and in contributing to the development of others.

A good member of the institution gives first priority to the:
a) personal demands of the manager.
b) demands made by the task.
c) the personal needs of other individuals in the institution.

People who do well in the organisation are:
a) competitive, with a strong drive for power.
b) competent and effective with a determination to get the job done.
c) competent and effective in personal relationships.

The institution treats individuals as:
a) though their time were at the disposal of people higher in the hierarchy.
b) equal partners committed to a common cause.
c) interesting and worthwhile people in their own right.

People are controlled by:
a) rewards and punishments.
b) the discussion of the criteria associated with the satisfactory completion of the job.
c) concern for others in the institution.

It is legitimate for people to control the activities of others if:
a) they have more authority in the institution.
b) they know more about the job in hand.
c) it is accepted that they will thereby contribute to the learning of others.

People work together when:
a) they are required to by higher authority.
b) their joint collaboration is necessary in order to get the job done.
c) the collaboration is personally satisfying.

The purpose of competition is to:
a) gain an advantage for oneself.
b) increase the capacity to get the job completed.
c) draw attention to one's own personal needs.

Total your score for all the (a) statements and then all the (b) and (c) statements.

The set of statements which score most highly will reflect the dominant ideology of the institution.
Analysis:

(a) statements refer to aspects of an authoritarian ideology.

(b) statements refer to an ideology that is concerned with completing the task, getting the job done.

(c) statements indicate that the dominant ideology is "person-centred" so that the needs of people within the institutions are given priority on the grounds that satisfied people make better contributors to the institution.

REPORT BACK
Did the results of the analysis surprise you at all? The real purpose of the analysis is to help you to reflect on various aspects of the ideology of the institution. It might be possible for you to identify aspects of that ideology where changes could be made in order to improve the training.

The greater the match between institutional values and an individual's values then the greater the ease with which they can enter in a psychological contract with the organization. People deal with a "bad fit" between themselves and the organization in various ways, such as by trying to change the organization, by limiting their involvement in it, or by attacking it in various ways.

An institution that is genuinely concerned with the development of individuals will espouse the following values:

respect, genuineness and empathy between people.
co-operation between all people in achieving shared goals.
continuous self-evaluation and openness to change.
the development of individual strengths.
willingness to confront and solve problems.

The values listed will contribute to an effective institution. Our final checklist raises questions about the effectiveness of the institution.

The effectiveness of the institution

How is the personal and career development of all the members of the institution catered for?

Do individuals receive constructive comments about their work?

Do people attempt to see each others' points of view as part of a normal routine?

Are people given the opportunity to take part in the making of those decisions that will directly affect them?

What are the signs that people are valued and cared for?

To what extent do people deliberately seek to achieve consensus rather than always compromising or going with a majority vote?

What are the ways in which people can air their grievances?

Answers to the Checkpoint on Departmental Self-Evaluation (see page 242)

1. If a department is to be efficient the members, even those of a temporary status, must feel part of the team. Once this is established almost all the points raised in Questions 2 to 7 will, consciously or unconsciously, follow. At the same time all members of the training staff should feel effective members of a corporate body; a department cannot exist in isolation.

2. It is generally agreed that departmental meetings should be called by Heads of Department and held on a regular basis, depending on the size and "nature" of the department. Formal meetings should be held once a month and informal meetings could be held at intervals throughout the term.

3. Initially consultation should take place at Departmental level involving every member of the department. The final recommendations are the responsibility of the Head of Department who should show the final draft recommendations to all members of the department before submitting them to his superiors. Continuity and commitments of staff to other departments might be a major concern, and in this respect the over all head of training will have to study the needs of each department and a compromise may have to be effected and accepted. The head of training should explain the overall planning policy so that trainers may understand both the relevance of and the necessity for involvement of other trainers. There must remain an avenue open for the individual who is dissatisfied to consult the head of training.

4. Training programmes should be drawn up by the Head of Department in consultation with members of the department. The training programme should be flexible enough to allow for ·experiment providing it is looked at regularly, i.e. every year. Areas of work which have failed to motivate trainees should be reconsidered and new ideas put into action with a more thorough revision every two years.

   All members of the department should have a copy of the training programme and all departmental programmes should be accessible to all trainers.

   New members of staff should receive copies of training programmes well in advance, supported, if possible, by an explanation of where he fits into the department.

5. Individual trainers should keep records of their work, and that the same should be checked by Heads of Departments at frequent intervals. Records are considered useful:
   a) for personal reference
   b) as a guide to ensure adherence to the training programme
   c) for reference in the event of a prolonged absence.

Component 6:

Reviewing Self-Evaluation

 Key Ideas

The importance of trust; the process and the product of training; approaches to trainer self-evaluation; time management; motivation; induction of new trainees; working with other people; the training environment; self-evaluation and trainer credibility.

Key objectives

The intention of this Component is to emphasise certain major aspects of self-evaluation. This particular Component is to be thought of as a revision exercise whereby you are able to reflect on the concept of self-evaluation in a variety of contexts.

Introduction

In the final part of this Study Unit I wish to return to some of the key issues raised in the components dealing with trainer, trainee and institutional self-evaluation. By way of a revision exercise I intend to return to these key issues in a slightly different way to that originally presented.

If self-evaluation is to be more than a hollow exercise it must take place in an atmosphere of trust. Self-evaluation is best thought of as a process in which individuals at all levels in an institution are free to ask themselves and others about the work that they are doing. This process will reveal weaknesses both in people and in the institution. It will also reveal strengths that can be developed. However, nothing can be revealed if the atmosphere of trust that I have referred to is absent.

Trust takes time to grow. Self-evaluation may best be begun at a private, personal level, or with respect to the less sensitive or contentious issues in the institution. If it can be seen as bringing benefits to the institution then there will be a demand for more self-evaluation. However, these benefits will only be recognised if some mechanism exists for "feeding" back this acquired information into the institution. Only then can changes be made as part of the constant process of reviewing.

Regarding all aspects of self-evaluation there are certain key questions that must be asked. These questions should be asked in relation to any initiatives in self-evaluation.

1. What prompted the organisation to become interested in self-evaluation?

2. Who devised the self-evaluation documents?

3. What kind of approach was used and where did the idea come from?

4. What instruments were used and why did they have their particular emphasis?

5. What happens to the evaluation reports if any are produced?

6. What are the outcomes if no formal report is sought?

7. What kinds of problems were encountered?

8. What action, if any, does the institution take on the completion of an evaluation?

9. How frequently would any individual or organisation be expected to embark on a full-scale self-evaluation?

10. What is the role of outsiders in self-evaluation?

All of these questions take for granted one central assumption. This assumption is absolutely critical for without it no evaluation can occur.

▰▰▰ Checkpoint

What is the absolute critical assumption to which I am referring?

REPORT BACK
The assumption is that you are completely clear about your criteria for making judgements. At this point you may care to refer to Component One again.

___

▰▰▰

Initiating self-evaluation

Think about self-evaluation in the context of your own institution. Make a list of all of those items that could be the subject of self-evaluation. Now rank order those items so that number one on your list is the least threatening or sensitive item and the final number is the most threatening or sensitive.

___

It's my nose isn't it? Well if it isn't my nose it must be my feet.

Trainer self-evaluation

You will recall that trainer self-evaluation should involve the evaluation by trainers of their own training performance. This will include the evaluation of the process of training including trainer/trainee interaction, and the product of the training. The essential feature is that this exercise is conducted by the trainer himself.

The process of training refers to that which directly involves trainees and contributes to their educational experience. Processes can include transactions which take place outside the formal training activities such as those transactions which involve the welfare of the trainee.

The product of training refers to the trainee learning outcomes. Please remember that the product is not necessarily confined to the acquisition of knowledge or skill. It may, and in some instances certainly should include development in the areas of the trainees' values and attitudes.

How might trainer self-evaluation be conducted? Two distinct approaches seem to emerge.

— **Meeting-based.** This includes evaluations conducted through staff meetings, working parties, conferences, courses, (and in the case of the individual trainer working alone, through personal reflection).

— **Research-based.** This describes those exercises in which there has been some formal and fairly systematic effort to collect and analyse 'data'. Two particular research approaches can be identified.
(i) **quantitative** — data might include test results, results of public examinations and the use of interaction schedules.
(ii) **qualitative** — data here might include diaries, interviews, and video recordings.

There are, as always, a series of questions which you as trainers may care to ask of yourselves. As has often been the case these questions will, by the manner in which they are posed, indicate that certain things are more preferable than other things. That said, what are these questions?

Questions
How often did I
  talk to people in their free time?
  go into other rooms to see trainees at work?
  teach?
What time did I give to meeting staff individually and in groups?
How much time did I spend out of the organisation
  at conferences or in-service courses?
  elsewhere?
Was this time
  (a) necessary?
  (b) useful to the service?
How much time did I spend on administration and meetings?
How much time did I give to visitors?
Do I need to try to change the time distribution revealed by the answers to questions above?

▰▰▰

How do I manage my time?

Try and answer those questions above for yourself. Are you satisfied with the answers? More questions will follow.

___

What do I see as the priorities for the organisation in the next term/year/five years?
To what extent is my view shared by others?
Are any institutional changes desirable or necessary?
Am I satisfied with the training programme?
Does every person in the institution know to whom he or she is immediately responsible and for what?

Am I confident that there is a system for looking after the interests of every trainee?

How available am I — formally and informally?

Do other staff feel I am interested in their professional development and advancement and their personal welfare?

When, for example, did I last speak to:
(a) the part-time trainer in so-and-so department?
(b) a cleaner?
(c) the new trainer in such-and-such department?
(d) the second in charge of department X?
(e) the head of department Y?

Who needs promotion?

How accurate is my awareness of the load carried by different individual trainers?

How accurate is my awareness of the load carried by non-teaching staff?

How appropriate is the load carried by yourself? (Don't leave yourself out of the equation).

What is the first impact of the institution on visitors? Do I know what impression is given to telephone callers?

It is possible that some serious thought should be given to the use of one's own time. In addition to that it is essential that there should be careful planning regarding the induction of newly appointed trainees and the appropriate allocation of time and resources for the in-service training of all trainers.

New trainers and in-service training.

What arrangements are made for applicants for posts to acquaint themselves with the training prior to interview?

What are the arrangements for integrating new members of staff and ensuring that not only are they involved but feel themselves to be involved in the organisation's life and decision-making?

What are the organisation's arrangements for staff development? What procedures are followed for induction? How are decisions made about appropriate in-service courses or conferences for individuals, for groups of staff or for the whole staff? What "reporting-back" arrangements are made on return from courses or conferences? What are the arrangements for covering classes for short-term absence? Can they be improved?

Any attempt at self-evaluation must take account of what, in the institution's view, the training programme is all about. In coming to a view you trainers will be affected by the general climate of opinion in society at large as well as by your contact with other professionals within the organisation and other trainers elsewhere. The act of self-evaluation will help to clarify what it is attempting is right. It should be preceded by an attempt to identify short-term and more distant objectives. It may, indeed, lead to changes in some of these.

There are, as you will be well aware, a number of motivational factors which will operate to render trainers more or less effective. The following points spell this out quite clearly.

Poor training

How can we help people to learn relevant skills quickly?

Are we lacking the right kinds of skills? Is there not enough time to take training seriously? Are new skills not being acquired efficiently by the organisation? Does management training tend to be unplanned? Is there a failure to get people to update their skills? Is quality suffering through lack of skill? Do newcomers find it hard to adjust to current practices?

Remuneration

Is there any discontent with salary policy? Are holiday arrangements poor? Is there sick pay/insurance protection? What social facilities?

Security

Are trainees insecure in the job? Is there a threat of redundancy? Do bad employee relations cause major upheavals at times?

Personal development

Does the institution ignore personal development? Is opportunity given to gain new experiences? What is the effort to develop individual skills?

Involvement

Does high level management appear to be unconcerned with your views? Are you consulted? Is there any systematic effort to identify employees' views?

Trainer Motivation

Once again I am going to ask you to rank order the motivational factors in order of importance as you see them. Think about your own situation. Rank order the factors listed so that number one is the most important factor and number five the least important factor. How do you imagine that this ranking will affect your approach to self-evaluation?

Trainee self-evaluation

In this section of this component we will begin by asking questions about the ways in which new trainees are introduced to their programme. You might care to reflect on the importance of this introduction to the procedure that is adopted to enable the trainees to engage in their own self-evaluation.

How are new trainees welcomed on to the programme?

What is the system of personal and individual attention to trainees? How well is it working and are there any ways in which we can improve it?

To what extent are trainees fully informed about further and higher education.?

What opportunities are given for the development of intiative and responsibility?

Then again the trainees as part of their own self-evaluation may wish to reflect on their own working practices. The following check list of statements is designed to help trainees to reflect upon the ways in which they work in relation to other people.

However, in order to see it in operation I thought that you might like, first of all, to apply it to yourself. The question is, "How well do you work with other people?" If you can apply this checklist to yourselves in the first place you will be better placed to ask others to apply it to themselves.

How Well Do I Work with Other People?

Indicate the place on the scale that describes you as you usually act in the group.

Pick out the three or four which you would most like to change.

1. Ability to listen to others in an understanding way:
   ....
   Inattentive and insensitive   Observant and sensitive

2. Ability to influence others:
   ....
   No influence   Dominant

3. Tendency to build on the ideas of others:
   ....
   Go my own way   Use their ideas

4. Likely to trust others:
   ....
   Distrust   Trust

5. Willingness to discuss personal feelings:
   ....
   Reticent   Free

6. Willingness to be influenced by others:
   ....
   Resistant   Influenced

7. Tendency to seek close relationships with others in a group:
   ....
   No interest   Seek close relationships

8. Reaction to critical comments about oneself or disagreement with one's opinions:
   ....
   Defensive   Receptive

9. Awareness of the feelings of others:
   ....
   Unaware   Sensitive

10. Reaction to conflict and antagonism in the group:
    ....
    Avoidance   Creative acceptance

11. Reaction to expressions of affection and warmth:
    ....
    Embarrassed   Pleased

12. Clarity in communicating my thoughts to others:
    ....
    Unclear   Clear

13. Awareness of oneself and of the effect of one's behaviour on others:
    ....
    Unaware   Aware

14. Contributing original ideas:
    ....
    Seldom   Often

Institutional self-evaluation: the training environment

In the context of institutional self-evaluation some consideration should be given to the actual training environment that the institution presents. This cannot be ignored. Indeed the answers that emerge about the training environment may say more about the training than any previous consideration.

The Training Environment

What is the general appearance of the areas where the training occurs? What are the arrangements for ensuring that these areas are kept in a state of good working order? Could the appearance be improved?

How would one describe the noise level and the kinds of noise at various times and places?

Is the reception of visitors friendly and helpful, especially unscheduled visitors?

How well lit and heated are the training areas?

What sort of facilities are available for relaxation?

How well cared for are the materials used by the trainees?

What procedures are there for a regular review of the provision of materials and equipment?

How is waste of materials and other resources (including trainer and time) avoided?

Conclusion

By and large the product of the training will speak for itself. However, the process of the training may be a more problematic area. Some final thoughts on evaluating the process of the training might be appropriate.

First of all, how should you proceed with this aspect of evaluation?

Paper-and-pencil instruments are typically more effective for process evaluation than asking people to talk about their reactions. This is due most often to hesitancy on the part of the participant to openly discuss critical reactions or reactions that deviate from the usual response of the group. Sometimes a group has built sufficient rapport, and trust in themselves and in the trainer, to make oral evaluation possible and of value to all concerned. In fact, oral evaluation can be built into the training process as an activity to improve participant feedback skills. I would suggest that this is actually a feature of the training process.

Secondly observation of the reactions of the participants is perhaps the process evaluation technique that trainers rely upon most often. Most trainers frequently monitor body language, intonation patterns of voice, seating arrangements, and so forth, to understand how the group is responding at any given point in the training. This observation, as well as how the trainer reacts to his observations, is often automatic and occasionally unconscious. In that case, of course, no permanent record of observations is made; nor are these observations validated by the participants. For these reasons, paper-and-pencil instruments, which may even be filled out anonymously, are typically most appropriate for process evaluation.

Whatever the method used, the following process variables are important to evaluate:

1. Degree to which the programme format and content met the training needs of the group.
2. Extent to which the tone and pace of the training was comfortable for the group.
3. Ability of the trainer to track and describe accurately the group dynamics.
4. Extent to which the trainer helped to generalize training principles to the actual, work setting.
5. Degree of openness, spontaneity, humour, and energy exhibited by the trainer.
6. Degree of consistency between the trainer's style and the materials and exercises he or she presented.

There are many ways in which evaluation information will be useful. The most obvious advantage is that of immediate feedback to the trainer. The trainer will receive reactions about how well the training process was conducted, as well as how the training was received by the trainees.

Finally, please remember that asking members to participate in the evaluation generally increases the trainer's credibility. When evaluation is emphasized as an important part of the training, people tend to develop confidence in the trainer as an ethical and conscientious professional. Also, most participants are eager to provide information that will validate programme strengths and improve weaknesses for future participants. Furthermore, most participants in training welcome the opportunity to react to what has happened to them. And they will react whether you are aware of it or not. Deliberately developing an awareness of these reactions will prove to be an invaluable training tool.

 Tutor seen work

Some Methods

Throughout the course of this Study Unit certain procedures have been operating. My suggestion is that these are the sorts of procedure or processes that can be used to embark on self-evaluation. To conclude I would ask you to review this Study Unit as a whole and make a list of the kinds of procedures or processes that have been presented. You might care to adapt some of them for use in your own situation.

Further reading

Elliott-Kemp, J. & Williams, G. *Improving Your Professional Effectiveness* PAVIC Publ.

Mortimore, Jo *Profiles in action* Further Education Unit.

Tutors Self-Monitoring Inventory Youth Education Service.

Cooper, C. L. & Makin, P. *Psychology for Managers* The British Psychological Society.

Cinnamon, K. & Matulef, N. *Effective Supervision* Applied Skills Press.

Objectives for this study unit

The objectives for this Study Unit are as follows:
1. For you to understand the connection between training and evaluation.
2. For you to be able to define self evaluation.
3. For you to be aware of the different factors involved in self-evaluation in a training context.
4. For you to gain an understanding of self-evaluation as it applies to you.

As a result of working through this Study Unit you should have a clear idea of the advantages and disadvantages of encouraging trainee and trainer self-evaluation against the broader context of training in general. Finally you should have some specific ideas on how to encourage trainee self evaluation, engage in self-evaluation for yourself and appreciate the value of these processes.

You should also have arrived at an understanding of the purposes of institutional self-evaluation. You should have become acquainted with particular areas associated with institutional self-evaluation and become familiar with the check lists and questions that can be raised about those areas. This familiarity is intended to help you to initiate the process of institutional self-evaluation within the context of your own institution.

Study Unit 6

The Results of Assessment

Component 1:

Results — What are they?

Key Words

 Product of Assessment; Results; Use of Results; Methods of Assessment; Numerical and Non-Numerical Results; Administration; Descriptive Results; Hybrid Results; Profiles.

Introduction

Assessment produces results! Whenever we assess anything, we end up with a product i.e. some form of results. The range of such results is, of course, enormous — varying from a 'mental note' of some casual and informal observation, to a comprehensive set of numerical data (maybe collected over a long period of time) used to make major decisions (e.g. the award of a university degree).

Whenever we undertake any form of assessment, we need to be quite clear as to why we are doing it, what form the results will take and how we intend to use those results. All these topics have been considered earlier in this Package, in particular in the first two Study Units. As it may be some time since you worked through those Units, you will find it useful at this point to go back and browse through them again, looking for any clues about the relationship between assessment itself and the results.

Just as a reminder, in the Introduction to Assessment (Study Unit One) we looked at the differences between:

* formal/informal assessment
* formative/summative
* coursework/examination
* internal/external
* norm/criterion/mastery
* continuous/terminal/certification
* individual/group
* before/after

to name but a few!

We also considered what is being assessed (e.g. knowledge, skills, attitudes). All these factors will have a bearing on the nature of the results obtained.

The problems of implementing any assessment programme or scheme were dealt with in Component 4 of SU 2, where reference was made to record keeping. The next Component concentrated on a simple introduction to collecting and using numerical data, and this was followed by an introduction to evaluation — using the results to decide what to do next.

However, you may have noticed that apart from Component 5 of SU 2, very little was said about the results themselves — the forms they might take and how to collect and process them. The reason for this was that we needed to wait until the range of possible assessment methods and techniques had been covered in Study Units 3 to 5. We are now in a position to be able to look carefully at 'the results of assessment'.

The Results of Assessment

It is obviously a complete waste of time implementing an assessment scheme if the results are then immediately discarded. The reasons for assessing (Components 1 and 6 of SU 1) should govern the use that will be made of the results and indicate their importance. But it is also clear that different **methods** of assessment will produce different types of results. We need to be aware of what those different types are, so that we can use them correctly and to best effect.

Study Units 3 to 5 have introduced you to a wide range of assessment methods and techniques, each of which will produce results of a particular type.

▰▰▰▰ Checkpoint

Make a list of about a dozen different **methods** of assessment (e.g. practical tests) referred to in SUs 3-5.

I expect you found it difficult at times to distinguish between a method (e.g. objective tests, interviews) and the various 'techniques' (e.g. variety of test items, types of questioning) which might be used within any method. However, I hope you recognise the methods in the following list:
Standardised tests
Objective tests (e.g. multiple-choice)
Short answer tests
Structured questions
Essays
Logs and diaries
Questioning (Oral, or written questionnaires)

Interviews
Profiles
Appraisal forms
Observation
Simulations
Practical tests
Checklists
Rating Scales

For our purposes, it is not necessary to re-consider every possible assessment method, but to choose a sufficient number of different ones which can be used to demonstrate and discuss the different types of results obtained.

Objective Tests

Let's begin with an easy one — objective tests (which could include standardised tests). The results are invariably in numerical form. Individual marks are added up to produce a total score — a number. The processing of such numerical results will shortly be dealt with in Components 2-4 of this Study Unit. Individual results can be compared — in some cases against established norms — and should be reliable and hopefully valid. Remember that with some standardised tests, the measurement of two or more different attributes may be included in the same test, giving a series of scores (e.g. the 16PFQ — personality factor questionnaire — measures 16 different characteristics). Nevertheless each sub-total is a **separate** numerical result.

Scores from objective tests can be manipulated in various ways, collected in groups/sets, converted into standard scores, and generally processed and analysed using a variety of statistical techniques. Tests can be designed to give scores which are spread out over a wide range (norm-referenced) or are clustered around a high mark i.e. geared to a high success rate (criterion-referenced).

Essays

In this category we can include short answer tests, structured questions, and many traditional written examinations. Again the results are usually expressed in numerical form, but we need to be alive to the fact that the marking will have some degree of subjectivity in it. The reliability of individual scores is therefore lower than with objective tests, and this must be borne in mind when examining and analysing them. The danger is that once a score is written down in numerical form we may regard it as an exact and 'fixed' figure.

Logs and diaries

At the other end of the scale we have logs and diaries. Some projects will no doubt fall into the same category. These methods focus on the processes of activity, learning and recording/indicating progress. The results are basically in the existence of the completed document, rather than any attempt to attach a grade or score to it.

Observation, Interviews, Oral Questioning

The results of using any of these methods will vary considerably in character, depending on how the method was being used. When used for assessment purposes, these methods will concentrate on what is happening, or has happened, during or at the end of some training activity. The results will generally be descriptive i.e. in the form of words rather than numbers, unless a detailed schedule is being used which counts the number of times particular events occur.

Checklists, Rating Scales, Profiles

These methods produce results of an intermediate type, in which individual items often give scores on some sort of scale, however rudimentary. Thus there appears at first sight to be an easy way of 'converting' the points along the scale into numbers, but as we shall see this can be misleading, and any attempt to combine results from different items is of doubtful value.

Obtaining the Results

Administration

To back-track a little, when undertaking any form of assessment it is important to ensure that the administration of the 'test' is correct. If there is a time limit — stick to it! If there are instructions to be read out, or specimen test items to be completed — follow the rules precisely. If equipment or materials are needed — make sure they are there. Conduct the assessment under suitable conditions (accommodation, lighting, resources, no noise etc.). Be prepared for the unexpected. Try to avoid interruptions, distractions and disturbances of any sort. The quality of the results will depend on the effort put into the administration of the assessment procedures themselves.

Following on, it is vital that the results obtained are collected together immediately. In the case of observations and interviews, allow time for writing out and recording. By tomorrow you may have forgotten! Don't leave things to chance — be methodical. There is often more trouble over one 'lost' result than . . . It doesn't matter what form the results take, they must be a correct and adequate record of what took place. So, assuming you now have a nice pile of results, what do you do with them?

Marking

The actual marking of the results, if it is not done at the time (e.g. as in practical tests) should be relatively straightforward, even though in many cases it is laborious and time-consuming. Standardised and objective tests may have special procedures to facilitate marking (e.g. grids, overlays, computerised systems). Where subjectivity in marking occurs, detailed marking schemes and/or double-marking by two or more trainers may be used. Where the results are numerical, they should be easily obtained, and are then available for processing and analysis.

Problems are more likely to arise where the results of assessment are not merely numerical, and we shall now spend some time considering such results.

Non-Numerical Results

Having talked in fairly general terms so far in this Component, the best way of tackling this topic will be to look at specific examples.

Descriptive results

Several trainees have been asked the question "How do you deal with a difficult customer?" You have transcripts of their replies, and are trying to find some way of analysing and summarising them, so that you can report back to the trainees on their results.

Suggest how you might examine and analyse their replies.

There are a number of techniques that can be used, depending on the length and number of the replies (and the time available). The simplest way is to identify 'key words' which are used again and again (e.g. smile) and see how many of these each trainee uses. A more sophisticated form of this technique is called content analysis, which is somewhat similar to the 'critical incident' method of identifying those reported 'incidents' (not simply single words) which seem critical to the success or failure of a venture.

So even when the results consist only of words, it may be possible to analyse them and compare them in some way.

Hybrid results
Most results which are not simply numerical are often a mixture of words or ideas which are linked in some way to a basic numerical representation. For example, let's take the classical five-point scale, using an example from Component Six of SU 3.

Example: Five-point Scales

Directions: Indicate the degree to which the trainee performed. The numbers represent the following values:

5 — outstanding
4 — above average
3 — average
2 — below average
1 — unsatisfactory

1. To what extent did the trainee exhibit skill in the use of:
   a. Layout and measuring tools   1 2 3 4 5
   b. Cutting edge tools   1 2 3 4 5
   c. Boring and drilling tools?   1 2 3 4 5
2. Did he select the proper tools for the job?   1 2 3 4 5
3. Did he use the tools properly?   1 2 3 4 5

What did you see as the dangers in using a rating scale of this type?

1. It gives a false sense of quantification.
2. The numbers (points on the scale) are only vaguely defined.
3. The intervals between the numbers are unlikely to be the same in degree (e.g. the difference between 'average' and 'above average' may not be the same as the difference between 'above average' and 'outstanding').
4. The interpretation of the meaning of each number and the application of the scale will vary from trainer to trainer.
5. There is no scope for scoring intermediate values.
6. Not all the items may lend themselves to a five-point scale (e.g. item 2 above which may simply require a 'Yes/no' answer).

In this example, each item is recorded separately to give a 'profile' of the overall assessment. Let's look at a set of results:

```
1 a  1  2  3  4  5
  b  1  2  3  4  5
  c  1  2  3  4  5
2    1  2  3  4  5
3    1  2  3  4  5
```

What does this suggest to you?

Well, it seems to me that the trainee selected the proper tools, and started off in an 'average' way but then his performance became unsatisfactory.

The great danger with this method of assessment is that we may try to 'add the scores together' to give a total or average — in this case 12 or 2.4. Now 2.4 is just below average, and we have lost sight of the important fact that the trainee's use of the tools (the really important thing) was unsatisfactory.

Suggest a way round this.

Stick to the original 'profile' or detailed set of scores, or weight the individual items to give greater significance to the important ones, e.g. by multiplying scores on 1(b) and 1(c) by, say, 2 and on item 3 by, say, 3 or 4.

Similar scales are often used to 'measure' the extent to which attitudes or approaches to a topic may have changed as a result of training (e.g. hygiene, safety).

The simplest and most common way of doing this is to choose a series of statements which are **decisively favourable or unfavourable,** and then score them 1, 2, 3, 4, 5 or 5, 4, 3, 2, 1 accordingly. For example:

	Strongly Disagree	Disagree	No Strong Opinion	Agree	Strongly Agree
Safety is all important	1 (Scores)	2	3	4	5
There's no need to worry about safety	5	4	3	2	1

An equal number of items (say 10 of each type) are then arranged in random order to form the questionnaire. Scores on individual items are then added up to give a total result. This is 'better than nothing', but these totals should not be regarded in any way as clear-cut and absolute values, since the degree of 'for/against' represented by each individual item can only be approximate, and the items often appear to be simply repeating each other, since they are restricted to opposing points of view.

A similar technique is to take a number of pairs of opposing statements and ask the trainee to allocate 10 marks **between** each pair. Scores on positive (or negative) statements are then added up to give a total for each individual. For example:

	Score Allocated
It's better to give employees both good and bad news because most people want the whole story, no matter how painful	_____
It's better to withhold unfavourable news about business because most employees really only want to hear the good news.	_____
TOTAL	10

With ten pairs of statements this gives a convenient maximum score of 100.

A better method is to collect together a large number of statements covering all shades of opinion and ask a number of people to 'judge' them for degree of positive attitude towards the topic being studied. This is generally done using an 11-point scale. Items are then selected which have been marked consistently by the judges, and which cover the whole range. Here are a few examples on safety:

	Scale Value (Percentage)
It is a great mistake not to learn about safety	91
Knowing about safety is desirable	69
'Safety' is one of the less interesting topics	25
Learning about safety is silly and unnecessary	3

Selected items are presented in random order without the scale values, and trainees are asked to tick or mark any items which they feel express their opinion. The average score of those items ticked by each trainee is then calculated. (Note that in 'sensitive' areas it may be necessary to ensure that replies are anonymous, if honesty in anwering is to be guaranteed!)

Both the above methods can be used for finding out, say, what trainees thought of a particular training programme. Remember that, when used in this way, these methods are designed particularly to give a single score for each trainee for comparison between trainees. If you are interested in reactions to specific features of a training programme, a simpler way is to present a list of appropriate statements, and then count the number of times each statement is ticked by the trainees. For example:

Items from a questionnaire given to 30 trainees	No of ticks (Agreement)
I found the whole programme boring	5
I liked being able to work at my own speed	21
I found the methods of presentation irritating	7
I liked the variety of activities	15
I would not recommend this training programme to my colleagues	4

In this case the 'profile' of results can be examined in detail to give guidance on future planning and decisions.

Of course the 'five point scale' method can also be used in a similar way to **count** the number of times each box is ticked, for example:

	Strongly Agree	Agree	No Strong Opinion	Disagree	Strongly Disagree
The trainer knows best what the trainee needs to learn	2	11	4	5	1
		(Ticks, Total 23)			
Trainees should be allowed to discuss whatever they want, even if this means the course content is not covered	—	2	2	16	3
It is important that the trainer sets up objectives before the course starts	9	13	1	—	—
If a trainee fails to get what he wants from a course, it is his own fault	—	—	4	18	1

What tentative conclusions would you come to about the group of 23 trainees who replied to the above items?

Well, it would appear that these trainees are relying fairly heavily on the trainer a) to decide what they should learn, and b) to take overall responsibility for that learning.

So this type of straightforward counting of ticks can build up a profile of results which can be usefully analysed and interpreted. However, apart from this technique, these hybrid results give a veneer of quantification which can be very misleading, and at best can only be taken to indicate general tendencies and give rough guidance.

Profiles

Much effort in recent years has gone into the development of profiles, designed to indicate and record a trainee's degree of proficiency in a wide range of achievements and skills. Profiling was covered in detail in Components 4 and 5 of Study Unit 4. When considering the **results**, it must be remembered that since profiles are deliberately designed to avoid comparisons between trainees, any totalling or global assessment is unnecessary. The allocation of scores to individual items would be against the spirit of the technique, even though each attribute is often defined and categorised from a 'basic' to a 'high' degree of proficiency.

Thus each completed profile should be taken to be a unique set of results, and no attempt to score or quantify it should be necessary. In other words, those statements which have been ticked (or chosen in some way) form a separate collection of items 'profiling' the individual trainee's achievements or standard of performance.

Summary

In this Component we have considered the different types of results that are produced by the various methods and techniques of assessment. A basic distinction has been made between numerical and non-numerical results, and the range of non-numerical results has been examined in some detail. Suggestions for dealing with such results have been made, and the dangers of rough and ready attempts at quantification highlighted.

We are now going on to look at the processing of numerical results (in Components 2, 3 and 4) before considering how to record the results of assessment in the final Component, number 5, of this Study Unit.

Component 2:

Processing Numerical Results I

Introduction

The first Component of this Study Unit has been dealing with the **results** of assessment — taking a look at the reasons for obtaining results as well as the different forms those results might take depending on the method of assessment used.

In Components Two, Three and Four we are going to consider what we can do with results which are in the form of numbers which lend themselves to mathematical processing. When assessment procedures produce numerical results, our aim should always be to make as much sense as possible of the results and to use them to provide maximum information. However, we all know that extreme caution must be exercised whenever we start to manipulate numerical data, as it is very easy to make incorrect or unjustified interpretations — or even to deliberately mislead! 'Lies, damned lies and statistics' is a well-known quotation. But when correctly used, statistical techniques can, and should, enrich our understanding of the results of assessment.

A start was made in Component Five of Study Unit Two of this Package, which was entitled "Collecting and Using the Data". You will find it useful to refer back to that Component from time to time, and maybe to work through it again quickly.

The nature of numerical results

The Introduction to Component Five identified the nature of the type of numerical data we are concerned with again here, namely 'performance' data in the form of scores or marks set along a numerical scale. Such a scale normally consists of a series of intervals which are generally designed (or sometimes assumed!) to be equally spaced along the scale. The key feature of such scales is that differences obtained by subtraction **anywhere along the scale** can therefore be compared. This is in contrast to ranking (e.g. order of finishing in a race) where the intervals between the rankings are not equal, and differences are not numerically comparable. As this distinction is of vital importance, here is a Checkpoint to make sure that you can discriminate between the two types of result.

▰▰▰ Checkpoint

Which of the following examples are on an ordinal (ranking) scale and which are on an interval scale?
1. Shoe sizes (e.g. 5 to 11).
2. Lining up a group with "tallest on the right, shortest on the left" and then numbering them.
3. A seven-point scale from extremely happy to extremely unhappy.
4. Temperature scale (e.g. Centigrade).
5. First, second, third etc. in a competition.
6. A list of times taken by different trainees to complete a practical task.
7. Scores on a standardised intelligence test.

2, 3 and 5 are ordinal; 1, 4, 6 and 7 are interval.

Although number 3 may seem to be an interval scale, with the seven points spread out along a 'line', it is inadvisable to treat it as such, since the points are unlikely to be anything other than 'in order', and any suggestion of equal intervals between them could be misleading.

*Number 6 is an interval scale because time differences can be obtained by subtraction. (In fact this is an even higher level of measurement, a **ratio** scale, since multiplication and division are now possible, e.g. one trainee might take 'twice as long' as another. This scale may be said to have a 'true zero', unlike any of the others in the list.)*

Number 1 is an interval scale because the difference between, say, sizes 5 and 6 is presumably equivalent to the difference between sizes 10 and 11. ('Foot length' in centimetres would be a ratio scale, but shoe sizes are arbitrary numbers, e.g. size 10 is not twice as large as size 5.)

With 'performance' data, in addition to the scores being on an interval scale, we also expect them to be based on formal, rather than informal, assessment procedures, and to be objective rather than subjective. In other words the results would be consistent regardless of who set up and monitored the procedure and decided on the scores. So individual subjective judgements should be excluded. In practice this is often difficult to achieve, particularly in trying to produce a single score (e.g. a percentage figure) when assessing a lengthy response or document (e.g. essays, assignments, projects) but nevertheless it represents an ideal to aim for.

Even when the results are objective, (i.e. there is no doubt about the actual scores obtained) we need to be alive to the fact that an individual's score is not an absolute fixed value as, for example, a measurement of height would be.

▰▰▰

List as many reasons as you can, which might indicate that an objective score obtained in a performance test could be suspect.

* *The trainee could have cheated!*
* *The trainee could have been feeling tired or unwell*
* *The trainee could have been lucky/unlucky in guessing some of the answers*
* *The trainee could have chosen some of the right answers for the wrong reasons (and vice versa)*
* *The environment (noise, heat, lighting, time of day) may have affected the trainee's performance*
* *The trainee may have done the test (or a similar one) before and thereby achieved an artificially high score*
* *The individual items making up the test may not be comparable, or the weightings used may be suspect*
I hope you feel you can agree with these reasons, and have managed to think up some more of your own.

Remember also, as was pointed out in Component Five of SU 2 on "Collecting and Using the Data", that even when two trainees obtain identical scores of, say, 60, these are very unlikely to represent the same collection of individual scores.

Finally, any actual score can only be the result of sampling the trainee's complete 'repertoire' of possible behaviour. Any such sample, if carefully chosen, is likely to be reasonably representative, but is still liable to error.

As trainers, we are somewhat reluctant to admit that the results of assessment are subject to error, but we need to be aware of the questions that should be asked whenever we are handling such results. This is particularly important in the case of numerical data, where we can be lulled into a sense of false security about the so-called objective nature of such figures. A score of 60 could so easily have been a few marks higher or lower!

Making sense of the results

We should perhaps remind ourselves of the reasons why we may decide to **record** the results of assessment, as this should also indicate the ways in which we may need to process the results.

■//▰

Make a list of the basic reasons why we may decide to record the results of assessment.

(I hope you can see what I am getting at in this question. If you are doubtful, have a look at the first reason given below, and then try to list some others.)

1. *Simply to record the individual's performance, as an item of useful information.*
2. *To compare with the same individual's scores on other tests/occasions (e.g. as in golf).*

3. *To compare individuals one against another, and to see where an individual 'lies' within the set of scores.*
4. *To compare the collective scores of different groups on the **same** assessment procedures (e.g. monitoring, quality control, comparing different training methods).*
5. *To set standards (e.g. pass/fail levels) and monitor them over time (requires a fairly large number of scores).*
6. *To enable us to study the relationships between scores on **different** assessment procedures.*
7. *To predict future performance.*

The first one or two reasons would seem to require very little in the way of mathematical processing, but as we go on through the list the need for such processing becomes more apparent.

If, as trainers, we are dealing with only a few trainees, then probably all we need to do is to ensure that tests are as valid and objective as possible and administered under standardised conditions. Results can then be recorded and directly compared without any need for further processing. As the number of trainees increases, however, so does the need for more sophisticated ways of describing and comparing the results of assessment.

At this point you will find it useful to read quickly through Component Five, starting at Individual Scores (near the beginning) and paying particular attention to Table 2 (set of scores arranged in rank order) and the sections on The Mean, Distribution or Spread, and Standard Deviation.

Descriptive Statistics

Values (statistics) such as the mean and standard deviation are **derived** from a set of scores in order to allow us to **describe** the form and nature of the scores in an abbreviated but convenient and useful way. Such statistical techniques are only tools, and as in most situations there is a 'right tool for the job'. What we need to develop is a toolbox of such techniques. This will enable us to choose and use the correct tool for the job we are trying to do.

For the moment we are going to concentrate on descriptive statistics, the branch of statistics which is concerned solely with describing a collection of data without making any inferences from it (such as considering the relationships between scores on different tests). When we have more than about twenty individual scores in a group, or when we want to compare sets of scores, we will need to use these techniques.

Here is a set of scores obtained by 100 individual trainees taking the same performance test at the end of a course of training. The scores have already been arranged in order from highest to lowest.

TABLE 1

90	73	66	61	53
85	72	65	61	53
83	72	65	60	53
83	72	65	60	53
83	71	65	59	53
82	70	65	58	53
81	70	64	58	52
79	70	64	58	52
78	70	64	58	52
78	69	63	58	51
78	69	63	58	51
76	68	63	56	50
76	67	63	56	50
76	67	63	56	45
75	66	62	55	43
75	66	62	55	43
75	66	62	55	38
74	66	61	54	36
74	66	61	54	30
73	66	61	54	26

The range is 90—26 = 64

The mean (or average) score can be calculated by adding up all the scores and dividing the number of scores (100). As this is a rather tedious operation when the number of scores is more than about 30, you may find it useful to find the **median** (middle) score, i.e. the one halfway down (or up!) the set of scores. Obviously this can only be done when the scores have been arranged in order of magnitude, as in Table 1.

In this case the median is **63** (50 scores above and 50 below). Notice that no real calculation is required to find this value. Incidentally the mean is **62.98** i.e.

$$\frac{90+85+83+\ldots\ldots+30+26}{100}$$

But don't expect the median always to be so close to the mean.

Any further interpretation is made difficult by the size of the array of 100 scores — we need to simplify them somehow. As a first step we may decide to group together those scores which are identical, and to express them as the frequency (number of times) each score occurs.

TABLE 2

90-1	73-2	63-5	52-3
85-1	72-3	62-3	51-2
83-3	71-1	61-5	50-2
82-1	70-4	60-2	45-1
81-1	69-2	59-1	43-2
79-1	68-1	58-6	38-1
78-3	67-2	56-3	36-1
76-3	66-7	55-3	30-1
75-3	65-5	54-3	26-1
74-2	64-3	53-6	

It may also help our interpretation if we decide to include zero frequencies in the table, e.g. 90-1, 89-0, 88-0 etc. Obviously the sum of the frequency columns (1+1+3+1 . . . . . +1) must be 100 i.e. the number of individual scores.

However, it is still rather difficult to take in the total picture, so the next step would be to group the scores together in sets covering a range of, say, five marks each. The overall range (in this case 64) will indicate a suitable range for each set — we probably need about 10 to 15 sets.

These sets are called **classes,** and the range of scores included in each class the **class interval**. It is advisable to arrange the classes so that the mid-value of each one is a convenient round number, and we must remember that the upper and lower limits of each class are continuous with adjacent classes. If you look at the example set of 100 scores, you may decide to use class intervals of five marks, based on mid-points which are multiples of five, namely 90, 85, 80 . . . . 30, 25. Thus the first class will range from 92.5 to 87.5 (half a class interval either side of the mid-point). In terms of **actual** scores, of course, this class would include any scores of 92, 91, 90, 89 and 88, but the class interval is 92.5—87.5 (=5) and **not** 92—88 (=4).

If we use a tally table alongside the list of classes to record the individual scores, we won't even need to arrange the scores in numerical order first of all, although we will of course need to inspect the total array of scores in order to find the highest and lowest ones and establish the range, before deciding on the classes and class interval.

TABLE 3

Scores	Tally	Frequency
88—92	I	1
83—87	IIII	4
78—82	IIII II	6
73—77	IIII IIII I	10
68—72	IIII IIII IIII II	11
63—67	IIII IIII IIII IIII IIII IIII IIII I	22
58—62	IIII IIII IIII IIII IIII II	17
53—57	IIII IIII IIII IIII IIII	15
48—52	IIII III	7
43—47	III	3
38—42	I	1
33—37	I	1
28—32	I	1
23—27	I	1
	N =	100

This arrangement of frequencies in tabular form is called a **frequency distribution**. Notice again that this table has been produced without the need for any real mathematical calculations.

The immediate effect of this grouping is to highlight the fact that most of the scores are clustered together in a few classes around the mean. In fact 82 of the total of 100 are in the middle six classes between 48 and 77. The price we have had to pay for this grouping is that the table doesn't tell us how the individual scores are distributed within any class.

For example, in the class 73—77 with a frequency of 10 scores, we don't know how many scores of 77, 76, 75 etc. there really were (unless we go back to the original list of individual scores). But for convenience in any subsequent calculation we assume that the average of the scores in any class lies at the mid-point of that class, e.g. the 10 scores in the class 73-77 are assumed to have a **mean** score of **75**.

Go back to Table 1 and calculate the actual mean score of the 10 scores between 73 and 77.

$$\frac{76+76+76+75+75+75+74+74+73+73}{10} = 74.7$$

Obviously the larger the class interval (and the fewer the classes) the greater will be the errors that are likely to result from this assumption. Hence the need for at least 10 classes (in most cases). Any errors produced by grouping are then likely to be negligible.

The array of scores (frequency distribution) in Table 3 is now much easier to visualise, but it can be made even clearer by displaying the information in graphical form. There are two simple ways of doing this.

The histogram (From the Greek word Histos = Mast)

A histogram is a graph of frequencies plotted as vertical columns above the various classes, remembering that the scale of scores shown along the horizontal axis is regarded as continuous. For the frequency distribution in Table 3 it would look like this:

Figure 1 Histogram

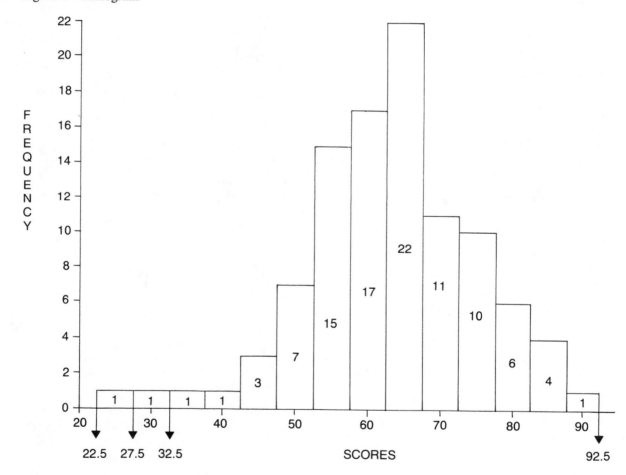

Notice that each vertical column has the full width of its class, so there are no gaps between adjacent columns. I think you will agree that this graphical representation makes the figures 'come alive' in a way that is much easier to visualise than when they are simply arranged in a table of frequencies.

In practice it is easier to construct a histogram on graph paper rather than on plain or lined paper, and nowadays many statistical computer programmes will produce histograms automatically, from data which has been entered. The histogram looks effective, but can be somewhat tedious to produce manually.

The frequency polygon

In a histogram, when class intervals are equal, the height of any column represents the **frequency** for that particular class. If we take the mid-point of the top of each column (which is vertically above the mid-point of its class) and then join them up to adjacent mid-points by straight lines, we produce a **frequency polygon.**

Figure 2 Histogram with frequency polygon superimposed on it

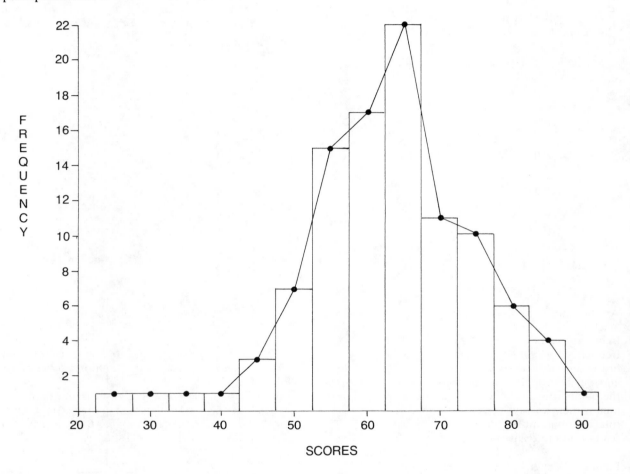

Figure 3 Frequency polygon

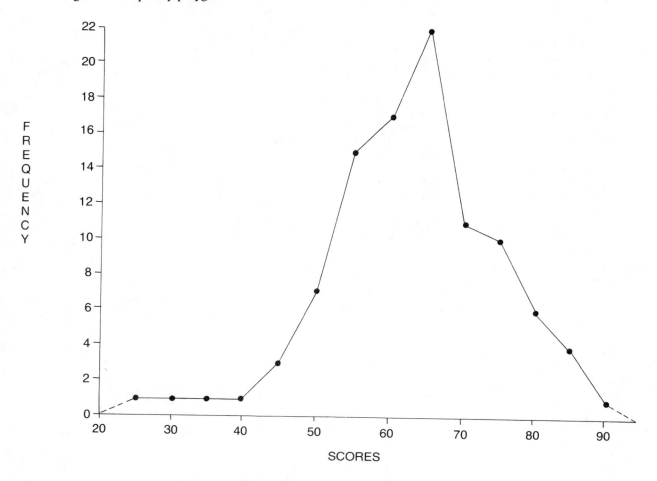

As the ends may look untidy, it is quite usual to 'anchor' them to the next adjacent classes, where the frequency is, of course, zero. The construction of a frequency polygon is therefore easier than a histogram, since we only have to plot a series of points and join them up. But we must remember that it is only the points which have any significance, and the lines joining them are only there to make it easier to see the total distribution. We must resist the hypnotic urge to read off intermediate values, which are meaningless!

Figure 4 Section of frequency polygon

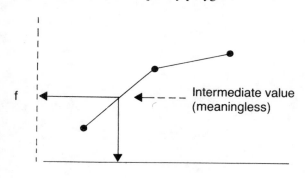

Also, different frequency polygons and histograms can only be directly compared if the total number of scores is the same for each, unless proportional frequencies (e.g. percentages) have been used. In many cases, however, a simple comparison of means may be sufficient.

Note that the construction of a histogram or frequency polygon is a final step following on from the procedures for producing the frequency distribution (as in Table 3). It is not a substitute!

▰▰▰

Draw up a set of step-by-step instructions for processing a set of scores (say about 50), in order to display them in the form of a frequency distribution, histogram and frequency polygon. Assume that the scores have been written as a single list in any order.

Here are the first three instructions to start you off:

1. Examine the scores to find the highest and lowest and establish the range.
2. Divide the range by a convenient number between 10 and 15 to establish the class interval (a convenient round figure).
3. Select a suitable number (e.g. a multiple of 5) for the mid-point of the highest class.

*Obviously from now on your list will not look exactly
the same as mine. A lot will depend on how much
detail you have decided to include.*

4. *Draw up a table of classes (e.g. 78—82, 73—77) in
vertical descending order in one column.*

5. *Construct a tally table alongside the above column,
entering a mark for each of the original scores as
you check through them. (It is a good idea to put a
cross through each of the original scores as it is dealt
with, in case you lose your place or get distracted).*

6. *Construct a column of frequencies alongside the
tally table by adding up the number of marks in
each class.*

7. *Check the total of the frequency column, to make
sure it equals the number of original scores.*

8. *Construct a histogram on graph paper, using
suitable scales for the vertical (frequency) and
horizontal (scores) axes. Remember to use the full
class interval for each column.*

9. *Construct a frequency polygon, plotting each
frequency above the mid-point of its class, and
joining the two end points up to the baseline at the
mid-points of the next (empty) classes.*

The advantages of drawing up a 'recipe' of step-by-
step instructions like this should be obvious,
particularly if it deals with the sort of task which we
only do occasionally. Then all we have to do is to take
out this job-aid when required and work through it
systematically.

Summary

This is a convenient point at which to take stock. In this
Component we have been considering what we can
and should do when the outcome of assessment is in
the form of numerical results. The reasons for treating
such results with caution were outlined, along with the
reasons why we may decide to record such results.

As the number of individual scores increases, the
need to start to use the techniques of descriptive
statistics was established. This led on to ways of
ordering and grouping a set of scores in order to
present them in ways which can be easily visualised,
namely by the use of a frequency distribution table, a
histogram or a frequency polygon.

Finally, we need to remember (yet again!) that the
only real **calculation** we have had to make so far in
processing a set of numerical results is to **add up** the
scores and **divide** by the number of scores, in order to
find the mean. The tables and graphs have all been
produced by inspecting, comparing, ordering and
simple counting.

Component 3:

Processing Numerical Results II

Key Words

 Frequency curve; area under the curve; skewed curve; mean of grouped data; standard deviation of grouped data; range and standard deviation; normal curve; percentages (proportions) of particular areas under the curve; standard scores.

Introduction

Having dealt with ways of presenting a fairly large set of scores in a condensed but orderly and representative manner, we can now go on to look at some other techniques which we may wish to use, particularly when comparing one set of scores with another. We are still firmly within the area of descriptive statistics, and are not yet concerned with making any inferences about relationships or predictions.

At the end of the previous Component we learnt how to construct a frequency polygon. Let's begin this Component with another graph based on frequencies — a frequency curve.

The frequency curve

If we take a frequency polygon and remove the 'kinks' by drawing over it a smooth curve, we produce a line graph called a frequency curve. This is a continuous line (not a series of points joined up for convenience) and is based on a **totally different concept** from a frequency polygon, in spite of the apparent similarity.

"These scores seem very low this time, I wonder why?"

Figure 1 Frequency curve

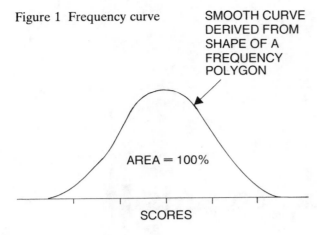

SMOOTH CURVE DERIVED FROM SHAPE OF A FREQUENCY POLYGON

AREA = 100%

SCORES

With a frequency curve, the **area under the curve** is taken to represent the total number of scores, i.e. 100%. Vertical strips or sections of that total **area** will represent an appropriate portion of the total number of scores. For example, if the curve is symmetrical either side of the mean, then the two halves of the total area, to the left and right of a vertical line drawn above the mean, will each represent 50% of the total number of scores. If the curve is not symmetrical, then the mean will not divide the total area into two equal halves, and more than 50% of the total scores will lie on one side or the other of the mean. Only areas can be compared, and there is no vertical scale of frequencies, as in a frequency polygon.

Figure 2 Frequency curve

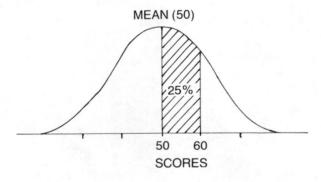

MEAN (50)

25%

50   60
SCORES

If 25% of the total area under the curve lies between scores of 50 and 60 on the scale, then 25% of the total number of scores are between 50 and 60.

▰▰▰ Checkpoint

If the curve in Figure 2 is symmetrical, what percentage of scores lie above (and below) 60?

25% above and 75% below. If, say, we wished to select the top 25% of the group for more advanced training, then a score of 60 would be the appropriate cut-off point.

We will be looking at other uses for the frequency curve later on, but let us consider one straightforward use now.

The frequency curve is basically derived from a frequency polygon, and is then used as a shorthand way of expressing the outline **shape** of the distribution of the scores, within the overall range and either side of the mean.

▰▰▰

If the scores obtained by a group of trainees on a performance test produced a frequency curve like this, what do you think has happened? (If you prefer to imagine a simple set of test scores, consider the following: 10 9 9 8 8 8 6 6 4 2; mean 7)

Figure 3 Frequency curve (skewed to the left)

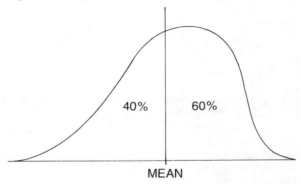

40%   60%

MEAN

Well, it could be that the test is too 'easy' for most of the trainees, or assessment is geared to a fairly high success rate (if, say, using the simple figures given, a score of 6 or more is regarded as a pass) and the test is designed accordingly. In the latter case, a frequency curve 'skewed to the left' (the longer tail is to the left) is quite acceptable.

If, however, we obtain a curve which is skewed the other way, then the majority of trainees are obtaining low scores and the test is too difficult. Here is such a smoothed curve obtained as a result of administering a test (not a performance test) to nearly 1,000 trainees.

Figure 4 Frequency curve (skewed to the right)

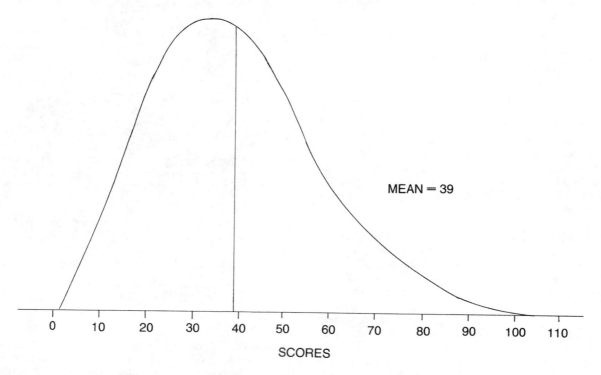

MEAN = 39

SCORES

In this case the test had too high a 'ceiling', and the majority of the trainees scores were clustered at the lower end. This 'bunching' meant that the test was not discriminating well between individual trainees' scores at this lower end. The frequency curve served to highlight this, as well as illustrating the overall distribution of scores.

Let us now leave the frequency curve for the time being and take another look at that most useful statistic, the mean or average of a set of scores.

The mean of grouped data

Once we have grouped the scores together into classes, we may decide to use this frequency distribution to find the mean, rather than go back to the original scores. Nowadays you would normally be using an electronic calculator to add up the figures and do the calculations, but it is still good practice to write them down as we go along. Let's use the set of 100 trainees' scores from Table 3 of the previous Component.

Table 1 Frequency distribution (tally table omitted)

Scores	Class Mean	Frequency	Frequency × Score (Class mean)
88-92	90	1	90
83-87	85	4	340
78-82	80	6	480
73-77	75	10	750
68-72	70	11	770
63-67	65	22	1430
58-62	60	17	1020
53-57	55	15	825
48-52	50	7	350
43-47	45	3	135
38-42	40	1	40
32-37	35	1	35
28-37	30	1	30
23-27	25	1	25
		100	6320

The mean is therefore 6320/100 = **63.2**

The calculation can be made simpler by the use of various tricks, e.g. working in units of the class interval (e.g. 18, 17, 16 etc. instead of 90, 85, 80 etc.) and then multiplying by the size of the class interval (5) as a final step, but if you are using a calculator it is hardly worth it, since the calculator's memory can be used to store the total as you go along.

Write out the instruction in words for **performing the above calculation** to find the mean of grouped data.

Multiply each frequency by the mid-point of its class, add up the products and divide by the total frequency (number of individual scores).

If you prefer to see this expressed as a formula, using normal conventions, then

$$\bar{X} = \frac{\sum fx}{N}$$

where $\bar{X}$ = the mean or average
$\sum$ = "the sum of"
f = frequency
x = raw score or mid-point of the class
N = number of individual scores

The actual mean of the original set of scores is **62.98** (see Component 2 text following Table 1). The mean calculated from grouped data is **63.2**, the difference being a small error caused by using grouped data (e.g. the final four scores were actually 38, 36, 30 and 26; not 40, 35, 30 and 25 as used in the Table above, although in this case the sums of these four happen to be the same!).

If we have drawn a histogram or frequency polygon to illustrate the spread or distribution, and we also quote the mean score, then we will have a good overall picture of the scores. However, when we wish to compare sets of scores (e.g. different groups of trainees taking the same test or the same group taking different tests) it is difficult to compare frequency polygons (unless the groups are the same size), and in any case it is a rather laborious procedure. So we may decide to calculate the standard deviation for each set of scores. This is the single figure which best expresses the way in which the scores are spread out or distributed either side of the mean — but it will **not** indicate if the distribution is unusual in any way (e.g. skewed to the left or right). Nevertheless if we know the mean and standard deviation of a set of scores we have the best simple shorthand view of them, and the basis on which to compare them with other sets of scores.

The standard deviation of grouped data

The reasons for using standard deviation as the best indication of the spread of a set of scores were outlined towards the end of Component 5 of Study Unit 2. By squaring the amount by which each score varies (deviates) from the mean score, we eliminate negative values and give more weight to extreme scores. Mathematically, this is the best way of expressing the spread or distribution of the scores. Basically, the standard deviation is the square root of the mean of the squares of the deviations from the mean — quite a mouthful!

What it boils down to is that we find out how far each score varies (deviates) from the mean score, square that deviation, add up all the squared deviations, divide the total by the number of individual scores, and find the square root of the result! Let's take the simple example used earlier above Figure 3. (This example is given to show the procedure. We wouldn't normally bother to work out the standard deviation for such a small set of scores — which are skewed anyway.) Notice the considerable effect of a single score (2) some distance from the mean (7).

Table 2 Standard deviation (using deviations from the mean)

Score	Frequency	Deviation	fd	fd^2
10	1	+3	3	9
9	2	+2	4	8
8	3	+1	3	3
(Mean = 7)				
6	2	−1	−2	2
4	1	−3	−3	9
2	1	−5	−5	25
N =	10		$\sum fd^2 =$	56

(d = deviation from the mean)

$$\text{Standard Deviation} = \sqrt{\frac{56}{10}} = 2.37$$

In practice this would be a very tedious way of doing it — even if the mean happened to be an exact whole number, which is unlikely. Fortunately we can use a derived formula which enables us to calculate the standard deviation from original (raw) scores or grouped data. We will, however, still have to square the scores and find a square root, but even simple calculators nowadays have a square root facility.
The formula is

$$\text{Standard deviation} = \sqrt{\frac{\sum fx^2}{N} - \left(\frac{\sum fx}{N}\right)^2}$$

We have already come across $\dfrac{\sum fx}{N}$. What is it?

The mean (average) score, $\bar{X}$.

___

The full procedure, using the same simple example, would look like this:

Table 3 Standard deviation (using raw scores)

Score	Frequency	fx	fx²
10	1	10	100
9	2	18	162 (i.e. 18×9)
8	3	24	192
6	2	12	72
4	1	4	16
2	1	2	4
N = 10		$\sum fx = 70$	$\sum fx^2 = 546$

Standard deviation =
$$\sqrt{\dfrac{546}{10} - \left(\dfrac{70}{10}\right)^2} = \sqrt{54.6-49} = \sqrt{5.6} = 2.37$$

Note this gives exactly the same result as before. The figures in the final column are much larger than before, but any calculator can easily cope with them. For the set of 100 scores used previously in Table 1:

Table 4 Standard deviation (Grouped data)

Scores	Class Mean	Frequency	fx	fx²	
88-92	90	× 1 =	90	8100	
83-87	85	× 4 =	340	28900	(340×85)
78-82	80	6	480	38400	
73-77	75	10	750	56250	
68-72	70	11	770	53900	
63-67	65	22	1430	92950	
58-62	60	17	1020	61200	
53-57	55	15	825	45375	
48-52	50	7	350	17500	
43-47	45	3	135	6075	
38-42	40	1	40	1600	
32-37	35	1	35	1225	
28-37	30	1	30	900	
23-27	25	1	25	625	
		100	6320	413000	

Standard deviation =
$$\sqrt{\dfrac{413000}{100} - \left(\dfrac{6320}{100}\right)^2}$$
$$= \sqrt{4130 - (63.2)^2}$$
$$= \sqrt{4130 - 3994.24}$$
$$= \sqrt{135.76} = 11.65$$

The actual process of working out the standard deviation using a calculator is not as daunting as the above table would seem to suggest, since running totals can be stored in the memory. Many calculators are in fact programmed to work out a standard deviation from a set of raw scores entered individually, although they may use a slightly different version of the formula given above.

Using a calculator, check the figures in the above table and the resulting standard deviation.

I hope you agree with the result!

___

What, then, does the standard deviation tell us, apart from giving a general indication of the spread of the scores? The first thing you can do is to compare the standard deviation (**11.65**) with the range (**64**). In most cases, where we have a reasonable number of scores, the range will be roughly six times the standard deviation. If it is not, we should begin to wonder if something unusual has happened (e.g. too many or too few extreme scores; frequency polygon considerably skewed). We also need to be aware of the way in which many sets of scores conform to a general pattern of distribution, as indicated by the 'normal' distribution curve.

"Who says we're not normal?"

The normal curve

If we obtain sets of physical measurements of naturally occurring features (e.g. individuals' heights, weights, finger spans, vital statistics) we tend to find that the resulting frequency polygons or curves conform to the same shape. This frequency curve is called **the normal distribution curve**, and it can be expressed as a precise mathematical equation. The curve of this distribution shows us (no surprise!) that most measurements are 'about average'. Also the curve is symmetrical about the mean, therefore half the measurements lie on either side of the mean. The normal curve looks like this, with units of the standard deviation shown along the horizontal scale.

Figure 5 The normal curve

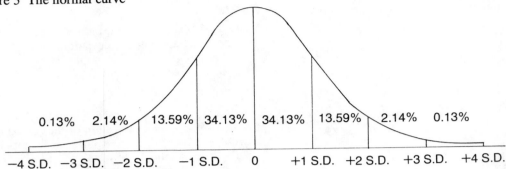

| 0.13% | 2.14% | 13.59% | 34.13% | 34.13% | 13.59% | 2.14% | 0.13% |

−4 S.D.   −3 S.D.   −2 S.D.   −1 S.D.   0   +1 S.D.   +2 S.D.   +3 S.D.   +4 S.D.

The most important thing to note is that roughly 68% (just over two-thirds) of the measurements lie between the mean and one standard deviation either side. Also, over 95% of measurements are within two standard deviations either side of the mean. So **very** tall or **very** short individuals are rare — as we well know!

You have given a large group of trainees a written test, and have worked out that the mean of the scores is 60 and the standard deviation is 12. Assuming that the scores are normally distributed, roughly
a) what percentage of trainees scored above 72, and
b) what percentage of trainees scored above 48?
Estimate the range of scores (excluding the very rare extreme scores).

16%, 84%, 72 (24-96) i.e. six times the standard deviation.

We tend to assume (unless we have good reason to believe otherwise) that sets of scores of ability, attainment, personality traits etc. are normally distributed, and therefore we apply our knowledge of the normal curve to them. A good example of this is in intelligence testing, where usually scores obtained from the results of testing large numbers of people are adjusted so that 100 represents the mean or average and the standard deviation is 15.

Obviously if a particular set of scores is obtained from a limited number of results, say less than 30 or 40, it is unlikely that the frequency polygon produced from them will look exactly like the normal curve, but there will generally be a marked similarity. The normal curve can be used as a model and is a useful yardstick to which we can refer.

There are times, however, when we have no choice but to refer to the normal curve and its particular characteristics. If we know, from previous results, that a test produces a certain mean and standard deviation,

then it is possible to see exactly where any particular score lies. For example, if the mean is established as 60 and the standard deviation is 12, a score of 84 is two standard deviations above the mean and is only surpassed by about 2 or 3 people in a hundred. Similarly, of course, a score of 36 . . . . ! What we are doing is converting the raw score (e.g. 84) into units of standard deviation (+2) away from the mean.

Tables which are included in any published set of statistical tables enable us to convert any such values, not just those which give round figures.

Standard scores

The process of converting raw scores into scores based on the normal curve gives a scale of **standard scores**. The simplest form of standard score is the "z" score, where we just use units of standard deviation as the scale (e.g. +1.5, −2.3). However, this introduces negative values, and the mean becomes zero, which makes comprehension difficult.

A commonly used scale is to let the mean = 50 and the standard deviation = 10, giving what are called 'T' scores and a normal range from about 20 to 80. Note however that this results in over two-thirds of the scores being between 40 and 60.

IQ scores are another example of standard scores.

Figure 6 The normal curve and standard scores

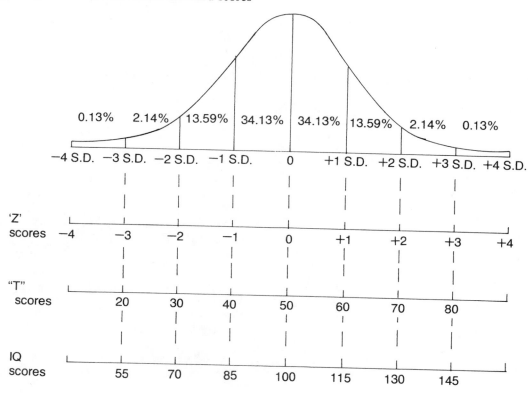

The use of standard scores is essential if we wish to **combine** different sets of scores, but let's leave consideration of that problem to the next Component. Meanwhile, here's a Checkpoint to round off this one.

A particular test of general ability gives raw scores with a mean of 40 and a standard deviation of 8. Convert the following raw scores obtained by four trainees, into intelligence quotients (Mean 100, standard deviation 15).

40, 52, 32, 64.
Which of these scores is the most unlikely one?

100, 122.5, 85, 145.
(145 is the most unlikely one, about 1 in 1,000)

Summary

In this second of the Components dealing with the processing of numerical results, we have looked at the frequency curve, where the area under its outline represents the spread or distribution of a set of scores. Practical applications were considered, along with ways of calculating the mean and standard deviation of grouped data. Finally, we looked at the normal curve and procedures for converting raw scores into standard scores based on the normal distribution.

The problems of combining sets of scores will be looked at next, before we leave descriptive statistics to move on to look at the techniques we will need to use to examine possible relationships between sets of scores and the problems of trying to make predictions.

Component 4:

Processing Numerical Results III

Introduction

When a group of trainees have taken several tests, it is common practice to combine the scores obtained by each individual in order to obtain a single total score. Comparisons between these total scores can, however, be very misleading. Let us take an example, where a group of trainees have taken three tests giving the following figures.

Table 1 Test figures

TEST 1	Range 0—100	Mean 50
TEST 2	Range 30—70	Mean 50
TEST 3	Range 20—80	Mean 50

Now let us consider what would happen if we added together the scores obtained by three fictitious trainees, A, B and C.

If A came top in Test 1 and was average in the other two, then his total score would be 100+50+50 = **200**.

If B came top in Test 2 and was average in the other two, then his total score would be 50+70+50 = **170**.

If C came top in Test 3 and was average in the other two, then his total score would be 50+50+80 = **180**.

This method of simple addition favours the trainees who do well in the tests where the marks are widely spread. This may be acceptable if Test 1 is felt to be the most important one, but if that is the case it would be better to 'weight' Test 1 scores by multiplying them up (e.g. by a factor of 2) or marking the test out of a higher total, rather than simply relying on a wider range. Note that it is the variation in the range (and therefore the standard deviation) which produces this effect. If, say, we decided to raise all the scores in Test 2 to give a range of 50-90 and a mean of 70, then this would not affect the ranking of the overall results, which would become

A = 100+70+50 = 220
B = 50+90+50 = 190
C = 50+70+80 = 200

In other words, this has simply added 20 to each total.

If we want to give equal weight to each of the three tests, then we must convert each set of scores to standard scores having the same standard deviation. Giving added weight to any particular test should then be dealt with subsequently, before each individual trainee's scores are combined.

Converting raw scores into standard scores

Let us take the 100 scores used in the two previous Components, having a mean of 63.2 (grouped data) and a standard deviation of 11.7. We have decided to convert them to "T" scores having a mean of 50 and a standard deviation of 10. As a 'visual aid', it is useful to draw the two scales alongside each other for comparison purposes.

The Results of Assessment

Figure 1 Raw and standard scores

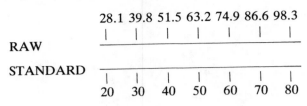

We can use this figure as a check to spot any large errors in our subsequent calculations!

Each individual score is then converted as follows:

Standard Score =

St. Score Mean + $\dfrac{\text{St. Score S.D.}}{\text{Raw Score S.D.}}$ (**Raw Score** − Raw Score Mean)

This looks more frightening than it really is! In our case

Standard Score = $50 + \dfrac{10}{11.7}$ (Raw Score − 63.2)

e.g. for raw scores 70 and 50

Standard Score = $50 + \dfrac{10}{11.7}$ (70 − 63.2)

$= 50 + \dfrac{68}{11.7}$ = **55.8**

Standard Score = $50 + \dfrac{10}{11.7}$ (50 − 63.2)

$= 50 - \dfrac{132}{11.7}$ = **38.7**

Standard scores will normally then be given to the nearest whole number, e.g. 56 and 39 for the above two examples. If you have access to a microcomputer it would be quite easy to write a short programme to undertake these conversions, and maybe produce a table of raw versus standard scores.

▰▰▰ Checkpoint

Try to explain in your own words (maybe to a sympathetic colleague!) **why** it is necessary to convert sets of raw scores to standard scores before combining them. Note down the main points of your argument/explanation.

I hope you managed to do this without too much 'looking back'!

▰▰▰

Write out a set of step-by-step instructions (similar to the ones in the final Checkpoint in Component Three) for converting a set of raw scores into standard scores.

1. Calculate the mean and standard deviation of the raw scores.
2. Decide the scale you wish to use for the standard scores (mean and standard deviation).
3. Draw the two scales alongside each other for comparison purposes (say between three standard deviations either side of the mean).

4. Convert each individual raw score into its corresponding raw score, using the formula
Standard Score =
St. Score Mean + $\dfrac{\text{St. Score S.D.}}{\text{Raw Score S.D.}}$ *(**Raw Score** − Raw Score Mean)*

5. Enter the standard scores (probably to the nearest whole number) alongside the trainees' names on the relevant document or record sheet.
(6. Combine with other standard scores as appropriate.)

If we then decide, say, that Test 1 is twice as important as the other two, then we simply multiply each standard score on Test 1 by 2 before adding it to the standard scores on the other two Tests.

Inferential statistics

When examining sets of scores obtained by a group of trainees on different tests, we may have noticed that the trainees who do well (or badly) on one test are often the ones who also do well (or badly) on the other tests. We may decide that we would like to examine these relationships in order to look at the degree of similarity between the results of the different tests. If, for example, the rankings of the trainees on two tests were exactly the same, then why bother with the second one?

Once we move away from pure description of scores into this new area, we are entering the field of **inferential statistics**, e.g. we are making inferences about the degree of any relationship between two sets of scores. The first thing to notice is that our scores now come in pairs, e.g. two different scores obtained by the same trainee on two different tests. Another example might be if we decided to examine the relationship between the heights and weights of individuals, where each individual would have a height and a corresponding weight. Notice that the units of measurement do not need to be the same for the two tests.

▰▰▰

Do you think that we need to standardise the scores?

No, because we are comparing them and not combining them.

Scatter Diagrams

As in the case of descriptive statistics, the simplest way of visualising the information is to display it in graphical form. This is done by means of a **scatter diagram** which, as the name indicates, shows in diagrammatic form the way in which the pairs of scores are scattered or spread around in relation to each other. Each pair of scores is plotted as a single point on a diagram.

Figure 2 Scatter diagram

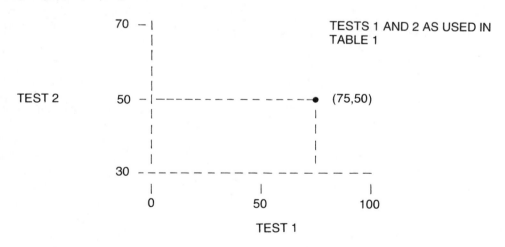

The first scale is drawn along the horizontal axis and the other one up the vertical axis. (They don't need to be the same overall length, but the diagram will look better if they are roughly comparable.) Any pair of scores (e.g. 75,50) is then indicated by a dot. As before, it is easier to construct the diagram on graph paper rather than on plain or lined paper.

Let us look at some examples of the types of diagrams we might expect, where a number of points have been plotted. The technical term for this relationship between scores is **correlation**, and the degree or extent of the relationship is expressed as the **correlation coefficient** (r), which can vary between +1 (perfect correlation) to −1 (perfect inverse correlation), with 0 representing no relationship at all. For example, we would expect a moderately high positive correlation between the heights and weights of a group of individuals (the taller people will tend to be heavier) and a negative correlation between the ages of a number of 2p coins and their weights (the older coins will tend to be worn and weigh less). A zero correlation occurs when the two measurements are completely unrelated, e.g. the weights of a group of individuals and the total values of the coins in each of their pockets/purses. We are usually interested in positive correlations, i.e. between 0 and +1.

Figure 3   Scatter diagrams

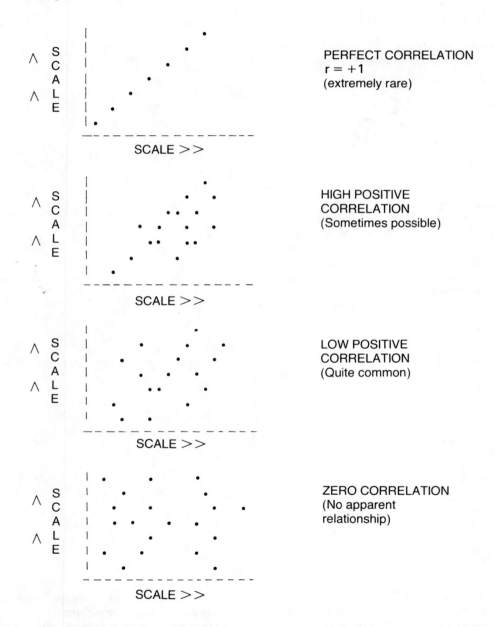

PERFECT CORRELATION
r = +1
(extremely rare)

HIGH POSITIVE
CORRELATION
(Sometimes possible)

LOW POSITIVE
CORRELATION
(Quite common)

ZERO CORRELATION
(No apparent
relationship)

If the scores are normally distributed we would expect to see a concentration of points near the middle of the diagram (remember that 68% of scores lie within one standard deviation of the mean in each set, if normally distributed). This probably doesn't show up well in the above simple diagrams.

Producing a scatter diagram from paired sets of results may simply be for general interest, but we may have more important reasons for looking at correlation. We may be interested in

a) How closely two different versions of a test, which are designed to measure the same feature, do in fact compare

b) How reliable a test is, by either comparing scores when the test is given twice to the same trainees (test-retest) or comparing scores on one half of the test with scores on the other half (split-half), and possibly

c) Whether scores on one test can be usefully used to predict scores on the other (e.g. selection test scores and end-of-training performance).

The scatter diagram is a useful first step, and it will certainly indicate whether any further effort is likely to be worthwhile or not, but to obtain more precise results we will have to resort to computation.

Rank-order correlation coefficient

The simplest way of calculating a correlation coefficient is to work out the rank order for each set of scores, and then use these rankings. This method can be used whenever the available data can be ranked, so it can be used with ordinal as well as interval data.

Work out the rank orders for each of these sets of scores:

TABLE 2   Test scores

	TRAINEES									
	A	B	C	D	E	F	G	H	I	J
TEST 1	50	49	64	69	60	63	54	51	58	52
TEST 2	42	45	56	59	44	51	57	49	52	55

(By all means draw a scatter diagram for your own interest if you wish — and try to guess the value of the correlation coefficient from it)

You should have

TEST 1	*9*	*10*	*2*	*1*	*4*	*3*	*6*	*8*	*5*	*7*
TEST 2	*10*	*8*	*3*	*1*	*9*	*6*	*2*	*7*	*5*	*4*

The rank-order correlation coefficient is calculated by finding the differences between the rankings for each pair and then squaring them, before entering the following formula:

Rank-order correlation coefficient (called 'rho') = $1 - \dfrac{6\sum d^2}{N(N^2-1)}$

where d = a difference between rankings
and   N = the number of **pairs** of rankings.

It will be easier to lay out the information in tabular form:

Table 3   Rankings

	RANKINGS		DIFFERENCE	
TRAINEE	TEST 1	TEST 2	d	d^2
A	9	10	1	1
B	10	8	2	4
C	2	3	1	1
D	1	1	0	0
E	4	9	5	25
F	3	6	3	9
G	6	2	4	16
H	8	7	1	1
I	5	5	0	0
J	7	4	3	9
	N = 10		$\sum d^2 =$	66

Note: It is not necessary to put either set of rankings into numerical order, 1, 2, 3 etc., but it would probably look neater and aid visual assessment of possible correlation. As 'd' is being squared, the use of + and − signs is not necessary.

Work out the rank-order correlation coefficient, given that $\sum d^2 = 66$ and N = 10. What does the result suggest?

$$rho = 1 - \frac{6\sum d^2}{N(N^2-1)} = 1 - \frac{6.66}{10.99} = 1 - \frac{2}{5} = \frac{3}{5} = +0.6$$

A rho of +0.6 indicates a moderate positive relationship, and could represent the value we would get by comparing results on, say, a theory and practical test covering the same topics. If we were comparing parallel versions of a test we would expect rho to be at least +0.8. Obviously the larger the number of trainees the more reliable the result will be.

Notice that, as with standard deviation, the larger differences (e.g. 5) have a considerable effect on the final result, due to the use of squared values (e.g. 25). If all the differences had been zero, then the second part of the formula would become zero, and rho would be +1, which should be no surprise.

You might like to work out rho when all the rankings on the second test are exactly opposite to those on the first test.

You should get −1 (i.e. the second part of the formula should give −2).

If trainee E had missed either test and been left out of the above Table, would rho have
A been much the same
B been considerably reduced
C been much larger
D become negative?

C been much larger (as the second part of the formula would have been less).

This is a convenient and easy way of working out a correlation coefficient, and if rankings are all we have got to go on, then it is the only way (although there are other versions of the rank-order method). However, in our case we have used raw scores to obtain the rankings, thereby losing the fine detail of the way in which the raw scores were arranged. For example, on Test 1 scores of 69, 64, and 63 have become rankings 1, 2 and 3, thereby losing sight of the large difference between 69 and 64. If we have the raw scores, it is more accurate to use them directly to obtain what is called the product-moment correlation coefficient (r). Unfortunately this is a rather more complex exercise — unless you happen to have a calculator with the built-in facility to calculate r.

Product-moment correlation coefficient

As we have tended to work with the raw scores directly when calculating means and standard deviations, rather than revert to any one of a number of 'tricks' to make the computation easier, let's carry on and use them again here. To keep the figures simple, we'll stick to the ten pairs of scores given in Table 2. The raw score formula, which is terrifying to look at, is

$$r = \frac{N.\sum XY - (\sum X)(\sum Y)}{[N.\sum X^2 - (\sum X)^2][N.\sum Y^2 - (\sum Y)^2]}$$

where

N	=	Number of pairs of scores
X	=	A raw score from the first set
Y	=	A raw score from the second set
$\sum XY$	=	Sum of the products $X \times Y$
$\sum X$	=	Sum of X scores
$\sum Y$	=	Sum of Y scores
$\sum X^2$	=	Sum of squares of X scores
$\sum Y^2$	=	Sum of squares of Y scores

When you've got your breath back, look at this formula item by item and you'll realise it's not in fact all that complicated. It just goes on a bit!

So we will need to lay out a table where the columns will give us the desired values for adding up, before entering them in the formula.

Write down the headings which you think will be needed for the columns in the table.

$X \; Y \quad X.Y \quad X^2 \; Y^2$
This is the usual order, but it isn't critical.

Table 4 Product-moment correlation coefficient

	TEST 1 (X)	TEST 2 (Y)	X.Y	X²	Y²
A	50	42	2100	2500	1746
B	49	45	2205	2401	2025
C	64	56	3584	4096	3136
D	69	59	4071	4761	3481
E	60	44	2640	3600	1936
F	63	51	3213	3969	2601
G	54	57	3078	2916	3249
H	51	49	2499	2601	2401
I	58	52	3016	3364	2704
J	52	55	2860	2704	3025
	$\sum X$ 570	$\sum Y$ 510	$\sum XY$ 29266	$\sum X^2$ 32912	$\sum Y^2$ 26322

$$r = \frac{N.\sum XY - (\sum X)(\sum Y)}{[N.\sum X^2 - (\sum X)^2][N.\sum Y^2 - (\sum Y)^2]}$$

$$r = \frac{10.29266 - 570.510}{\sqrt{[10.32912 - 570.570][10.26322 - 510.510]}}$$

$$= \frac{292660 - 290700}{\sqrt{[329120 - 324900][263220 - 260100]}}$$

$$= \frac{1960}{\sqrt{4220.3120}} \quad = \frac{1960}{\sqrt{13166400}}$$

$$= \frac{1960}{3628.5534} \quad = +0.54$$

If you are using an electronic calculator, the memory can be used to add up in each column as you go along, and you won't need to write each figure down as in the Table. Also, the working out of the formula can be simplified. This is the best version of the formula to use with a calculator (or computer) which can easily cope with the large numbers obtained.

Compare this value of r with the value of rho obtained earlier. It seems reasonable to expect the more accurate result (r) to be slightly smaller than rho in this case.

Any set of statistical tables should include a table giving critical values of r in relation to the number of pairs of scores. The larger the size of N, the smaller the value r would need to be in order to indicate a high degree of correlation.

As suggested earlier, we may be interested in correlation out of interest or curiosity, or we may be comparing test and re-test scores, or comparing scores on odd-numbered items in a test with scores on even-numbered items (split-half technique). A much more important use would be if we have to consider the validity of a test used for selection purposes.

Validity of Selection Test(s)

Does a selection test really measure what it is supposed to measure, i.e is it valid?

This is usually a very difficult question to answer!

Suggest any reasons you can think of why it may be difficult to decide whether a selection test (e.g. a test of numerical or spatial ability) is valid.

This Checkpoint was deliberately introduced here to try and make you rely on your own experience, rather than on something you've just been told!

What we are really chasing is predictive validity i.e. does the test predict how a prospective employee is likely to perform later on. An intelligence test may give a valid measure of intelligence, but it doesn't necessarily follow that people with high IQ's will be most successful at a particular job.

Difficulties in establishing validity may be caused by
a) not knowing how those who 'failed' the selection test would have performed later on (if selected)
b) drop-outs between selection and any later measurement of performance will interfere with the results
c) (a) and (b) combined will leave us with a 'biased' sample of individual scores
d) measurements of performance on-the-job or at the end of training take place a long time after selection testing, and many other factors will have intervened to affect performance.

Nevertheless many attempts have been made to assess the predictive validity of selection procedures (e.g. "O" and "A" level results as predictors of performance in higher education) and a number of classic studies have emerged. The Armed Services, Civil Service and many large organisations have developed highly sophisticated selection procedures, many of them based on long experience and studies of predictive validity. A twenty-five year study of naval officers identified a number of significantly high correlation coefficients between various measures, e.g. initial training results were found to be particularly

well correlated with long-term success. Unfortunately we can't all afford to wait twenty-five years to decide on the validity of our tests!

Provided we can obtain for each trainee a selection (or entry) test score and some later measure of performance, then we can work out the correlation coefficient between them. However, we must not be too alarmed if the coefficient is not as high as we would like or expect, as we must bear in mind the difficulties we identified earlier. It is often a good idea to use several selection tests and then compare them later on, in order to weed-out the less effective ones.

Summary

The degree of relationship (correlation) between two sets of scores can be examined by drawing a scatter diagram. The scales (means and standard deviations) do not need to be similar, and indeed the two measurements may be quite different (e.g. height and IQ). A correlation coefficient may be calculated from either rankings or raw scores using each pair of measurements obtained. The reliability of a test may be assessed, or the predictive validity of one measurement in terms of the other.

 Tutor Seen Work

Produce a short report incorporating the use of statistical techniques developed in these Components, based on assessment results obtained by your trainees. The report should cover and explain the advantages of using such techniques, the sources and types of data, the techniques themselves and conclude with an interpretation of the results.

Conclusion

In these three Components (2, 3 and 4) we have developed ways of displaying and processing the results of assessment, where such results are in some numerical form (scores or rankings). The field of statistics is immense, and we have only been able to scratch at it, but the tools we have been working on should enable you to make the best and most appropriate use of your trainees' results, avoiding the most common pitfalls and dangers. Having obtained and processed the results, the next and final Component in this Study Unit will consider procedures for recording the results of assessment.

Further reading list

Crocker, A.C. *Statistics for the Teacher,* NFER
Moroney, M. J. *Facts from Figures,* Penguin
Milton Smith, G. *A Simplified Guide to Statistics,* Holt, Rinehart and Winston
McIntosh, D. M. *Statistics for the Teacher,* Pergamon
Pidgeon, D. and Allen, D. *Measurement in Education,* BBC
Guilford, J. P. *Fundamental Statistics in Psychology and Education,* McGraw-Hill
Lewis, D. G. *Statistical Methods in Education,* ULP
Lindley, D. V. and Miller, J. C. P., *Cambridge Elementary Statistical Tables,* CUP

Component 5:

Recording the Results of Assessment

Key Words

 Recording; permanent record; use of recorded results; time-scale; access and confidentiality; types/ways of recording; computerised recording; database; spreadsheet; maintenance of records.

Introduction

Having gone to the trouble of using assessment procedures and obtaining results, it would seem sensible to decide that those results should be recorded in some way. Hopefully, however, any decision to go ahead with recording the results will be based on firmer ground than simply the fact that they are there!

By recording we mean collecting together and writing down the results, in whatever manner seems appropriate, to form a permanent or semi-permanent record of them. And that is where the trouble usually starts!

In this Component we shall be looking at the various topics that arise whenever we decide to record the results of assessment. "Why should we bother?" will lead on to "What to record?" and associated questions relating to the possible uses of recorded results. The thorny problems of access and confidentiality will be dealt with, and then we will look at different methods of setting up a recording system. Finally, we will consider the maintenance/up-dating of the records and the need for frequent re-consideration of the results as a whole.

When you have finished this Component you

"Oh, those are their scores on the last test".

should be in a position to decide what assessment results you want to record and why, and then to set up and operate appropriate recording and retrieval procedures.

Why and what to record?

The questions of 'why' and 'what' to record are best turned around and considered in terms of possible uses for the recorded results. If the results are **only** going to be used for immediate decisions (e.g. pass then continue; fail then drop out) there would seem to be little point in recording the detailed results for posterity, once action has been taken. On the other hand, if the results are being carried forward to form part of a cumulative long-term assessment, then there is every need to record them.

As has already been mentioned in this Study Unit and elsewhere in this Package, assessment results may be used for a number of different purposes and be of interest to different people. A single result will be of interest to the trainee and the trainer concerned; collections of results will be of interest to the training department and maybe the organisation. External bodies may also be interested, both with individual and collective results — particularly if they are involved in certification of successful trainees or approval of courses of training.

So the **uses** to which the results are likely to be put should answer the questions 'why' and 'what' to record, or at least give a good lead. We must, however, consciously avoid the tendency to say "If it's there, we might as well record it". We need to be quite ruthless at times if we are to avoid information overload!

Checkpoint

Imagine you are responsible for running a training course which has the following assessment procedures:

a) weekly progress tests which are designed to give individual trainees feedback on their progress and reinforce the week's work.

b) monthly group projects which are assessed by the trainer with, hopefully, constructive comments and advice for each group.

c) informal questionnaires used to obtain trainees' reactions to various aspects of the course.

d) performance tests given at the end of each completed section of the course.

e) cumulative profiles of each individual trainee's progress during the course.

Which of the above results would you wish to record?

Well, I would certainly want to record d) and e). The results of d) would be used to give a cumulative record of performance. The results of e) may need to be recorded during the course, but at the end they may be converted into a written report or single score or grade, for later use. In this case the 'fine detail' can then be discarded. However, comprehensive profiles are increasingly being used to chart each individual trainee's progress and attainment. Such documents are themselves records, indicating the degree of competency reached in a number of stated areas of performance. Any such profile 'stands on its own' and the information it contains will not normally be combined or compared with other trainees' profiles. Remember that Components 4 and 5 of Study Unit 4 dealt with profiling.

The first three would seem to be designed to give feedback at the time, rather than provide data for long-term recording.

The time-scale for recording

The above Checkpoint raises the next issue, which is related to the use of recorded information, and to which reference has already been made indirectly, namely, for how long are the results significant? Common sense would suggest that results which are only used for immediate purposes need not be formally recorded, but the longer the time-scale over which the results are likely to be used, the greater the need for rigorous formal assessment procedures and clear recording of the results. For example, results of external examinations leading to academic or professional qualifications must be correctly and clearly recorded. In the case of, say, the driving test, if the result is a 'Pass' then only that fact needs to be recorded, but in the case of a 'Fail' it is usual to indicate (i.e. record) those sections of the test on which failure occurred. This record will become redundant and can be discarded after the next test.

Figure 1

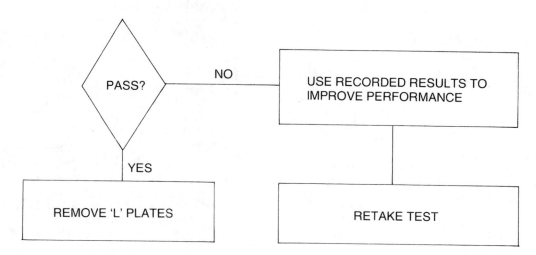

It is also often the case that the results of several assessments of an individual are compounded and used as a basis for a written 'report' which then forms an important part of the recorded results. Decisions may then have to be made as to if and when the original items of information can be discarded.

Results should only be recorded if they will be needed for future use, and the nature of that use should govern exactly what needs to be recorded. Once used, the results should be discarded if no longer needed. Remember, however, that 'future use' is not always clear-cut. For example, records that lie dormant while an individual remains with a company may have to be referred to when another prospective employer asks for a reference.

Access and confidentiality

This last example leads in to the next consideration, that of access. Once the results of any assessment have been recorded, there needs to be a clear understanding as to who has access to the records. This is a matter of weighing up ease of access against the need for confidentiality.

The more formal and critical (e.g. in terms of promotion prospects) the records, the greater the need for confidentiality, but this raises its own problems. Simply to stamp "PRIVATE AND CONFI-DENTIAL" on the records is meaningless — unless the organisation has an established security policy covering such categories of classification. There is often a tendency to try to raise one's status and importance in an organisation by regarding recorded information as 'special' in some way and only available to certain individuals. On the other hand, where any recorded information might be seen as personal and 'sensitive', the rights of individuals must be protected and respected. For example, marks and grades might not be seen as very 'private', but written reports, appraisals and profiles based on more global assessments might need to be carefully guarded. This is an area of concern in society as a whole — reference will be made later on in this Component to the Data Protection Act.

In broad terms, how would you ensure the confidentiality of any recorded results of assessment?

Well, I don't know what you have written, but one way would be to make a named individual the custodian of such records, and restrict access to clearly identified personnel only.

If, however, records are too heavily guarded, suspicions will arise as to exactly what is contained in those records!

Types of recorded information

Just a quick reminder that we may decide to record a number of different types of results, including such things as

individual scores/grades/assessments or groups of such scores, which may be performance (objective) test results, examination results, subjective assessments etc.,

written reports (various categories),

reaction information,

judgemental information/evaluation.

The form and type of such information will to some extent govern the way in which we decide to record it.

Ways of recording the results

If we are setting up some system for storing (recording) the results of assessment, then we need to consider ways of storing, retrieving, manipulating and presenting the information. If, for example, the results are written out on report sheets, and all we may ever need to do is re-examine them, then a simple manual filing system of sheets/folders/wallets may be quite adequate. Your GP may use a system like this for patients' individual records. Another straightforward way is to use a card index system, where results are recorded directly onto cards which can then be consulted as required. Some manipulation of the records (e.g. sorting, selecting) is then possible, depending on the degree of sophistication of the system.

So, individual records can be held in files or on cards, and grouped records and summarised information can be prepared and presented on separate sheets (in tabular or diagrammatic form, e.g. histograms or scatter diagrams).

At this point, a word of caution! If your needs are satisfied by the 'paper' techniques mentioned so far, there is no need to consider anything more elaborate, such as computerisation of the results. It is pointless to spend time entering information into a computer system if all you ever need to do is to retrieve the information in the same form. But there are tremendous advantages to be gained by using computers where appropriate, and powerful new and exciting ways of processing and presenting information can be easily devised.

Computerised recording of results

If you have access to a microcomputer system you might be considering using it to record the results of assessment. To make the best use of the computer you will need to have a printer attached to it, and hopefully a disc drive. Let's assume that all this is available, and see what benefits there are to be obtained from using a computer. You will find it useful to have both a database and a spreadsheet programme/facility. These are available at relatively low cost from various sources for all the popular microcomputers.

Using a database programme

If you are already familiar with the use of a database programme on a microcomputer, please feel free to scan quickly through this section and move on to later sections of the Component.

At first sight, a database programme would seem to provide simply a replacement for a manual card index system. **Records** are set up, each one based on a number of **fields** with **titles** specified by the user. Information is entered, record by record, and stored on disc in a **file**. Any record can be accessed and displayed on the screen, and the records can be printed out in any convenient form as specified by the user, e.g. horizontal or vertical format, full or partial records, fields in any chosen order. Thus, for any purpose, only the **necessary** information need be printed, thereby avoiding cluttering up the print-out with unwanted information.

The 'power' of the database, however, really comes into play when we use it to

a) search for particular records or 'sets' of records (e.g. all those scoring above/below a certain mark on a test)

b) sort the records into any required order (e.g. surnames in alphabetical order).

The ways in which a) and b) are performed vary from one database to another, and need not concern us here. Suffice it to say that they all work — it's simply that some methods are quicker than others. Once you are familiar with a system, you will discover its ability to 'search and sort' is of tremendous value in processing, analysing and displaying results. It won't be long before you wonder how you ever managed without it!

Note that if you only have a single set of results, and are not likely to have to deal with a similar set in the future, then it will probably not be worthwhile setting up a database — unless you intend to do a lot of manipulation of the results.

Let us now be more specific and look at a **very** simple example. This is actually based on MASTERFILE II (from BEEBUG) using a BBC microcomputer. Up to 18 fields can be specified for each record, and the total number of records is only limited by the storage capacity of the disc system — unlikely to cause any problems.

Imagine you have a group of trainees who have taken four 'tests' A, B, C and D. (We said it would be a simple exercise!) You decide to set up a database for them on the computer. Normally, much of the effort would go into planning very carefully exactly what each record should contain, e.g. how many fields, order, titles, lengths (number of characters), alphabetical or numerical data. All this will depend on how you may need to manipulate and display the information later on. This is entered as a specification (description) for the **file** and is stored on disc along with the records, but in a separate (descriptor) file.

TABLE 1   RECORD SPECIFICATION

Field Number	Title	Size (Maximum Number of Characters)
1	Initials	5
2	Surname	20
3	Test A	5
4	Test B	5
5	Test C	5
6	Test D	5
7	?	5
8	?	5
9	?	5

Fields 7, 8 and 9 have been included for possible later use. A 'Remarks' field is often also useful at the end of each record for unanticipated comments etc.

Now here is record Number 1 as entered:

TABLE 2   INDIVIDUAL RECORD

Record: 1

Field	Data
1 In.	A.
2 Surname	ARCHER
3 Test A	5
4 Test B	4
5 Test C	3
6 Test D	6
7 ?	
8 ?	
9 ?	

This is approximately how it would appear on the screen, and it can be printed out in the same format.

When several records have been entered, we can obtain print-outs such as the following:

TABLE 3   LIST OF RECORDS

REC.	In. Surname	Test A	Test B	Test C	Test D
1	A. ARCHER	5	4	3	6
2	B. BRIDGE	4	2	4	3
3	C. CARTER	5	5	5	4
4	D. DOVER	4	6	6	5
5	E. EDGE	3	2	1	2
6	F. FRINGE	4	5	4	3
7	G. GOLD	6	7	5	6
8	H. HOWARD	4	5	6	5
9	I. INSKIP	3	5	4	4
10	J. JOKER	6	5	7	4
		44	46	45	42
		4.4	4.6	4.5	4.2
		1.0	1.5	1.6	1.2

Number of records is 10

Note that this particular database prints out totals, means and standards deviations for those fields which have been identified as containing numerical data — a useful added bonus. The database really 'comes into its own' when we decide, say to sort the records into order on field 3 (results of Test A). A print-out then gives:

TABLE 4   SORTED RESULTS

REC.	In. Surname	Test A
7	G. GOLD	6
10	J. JOKER	6
3	C. CARTER	5
1	A. ARCHER	5
8	H. HOWARD	4
6	F. FRINGE	4
2	B. BRIDGE	4
4	D. DOVER	4
9	I. INSKIP	3
5	E. EDGE	3
		44
		4.4
		1.0

Number of records is 10

The above table is based on a choice of fields 0 (Record Number), 1, 2 and 3 only.

We could search the records for, say, those trainees scoring above 3 on Test A and **also** above 4 on Test B. A print-out then gives the following (records 1, 2, 5 and 9 are automatically omitted):

TABLE 5   RESTRICTED LIST

REC.	In. Surname	Test A	Test B	Test C	Test D
3	C. CARTER	5	5	5	4
4	D. DOVER	4	6	6	5
6	F. FRINGE	4	5	4	3
7	G. GOLD	6	7	5	6
8	H. HOWARD	4	5	6	5
10	J. JOKER	6	5	7	4
		29	33	33	27
		4.8	5.5	5.5	4.5
		0.9	0.8	1.0	1.0

Number of records is 6

Note that the totals etc. are now based on the revised list — not that they are likely to be of much use to you in this case.

▰▰▰

Look at records 1, 2, 5 and 9 in Table 3 and check their scores on Tests A and B. Is Table 5 correct?

I hope you agree that it is!

Recording the results using a database enables you to manipulate the data in various ways and print it out in any suitable format. It is this flexibility which cannot be achieved by any manual system of recording.

A simple database is very good at searching through and sorting individual records, but if we need to collect together and process the results, a spreadsheet programme will be more powerful and useful. For example, we may want to add together several scores obtained by the same individual, or weight them in some way, or maybe standardise them. This is a tedious operation if done manually for each individual, but in a spreadsheet it is done quickly and automatically.

Using a spreadsheet programme

A spreadsheet consists of a rectangular grid of **boxes**. Usually the columns are **lettered** from left to right and the rows **numbered** from top to bottom for reference purposes. Each box therefore has a unique location, e.g. A1, B10, G25. The width of columns can be varied. Any box can contain alphabetical or numerical data, and any box can be provided with a 'formula' for calculation, the **result** of which is then displayed in the box automatically.

Again, let us take our simple example and enter up the data into a spreadsheet.

TABLE 6   SPECIMEN SPREADSHEET I

TRAINEES	SUBJECTS				?	?	?	(A+B+C+D+ETC) TOTAL
	A	B	C	D				
A. ARCHER	5	4	3	6				18
B. BRIDGE	4	2	4	3				13
C. CARTER	5	5	5	4				19
D. DOVER	4	6	6	5				21
E. EDGE	3	2	1	2				8
F. FRINGE	4	5	4	3				16
G. GOLD	6	7	5	6				24
H. HOWARD	4	5	6	5				20
I. INSKIP	3	5	4	4				16
J. JOKER	6	5	7	4				22
?								
?								
?								
COL. TOTAL	44	46	45	42	0	0	0	177
N	10							
AVERAGE	4.4	4.6	4.5	4.2				

This particular spreadsheet is based on PERFECT CALC using a TORCH Z80 processor fitted into a BBC microcomputer. Similar results would be obtained with, e.g. INTER-SHEET (from Computer Concepts) and a BBC micro.

The spreadsheet has been deliberately set up to allow for expansion, i.e. extra trainees or test results (although the extra columns and rows could always be inserted later). Again, it would hardly be worth setting up a spreadsheet to process a single set of figures, since much of the effort goes into the original design. Once set up, however, all the calculations are performed effortlessly and automatically, and the spreadsheet responds immediately to any changes or new information as entered. Thus row and column totals, averages etc. are immediately available.

Numerous calculations can be set up using formulae. For example, we may decide that scores on Test A should be weighted by a factor of 1.5 — a column can be set up to do this. Or we may decide to record A squared for later calculations — again no problem!

TABLE 7   SPECIMEN SPREADSHEET II

TRAINEES	SUBJECTS				(A+B+C+D) TOTAL	1.5*A	A*A
	A	B	C	D			
A. ARCHER	5	4	3	6	18	8	25
B. BRIDGE	4	2	4	3	13	6	16
C. CARTER	5	5	5	4	19	8	25
D. DOVER	4	6	6	5	21	6	16
E. EDGE	3	2	1	2	8	5	9
F. FRINGE	4	5	4	3	16	6	16
G. GOLD	6	7	5	6	24	9	36
H. HOWARD	4	5	6	5	20	6	16
I. INSKIP	3	5	4	4	16	5	9
J. JOKER	6	5	7	4	22	9	36
COL. TOTAL	44	46	45	42	177	66	204 (SUM A*A)
N	10						
AVERAGE	4.4	4.6	4.5	4.2	17.7	6.6	20.4

Note that if we have decided to display the figures in integer (whole number) form, then 7.5 for example is shown as 8. It is however stored in the memory as 7.5 and the column total is correct (66).

If we add the scores for an additional trainee, all the figures are automatically adjusted — you can throw your rubber away! Similarly if we alter any of the recorded scores the whole spreadsheet is re-calculated.

TABLE 8   SPECIMEN SPREADSHEET III

TRAINEES	SUBJECTS				?	?	?	(A+B+C+D+ETC) TOTAL
	A	B	C	D				
A. ARCHER	5	4	3	6				18
B. BRIDGE	4	2	4	3				13
C. CARTER	5	5	5	4				19
D. DOVER	4	6	6	5				21
E. EDGE	3	2	1	2				8
F. FRINGE	4	5	4	3				16
G. GOLD	6	7	5	6				24
H. HOWARD	4	5	6	5				20
I. INSKIP	3	5	4	4				16
J. JOKER	6	5	7	4				22
K. KLOWN	6	4	5	8				23
?								
?								
?								
COL. TOTAL	50	50	50	50	0	0	0	200
N	11							
AVERAGE	4.5	4.5	4.5	4.5				

The scope of spreadsheet techniques depends solely on your ingenuity and the time available for development. All normal mathematical calculations are possible, and the results can at any time be printed out or stored on disc. Tables 6 to 8 were prepared using the spreadsheet programme, then stored on disc and inserted automatically into this text at the appropriate points.

Most spreadsheets can be linked to programmes which will present selected information from a spreadsheet in graphical form, e.g. pie charts, bar charts, line graphs.

Given scores obtained by 25 trainees on two tests, you wish to record them and calculate the product-moment correlation coefficient (r) between them, displaying the results in tabular form. You may want to do the same thing with several other sets of scores. Would you use a manual method, a database or a spreadsheet?

A manual method will leave you with a lot of calculations to perform (see Component 4), unless you have an advanced statistical calculator or can obtain a suitable computer programme. A database will not be very helpful, except to display the scores in tabular form and maybe give means and standard deviations. A carefully designed spreadsheet would automatically calculate squares, products (X×Y), totals etc. and perform the calculations necessary to find the value of r.

Data Protection Act

When we are considering the use of computers to record results, we need to keep in mind the requirements of the Data Protection Act 1984. Once you start to process information relating to individuals (personal data) using equipment which 'automatically processes' the information by non-manual methods, you may have to register with the Data Protection Registrar. The details of the Act and registration procedures are well covered in a series of Guidelines and other booklets obtainable from the
Office of the Data Protection Registrar,
Springfield House, Water Lane, Wilmslow, Cheshire,
SK9 5AX.

There are four categories of exemptions from all or parts of the Act, but the detail is quite complex and expert advice should be sought if you are in any doubt about whether you need to register or not.

Maintenance of records

Once records are started, it is important to devise a scheme for maintaining these records. You will need to consider when and how records should be up-dated, as well as how long they should be kept for. Weeding-out records which are no longer needed should be standard practice and a part of good 'housekeeping'. The 'sell by/best before' principle

could well be applied to the useful life-span of records! Up-dating is made easier if the records are readily available (e.g. on a computer database) but this has to be offset against the need to maintain confidentiality.

Reconsideration of need/usage

Along with maintenance you should build in regular appraisal and evaluation of why you need to record the results, what use is actually being made of the records (compared with the original intentions), whether the records are adequate etc. Once set up, it is easy to continue to record results even when the original reasons for doing so have disappeared. Stop, think and question from time to time. Why are we doing this?

This really takes us back full circle to the beginning of this Component and the key point about the uses to which the results are likely to be put. This should be the guiding principle throughout.

 Tutor seen work

If you 'skipped' the TSW at the end of Component 4, you should have another look at it, to see whether you could now attempt it – particularly if you are able to use a database or spreadsheet programme on a computer. By all means re-word the task to suit your own situation.

What next?

The next and final Study Unit in this Package will pick up and develop the wider uses of the results of assessment to assist in evaluation of training.

Objectives

When you have completed this Study Unit you should be able to
* list the main methods of assessment and indicate the types of results they produce
* distinguish between numerical, descriptive, hybrid results and profiles
* list the dangers of combining scores from items on a rating scale
* describe the main features of numerical data (e.g. obtained from using an objective or performance test)
* group a set of scores into suitable classes, and then calculate the mean and standard deviation
* construct a histogram and frequency polygon
* describe a frequency curve, and discriminate between it and a frequency polygon
* describe the main features of the normal curve, and perform simple calculations based on its standard characteristics
* explain why it is necessary to convert sets of raw scores into standard scores before combining them
* convert raw scores into standard scores, given the means and standard deviations of both sets
* construct a scatter diagram on graph paper for a set of paired scores
* calculate a rank-order and product-moment correlation coefficient, and discuss the significance of the results

* decide which results of assessment should be recorded, and justify the decision
* indicate ways of recording results while ensuring confidentiality
* choose appropriate methods for recording the results of assessment
* identify the main problems in long-term storage and maintenance of records.

Study Unit 7

Evaluating the Results of Assessment

Component 1:

An Introduction to and Discussion of Context

Key Words

 Assessments; appraisal; evaluation; effectiveness; personnel; training programmes; work situation.

Evaluating the Results of Assessment: an Introduction, and a Discussion of the Context

This Unit deals with the range of problems that those responsible for providing training programmes encounter when they reach the stage of evaluation — a task that nearly everybody commends, but many find very difficult. When you have worked through this first Component, you should be better equipped to tackle the remaining Components in the following ways:

i) you should be familiar with distinctions that are often made between evaluation, appraisal and assessment;

ii) you should be aware of the complexities that lie under the surface of these three familiar words, and so escape falling into avoidable pitfalls;

iii) you should be aware of a range of reasons, often conflicting, why people undertake evaluation.

First then, we will briefly examine the three terms that will be frequently used in this unit: assessment, appraisal, evaluation. It is important to remember

a) that these three words do not denote entirely separate procedures;
   and

b) that different writers use these words in different ways — as a glance at a good dictionary will quickly show.

So what follows is an attempt to suggest how writers in the field of training and education tend nowadays to use these words. The word 'tend' must be stressed, since fashions can change quickly.

Assessment is usually used in relation to someone's performance: the skill, speed, accuracy, reliability, dependability, commitment with which a task or tasks is done. For convenience and speed of interpretation an assessment is often expressed in the form of a figure (e.g. 65%) or of a letter grade on a scale of agreed limits (e.g. Grade B on an A to E scale). It follows from this that assessors are most comfortable when what is to be assessed can be easily broken down into clear and measurable activities or processes. When the competencies to be judged are very wide, or very subjective (i.e. when they are open to apparently irreconcilable disagreements about what is important), assessment as described above becomes very difficult.

Appraisal is often used to denote a wider process of making judgements about the broad capabilities of a person, particularly when that person has a range of responsibilities which demand the use of judgement and the exercise of authority. Clearly, this term overlaps with assessment, and some writers write as though there is little difference. But it is worth noting that appraisals are less likely than assessments to produce fine scores such as percentage marks.

Evaluation is often given the widest use of all. Evaluation will include assessment and appraisal, but the word evaluation is typically used to describe the process through which a range of wider considerations is introduced. Evaluation has been defined as the process by which information and judgements are collected and used to influence future policy. We can put the same point in a different way. Assessments and appraisals are usually devoted to people's performances or skills. Evaluation will probably deal also with conditions of work, with the nature of an employee's job, with the quality of training and so on. Evaluation, in other words, can link assessment and appraisal to an organisation's corporate plan and manpower plan, in other words to the task of ensuring that the organisation remains strong and healthy.

The word 'policy' reminds us of another important point. Organisations are unlikely to undertake assessments or appraisals or evaluation simply for the sake of discovering interesting facts. They are much more likely to be done so that the organisation can benefit from the facts that are discovered — benefit by developing its policy on what products, processes and services it wishes to concentrate on, by developing its policy on pay and conditions of service, by developing its policy on training.

```
                    EVALUATION
        ┌─────────────────────────────────────┐
        │ APPRAISAL: of a wide range of       │
        │            qualities, such as       │
  ┌──────────────┐ commitment, ability        │
  │ ASSESSMENT   │ to use authority,          │
  │ of particular│ likelihood of              │
  │ skills and   │ benefitting from           │
  │ knowledge    │ training.                  │
  └──────────────┘                            │
        └─────────────────────────────────────┘
```

Assessment and Appraisal are linked to a wider review of policy: finding out weaknesses and strengths in organisation; in deciding on future plans etc etc.

▨▨▨ **Checkpoint**
Which word, **assessment, appraisal,** or **evaluation** would you probably use to describe the following situations?
Situation A
Middle managers undergo an annual _____ in which their general performance is reviewed (possibly through reports and a personal interview), and after which their suitability for promotion is decided.
Situation B
An organisation is worried because labour relations appear to be worsening, training programmes appear to be less than effective, and its ability to get new products quickly onto the market is under threat. The organisation commissions a general _____ of its own health.
Situation C
New equipment has been installed, effective use of which demands that all the employees using it can perform certain operations accurately within a given time. Training is provided. Employees may be transferred to the new equipment, only after a successful _____ of their skill in using it.
Did you find the task straightforward? It is common to find some hesitation in choosing amongst these three words, partly because, when we use them in everyday situations, we often replace one by another without thinking seriously about why we do this.
However, here are some answers. If you are finding yourself disagreeing with them, talk them over with your colleagues.
Situation A: the most apt word is 'appraisal'.
Situation B: the most apt word is 'evaluation'.
Situation C: the most apt word is 'assessment'.

Why evaluate?
From what has been said above, the following summary may be made about the process of evaluation. First, it is a complex process, incorporating but wider than assessment and appraisal. Second, it relates to questions of policy. Thirdly, the process is likely to be used when management is concerned to ensure that the organisation remains healthy.

These features of evaluation are likely to produce some bewildering and even angry reactions when it is tried in an organisation. Members of the organisation are likely in general to see evaluation as a 'Good Thing'; but some groups and some individuals may in practice find that evaluation is personally quite threatening. An evaluation may show that a particular person's or department's attitudes are unsatisfactory; and this may lead to the prospect of reprimand, or even threat of dismissal.

It may help now to take an example from an organisation such as a school or college, which is not an industrial concern, but which highlights the problems in a very clear way.

Suppose the school has a policy of **evaluating** its own effectiveness as an institution. As part of this evaluation, the school analyses its public examination results for the 16+ pupils. The discovery is made that, although results in most subjects are similar to those in other schools in the area, the results in modern languages (French and German) are markedly poorer — and not just in one year, but over several years. The school, taking the view that evaluation is the systematic gathering of information and judgements in order to guide policy, now experiences the complexities and pressures of the evaluation process as it faces the practical question, 'What should it do about what it has found out?'

The school has collected interesting evaluation data. What does it do with it?

i)   The assessments could form important evidence in the **appraisal** of the teachers of French and German, particularly of the Head of Department. In other words, a group of teachers may be called to account for performing below expectation. It may be found that the teachers are not very well qualified (further training needed?) or are lazy (formal reprimand needed?)

ii) The results (i.e. the **assessments**) of the pupils may lead to further enquiries into the pupils' motivation, industry, application. Is there some factor which is nothing to do with the quality of teaching that is leading to poor results? In other words, the explanation may not lie with the inadequacy of the day to day teaching in the classroom, but in the attitude the pupils bring to foreign languages. 'Foreigners should all learn English!' 'It's a waste of time!'

iii) The **assessments** may lead into enquiries about timetabling, books and materials. Do French and German have too little time, and too poor a budget? In other words, the explanation may lie with a bad **policy** directed by the senior management of the school.

It is now clear that an interesting social situation has been produced. To the Head of the school, the evaluation may look like the ideal chance to alter the timetable. To some pupils, the evaluation may look like an opportunity to get modern languages out of the compulsory timetable. To the Head of French, the evaluation may look like a chance either to secure a better budget or an early retirement for himself.

It is also clear that the evaluation quite clearly exposes many aspects of the life of the school. In other words, the task of evaluating assessments is not easily separable from that of evaluating other aspects of the organisation.

What can be evaluated? What is on the agenda?

Before we further consider the central question of **why** an organisation undertakes an evaluation, the illustration of the school suggests that it would be wise to analyse and set out the various aspects of an organisation that may be evaluated. Three broad aspects are worth examining.

People: those, who at whatever level, are on the payroll — whether their money comes as wages, salaries or fees. The evaluation may take the form of **appraisal** — of people's broad competencies and attitudes, particularly of those in the work force who need to have a wide interest in and commitment to the organisation because of the responsibilities they carry.

Assessment — of the work force's range of skills in relation to the inventory of skills, current and projected, that will enable the organisation to remain effective. Such assessments and appraisals need to be related to the organisation's programme of training.

Training Programmes. Is the training available

i)   relevant to tasks that the organisation requires people to do?

ii) available at the appropriate times to appropriate personnel?

iii) provided with the minimum of waste?

An example might make these points clearer. Several years ago, an organisation agreed to release employees one day a week for a course run at a local F.E. college. At the time, the course seemed very much in line with the organisation's training needs. Since that time, the organisation has changed its product range and the processes by which they are produced. The local course (which serves half a dozen other organisations) has not changed in the same way. Its relevance and usefulness have declined. An evaluation of this course (using the criteria of relevance and up-to-dateness) would conclude that no more personnel should be released to attend it.

The Work Situation.

i)   Are people satisfactorily placed within the organisation?

ii) Are jobs defined wisely, both in relation to the products of the organisation, and also in relation to employee satisfaction?

iii) Are relations within the organisation such as to foster good attitudes amongst employees.

iv) Is there a good programme of reward and promotion?

▰▰▰

During an internal evaluation of an organisation, the following data are produced. **What interpretations might be placed on it?** You may find it helpful to use the headings used above.

The organisation is a building company. Delays are frequently caused in completion of buildings because of faults in the standard of woodwork produced. Assessment of the employees working on wooden doors, panelling, window-frames etc reveals significantly low levels of skill. (Spend about 10 minutes on this. Then compare your own ideas with those given below.)

Under the heading of **people,** *you may have arrived at a variety of conflicting explanations: are the woodworkers lazy? Are they unmotivated because of poor pay? Do the rates of pay currently offered attract only personnel with poor potential? . . . and so on? Under the heading of* **training,** *you may have a similarly wide range. Was the training available before employment poor? Does the organisation offer few chances to improve? Is the course often used now out of date? What happens to employees who perform badly on these training courses? Under the heading of* **work**

situation, *you are likely to have put forward possibilities such as: is there poor site supervision? Is the overall sequence of operations poor in that the woodworkers are given too little time to complete their part of the process well? Is there poor reward for good quality work?*
Summary: the process of assessment tells us that the woodworkers concerned have poor carpentry skills. The process of evaluating these assessments gives a framework which links this problem with the general policies of the firm.

It will be useful now to look in greater detail at these three aspects: personnel, training programmes, work situation.

Evaluating Assessments on Personnel

If we ask the question: 'Why evaluate?' in relation to personnel, it is fair to give a broad answer, 'In order to keep the organisation as effective and healthy as possible.' Let us now look more closely at aspects of this.

Assessment and Appraisal
We drew a distinction above between these two terms. Return to section 1, and check that you are clear about and satisfied with this distinction.

Assessment
Personnel who have jobs that require a narrow or easily specified range of skills are likely to be assessed by means of suitable tests at the point of entry, and again during or after training. Suppose that sets of results such as the following are obtained for a workforce of 100.

Successful performance of the job depends upon the employee's knowing with instant recall 25 items of information, and being able to perform 12 manual acts within a specified time over a specified period. In Organisations A and B the following results are found.

Organisation A
Items of Information
Percentage of Employees able to recall N items of information

20+	items	20
15–19	items	30
10–14	items	30
5–9	items	20

Organisation A
Manual Acts

Able to perform	10,11,12	15
"	8,9	30
"	6,7	30
"	4,5	25
" fewer than 4		—

Organisation B
Manual Acts

Able to perform	10,11,12	85
"	8,9	10
"	6,7	5
"	4,5	0
" fewer than 4		0

Organisation B
Items of Information
Percentage of Employees able to recall N items of information

20+	items	85
15–19	items	10
10–14	items	5
5–9	items	0

When we try to evaluate these results, we could quickly reach the conclusion that Organisation A has a training problem. It is employing personnel who are likely to be holding up processes, causing damage, reducing efficiency. After a suitable training programme, the Organisation should expect to find that over 90% of these personnel should have scores in the top rows for each aspect, information and manual skill.

We might also conclude that it would be surprising to find Organisation A even surviving. Its employees cannot meet the necessary requirements in any credible way.

The schedules of information and skills that are required for the successful performing of the job form the **criteria** by which success is judged. If the schedule is clear, specific, relatively narrow and relatively easy to attain, then the Organisation should be satisfied only with the performances that are all (or nearly all) very good. It should be noted that employees' performances are being compared not with one another, but with the specific demands of the job.

Appraisal
In many organisations, the jobs performed by personnel can be arranged in a hierarchy. Jobs near the bottom can be specified as we did in the example above. As we move nearer to the top, the job descriptions are likely to take on characteristics of one or both the following types:
i) the range of knowledge and skills many become technically much more complex; and/or
ii) the range of knowledge and skills may become more diffuse, more difficult to predict, perhaps much more closely related to the broad characteristics of the employee as a human being.
Jobs of these kinds are **likely** to be linked to the person's use of his or her authority, the exercise of broad responsibilities, the making of a variety of judgements. How might an evaluation of the results of assessments of this type of job be undertaken?

For the first type, if the relevant inventory of skills and knowledge can still be produced, then an assessment can take place which is **in principle** the same as for the simpler job description given above. When an evaluation of the results of such an assessment is made, then the following points need to be remembered.
a) If successful completion of a very large proportion of the items of assessment is a requirement for holding the post, and if the items demand a very high level of intellect, and/or commitment, then the evaluation leads us to conclude that applicants for such posts may be rare, may have to be persuaded into the post by high income and very good working conditions. There is a reason for this. Studies into human abilities have suggested that whenever a range of skills and knowledge is called for beyond the simple and routine, then these skills and knowledge are not distributed **evenly** through the population. Instead, they are distributed **normally.** The skill of identifying bad peas on a conveyor belt is likely to be distributed evenly through the population. (As we say,

'Anyone can do it.') The skill of making an economic forecast of demand is likely to be nearer a normal distribution i.e. relatively few will be able to do it **well** even though the majority can make an average shot at it.

b) The assessment tests will almost certainly have been difficult to construct, and the scores will very probably need skilled interpretation by experts in the field.

Level of Skill or Knowledge

A **normal** distribution as distinct from an **even** distribution. If we take the area under the curve to represent the number of people likely to have a particular level of skill or knowledge, we can see that the majority of people fall into the medium level. Relatively few people are likely to possess the skill or knowledge to a high (or low) level.

If the diagram is a normal **curve** (not a polygon) there is no vertical 'scale' as such, since it is based on **proportions** of the area 'under' the curve.

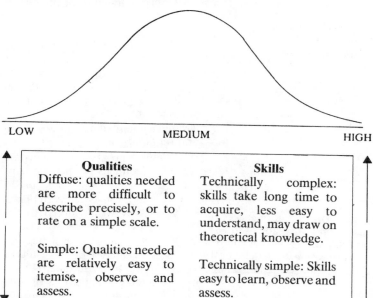

	Qualities	**Skills**
	Diffuse: qualities needed are more difficult to describe precisely, or to rate on a simple scale.	Technically complex: skills take long time to acquire, less easy to understand, may draw on theoretical knowledge.
	Simple: Qualities needed are relatively easy to itemise, observe and assess.	Technically simple: Skills easy to learn, observe and assess.

For the second type of post, the requirements will probably be stated in rather broad terms e.g. 'able to relate successfully with a range of people inside and outside the organisation'. Qualities of this kind being difficult to organise, without damage, into inventories of narrowly defined skills and knowledge, the task of judging success i.e. the task of appraisal inevitably becomes more subjective. An assessor's blind-spots, or private opinions may prevent him from undertaking appraisal well.

The **task of evaluating** in this case becomes therefore one that it is important and complex for the organisation to undertake. Reports from appraisers cannot be simply taken at face value; they need to be interpreted in the light of

(a) the relative scarcity in the population of large members of people who have the range of characteristics at a high level, and

(b) the policy of the organisation. Qualities that may be perfectly suitable in one organisation (e.g. aggression) may be ruled out in another.

We can now return to our opening question: why evaluate the results of assessments on personnel? We can give a number of answers.

(i) The process of evaluation requires us to look carefully at the assessment tests used, and at their results, to see whether the assessments were suitable for the task in hand.

(ii) The process of evaluation makes us cautious about the kinds of levels and types of success we expect to find in personnel assessment and appraisal. It can prevent us from making silly mistakes of interpretation.

(iii) The process of evaluation also reminds us of the importance of reviewing the types and opportunities for training provided by the organisation.

(iv) The process of evaluation takes us out into broader questions of the labour market, the availability of skills, the general policy on pay and conditions of service held by the organisation.

(v) The process of evaluation provides a means by which the organisation's arrangements for assessment, appraisal and training can be linked to its arrangements for general review and development, i.e. for developing its future policy.

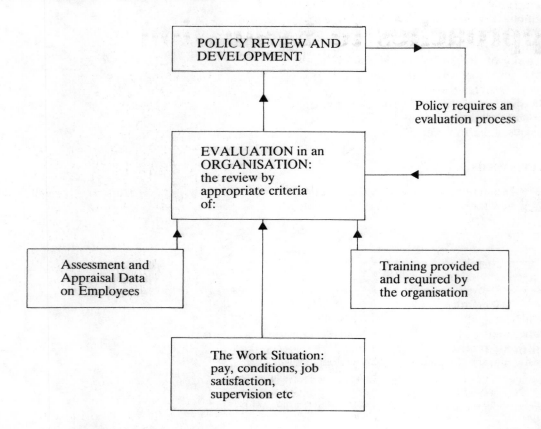

Component 2:

Approaches to Evaluation

Key Words

 Evaluation; goal orientated evaluation; decision orientated evaluation; transactional evaluation; goal free evaluation; adversary evaluation; illuminative evaluation.

Introduction

Now that you have worked your way through the first Component of this Unit you should have a pretty good idea of why you need to evaluate the results of any assessment programme you undertake.

▨▨▨ Checkpoint

How many reasons can you give for evaluating the results of assessment?

I don't know how many you have got but I hope your study of Component 1 has helped. If you are not too sure go back and read through it again.

What we shall be doing in this Component is to look at the different ways or models that you can use to help you with your evaluation. Many processes which we would place under the broad umbrella of evaluation arise naturally during learning. Examples of such evaluating could be:

— The puzzled faces and body language of learners in a workshop who have been asked by the organiser to undertake some task or other which indicate that more explanation of the task is needed.
— The teacher who, in a class, notices the same learning difficulty for many learners and calls together the whole group for additional discussion and help.

At the other end of the evaluation spectrum we could get a planned, highly organised and time consuming evaluation, of say, this multi-media distance learning package. The approaches to the above examples are likely to appear very different but each involves the collection and analysis of information to help many informed judgements about how worthwhile something is.

This Component will take you through some popular approaches to evaluation and hopefully clarify your ideas so that at the end of the Component you will be able to adopt one or more of these approaches yourself. This is going to be a difficult Component and will probably take a long time to get through — I would estimate twice as long as many of the others you have tackled.

▨▨▨

Can you remember the last meal you ate? Was it good or bad? Try and set out a process by which you could evaluate that meal.

I hope you rated the meal a success! However, what we are interested in, in this component, is how you came to rate your meal a 'good' one or a 'bad' one.

As you begin to read the literature in the field of evaluation — I hope you will do some extra reading! — you will begin to encounter different 'evaluation models'. These models serve mainly to bring together common elements of different approaches to evaluation and set the boundaries of the evaluator's role. In addition they provide a vocabulary so that people discussing evaluative issues can speak from a common basis. These different approaches to evaluation are set out in the table below and the rest of this Component sets out the main elements of each model, so that when you come to design your own evaluation programme you can choose the most appropriate approach.

TABLE 1: **MODELS OF PROGRAMME EVALUATION**

MODEL	EMPHASIS
Goal-orientated evaluation	Evaluation should assess individual progress and the effectiveness of change.
Decision-orientated evaluation	Evaluation should facilitate intelligent judgements by decision makers.
Transactional evaluation	Evaluation should depict programme processes and the value perspectives of key people.
Goal free evaluation	Evaluation should assess programme effects based on criteria outside the programme's own framework.
Adversary evaluation	Evaluation should present the best case for each of two competing alternative interpretations of the programme's value, with **both sides** having access to the same information about the programme.

Illuminative evaluation   Evaluation should study a change programme, how it operates and how it is affected by the situation in which it is applied: to discover what it is like to participate in the scheme and to discover the change programme's most significant features.

In evaluating, as in most activities, the same problem can be approached from a variety of viewpoints using a variety of approaches. We shall be looking at each approach illustrated in Table I setting out the main elements of each one. The approaches to evaluation in the rest of this Component were selected to represent the diverse views and practices to evaluate training programmes etc. Let us now take each of these in turn.

Goal-Orientated Evaluation

This approach is usually associated with the name of Ralph W. Tyler whose work evolved during the 1930's and 1940's at Ohio State University in the United States. In a study published in 1942 he set out the "objectives orientated" style of evaluation. He argued that decisions about programmes had to be based on the 'fit' between the objectives of the programme and **its actual outcomes.** If the objectives are achieved, decisions will be taken in a particular direction, if they are not then different decisions will have to be taken. Tyler argued that the advantages of the 'best fit' or 'congruence' approach to evaluation was that it evolved from an organised plan of programme development and that evaluation was an essential part of this development. Tyler set out the procedure of programme evaluation as follows:

(1) Establish goals or objectives
(2) Place objectives in broad classifications
(3) Define objectives in behavioural terms
(4) Establish situations and conditions in which attainment of objectives can be demonstrated
(5) Explain the purposes of the strategy to relevant personnel in the selected situations

(6) Choose or develop appropriate measurement techniques

(7) Collect data from performance of personnel

(8) Compare data with objectives.

The main element in Tyler's approach is the emphasis on objectives. The fact that objectives had to be defined gave firm reference points for evaluation and decision making. When formulating the objectives of a programme for evaluation purposes six main questions have to be asked.

(1) **What** is the nature of the content of the objective? (e.g. change in knowledge, attitudes and/or behaviour)?

(2) **Who** is the target of the programme? (Large scale or discrete groups)?

(3) **When** is the desired change to take place? (Short term or long term)?

(4) Are the objectives **Unitary** or **Multiple?** (e.g. are programmes similar for all users or different for different groups)?

(5) **What** is the desired magnitude of the effect (e.g. widespread or concentrated results)?

(6) **How** is the objective to be attained? (Voluntarily, mandatory or otherwise)?

From: Stufflebeam and Shinkfield (1985).

Tyler developed what became known as the "feedback system" in evaluation and saw evaluation as a recurring process. He argued that evaluation should provide those people involved with the programme with useful information that would enable objectives to be redefined if necessary.

Tyler laid the foundations for the first systematic approach to evaluation which was later to emerge as the "Management by Objectives" approach to developing organisations.

▰▰▰

Pause for a moment and write down other advantages of the Objectives approach.

How many did you get? I will list a few as well.
(1) Precise measurement of behaviour.
(2) Exploring data while the programme was taking shape.
(3) Getting rid of unwanted data.
I hope you can add to this list.

Tyler's ideas were the most important elements in approaches to evaluation for a very long time and even today his ideas are very strong and are used all the time. It is important, however, to look at the approach and try and pinpoint its weaknesses.

▰▰▰

See how many weaknesses you can find.

I don't know how many you got but see if yours correspond to any of mine.
(1) It is impossible to control all the variables in a programme.

(2) All objectives cannot be evaluated so how are you going to make a choice?

(3) Before and after evaluation designs assume that e.g. training programmes undergo little or no change during any given period. This rarely happens as is set out in some of the Components of Package **Five,** *Study Unit* **Three.**

(4) Concentration on seeking quantitative data by objective means may lead to the neglect of other data which may be very important to the study i.e. "subjective" or "anecdotal" data.

(5) Most studies have to be very big to get realistic statistical generalisations and are thus not very useful in a small firm or organisation.

(6) It fails to take into account the 'politics' of evaluation, (see Component 5 of this Unit).

I think that's enough from me at this stage but I hope you can add more of your own.

I have spent some time on the Tyler approach because, as I mentioned before, it is still a very important element of evaluation programmes.

▰▰▰

Set out the main elements of the Tyler approach and the arguments for and against this approach. Take about twenty minutes on this activity. Try and do this using the information already given. If not consult one of the references at the end of this Component.

I hope you were able to do this using the information already given.

Let us now go on to the second approach set out in the table.

Decision-Orientated Evaluation

This approach, as with all other approaches since Tyler, was developed as an alternative to the 'objectives approach'. It is sometimes known as the C.I.P.P. approach and was developed by Daniel Stufflebeam and his associates in the United States. The letters C.I.P.P. stand for: CONTEXT evaluation to help develop objectives, INPUT evaluation to help shape proposals, PROCESS evaluation to guide implementation, and PRODUCT evaluation to serve recycling decisions. Shufflebeam defined evaluation as follows: evaluation is the process of delineating, obtaining and providing descriptive and judgemental information about the worth and merit of a programme's goals, design, implementation and impacts in order to guide decision making, service needs for accountability and promote understanding of the process. It sets out three main purposes of evaluation: guiding decision making, providing records for accountability and promoting understanding of what is involved. It presents evaluation as a process not an event and includes the three steps of delineating, obtaining and providing information. The main elements of the C.I.P.P.

approach is set out in the following table and presents a convenient overview of the essential headings of context, input, process, and product evaluation.

TABLE TWO: C.I.P.P.

	Context Evaluation	Input Evaluation	Process Evaluation	Product Evaluation
Objective	To define the institutional context, to identify the target population and assess their needs, to identify opportunities for addressing the needs, to diagnose problems underlying the needs, and to judge whether proposed objectives are sufficiently responsive to the assessed needs.	To identify and assess system capabilities, alternative program strategies procedural designs for implementing the strategies, budgets, and schedules.	To identify or predict in process, defects in the procedural design or its implementation to provide information for the pre-programmed decisions, and to record and judge procedural events and activities.	To collect descriptions and judgements of outcomes and to relate them to objectives and to context, input and process information and to interpret their worth and merit.
Method	By using such methods as system analysis, survey, document review, hearings, interviews, diagnostic tests, and the Delphi technique.	By inventory and analyzing available human and material resources, solution strategies, and procedural designs for relevance, feasibility and economy. And by using such methods as literature search, visits to exemplary programs, advocate teams, and pilot trials.	By monitoring the activity's potential procedural barriers and remaining alert to unanticipated ones, by obtaining specified information for programmed decisions, by describing the actual process and by continually interacting with, and observing the activities of project staff.	By defining operationally and measuring outcome criteria by collecting judgements of outcomes from stakeholders, and by performing both qualitative and quantitative analyses.
Relation to decision making in the change process	For deciding upon the setting to be served, the goals associated with meeting needs or using opportunities, and the objectives associated with solving problems, i.e. for planning needed changes. And to provide a basis for judging outcomes.	For selecting sources of support, solution strategies, and procedural designs, i.e. structuring change activities. And to provide a basis for judging implementation.	For implementing and refining the program design and procedure, i.e. for effecting process control. And to provide a log of the actual use in interpreting outcomes.	For deciding to continue, terminate, modify or refocus a change activity. And to present a clear record of effects (intended and unintended, positive and negative).

From: Stufflebeam and Shinkfield (1985)

If you want to obtain more information about this approach you will find some of the references at the end of this Component helpful.

Let us now go on to the third approach in Table I.

Transactional Evaluation

This approach was developed by another American evaluator Robert Stake who published the approach in 1967.*He argued that few evaluators saw what they were evaluating "in the round". He noted that formal evaluations often focus narrowly on a few variables in a programme, e.g. outcomes associated with objectives, and that informal evaluations often reflect a few people's opinions but not carefully collected empirical data. He urged evaluations to recognise the shortcomings of their usual evaluation practices and to pay attention to all aspects of evaluation. This includes:

(1) Description and judgement of a programme
(2) A variety of data sources
(3) Analyses of congruences and contingencies

(4) Identification of pertinent, often conflicting standards
(5) Multiple uses of evaluation.

Fundamentally he noted that evaluating any programme requires that it be fully described and judged.

Stake's approach is set out in the diagrams below.

* I hope that you may already have read the simplified account of Stake's approach in Study Unit 2, Component 6 of this Volume.

TABLE 3

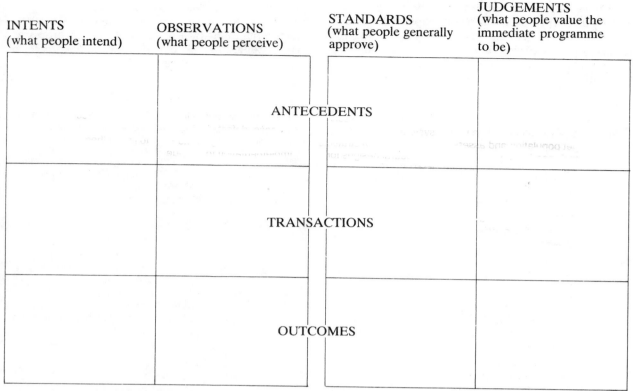

INTENTS (what people intend)	OBSERVATIONS (what people perceive)		STANDARDS (what people generally approve)	JUDGEMENTS (what people value the immediate programme to be)
		ANTECEDENTS		
		TRANSACTIONS		
		OUTCOMES		
DESCRIPTION MATRIX			JUDGEMENT MATRIX	

In Table 3 the rows distinguish the stages of the change process.
(1) Antecedents — the conditions that existed before the change is introduced.
(2) Transactions — the process of interaction as the change proceeds.
(3) Outcomes — the main effects of the change.
However these categories are not rigid as Stake himself points out.

> Transactions are dynamic whereas antecedents and outcomes are relatively static. The boundaries between them are not clear, e.g. during a transaction we can identify certain outcomes which are feedback antecedents for subsequent learning. These boundaries do not need to be distinct. The categories should be used to stimulate rather than to subdivide our data collection.
>
> (Stake (1967) p.258)

For each of these stages, we can distinguish four sets of relevant data (the columns in Table 3). The first set consists of INTENTS, the goals, aims and objectives that the trainer formulates, which are related to the antecedent conditions of the situation, the type of transactions that are to occur, and the performance outcomes that are to be hoped for. The next set consists of data arising from OBSERVATIONS which describe what actually happened (or at least is perceived to have happened) as opposed to what was intended to happen. Again, these can relate to the antecedent conditions, the transactions and the outcomes. The third set relates to STANDARDS, the expectations implicit in the original intentions transformed into a criterion or norm. What sort of transactions can be expected; and what sort of learning outcomes can be achieved? At the final stage we have JUDGEMENTS. Were the antecedent conditions satisfactory? Were the transactions as good (worthwhile) as they should have been? And were the outcomes acceptable?

The appeal of Stake's conception is that it extends such judgements back through the process of change itself and the conditions under which it occurs. In these cases of course, the judgement relies much more on a subjective assessment of the value of what is happening. The important point is that such a judgement is made at all.

The left-hand columns of Stake's diagram hold particular interest and require a further diagram to show the form of analysis required. Stake sees the analysis as having two aspects. The first concerns congruency: how well do the intentions correspond to the observations? The second is contingency: are the intentions logically coherent and do the observations show the expected correlations? Analysis of congruency can be seen as an exercise in empirical validation: how well are our intentions congruent with what actually happens? Analysis of contingency represents the testing of hypotheses, both logically and empirically: is it reasonable to assume that B should follow A? Does B in fact follow A? This distinction illustrates two kinds of analysis: intrinsic and empirical. For empirical analysis, experiment and observation **are essential, whereas intrinsic analysis relies upon thought and discussion.** Thus the analysis of observational contingencies may be at a premium in the formulation of hypotheses and in trying them out

in the workshop; standards may be central to the evaluation of a curriculum innovation. The important stance for any evaluator is responsiveness to the needs of the particular situation — in Stake's terms the appropriate portrayal of those classroom processes and products that relate most closely to the problems requiring solution (Stake, 1967).

TABLE 4. A representation of the processing of descriptive data. (Stake 1967, p.533)

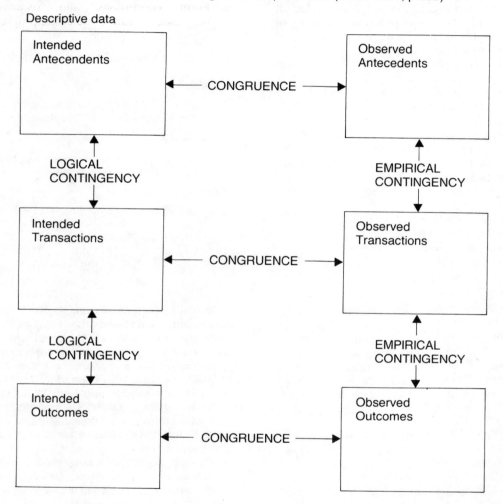

Take an example of any change process you have been involved in and try to see if it can be evaluated by Stake's framework.

I cannot give you an answer here as you are the only one who knows our own situation, but I hope you were able to come up with a clear answer — one way or another.

Let's now go on to the next approach.

Goal Free Evaluation

This approach was set out by an Australian called Michael Scriven. In an article published in 1967 Scriven argued that the goal of evaluation is always the same — to judge value. He argued, however, that the roles of evaluation varied enormously. They may form part of a training activity, a change process, an experiment with a small group or looking at training materials etc. He argued that the failure to distinguish between evaluation's goal (to judge the value of something) and its roles (constructive use of evaluative data) has led to the dilution of what is called evaluation so that it no longer achieves its goal of assessing value. He argued that evaluators too often, in trying to help the people involved to improve their programme, become co-opted and fail to judge the programmes. He argued that evaluation had two main roles. Formative, to assist in developing programmes and other objects, and summative to assess the value of the object i.e. training programme, once it has been developed. As the next two components will be looking at these different forms of evaluation I will not say more about them at this stage. Scriven published a key evaluation checklist to accompany his arguments and it reflects his view that evaluation evolves multiple dimensions, should employ multiple perspectives and must use multiple methods.

Key Evaluation Checklist

a. Characterize as objectively as possible the nature of the training programme to be evaluated.
b. Clarify the audience for the evaluation findings, including the commissioner of the evaluation and all other stakeholder groups.
c. Examine the background of the need for the evaluation and clarify the questions to be answered.
d. Inventory the financial and other types of resources that are available to support the development, maintenance, and evaluation of the programme.
e. Perform a functional analysis of the programme as it actually operates, especially in terms of what the participants actually do while participating in the programme.
f. Carefully examine which participants are actually using and benefiting from unique aspects of the progamme.
g. Assess the needs of participants that might be addressed by the training programme.
h. Search out standards that might have been evolved to assess training programmes; also derive other standards of assessment by means of analyzing the programme's functions and goals, and, in general, determine and assess the criteria of merit and the philosophical arguments pertaining to the programme.
i. Examine the implementation process to find what constraints attend the normal operation of the programme and to help discern the parts of the programme plan that are not feasible in the given setting or possibly only workable there.
j. Check all effects of the programme comprehensively.
k. Examine the possibility and desireability of exporting the approach to other situations.
l. Assess the various financial, psychological, and other costs of the training programme.
m. Identify and assess critical competitors to the programme.
n. Validate and synthesize all information obtained.
o. Form conclusions and recommendations regarding the future use of the programme in its setting and elsewhere.

From Stufflebeam and Shinkfield (1985).

Suppose you plan to evaluate a training programme using the Key Evaluation Checklist, summarise the steps you would follow.

Again I cannot give you an answer but make sure you understand all the items on the list.

The next approach on our original list is

Adversary Evaluation

The argument used for this approach was that in evaluation emphasis was being increasingly placed on providing information for decision making and the methodology of current approaches had not kept pace with this development. People involved in training and education at all levels have to increasingly justify their decisions and must realise the importance of effective communication with the public in such matters. The supporters of this approach argue that conventional evaluation approaches do not meet these changes and the solution to the problem lies in taking a judicial approach to the situation. The approach adopts and modifies concepts from both jury trials and administrative hearings as to how evaluations can focus clearly on a set of issues, rely on testimony for individuals, explore different aspects of issues by using two evaluation teams, enable a balanced point of view to develop and structure the deliberations of the programme decision makers.

Four stages for the implementation of this approach can be set out.

a. **The issue-generating stage:**
   1. A broad range of issues are identified relating to evaluation of the programme.
   2. Outcomes of any formative evaluation processes are used to help identify issues.
   3. Personnel involved in programme development are invited to help identify issues for evaluation.
   4. Issues may vary from original programme objectives.
   5. Interviews and other means are used to identify issues.

b. **The issues selection stage:**
   1. Issues are narrowed down to manageable size for the hearing (these should be specified).
   2. The part to be played by programme and other personnel in establishing the priority ranking is outlined.
   3. A special review panel (which should be described) checks the issues for relevance and puts them in written form.

c. **The preparation of arguments stage:**
   1. Two teams of evaluators are selected; they prepare contrary formal arguments.
   2. Specific points of contention are developed around each selected issue.
   3. Statements and data relating to issues are collected from various sources.
   4. Reference is made to data from any earlier evaluation(s) of selected issues.

d. **The hearing stage:**
   1. In a pre-hearing session, both teams review major arguments.
   2. With the hearings officer, rules of debate are determined.
   3. Specific questions are drafted to guide panel deliberations.

4. Details of panel composition, decision-making body, a number of sessions for the hearing are all determined.
5. The hearing occurs and the panel deliberates.
6. Recommendations ensue upon which decisions are made.

From Stufflebeam and Shinkfield (1985).

Also the arguments for and against this approach can be set out as follows:

a. **The pros of adversary evaluation:**
   1. Information scope; a wider array of information arises from both sides being represented, and confrontation encourages thorough substantiation of stances adopted.
   2. Quality of evidence; the ever-present possibility of challenge encourages precise documentation of evidence and a wariness of widesweeping statements.
   3. Predisposed ideas of both program personnel and evaluator are diminished; the adversary approach encourages evidence free of personal bias.
   4. The "yes-man" syndrome diminishes; the approach guards against appeasement by the evaluator of the decision maker's known leanings.
   5. Hidden assumptions are exposed; the approach helps reveal, clarify and eventually change underlying assumptions involved in opposing points of view; value premises come to light, and inconsistencies are clarified.
   6. Enforced openness; as a result, better decisions may be made.

b. **The cons of adversary evaluation:**
   1. Disparity in proponent prowess; a better defense may make the weak side of a case appear more attractive.
   2. Fallible arbiters; judges vary in their ability, and poor decisions will sway the outcomes of the hearing.
   3. Excessive confidence in the model's potency; inexperience with the law may give rise to undeserved praise for the efficacy of the model.
   4. Political matters receive too little contemplation; the evaluators may ride roughshod over political considerations, but these will remain no matter what decision is reached and disruption of future plans may result.
   5. Difficulties in framing the proposition in a manner amenable to adversary resolution; issues are not always approached in a manner helpful to uneventual decision making because decisions are often reached on the basis of complex and interrelated information.
   6. Excessive costs; almost invariably, the adversary evaluation costs more than a conventional evaluation of a similar programme.

c. **A balanced argument:**
   1. Remedies may be proposed for many of the arguments against the model.
   2. When finance is available, adversary evaluation may be considered particularly when large programmes need to be evaluated.
   3. Careful consideration must precede any study using the adversary approach.
   4. The model's enforcement of an open and honest approach, with bias held to a minimum, makes it unique among evaluation models.

From Stufflebeam and Shinkfield (1985).

Illuminative Evaluation

The last approach to evaluation we are going to look at is ILLUMINATIVE EVALUATION.

This approach was developed as an alternative to all other approaches to evaluation and grew out of research at the Massachusetts Institute of Technology in 1969. The most informative account of this approach is set out by two authors Malcolm Perlett and David Hamilton in 1977.

Illuminative evaluation takes account of the wider context in which training programmes function; thus its primary concern is with description and interpretation rather than with measurement and prediction. The aims of illuminative evaluation are as follows:

1. To study the innovatory programme — how it operates, how it is influenced by the various situations in which it is applied, what those directly concerned regard as its advantages and disadvantages, and how peoples' intellectual tasks and experiences are most affected.
2. To discover and document what it is like to be participating in the scheme.
3. To discern and discuss the innovation's most significant features, recurring concomitants, and critical processes.

Thus, it seeks to address and to illuminate a complex array of questions, helping the innovator and other interested parties to identify those procedures and those aspects of the programme seen to have had desirable results.

As Parlett and Hamilton point out, the adoption of illuminative evaluation requires more than an exchange of methodologies (from the traditional ones); it also involves new suppositions, concepts, and terminology central to the understanding of illuminative evaluation of two concepts, the "instructional system" and "learning milieu".

The Instructional System

Educational prospectuses and reports usually contain a variety of formalized plans and standards relating to particular teaching arrangements. Each of these may be said to constitute, or define an instructional system and to include a set of pedagogic assumptions, and details of techniques and equipment. A catalogue is an idealized specification of the scheme, a set of elements arranged to an optimistic, coherent plan.

Parlett and Hamilton point out that the traditional evaluator builds a study around innovations defined in this way. Having examined the blue-print or formalized plan and having extracted the programmes goals, objectives, or desired outcomes, the evaluator next derives the tests and attitude inventories to be administered. The aim is to evaluate the instructional system by examining whether it has attained its objectives or met its performance criteria.

This technological approach, however, fails to recognise the prospectus or report for what it is:

> It ignores the fact that an instructional system, when adopted, undergoes modifications that are rarely trival. The instructional system may remain as a shared idea, abstract model, slogan or shorthand, but it assumes a different form in every situation. Its constituent elements are emphasised or de-emphasised, expanded or truncated, as teachers, administrators, technicians, and students interpret and reinterpret the instructional system for their particular setting. In practice, objectives are commonly reordered, redefined, abandoned or forgotten. The original "ideal" formulation ceases to be accurate, or indeed, of much relevance. Few in practice take catalogue descriptions and lists of objectives very seriously, save — it seems — for the traditional evaluator.

The move from the discussion of the instructional system in its idealized form to a description of its implementation in practice may well represent moving into a new realm. This brings us to the second concept, the learning milieu.

The Learning Milieu

The learning milieu is the "social-psychological and material environment in which participants work "together". It represents a network of cultural, social, institutional, and psychological variables that interact in complicated ways to produce, within groups or courses, a unique pattern of circumstances (e.g. pressures, opinions, conflicts) which suffuse the teaching and learning that occur there.

According to Parlett and Hamilton, the configuration of the learning milieu, in any particular situation depends on the interplay of numerous different factors. As an example, there are numerous constraints (legal, administrative, and financial) on the organization of training, there are pervasive operating assumptions held by training staff; there are learning styles, and private expectations; and there are participants' perspectives, needs, and motivations.

It is important that the diversity and complexity of learning milieux is seen as a basis for the serious study of training programmes. Any program, and particularly an innovation, should not be thought of as being a self-contained and independent system. The introduction of an innovation sets off a chain of repercussions throughout the learning context. Most likely, unintended consequences arise that affect the innovation itself, changing its form and moderating its impact.

The main features of Illuminative Evaluation.

a. Illuminative evaluation as a general research strategy.

1. Illuminative evaluation aims to be both adaptable to meet the size, aims, and techniques of the evaluation and eclectic to give the evaluator a choice of research tactics.

2. The choice of strategy to be used arises from the problem to be investigated.

3. No one method is used exclusively or in isolation.

4. The evaluator makes no attempt to manipulate or control or eliminate situational variables, but takes as given the complex scene that is found.

5. The evaluator endeavours to delineate cycles of cause and effect and relationships between belief and practices.

b. The observation phase

1. The observation phase occupies a central place in illuminative evaluation.

2. The investigator complies a continuous record of events, transactions, and informal remarks.

3. The evaluator also documents a wide variety of other events such as meetings.

4. Discussions with and between participants are recorded and language conventions and metaphors discerned.

5. Parlett and Hamilton believe that there is also a place for codified observation, which makes use of schedules for recording patterns of attendances, eating, utilization of time and facilities, and the like; this information, however must be used with caution, as it is not likely to uncover underlying features of the programme.

c. The place of interviews.

1. Discovering the views of participants is crucial in the assessment of the programmes impact.

2. Course participants are asked about their work and also about the use and value of the programme from their perspective.

3. The type of interview chosen must be the most appropriate to elicit the type of information or comment sought.

4. Brief, structured interviews are convenient for obtaining biographical or demographic information, while more open-ended and discursive forms are suitable for less straightforward topics.

d. Questionairre and test data.

1. Though concentrating on observation and interview, the illuminative evaluator must not disregard paper-and-pencil techniques where these may prove useful.

2. Their advantage in large-scale studies is especially evident (although they may be used in small studies).

3. The results of questionnaires may be used later in a study to sustain or qualify earlier tentative findings.

4. Questionnaires should be used only after careful thought — and never in isolation.

5. Besides completing questionnaires, participants may also be asked to prepare written comments about the programme or to compile work diaries of their activities over a period of time.

6. Custom-built tests of attitude, personality, and achievement may be used (but without privileged status within the study) — and again, never in isolation.

e. Documentary and background information.

1. The historical antecedents of a programme should be recorded as these do not arise by chance.

2. Primary sources may be trapped, such as confidential data held on file, together with autobiographical and eye-witness accounts of the programme.

3. Tape recordings of meetings and examples of students' work may also prove useful in providing an historical perspective.

From Shufflebeam and Shinkfield (1985).

Conclusion

The main aim of this Component was to set out as clearly as possible the main approaches to evaluation in use today. I said at the beginning of this Component that the same 'problem' could be approached from a variety of viewpoints using a variety of approaches. The crunch question for you is to decide what approach to take when you are asked to carry out an evaluation. I am afraid that here I cannot be of too much help. There are few, if any, precise rules to follow as all the circumstances in organisations are different. However, I have found that the following list of questions has helped me a great deal in coming to a decision as to what approach approximates to what I want. I hope you will find the list as helpful once you have decided what type of evaluation you are going to undertake (and what approach). You will find the next two Components very helpful.

Questions for Evaluators

Planning

1. Why do you want to set up an evaluation? Why might other people want an evaluation to be set up?

2. How clear are you about the intended audience for the evaluation information?

3. Whose agreement must you get before starting the evaluation? Whose interest should you engage?

4. Who will be affected by the evaluation? How much should they be told about it? How, if at all, should they be involved in it?

5. Who might be interested in helping with the evaluation? How can that assistance be secured (or avoided)?

6. How open-minded are you about what you might find? How open-minded do you appear to others?

Organising and doing

7. How will you start? If it is to be a problem-centred evaluation how and by whom will the problems be identified?

8. Who will undertake the general planning of the evaluation?
9. How and by whom will the planning of the evaluation be carried out?
10. Which source of information will you draw upon?
11. Who will do the actual drafting of questionnaires, interview schedules, etc? What opportunities are there to involve participants in the work of evaluation?
12. Who will carry out the interviews, administer the questionnaires, etc?
13. Who will collate and analyse the information collected?
14. Who will produce the reports (if any)?
15. How much of (a) your time, (b) other people's time is available for the evaluation? Is it enough?
16. Do you have the other resources necessary to carry out the evaluation?

Information and its collection
17. How clear are you about what you want to find out? How clear do you need to be?
18. How can you exploit the routinely collected information?
19. How will you choose the appropriate methods of collecting the information?
20. Do you or your colleagues have the knowledge and skills necessary to use the various techniques of inquiry? If not, how can they be acquired?

Using the information
21. What kind of information might other people want from an evaluation? To what extent will you be able to (or should you) provide it?
22. What methods are available in your organisation for passing on information?
23. What new methods, if any, will you have to invent for passing on the information?
24. How likely is it that action will be considered or taken as a result of the evaluation?
25. How familiar are you with the ways decisions are taken about the course?
26. To what extent are you able to influence the processes by which decisions are taken about the course?
27. How will you engage the interest and support of the people with the authority to take decisions about the course?
28. What support might be needed by people who wish to change their practices as a result of the evaluation?

Acknowledgement: In this component use is made of material from Stufflebeam, D., and Shinkfield, A. *Systematic Evaluation,* published by Nijhoff Publishing, whose permission is gratefully acknowledged.

Component 3:

Formative and Summative Evaluation

Key Words

 Formative Evaluation; Summative Evaluation; 'Outsider' Evaluator; 'Insider' Evaluator; Monitoring; Personal Framework; Action Plan.

Introduction

In the previous Component when we were looking at Scriven's 'Goal Free Evaluation' he argued that any evaluation programme has two main roles, Formative, to assist in developing programmes, and Summative, to assess the value of the programme once it has been developed. This formative evaluation is an integral part of the developmental process. It provides continuous feedback to assist in planning and then producing the programme. It helps to improve the development and operation of the programme.

Summative evaluation, on the other hand may be used by administrators to decide whether the finished programme refined by use of the evaluation process in its formative role, represents a sufficiently significant advance on the available alternatives to justify the expense of adopting the programme on a permanent basis. To be really effective summative evaluation should be performed by someone who is not closely associated with the programme in order to enhance its objectivity, and the findings made public. It provides judgements about the extent to which the goals of the programme validly reflect assessed needs.

Formative Evaluation — assisting the Development

311

Summative Evaluation — was it a success?

This Component will outline the main steps you will have to take in order to carry out formative evaluation and summative evaluation.

It will be a good idea to use this Component when you are actually embarking on an evaluation programme, i.e. use the checkpoints as a check not just on your learning but also on the extent to which you are following the steps to lay out your own programme of evaluation.

▨▨▨ Checkpoint

Write down your working definition of a formative evaluation.

I do not know what you have written down but your definition must contain such features as, e.g. formative evaluation serves as a continuous feedback during the period of the planning and implementation of the planned change. The purpose is to influence the shaping and working of the progamme and to assist in any revisions which may be considered desirable during the development and implementation stages.

Right, let's now work our way through the major stages of a plan for formative evaluation.

Stage 1

Getting to know the proposed programme of change and working out what you are going to do.

Hello, I'm the evaluator

Getting to know a programme

This stage may sound easy but it is probably the most critical of the lot. It is the time when you establish your role in the situation and develop a relationship with those involved in the programme. It will also be a time to work out what you can achieve as an evaluator and again, very importantly, setting all this down on paper.

Information about any proposed programme of change, be it a large organisation wide one or a small department based one, will hopefully be contained in documents and descriptions. Study these very carefully and when you think you have got all the information you want then start talking to the people involved. Since formative evaluation depends on sharing information then talking to people must not only have the aim of obtaining information but in order to obtain this information a good trusting relationship must be developed with the people involved. If you are an 'insider' i.e. you are also a member of staff in the department or organization then establishing trust will be easier than if the evaluation is being carried out by someone from outside.

'Insider' and 'Outsider' Evaluation.

▨▨▨

Write down as many arguments as you can for and against 'insider' and 'outsider' evaluation.

I don't know what you have written but see if you have included the ones I am going to use as illustrations.

First of all the people involved with the programme of change should be fully conversant with it and these should be in charge of the evaluation. However, they may be emotionally involved and may also expend a lot of energy to ensure that the programme will succeed and will not want to see their 'investment' wasted. Factors such as these can make it difficult for those closely involved with the programme to be objective about it. One alternative is to bring in an outside 'expert' in evaluation who is also impartial and objective about the change. The main problem here is that the evaluation 'expert' may have no knowledge of the area that is subject to change. Probably the most appropriate arrangement is to have a mixture of the two approaches, i.e. someone who has knowledge of evaluation methods but who is a member of some other area of the organisation which is not being affected by the change. This approach has two main advantages.

(a) As a member of the same organisation you will find it easier to convince the staff you are on their side and not in an adversary position.

(b) Not being part of the programme of change will help to maintain objectivity.

While the attainment of mutual trust must be a gradual process some necessary areas must be made explicit very early on in the process.

(1) Identifying programme objectives.
(2) Choosing instructional materials.
(3) Identifying the primary characteristics of the programme.
(4) Members attitudes to change, i.e. how far are they prepared to go.

Once you have got as much information as you can about the proposed programme of change and the people involved you must convey to everyone a description of what you can and cannot do for them within the constraints of time, money and personal abilities. You should be quite frank about those areas in which you have expertise and those in which you lack competence. You should also have a tentative evaluation plan in mind which you can discuss with the others involved. Once you and the programme planners have come to an agreement about your role and activities, write it down. The work statement should include things like:

(1) An outline description of the evaluation questions.
(2) Data collection methods.
(3) A time table of activities.
(4) A schedule of reports and meetings.

Do not lay down any hard and fast rules at this stage making sure everyone sees them as tentative.

What you are doing at this stage of the evaluation process can be summed up by the following:

(1) Discussing
(2) Assessing possibilities
(3) Examining constraints
(4) Negotiating
(5) Exploring opportunities.

▨▨

If you are involved in an evaluation programme check to see if you have got all the information required. If you are not involved in an evaluation activity spend some time in thinking how you would tackle a proposed programme of change as the evaluator.

Spend about 15 minutes on this activity.

Stage II

Let's now go on to have a look at the second stage of the formative evaluation plan. This is the monitoring of the implementation of the programme of change. What you will be doing is investigating the match between the intentions of the programme as set out in the planning stages and what actually happens with the programme in action.

The problems of intentions and actions.

The formative evaluation serves as the eyes and ears of the programme planners and the information that is gathered may be used to:

(1) Pinpoint areas of programme strengths and weaknesses.
(2) Refine and revise the programme and maybe your own evaluation plan.
(3) Come to tentative conclusions about the cause-effect relationship between objectives and results.
(4) Draw some conclusions about the relative effectiveness of the programme.

At this stage the formative evaluator will be involved in two main activities.

(1) Collecting, analysing and interpreting data.
(2) Reporting back to the participants.

The extent to which the formative evaluator gets involved in the decision making process after the report stage will depend on the original contract and how involved the evaluator is with the programme, i.e. how much of an 'outsider' or 'insider' the evaluator is.

▨▨

If you are planning a formative evaluation try working out to what extent you should become involved in the decision making process. Remember the problems outlined in this component.

As I shall be discussing data collection, analysis and reporting in detail in Component 4 of this Unit, I will only make general comments at this stage. Ideally the formative evaluator should remain with the programme all the time in the style of a participant observer. Realistically because of constraints of time, money, geographical location etc. this will not be possible. The evaluator must then work out the best programme possible and decide on the best mix of approaches. These approaches will be the subject of Component four.

The evaluator must work out the best programme possible

Once you have reported the results of the first round of data collection the job of the people in charge of the programme and ideally taking in those involved as well, is to carefully examine what you have said and choose a course of action. Your own degree of involvement as I said above will be a matter agreed between you and the other people involved. On the other hand you can simply be an impartial carrier of information to the staff who will then have to take decisions themselves. However you can become much more involved calling attention to what you think are the programmes' successes and failures and call for certain courses of action.

We can show the process by means of a spiral diagram (see next page).

This diagram is based on, and adapted from the ideas set out by Kemmis et al. (1982) *The Action Research Planner*, Geelong, Dearen University Press. It sets out the 'Spiral for Action' which the formative evaluator can follow — I have found this process very useful.

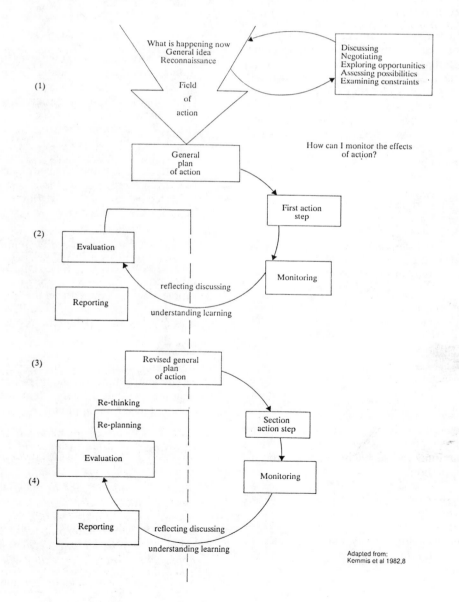

Adapted from:
Kemmis et al 1982,8

When you start your formative evaluation sequence you are involved in two main activities:
(1) Finding out what the situation is at that time.
(2) Helping the people involved to formulate a general plan of action.
Once the plan is to be put into action you are involved in monitoring, analysing and reporting the process. Your report is then used by the people involved to evaluate the situation and with your help formulate a revised plan of action which is then put into effect.

▰▰▰

For revision purposes translate the general outline plan set out above into your own personal framework as you would use it for a change programme you are involved in or you would hope to be involved in.

You should now be in a good position to get involved in a formative evaluation programme. However a word of warning — evaluating is like swimming — you have to get involved and doing it in order to learn it. We can only give you a general guide, it is up to you to jump into the water and see if you can sink or swim!!

'Summative evaluator at work.'

The results from a summative evaluation usually compiled into a report can be used for several purposes.
(1) To show outside interests e.g. the board of directors, that the programme has achieved its objectives.
(2) For filing for future reference.
(3) To be used as a planning document for other people who might want to duplicate the programme.
Summative evaluation usually follows a well known series of steps.
(1) Focus the evaluation — what knowledge etc. needs to be known and by whom.
(2) Select an appropriate evaluation design — you may want to go back to component two at this stage to refresh your memory.
(3) Collect data.
(4) Analyse data.
(5) Prepare report.
Although these various stages have been separated this is solely for illustration as the first two usually occur simultaneously as do stages three and four.

As I have mentioned before in order to learn how to carry out evaluation you have to actually do it so what I shall do is set out a series of questions to use as a guideline when planning your summative evaluation programme.

The Evaluator must get involved in the evaluation to find out if he can do it!

As we said in the introduction to this component, summative evaluation differs from formative evaluation in its timing, its audience and the evaluators relationship to the change programme. When the programme has been developed and implemented satisfactorily it is time to find out to what extent the programme has achieved the objectives and whether to carry on with it or abandon it.

▰▰▰

What do you think is the main function of the summative evaluation?

See if your answer corresponds to mine. I think the summative evaluator's main function is to collect, analyse and report data showing what the programme looks like and what has been achieved. Ideally the summative evaluator does not get involved apart from collecting data.

QUESTIONS to use as a guideline for planning a summative evaluation.
(1) What is the title of the programme to be evaluated?
(2) Who wants to know what?
(3) What is the programme's aim and objectives?
(4) What are the distinctive features of the programme?
(5) What are the peoples' views of the programme?
(6) Are there any plans for formative evaluation?

(7) Who are the various people involved with the programme?

(8) How is the programme going to be implemented?

(9) What will happen if the programme is not successful?

(10) What costs, implementation aspects and outcomes are you going to measure?

(11) What evaluation design are you going to use?

(12) What data collecting instruments are you going to use?

(13) What sampling strategy are you going to use?

(14) What approach to data analysis are you going to use?

(15) How are you going to record your data?

Questions 11 to 15 can be answered using Components Two and Four of this Study Unit.

(16) How are you going to plan and assemble your report?

(17) What form is the report going to take?

(18) What is the deadline for your report?

After working your way through this Component (and this comment also applies to Component Four) you may think I have used a very didactic approach. Yes I have, because as I have said before there are a very large number of books on the market which you can use to supplement these two Components — and as you can only learn to evaluate by actually doing it, all I have done is to give you a framework which you can use to guide your work; the rest is up to you!

Component 4:

Data Collection and Analysis for Evaluation

Key Words

 Data Collection; Questionnaires; Interviews; Observations; Closed and Open Questions; Interview Characteristics; Participant Observation; Sampling; Reliability; Validity; Triangulation; Objectivity; Data Analysis; Quantitative Analysis; Qualitative Analysis.

Let us now suppose that you have reached the stage in your evaluation and appraisal where you are quite clear on the kind of information you require to carry out the task. You are then faced with two main problems.

(1) How do I obtain the information?

(2) What do I do with the information after obtaining it?

These two tasks are inter-related as you must be thinking of what you are going to do with the information you are going to gather as you are planning to do it. I can think of some horrific examples of people embarking on massive programmes of data gathering before thinking how the results are to be analysed. All to often this leads to considerable wasted effort. The aim of this Component is to take you through the main methods of data gathering and how this data may be analysed. The Component will be divided into two sections, one on data collection and the second on analysis and reporting.

Section One: Data collection.

I am going to look at three main methods of data collection: Questionnaires, Interviews and Observation. I shall deal with just those three for two reasons. First of all I think that most people who get

involved in evaluation will probably only have time to use one or more of these, and secondly other Components and Units in Package Four have dealt extensively with many of the methods of Data collection, e.g. Component six of Study Unit four deals with interviews. I would strongly suggest that after you work you way through this Component to look through the other Study Units and Components of Package four and supplement your reading with some of those. I know this may take time but it will pay off in the end.

Questionnaires

Questionnaires are the most common method of collecting information.

Questionnaires are probably the most common method of collecting information. They are cheap to administer, can be sent to a large number of people and provided they are well designed are relatively easy to analyse. However, a word of warning. Questionnaires can be very difficult to design, finding the right words, the best layout and the method of distribution most likely to yield a good response is very skilled work.

It is all too easy to produce a questionnaire whose questions are ambiguous, instructions unclear, layout poor or information difficult to analyse later.

Right, let me now take you through some of the main elements of questionnaire construction and use. First of all the layout of the questionnaire can be as important as the wording of the questions. A badly laid out questionnaire can cause respondents to become confused and miss out questions. Lack of space can also be a problem as is too many questions.

▰▰▰ Checkpoint

What are the main types of questions do you think should be included in questionnaires?

I hope you kept it simple and did not get a very long list. I find it useful to stick to the two types open and closed. Here's an example;
(1) Did you find the training session useful? . . .
              Yes   No
(2) How useful did you find the training session? . . .
              Very . . . Not

(3) How useful did you find the training session? . . . .
Questions (1) and (2) are examples of closed questions whereas question (3) is more open ended. Although basically asking the same question, the information received from the above is likely to be different for each question. An even more open ended question might be:
(4) What were your reactions to the training session?
Answers to question (4) are likely to display the most differences depending on:
— How much time is available
— The amount of space given on the questionnaire
— How motivated the respondent is
— The number of people who respond.

The choice between using open or closed questions depends upon what information is required, the audience and the time available to write, answer and analyse the questionnaire. When open ended questions are asked, enough space must be left for the respondent to answer the question in his or her own words. This usually means allowing more space than you would ordinarily think necessary. Open ended questions will greatly increase the work of analysis because the replies must be categorised and graded, after the questionnaire has been administered. It's often useful to aim at including both open and closed questions in the same questionnaire to allow people to expand answers and express opinions as well as providing specific information. If closed questions are presented first the people completing the questionnaire will have their attention drawn to certain points and this may affect their answers to questions which follow. If open questions are used first the respondents are given freedom to express themselves before having their ideas focused by the questionnaire. A particularly useful combination for evaluation purposes is a closed question followed by an open one allowing the respondent to qualify the answer.

Construct a short questionnaire using closed and open questions on some subject you want information on. Try it out on your colleagues.

I do not know how you got on but keep the examples as we shall use them later on.

If you decide to use a questionnaire then a framework for developing it could be:

Framework for Questionnaire construction

A. Decisions about question content
1. Is the question necessary? Just how will it be useful?
2. Are several questions needed on the subject matter of this question?
3. Do respondents have the information necessary to answer the question?

4. Does the question need to be more concrete, specific and closely related to the respondent's personal experience?
5. Is the question's content sufficiently general and free from spurious concreteness and specificity?
6. Do the replies express general attitudes and only seem to be as specific as they sound?
7. Is the question content biased or loaded in one direction without accompanying questions to balance the emphasis?
8. Will the respondents give the information that is asked for?

B. Decisions about question wording
1. Can the question be misunderstood? Does it contain difficult or unclear phraseology?
2. Does the question adequately express the alternative with respect to the point?
3. Is the question misleading because of unstated assumptions or unseen implications?
4. Is the wording biased? Is it emotionally loaded or slanted towards a particular kind of answer?
5. Is the question wording likely to be objectionable to the respondent in any way?
6. Would a more personalised working of the question produce better results?
7. Can the question be better asked in a more direct or a more indirect form?

C. Decisions about form of response to the question
1. Can the question best be asked in a form calling for check answer (or short answer of a word or two, or a number), free answer or check answer with follow-up answer?
2. If a check answer is used, which is the best type for this question — dichotomous, multiple-choice ('cafeteria' question) or scale?
3. If a checklist is used, does it cover adequately all the significant alternatives without overlapping and in a defensible order? Is it of reasonable length? Is the wording of items impartial and balanced?
4. Is the form of response easy, definite, uniform and adequate for the purpose?

D. Decisions about the place of the questions in the sequence
1. Is the answer to the question likely to be influenced by the content of preceding questions?
2. Is the question led up to in a natural way? Is it in correct psychological order?
3. Does the question come too early or too late from the point of view of arousing interest and receiving sufficient attention, avoiding resistence, and so on?

Source: Selltiz, Wrightsman & Cook

'Avoid' Questions
1. Avoid leading questions, that is, questions which are worded (or their response categories presented) in such a way as to suggest to respondents that there is only one acceptable answer. For example:
   > Do you prefer abstract, academic-type courses, or down-to-earth, practical courses that have some pay-off in your day-to-day work?
2. Avoid highbrow questions even with sophisticated respondents.
   For example:
   > What particular aspects of the current positivistic/interpretive debate would you like to see reflected in a course of developmental psychology aimed at a trainer audience?

   Where the sample being surveyed is representative of the whole adult population, misunderstandings of what the researcher takes to be clear, unambiguous language are commonplace.
3. Avoid complex questions. For example:
   > Would you prefer a short, non-award bearing course (3, 4, or 5 sessions) with part-day release (e.g. Wednesday afternoons and one evening per week attendance with financial reimbursement for travel), or a longer, non-award bearing course (6, 7 or 8 sessions) with full-day release, or the whole course designed on part-day release without evening attendance?
4. Avoid irritating questions or instructions. For example:
   > Have you ever attended an in-service course of any kind during your entire career?
   > If you are over 40, and have never attended an in-service course, put one tick in the box marked NEVER and another in the box marked OLD.
5. Avoid questions that use negatives. For example:
   > How strongly do you feel that no one should enrol on the in-service award bearing course who has not completed at least two years full-time training?
6. Avoid open-ended questions on self-completion questionnaires. Because self-completion questionnaires cannot probe the respondent to find out just what he means by a particular response, the open-ended question is a less satsifactory way of eliciting information. (This caution does not hold in the interview situation however). Open-ended questions, moreover, are too demanding of most respondents' time.

   Source: Cohen and Manion (1984).

Interviews

Let's now take a look at the second way of collecting information — INTERVIEWS. Interviews can take several forms, ranging from very formal exchanges to very structured ordered sets of questions. A skillful interviewer can follow up leads, probe responses, and investigate motives and feelings. The form you select will depend on the subject, the kind of information that you need, the setting of your evaluation and the people you are talking to. "Closed" and "Structured" approaches to interviewing maintain great control for the evaluator, while open and shared approaches allow for more control from the informant.

Let me illustrate the main types of interview for evaluation purposes.

Easterby-Smith (1985) sets out the main types of interview for evaluation purposes

Types of Interview	Characteristics
1. Closed	Responses required within predetermined answer categories.
2. Structured	Interviewer's questions are predetermined, but answers are not restricted.
3. Open	A general guide or checklist of questions is normally followed, but there is flexibility about what is focused on.
4. Shared	The evaluator's problems/questions are shared with the respondent, and these are explored in whatever way seems appropriate.

Let's take a look at each of these interviews.

1) **Closed Interviews:**

   This is the most formally structured type of interview. The same information is required from each person and each is asked the same questions in the same order. The form from which the questions are asked is called the interview schedule and is in fact a type of questionnaire. In this type of interview people have little opportunity to introduce variations on your choice of answers.

2) **Structured Interviews:**

   Structured interviews are rather similar to open-ended questionnaires. The interviewer is expected to read out the question precisely as worded on the interview sheet, and the answer is then recorded on audio tape or/and in note form by the interviewer. It is then up to the interviewer to probe and inquire deeper around the answers to particular questions if appropriate. (The format allows for a degree of standardisation, and for some flexibility and exchange between the interviewer and the informant.)

Interviews

But because there is not much flexibility in the structure of the interview it is important that the evaluator has a good idea of what he is looking for at the outset, and is therefore able to provide a tight focus for the questions asked. This means that structured interviews are often most appropriate when focusing on a particular area of course (such as outcomes), and they may also adopt a particular technique (such as the critical incident technique discussed below). In the case of management training courses where participants disperse to different parts of the country or the world after its end, further advantage is that such interviews may be conducted by different individuals who have no prior contact with each other — and the results thus produced are likely to be reasonably consistent.

3) **Open interviews:**

   Open interviews normally employ a general guide or checklist of questions which can be embellished as the evaluator thinks fit. Provided the list of questions is not too long, it is often possible to conduct most of the interview without reference to the checklist — until the end when it is necessary to ensure that most of the specified areas have been covered. Thus open interviews can easily be conducted in very informal settings such as bars, on trains, and so on. Their main strength is in opening up questions of importance and in covering a wide range of possible areas that look problematic.

4) **Shared Interviews:**
   Shared interviews take a further step towards allowing greater control to the informant. It involves both interviewer and informant sharing their ideas, observations, and interests about say, what is taking place during a management course; and over several conversations they may come to a better understanding of what this is. The difference in role between the evaluator and the informants (as colleagues or participants) is simply that the evaluator's interest may be a continuing obsession whereas the informant's interest may be no more than a passing concern.

5) **Depth Interviews:**
   There is another form of interview which is occasionally discussed as a distinct type, but for our purposes I would locate it as either 'shared', or mid-way between that and 'open' interviews. This is the 'depth' interview (Ruddock, 1981) in which 'the subject is asked to follow and verbalise his own train of thought, without guidance'. It requires handling by interviewers who are skilled as counsellors or psycho-therapists since this kind of interview often gets into sensitive personal areas of anxiety, denial, obsession, or whatever. Such depths interviews may be very useful in identifying fundamental problems about the operation of educational programmes (as when a particular form of examination system is causing great anxiety amongst students which manifests itself in laziness or over-indulgence in drink). But apart from the obvious need for a highly skilled interviewer, it may be an extremely time consuming approach which involves looking for symptoms of anxiety and defensiveness to come up with the answers and solutions in like vein.

   From Easterby-Smith (1985)

Observation

Let us now go on to the third type of data collection technique namely OBSERVATION.

Observation as a technique for gathering information covers a variety of situations and approaches. This can be illustrated as follows:

1) Full participant   Full observer who
   who also observes   does not participate

   Observer who also participates
2) *Field notes*   *Check list*
   Diaries   *Sound recording*

   Field notes   Video recording
   Check lists

   From Easterby-Smith (1985)

The observations of a scientist studying a complex chemical reaction or some intricate biological change are quite different from the observations that most of us make as we go about our daily business, travelling to and from work, waiting for late trains, and walking in the rain. In the latter cases we observe willy-nilly, our senses bombarded by a large number of stimuli few of which we register consciously, and still fewer which

engage our attention. However, both sets of observations are made through a 'filter'. The scientist is using a framework for observations that he has developed and is using in a systematic way. While you and I are using our framework which is just as efficient in filtering information.

Observation

Thus we must see the extremes in the two diagrams not as mutually exclusive but as a continuum i.e. those to the right of the continuum being developed in a more systematic way.

Observation is more than just sitting and watching, it is looking with a purpose, using techniques to record or encode what is observed. The ability to observe is not innate or inherited but is developed systematically. The scientist 'observes' through a carefully developed framework or 'filter' the result of years of work by the scientific community while the casual observer 'sees' events through his own personal filter developed over a lifetime. I have no doubt that, like me, you have come home from a soccer match, switched on the radio and listened to the report on the match or read the many papers — How often have you completely disagreed with the report and said "I don't think we were at the same match".

Using a colleague question him about an event you have both seen. To what extent do you differ?

I am sure you will, as each of you are using your own personal filter to aid your perception.

This brings me to the main controversy surrounding observation as a technique. There are those who argue that all observations must be as "structured" as possible i.e. as near to the methods used by the scientist as possible. On the other hand there are those who argue that in the field of observing human behaviour the structural approach is too restrictive and that the rich variety of human behaviour can only be captured by the participant in the behaviour allowing for capturing a rich variety of behaviours.

Capturing a rich variety of behaviours.

I am not going to come down on the side of either but will outline the pros and cons of each approach. You make up your mind and develop your own approach.

By structuring the observations it is possible to maintain a focus on a particular aspect of the situation. Also the job of observing and recording is made easier. Structuring can be employed at several levels, from the classed and pre-ordained categories of a commercially available observation schedule through the observation schedule developed in situ by the observer, to a simple checklist.

Suppose you were going to observe up to one hour in your section or department. List down all those events you would include on a checklist and your reasons for doing this.

I have no idea what you have written but I think you will be surprised at the list.

Now write down the main problems you envisage in using your schedule.

Again I do not know what you may have written but I should imagine you have got quite a few.

Apart from the sheer physical problems of carrying out the task the main argument against this approach is that you only "see" what you have got on the checklist

thus leaving out a large amount of behaviour which may be very significant. This type of approach must use a schedule which is as watertight as possible.

What about using sound or video recording? Set down the pros and cons.

I hope you have mentioned that while these can allow for replay for observation, analysis and comment, they may be subject to the bias of the user — that is an interesting event — and the presence of the camera or tape recorder may upset the natural pattern of behaviour. (See Volume 7 for a detailed discussion of the observation of training).

The contrasting approach to the objective outside observer is the recording of behaviour by the participant observer using unstructured approaches. This type of observation has developed out of the argument that it is only possible to understand human behaviour when the observer gets the meanings behind the actions, i.e. you can only understand human behaviour by becoming a participant in the situation yourself. It is a method frequently used by Social Anthropologists. If the observer enters and becomes involved in the situation with as open a mind as possible, then things may be seen and recorded which could have been missed in a more structured situation.

Write down the main arguments for using participant observation.

I do not know what you have written but I hope your argument went something like this:
Participant observation is a good method to use when you are going beyond superficial explanation and judgements. You record to the extent that it is humanly possible everything you see and hear in a situation. You do not know what is trivial or irrelevant. For example people who make real contributions to labour-management relations are successful not only because they listen to what each side says is important or what appears to be superficially important, they assume they know nothing and go in fresh with as little bias as possible and listen and look. The most immediately obvious is not necessarily the explanation or even an important element in the problem.

Thus for participant observation:
(1) You try to make no judgements about what is significant.
(2) You record everything that is possible to record through straightforward description.

Try the following exercise. Observe a situation containing people for two minutes (at work if possible). Write up your notes and now answer the following questions.

1. Where was the situation?
2. Where were you in relation to it?
3. What did you do during the observation?
4. What was the placement of other people?
5. What were your and their body positions? Sitting, standing, walking? If people were just passing by, include them, if possible.
6. Did you describe the movements of people?
7. What time was it? What was the temperature? Weather conditions?
8. What did the people wear? What colours, materials, lengths, styles? Do not forget accessories, shoes, hats.
9. What did people look like? Height, weight, age, hair colour and style, any distinguishing characteristics?
10. What did people say? In what order did they speak? Did anyone not speak? What gestures and body movements occurred in speech or while listening to speaking? Were there any other sounds? What about sounds in the background?
11. Did any of the above change during the observation? When? How?
12. What other physical objects were present? What was their shape, size, colour, material, texture? Where were they placed in relation to each other? If you were in a room, what were the dimensions of the room and placements of windows? Did you describe curtains or other window coverings, pictures, light fixtures, electrical outlets?

From Kane E. (1985)

How did you get on? Are you satisfied that you captured that was going on? If not try again.

One final point about this type of method of Data collection. You may have already noticed it, this is the sheer amount of information that you accumulate using this method — is it worth it? Only you can decide!!

I will now pass on to a few other aspects of data collection which apply to all three approaches we have looked at, to a greater or lesser degree, and which you should bear in mind when using different approaches.

First of all there is the problem of **sampling.** We can define sampling as 'a group selected from a larger population so that we can make statements about this population as a whole'. The basic distinction in sampling is between probability and non-probability sampling. A probability sample is one in which the probability is that any element of the population will be included. In non-probability sampling the probability that a person will be chosen is not known and one cannot measure the sampling error. It is therefore difficult to generalise one's feelings beyond the study group. However other considerations such as going for a cheap, quick result may be more important.

Reliability — The extent to which a test would give consistent results if applied more than once to the same people under standard conditions. In ethnographic work reliability relates to the extent to which two observers would produce a consistent analysis of a particular aspect of the same social

situation. This is dependent on the accurate recording and checking of observations. Replication, one way of assessing reliability, is difficult in ethnographic research because of the reliance on natural settings.

Triangulation — The use of different research methods or sources of data to examine the same problem. If the same conclusions can be reached using different methods or sources, then no peculiarity of method or source has produced the conclusions and one's confidence in their validity increases. **Data triangulation** refers to the collection of varied data on the same phenomena, e.g. from different participants, different phases of fieldwork. **Investigator triangulation,** similarly involves collection of data by more than one researcher (preferably through adoption of different roles in the field) and **methods triangulation** involves the collection of data by different methods which entail different threats to validity.

Validity — Validity refers to the extent to which a test, questionnaire or other operationalization is really measuring what the researcher intends to measure. A test or questionnaire is said to have **concurrent** validity if it correlates well with other measures of the same concept; it has **content** validity when it samples adequately the domain which it is supposed to measure and **predictive** validity if it may be used to make accurate predictions of future performance. Concurrent validity and predictive validity may be classified as **criterion-related** validity as they both evaluate the test or questionnaire against some criterion assumed to be valid. **Construct** validity refers to the extent to which the test appears to conform to predictions about it from theory. Validity in ethnographic research refers to the extent to which the actors' expectations, perspectives, meanings etc. are accurately represented and reported in the research report. Validity is checked (e.g. by triangulation) throughout the research process. Validity is also used in a more general sense to refer to the validity of a piece of research as a whole (as opposed to the validity of particular measurements). In this respect it is concerned with the extent to which one can rely upon and trust the published findings of some research and involves an evaluation of all the methodological objections that can be raised against the research.

Objectivity — Observations or research findings are objective if they are independent of the particular observer or research methods — any other researcher performing the observation or the same researcher using different methods would get the same result. One way of trying to achieve objectivity is to set up precise and explicit rules to govern how the observations shall be made and how they may be interpreted. Another is to use triangulation to identify the influence of reactivity. The demands for objectivity vary between research styles but are particularly strong where the 'scientific' nature is emphasized: e.g. one of the basic assumptions in experimental work is that the personal influence of the experimenter should be nil. Many would suggest, however, that this is an ideal which can never be achieved.

Data Analysis

I would now like to move on to the other main element of this component, that of data analysis.

Data collected by means of Questionnaires, Interviews, Observation, Diaries or any other method mean very little until the data is analysed and assessed. Gathering large quantities of data in the hope that something will turn up is not recommended as it can lead to frustration and a lot of wasted effort. One key function of analysis of any data is to communicate the value of the findings, the other key key function is to convince your audience that the results can make a contribution to the level of information about a situation aid decision-making etc.

Try and work out a working definition of Data Analysis.

I do not know what you have written but compare your definition with mine. Data analysis involves the ordering and structuring of data to produce knowledge. This definition of analysis is a broad one and embraces both the quantitative and qualitative approaches. In this part of the component I will deal with each part in turn.

---

1. Quantitative Analysis

Common purpose of analysis

Purpose	Aim of the analysis	Applicable techniques
1. Description	(Concept formulation (	(Factor analysis (Cluster analysis
	(Classification	(Discriminant analysis
2. Construction of measurement scales		(Regression on surrogate (variables

Adapted from: Howerd K. and Sharp J. H. (1983)

In general the nearer any technique of analysis is to the bottom of the list in the above diagram the more conditions have to be fulfilled before it can be applied. I am going to concentrate on descriptive analysis because this is as far as most evaluators will wish to go. Beyond this analysis becomes rather complicated and is only used in specialised research.

The first aspect to remember is that data analysis like a report, is just like telling a story. You start out with a general description or idea of what is going on. You then go into more detail giving examples to illustrate your points. At the conclusion you should provide a summary of your main findings. In analysing your information, whether on your own, or if appropriate with a computer, you will be categorising information, trying to see problems and relationships.

In descriptive analysis there are two main methods. Firstly there is univariate analysis when you look at one variable at a time. Suppose you are gathering information about a new training programme. You have to ask yourself two questions:
(a) What are the main variables involved?
(b) How is each variable distributed?

While the answer to the first question is relatively easy to obtain, the answer to the second is found by the use of the techniques of frequency distributions and standard deviations. To find out more about these statistical techniques you have to go back to the earlier Study Units in this Volume.

Secondly there is bivariate analysis. Once you've got a fairly clear idea of the broad outline of your data you may want to carry the analysis a step further, e.g. you want to see the association or relationship between two variables. This relationship can be detected quite easily using a scatter diagram in which one variable is plotted against another. The quantitative equivalent of the scatter diagram is the correlation coefficient. Again go back to the previous

Study Units in this Package to find out how to use these. One word of caution: just because two variables are associated do not assume that one **causes** the other. Correlation makes no statement about causality. This is a very important point to keep in mind when reporting the results of formative evaluation. If you infer that one event causes another to happen then entirely wrong decisions may be made as a result.

2. Qualitative Analysis

Data which is obtained by participant Observation has to be analysed in a completely different way. Here the evaluator is concerned both with exploring and describing intentions, motives, perspectives and cultures and with developing theories regarding how these social meanings relate to the situations faced by the people concerned. What distinguishes qualitative analysis from most work in quantitative analysis is a greater emphasis on the importance of linking the researchers own analytic concepts with the terms in which the people themselves understand their solutions and actions. Qualitative analysis begins by trying to describe the perspectives and actions of the people involved in the scene being studied. It then seeks to build concepts on those of the participants in such a way that they incorporate and explain those social meanings.

▰▰▰

How might you investigate the introduction of a training programme or a problem of staff performance, say, in a department using a qualitative approach?

I do not know what you have written but the main point you must have is that you begin by analysing how the people who are affected by the programme or problem see the process and the several meanings embedded in any actions they take as a result. What we as evaluators are doing, is trying to "see" and "explain" the situation from the point of view of the people involved. Thus there is a very close relationship between Data collection and analysis in this approach. One of the problems is that it usually results in a failure to produce data which is open to statistical analysis and this makes the problems of representation and control more difficult. The other major problem is that the evaluation can become involved in the "politics" of the department or organisation which could have a profound effect on the Data, its analysis and what is done as a result. The problem of the politics of evaluation is the subject of Component Five of this unit.

Summary

What I have tried to do in this Component is to take you through the main aspects of the three main approaches to data collection in evaluation and appraisal. The extent to which you use any or all of these will depend on what you want to do. If you have worked your way carefully through the first few Components of this Unit you should now be in a pretty good position to make a choice.

Acknowledgement: Cohen L. and Manion L. (1985) *Research Methods in Education* published by Croom Helm. Easterby-Smith M, (1985) *Evaluation of Management Education, Training and Development,* published by Gower and Kane E, (1985). *Doing Your Own Research,* published by Marion Boyers whose permission is gratefully acknowledged.

Component 5:

The Politics of Assessment and Evaluation Inside the Organisation

---

Key Words

 Hierarchy; power; authority; status; organisational health; the politics of human interaction.

Evaluation, it was agreed in the first Component of this Unit, is the gathering of information and judgements so that future policy can be influenced. Assessment and appraisal consists of the gathering of data about people's competencies, skills and attitudes. Both processes, in other words, are likely to involve the assessing of a good deal of knowledge of a personal kind. It is often said that knowledge is power. So it is not surprising that assessment and evaluation are linked closely to the ways in which power is claimed, authorised and used in an organisation. To talk about power and its distribution is to talk about politics. (It is important to remember that, although the word 'politics' is mainly used in relation to the interplay of policies put forward by political parties, it is also used to describe the interplay of groups inside organisations.) So in talking about these links, we shall be talking about the politics of assessment and evaluation.

When you have worked through this Component you should

(i) be more aware of the close links, sometimes overt, sometimes covert, between the processes of evaluation and assessment and the general processes by which policy is established, carried out (or blocked) and changed in the organisation;

(ii) be more sensitive to the varied ways in which human beings may use their authority to require that others shall be assessed or appraised, or may

react to the findings of the appraisal or assessment process.

Both of these aspects are of direct practical concern for those whose task it is to ensure that training is organised as effectively as possible to ensure the good health of the organisation.

It will be useful to give a brief analysis at this point of a number of ideas, each of which can throw light on the problems we now wish to examine, because they are frequently used in discussion of organisation.

Hierarchy. Most organisations, if not all, have a structure which is hierarchical i.e. the people in it know that they are in grades according to power, authority, status, income. Those at the top of the hierarchy, as part of the general responsibility they hold for keeping the organisation healthy, have the power to commission assessments and evaluations. This right, this process may in certain circumstances make those lower down in the hierarchy suspicious of the motives behind a programme of assessment. Is it simply another means of asserting power over subordinates? Is it a way of preparing people for redundancies to come?

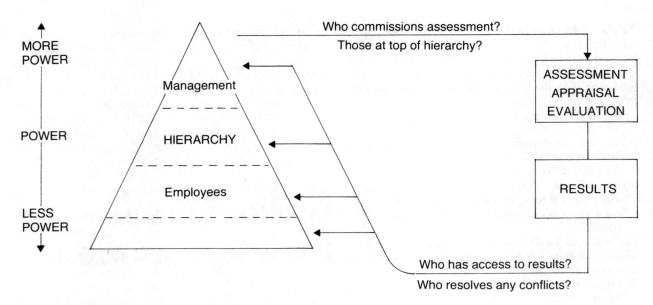

Diagram 1 The organisation as a hierarchy

Power is a second idea that has a bearing on the process of assessment and evaluation. A person has power in so far as he can require others to carry out his instructions. Power is an important aspect of hierarchy. The results of assessments and appraisals may have strong implications for those with power; the results give them the opportunity (and the duty) of controlling or influencing the careers in the organisation of those who are subordinate to them.

Organisational health. The human body has health when the limbs and organs that comprise it work together effectively and harmoniously, and succeed also in keeping under control harmful attacks (e.g. of viruses) from the outside. An organisation can be said, in a parallel way, to have health if its component parts work together effectively and harmoniously and succeed in keeping off the threats of competition from other organisations. One reason why organisations undertake assessments and evaluations is the same as that why individuals seek medical examinations; they wish to remain healthy. If we pursue this analogy, we see that, just as it is vital for a doctor's diagnosis to be heeded, whether the treatment concerns the brain or the little toe, so it is vital for the results of assessment to reach the top of the hierarchy as well as the bottom, even where the results are threatening.

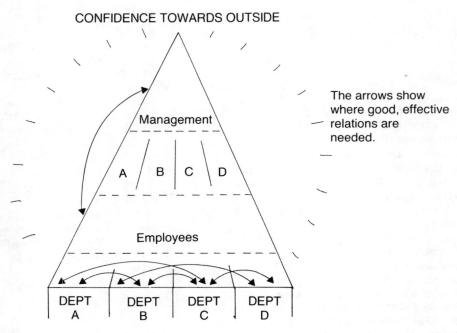

Diagram 2 The Idea of Organisational Health

◢◢◢ Checkpoint (spend about ten minutes on this exercise)

Imagine that an assessment and evaluation has been carried out on aspects of organisation where you have a training responsibility. The results are critical of

(a) **senior management**, who are criticised for weak organisational planning, in that they have failed to set up a properly trained design department;

(b) **the delivery department**, where labour is strongly unionised, whose working practices lead to frequent delays;

(c) **an off-site branch**, which supplies partly assembled components (using a good many part-time women operatives) where quality control has been poor.

List briefly the key features of the actions which would follow the receipt of these evaluations (a) in an organisation that is healthy and (b) in an organisation that is unhealthy.

When you have done this, however sketchily, you should be in a better position to follow the next section.

Politics at Work in an Organisation: Using an Example to Illustrate some key ideas

In the Checkpoint illustration, we suggested that an assessment and evaluation exercise, perhaps done through an external agency, has revealed three different types of problem. We may call these problems political because they are likely to lead to difficulties of relations for the groups inside the organisation, particularly where these relationships involve the use of powers. You have made a personal and quick attempt to analyse these problems. It will be useful now to take this analysis further.

Criticism of Senior Management

The organisation has been criticised for failing to set up a properly trained design department. We can ask the following questions about this criticism.

i) Where did it come from? It is possible that members of the senior management team have made this criticism. It is possible that the criticism has come from members of the organisation who are at a lower level than senior management but who have bad direct experience of the problems caused by the lack of such a department. For example, sales staff may have received hostile customer comment.

It is also possible that the criticism has come from the evaluation specifically commissioned by senior management and achieved through the use of an outside agency e.g. a management consultant.

ii) Does such a criticism easily reach senior management? If an outside agent is being used, it is likely that the criticism will reach the senior management team without difficulty. If the criticism comes from, say, subordinates in the sales department, it is possible that it will be filtered out by others who do not wish to give offence, or do not wish to 'rock the boat', or who feel that it is in some way not proper for subordinates to offer criticism to superiors. If blocking of this kind is common, then we may have a sign of organisational ill-health. Or if we put this in a rather different way, employees who are regularly assessed themselves may feel resentful if power is being used in the organisation to prevent criticisms of senior management from reaching the management.

iii) What happens when the criticism reaches senior management? In an unhealthy organisation, it is likely that the point of the criticism will be lost in personal recrimination, or will not be properly built into a review of the corporate plan or the manpower plan.

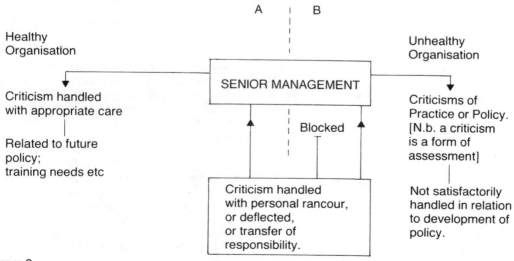

Diagram 3
Criticism (as a form of assessment) handled in (A) a healthy organisation and (B) a unhealthy organisation. The criticism in this case is levelled at senior management.

In a healthy organisation, the criticism will be considered in relation to the purposes and future planning of the organisation. Individual jealousies, private fears and personal blindspots of vision are likely to be overcome by a general desire to ensure the future success of the firm.

If the result of these deliberations is that a design department should be set up there, then a training demand follows.

The organisation's manpower plan will need to be changed, so that either by (i) recruiting new staff who already have appropriate design training and experience or by (ii) retraining existing staff, a suitable department can be set up. If the second of these approaches is included in the plan, then the necessary time, money and opportunity for the necessary assessment and training (internal and using external agencies) must be provided.

From this example, however brief the treatment, we can list a number of important points that link evaluation, the internal policies, the organisation, and training.

1. Training needs can directly follow from high level managerial decisions.
2. These decisions may be reached only after considerable internal debate, discussion, and resolving of disagreement at high level.
3. Organisations that are unhealthy may block routes through which criticisms can be channelled, and so may block the provision of necessary training.
4. Decisions at all levels are made by human beings, and so the part played by ambition, jealousy, timidity and stupidity can never be ignored.

Criticism of the Delivery Department

The criticisms here appear to be directed at people much lower down in the hierarchy. There are poor working practices which lead to delay in deliveries; those responsible are presumably drivers of vans or lorries, loaders and packagers, together with the supervisory staff. It may be also that senior management have, for a variety of reasons, been unwilling to intervene in the problem.

Let us take the same sequence of questions as we did when considering the case of senior management.

i) Where did the criticism come from? The facts are that drivers are claiming that by company agreement they will not undertake journeys that take their hours of work beyond 6.00 p.m. This claimed agreement means that the organisation may fail to meet many afternoon delivery times, and that drivers have dead time within the paid working day.

Who will report these facts and try to change them? The highly unionised drivers will not.

Their immediate supervisors may play down the problem, hoping for a quiet life. Returns of hours may be massaged, or even falsified, in order to suggest that the problem is not serious.

Management may be aware, but unwilling to intervene.

ii) Does such a criticism easily reach the senior management team? The answer is likely to be 'No', unless the organisation has very clear review procedures, and regularly examines conditions of service documents. Even though the poor practices are a drag on the finances and reputation of the organisation, there may be little enthusiasm for tackling the problem.

iii) What happens when the criticism reaches the senior management team?

In an unhealthy organisation, it is likely that the problem will be dodged or postponed. Or alternatively, that some strong over-reaction will lead to a confrontation, which in turn might lead to a strike, or a protracted period of bad relations.

In a healthy organisation, we might expect some or all of the following, each of which arises out of the politics of evaluation and each of which has implications for training.

a) The senior management team would accept its duty to tackle the problem. It would take appropriate advice on matters of law e.g. drivers' hours and on the conditions of service agreements already negotiated with drivers. It would look into the practicalities of changes, and over what time period.

b) It would look into the levels of training provided for supervisors in the delivery department. How useful a view of their own job do they have? Are they able to take advantage of alternative ways of devising schedules, or rosters? Are they able to liaise effectively with other departments? Such an evaluation (resulting from the earlier evaluation that work practices were inadequate) would now indicate how much more training needed to be given to supervisors.

c) Senior management would look at the likely consequences of changing the drivers' work practices. Questions of the following kinds would help identify what training would help. Can the drivers be motivated to accept change? Cash? What information do they need to master in order to see the need for change?

What can be done with or for any employees who cannot or will not accept change?

Are there ways in which drivers could be helped to get greater satisfaction from their job? Would job rotation or work in teams help? What training would be needed in order to secure job rotation or team working?

From the case of the delivery department, similar conclusions follow as did from the case of the design department.

i) Training needs are often directly related to high level management decisions.

ii) These decisions may be reached only after a good deal of discussion and debate at high level. Much disagreement may need to be tackled at this stage.

iii) Organisations that are unhealthy may block routes through which criticisms can be channelled. Indeed, the channels may not even be there in the first place.

iv) Management decisions will affect other human beings. The part likely to be played by fear, awkwardness, misunderstanding, anger and suspicion must not be forgotten. A good programme of training, which picks up these very human as well as the technical aspects, may help us prevent the worst effects.

Criticism of Quality in an Off-Site Branch

This third example raises many of the same points as have the two previous ones, but also some significantly different ones. It will still be useful, since we are still trying to link the 'politics' of the organisation to the provision of training, to take the same questions as before.

i) Where did the criticisms come from?

They are likely to have originated with customers (who are the ones most likely to experience the consequences of poor quality control). Such complaints may well have reached the headquarters of the organisation directly, rather than coming through the branch site.

Questions: will management or supervising staff at the branch feel threatened by such a process, and so try to play down the difficulties, even if they know them to be real? The criticisms may equally well have come from managers/supervisors from the main site, who have made observations during one of their visits — observations which have led to a formal, but covert assessment of the quality of products coming from the branch site.

ii) Do such criticisms easily reach senior management?

Although much here may depend on the magnitude of the shortcomings, there may be people in the organisation who wish to block direct, straightforward consideration of the problem. To raise this, however, is to move to the next question.

iii) What happens when criticisms reach management?

In the healthy organisation, a complaint would lead to a systematic assessment of the difficulty. Is there under-or-over-manning? Do employees at the branch site lack access to the same training opportunities as at the main site? Is the equipment used less adequate? And so on, as we have seen in the two previous examples.

Assessment of workers' performance would, in other words, be carefully related to a more general evaluation of the contribution made to the corporate plan by the branch site, and to the general norms and expectations stated in the organisation's manpower plan. Any further training proposed to put the problem right would, similarly, be related to these general requirements. Likewise, a careful policy of appraisal of management and supervisory staff at the branch would be needed.

However, in an unhealthy organisation there may be employees at widely different levels of the hierarchy who see life at the branch site as a 'cushy' placement, and wish to divert, or explain away any criticisms. Any offers or requirements of further training may all be seen as intrusions by 'big brother'. Equally, there may be some on the main site who, irrespective of the quality of work produced on the branch site, would like to see it closed. Any assessment may therefore be captured and used by such people.

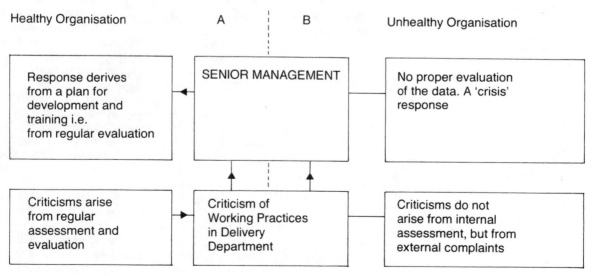

Diagram 4

The politics of assessment and evaluation in practice. The criticism, this time, concerns employees in one department.

Some General Points about the Political Aspects of Assessment, Evaluation and Training

Organisations are staffed by human beings. Human beings vary in age and experience, have different temperaments and abilities, different outlooks and interests, may have feelings of aggression, jealousy, and suspicion, or fears of inadequacy. Any policy of assessment and evaluation is inevitably carried out against this background.

Specific, defined skills, particularly of a technical kind e.g. of disassembling for repair a new type of gear box, can be improved by programmes of training (with associated assessment of performance). The more broad and deep-seated features of temperament, outlook and ability mentioned are not, however, so easily modified. Their effects on performance and relations in an organisation can be disastrous; the task, therefore, of a good organisation is to exploit this range and variety as positively as possible.

The human beings that make up the staff of an organisation are inevitably located in a hierarchy. The distribution of power, responsibility, and authority is not even. Those who hold authority, responsibility and power have the opportunity to create conditions in which the range of talents is used positively.

Assessment and appraisal of employees takes place in the situation described above. The fairly straightforward tasks of assessing performance become complicated when we have to take into account the varied attitudes (e.g. of fear, of suspicion, of ambition) of those who participate in the assessment.

Assessment and appraisal are also related to **evaluation** i.e. to those wider questions about the work situation, about pay, conditions, motivation, about the wisdom of the organisation's corporate plan.

The idea of organisational health is useful to denote an organisation to which people at all levels can show loyalty and commitment, and for which they are prepared to overcome some at least of their own emotional hang-ups. An organisation is unlikely to be healthy where those high up the hierarchy seem preoccupied with their own status, privileges.

To develop an organisation that is healthy is a different task from providing training for meeting specific needs and deficiencies. Both need to be attempted. To provide training for employees who have no motivation to benefit from it may be a waste of money.

The term politics may seem an intrusion into the world of business and industry, but it is often used to denote the interplay of people and groups in an organisation, and so, by extension, to denote the range of conflict we have been talking about. These human factors cannot be ignored. They form the soil in which the organisation's activities either prosper or fail.

THE ORGANISATION

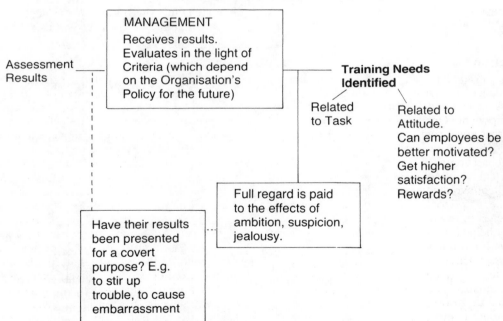

Diagram 5
Evaluating and Acting Upon the Results of
Assessments: a Diagram showing how Human
Reactions and Emotions Intervene

Component 6:

Using the Results of Evaluation for Future Planning

Key Words

Assessment; appraisal; evaluation; profiles of employees; policy development; corporate plan; manpower.

Introduction

In this Unit so far, you have deepened your understanding of a range of topics associated with the tasks of assessment and evaluation.

In Component One, you were introduced to problems that arise from the often confusing way in which people use words such as evaluation, assessment and appraisal. Suggestions were made for a more systematic use of these terms, in particular so that you might avoid common pitfalls.

Component Two took you through some examples of approaches to evaluation, with the idea that you should be helped in deciding which is the most appropriate for you in your situation.

Component Three introduced you to a distinction made by many evaluators, that is the distinction between 'formative' and 'summative' evaluation. The term 'formative' draws attention to the fact that it is often important to evaluate a development while it is being put into practice. The term 'summative' reminds us that it is also important to take a careful look at the outcomes of new developments.

Component Four gave details of the most common methods of obtaining information for evaluation, and of handling that information in such a way as to give meaningful and helpful analyses of your problems.

Component Five took a look at the 'political' aspects of evaluation. Nearly all evaluation has a political aspect, in that the process of information gathering may threaten people and upset their sensitivities, while the results may present some unwelcome challenges.

Nevertheless, those in organisations who have a responsibility for training undertake them, at expense of time, effort and money. Why? The answer is that there is assumed to be a pay-off; if the operations are done well, then the organisation will become more viable, more effective, more efficient, more healthy.

This Component will be devoted to the links between evaluation and subsequent action. After working through it, you should be much clearer about the nature of these links, and in a better position to appraise the success, or likely success, of your own organisation in this vital aspect of its work.

Let us start by breaking down the title of the Component, **Using the results of evaluation for future planning** into two areas for analysis:

i) the results of assessment and evaluation, and
ii) future planning

We then need to ask certain questions so that we can establish clear links between the two.

The results of assessment and evaluation

What kinds of information are we likely to find under these headings?

Profiles of employees

If the organisation operates a systematic profiling of its employees, information of the following sorts will be available. Data about employees' ages, sex, length of service. Data from assessments (either from blanket testing of employees, the tests of course varying from occupation to occupation, or from tests given to representative samples of employees), which will give the types of skills currently available amongst what numbers of employees.

These skill profiles are likely to be made up of different types of data.

i)   Some assessments or appraisals will have painted broad brushstroke pictures of employees' characteristics e.g. their broad intellectual abilities, their broad aptitudes, their broad social characteristics e.g. ability to relate well with other employees. These features of employees may be to some extent modifiable or developable particularly if the organisation is generally healthy, but the general characteristic features will represent the reservoir of abilities on which the organisation can draw.

ii) Some assessments will have painted detailed pictures of specific clusters of skills, quite possibly of skills that have been developed by training provided by or through the organisation. If the patterns of skills available are unsatisfactory, then the explanations may lie in one or both of the following: either the reservoir of abilities (see above) is inadequate, (in which case the organisation may have to reconsider its recruitment, promotion and severance policies), or the training provided is inadequate in type, extent or timing.

Evaluations of the training programmes previously provided by or through the organisation

Let us take, as the neatest way of exploring this point, two examples:

First, a situation in which the organisation uses an outside agency, a local college, in order to achieve training. The organisation, wishing to computerise its records of stock, and being rather small, decides that it will send selected employees to a course in a local college designed to develop a general understanding of computerised records. The course, however, turns out to be rather theoretical (raising problems of programme design that are outside the demands placed on the employees concerned) and rather general (in that it deals with the general advantages of computerised records, rather than giving skills specific to the task of setting up and sustaining a system of stock records). As a consequence, the employees claim that the course is of little direct use, that parts of it are too difficult, and there are some problems over attendance.

The college assesses the employees on the course, and these assessments form part of the collection of data that we were considering in the section above. These assessments, however, are not of any particular use since they are based on performances on a course which is seen not to meet the organisation's need (and on which employees may have performed less than their best since they appear not to value it). Nevertheless, the organisation has a commitment and a budget for external training, so employees continue to be released, and data about their performances recorded.

Clearly some kind of evaluation procedure is needed if these assessments are to contribute to the general development of the organisation. This illustration will be elaborated in a later section of the component.

Second, a situation in which the organisation has provided its own training. Let us take the case of a chain of restaurants. There have been complaints from customers about the standard of service provided by waiters. The training section of the restaurant group organised short, intensive on-site sessions of training, dealing with the serving of food, with addressing customers, and with problems caused by difficult members of the public. The sessions go reasonably well, though some staff feel resentful that the training implies an unjustified criticism of them, and there have been marginal losses of trade, in that over the period of training, the restaurants have been opened thirty minutes later on one day a week. However, in spite of these marginal losses of trade, the general evaluation of the training is favourable. However, a change in the chain's corporate plan has made much of the effort useless. The new corporate plan, published shortly before this period of training ends, is that the restaurants will turn over to a self-service system. Each restaurant will have a new image, new layout, new decor, but, most importantly, significantly different types and numbers of staff, with significant shifts in the way that they relate to the public.

Hence, although the narrow evaluation of the

training is favourable, the broad evaluation is that it has been pointless, counter-productive and wasteful.

▰▰▰▰ Checkpoint

Use the above analysis in relation to your organisation. You will find it useful to list your observations under these or similar headings. (Take about 10 to 15 minutes on this.)

1. Is general data easily available about employees (e.g. age, educational background, length of service)?
2. Is data available about
   i) assessments and appraisals of employees, where appropriate related to
   ii) the types, level, duration and dates of training provided?
3. Are there procedures for the evalution of this data i.e. for relating it to the general policies of the organisation, to policy on pay and conditions, to

investigations of the various jobs done by employees in terms of interest or motivation offered?
4. Are these procedures regular or occasional or thought about only in times of crisis?

Having taken 15 minutes or so to think about these questions, if you find you are unable to answer them satisfactorily, then you can proceed to the rest of this Component, but you will find it important to pursue these questions on another occasion.

We started this Component with the reminder that organisations made the effort to assess, appraise, and evaluate on the assumption that there was a spin-off; the organisation would use the data produced in order to become more effective. In other words, there has to be a link between these processes and the future policy of the organisation.

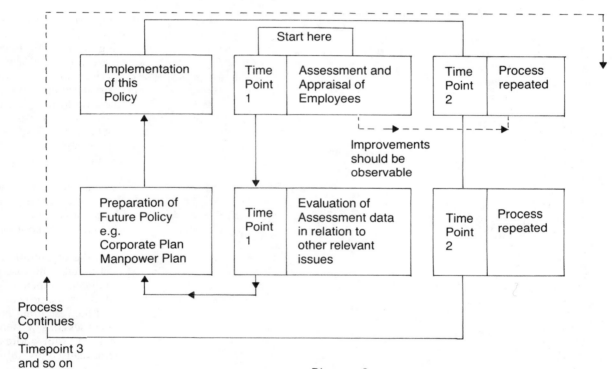

Diagram 2
Making Use of Assessment, Appraisal and Evaluation

These connections can most easily be understood by reference to the diagram. The diagram brings out two important points:

1) The value of the assessment, appraisal and evaluation procedures should lead to policy review and development, with the expectation of finding, as the process moves to Timepoint 2 (then Timepoint 3 and so on), observable improvements.
2) The task is not a 'one-off', but part of a regular cycle.

Preparation of Future Policy: using the Results of Assessment, Appraisal and Evaluation

The internal structure of organisations (i.e. the ways in which managers' responsibilities are allocated, the kinds of committees set up, the procedures for consulting with trade unions, etc) are likely to be varied. Likewise, as was pointed out in Component 5 of this Unit, all organisations have to allow for the interplay of human beings, with their complex and often conflicting attitudes, fears and ideas. Nevertheless, all organisations have to face the two major tasks, **however they are described**, of producing

1) a corporate plan and
2) a manpower plan.

If we wanted to use different words, we could say that the production of these two plans amounts to the production of future policy (the phrase used on the diagram).

Policy is a term used for the process by which evidence is reviewed, various options are looked at, and most wise course of action adopted.

It is now possible to look in some detail at the links between the assessment and appraisal of employees, the evaluation of these assessments and appraisals, and the establishment of policy.

Using assessment data
FIRST ILLUSTRATION
Let us begin by returning to the case of the restaurants. The central problem was that of the standard of service provided by waiters. The problem was serious in that it had provoked complaints from customers. The problem of bad service was, however, tackled in that restaurant chain in a very unsatisfactory way. Let us see how it might have been done in a healthier, more effective organisation.

Look at diagram 2.

If the organisation had been more effective than it apparently is, then its own programme of employee **assessment** would probably have diagnosed that waiters were performing poorly. However, whatever is the general condition of the organisation, the arrival of customer complaints would have provided data to be added to whatever was already known.

The facts of poor service being known, the organisation can move to the **evaluation** stage. What is the context of the poor service? Is supervision poor? Are staff relationships and morale low? Why? Are conditions for employees poor? Are there delays in the kitchens for which waiters are being blamed? Are clients at this branch, for some reason, hypercritical?

If these wider evaluation questions are answered in such a way that the problem still lies with the waiters, then the organisation can continue by asking further questions.

a) What are the general characteristics of the waiters employed? Age: are they too old for retraining? General attitude, outlook and temperament: are there deep-seated features which might make them unamenable to training?

b) Are there alternatives and better people in the area who might be employed? Example: would a change to waitresses help?
c) Are there conditions, which the organisation can control, a change of which might help? This question has already been asked, and preliminary answers suggest that conditions in the restaurant, for example, are **not** the cause of bad service. But the question is still relevant, because a different change, such as an increase in pay, might lead to the easier recruitment of others, and might overcome some of the poor approaches of the existing waiters.
d) Are there conditions, which the organisation **cannot** control, but which have a bearing on the problem? For example, is there a general shortage of suitable employees in the area, because new and expanding industries nearby are offering higher pay and very attractive working conditions?

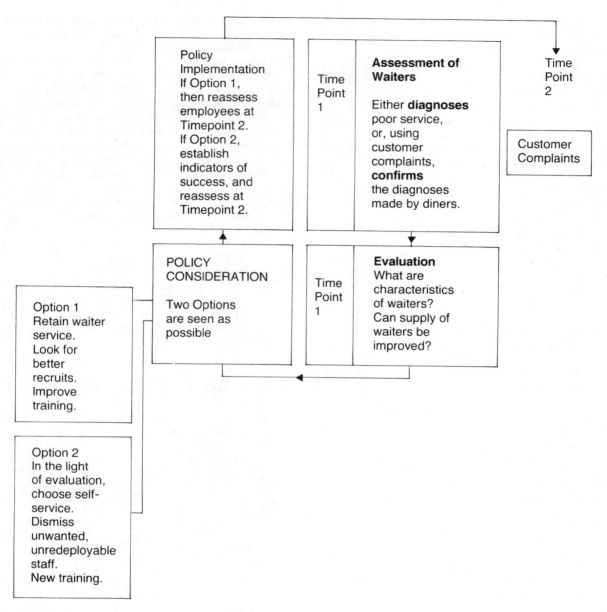

Diagram 3
Evaluation of the Results of Assessment as an aid
to Policy Development

So far then, the organisation has its assessment/ appraisal data; it also has evaluative data on other relevant factors. If the problems are to be put right, then the data has to be brought into the **policy-making** stage.

A policy review would examine various options. One group of options would be confined to the specific approach of improving waiter service. One reasonable conclusion could be that the staff of existing waiters was unlikely to benefit from training. Therefore, an alternative work force should be recruited and trained. If the corporate plan of the restaurant was such that waiter service was an integral feature of the house style, then this option looks the only acceptable one, even though the manpower plan that results from it is likely to be fraught with difficulties.

Once the revised manpower plan is in operation, then an appropriate assessment process will have to be undertaken at what in the diagram we have called Timepoint 2.

If, however, the corporate plan of the restaurant chain is open to the idea that some of its branches would be run on self-service lines, then the data yielded by the evaluation could be used as strong evidence for such a change. Once the changeover has been agreed, the relevant planning of layout, counters etc will be handled via the corporate plan, but an alternative training plan for counters and clearing staff will have to be worked out. And with it, there will be an appropriate staff assessment scheme, which can be implemented at whatever seems a wise timing of Timepoint 2. This staff assessment scheme will, of course, be linked to a more general plan for evaluation of the whole situation.

What features are built into this scheme that are likely to prevent the waste and confusion that ensued in the first presentation?

SECOND ILLUSTRATION

It will be useful now to return to the example of the organisation that used an outside agency (a college) to provide training on computerised records. You will remember that, because the organisation had no clear procedure for evaluating the courses provided, it was continuing to send employees, in spite of the ineffectiveness and irrelevance of the course.

An alternative and more satisfactory ending to the story might have been as follows – using the diagram that we used for the waiter training in the chain of restaurants.

At Timepoint 1, employees are attending the course. On completion, the college sends to the organisation the course assessments. However, before the organisation records and acts on these assessments, it now introduces an evaluative element. First, it interviews a selection of high, low and medium achieving employees, and asks for their views on the courses. The employees' comments on the over-theoretical and over-general nature of the course would be quickly heard. Second, the organisation asks for detailed, up-to-date syllabuses of the course, together with examination papers etc. When training managers look in depth at these documents, they realise that the employee-students' comments are to be taken seriously.

Training managers now have the task of linking this information to the general training policy of the company. An analysis of the situation leads to these key points.

1) They note the company's commitment to effective training. They conclude that some sort of training must be continued.
2) They consider two options:
   (a) providing their own on-site training;
   (b) continuing to use the college, but insisting on a changing course.
3) Given other pressures on the on-site programme, they choose to retain a college-based course.
4) They then raise their worries with the college staff. After some initial misunderstandings, and some suspicion, the college staff agree both to visit the organisation regularly and also to change the course, relating the practical work requirements directly to the organisation's needs.
5) The next group of employees undertake the revised programme, and at Timepoint 2, a much more satisfactory set of responses is found. The organisation finds the course directly helpful, and contact with the college has also helped them to develop their computerisation in one or two ways that had not been foreseen.

A number of general points may now be made about the links between assessment, evaluation and the development and implementation of organisational policy.

Data about assessment and appraisal should not be taken at its face value. Questions need to be asked about the content of the training or courses on which it is based. Is the content relevant, well-taught, up-to-date? Questions also need to be asked about the assessment process. Were the assessments fair? Did they cover the training effectively? These and similar questions constitute an **evaluation** of the data.

Evaluations likewise remain sterile unless they are related to the current and future policies of the organisation e.g. as in its corporate and manpower plans. Data from assessment may lead to a modification of policy. Policy may lead to a shift in training and assessment.

Tutor Seen Work

This final Study Unit contains many Checkpoints which you may wish to treat as Tutor Seen Work, specially as they relate to your own situation/organisation. Select one or two to develop as Tutor Seen Work.

The objectives of this Unit are

That you should deepen your understanding of, increase your skill in working on, and better see the point of the tasks of assessment and evaluation in the field of training.

In particular, the six Components have focussed, with these four objectives in mind, on a range of specific topics which should have increased your ability to carry out the work of assessment and evaluation.

Component One focussed on the skill of teasing out problems, particularly when they come wrapped in puzzling labels.

Component Two focussed on developing your ability to decide which approaches to evaluation would best suit your situation.

Component Three was designed to help you see, and use, the complementary roles of formative and summative evaluation.

Component Four showed you how to obtain and make use of appropriate information.

Component Five was designed to increase your awareness of the human difficulties that evaluation brings to light.

Component Six looked forward, with the intention of helping you to see why evaluation is widely undertaken, in spite of the difficulties it brings, and what benefits can accrue.

Useful Books

Easterby-Smith, M. (1986) *Evaluation of management education, training and development.* (Gower).

Kane, E. (1985) *Doing your own research* (Marion Boyers)

Legge, K. (1984) *Evaluating planned organisational change* (Academic Press)

Pugh, D. S. N. (1984) *Organisation theory: selected readings* (Penguin)

Tyson, S. and York, A. (1982) *Personnel management* (Made Simple Books, Heinemann)

Voluntary Package Assignment (VPA)

This Package has been written by a number of authors and each Study Unit contains one or more pieces of Tutor Seen Work (TSW). If you have completed all of these you will have received in a substantial way the content of this Package and you should consider this as the completion of the VPA. You may, however, have omitted a number of items of TSW or have received suggestions from your tutor about revising or expanding an item of TSW.

We suggest that you **either** complete one or more of the items of TSW which you previously left aside **and/or** you revise or expand an item of TSW already submitted.